High-Speed Rail and Sustainability

T0313162

High-speed rail (HSR) is being touted as a strategic investment for connecting people across regions, while also fostering prosperity and smart urban growth. However, as its popularity increases, its implementation has become contentious with various parties contesting the validity of the socioeconomic and environmental objectives put forward as justification for investment.

High-Speed Rail and Sustainability explores the environmental, economic and social effects of developing an HSR system, presenting new evaluations of the proposed system in California in the US as well as lessons from international experience. Drawing upon the accumulated experience from past HSR system development, leading experts present a diverse set of perspectives as well as diverse contexts of implementation. Assessments of the California case as well as cases from Japan, France, Germany, Italy, Spain, Taiwan, China and the UK show how governments and stakeholders have bridged the gap between the vision and the realities of connecting metropolitan regions through HSR.

This is a valuable resource for academics, researchers and policy-makers in the areas of urban planning, civil engineering, transportation and environmental design.

Blas Luis Pérez Henríquez is the Founding Director of the California – Global Energy, Water & Infrastructure Innovation Initiative, Stanford University, USA.

Elizabeth Deakin is Professor Emerita of City and Regional Planning at the University of California, Berkeley, USA.

Routledge Explorations in Environmental Studies

High-Speed Rail and Sustainability

Decision-making and the political economy of investment

Edited by Blas Luis Pérez Henríquez and Elizabeth Deakin

LONDON AND NEW YORK

from Routledge

First published 2017
by Routledge
2 Park Square, Milton Park, Abingdon, Oxon OX14 4RN

and by Routledge
711 Third Avenue, New York, NY 10017

First issued in paperback 2018

Routledge is an imprint of the Taylor & Francis Group, an informa business

British Library Cataloguing-in-Publication Data
A catalogue record for this book is available from the British Library

Library of Congress Cataloging-in-Publication Data
Names: Perez Henriquez, Blas Luis, editor. | Deakin, Elizabeth, editor.
Title: High speed rail and sustainability : decision-making and the political economy of investment / edited by Blas Luis Peìrez Henriìquez and Elizabeth Deakin.
Description: New York : Routledge, 2017. | Series: Routledge explorations in environmental studies
Identifiers: LCCN 2016028153 | ISBN 9781138891975 (hb) | ISBN 9781315709406 (ebook)
Subjects: LCSH: High speed trains--Economic aspects. | High speed trains--Environmental aspects. | High speed trains--California--Evaluation. | Public administration.
Classification: LCC HE1031 .H54 2017 | DDC 385--dc23
LC record available at https://lccn.loc.gov/2016028153

ISBN 13: 978-1-138-62588-4 (pbk)
ISBN 13: 978-1-138-89197-5 (hbk)

Typeset in Goudy
by HWA Text and Data Management, London

Contents

Figures

Tables

Contributors

Ander Audikana
Postdoctoral Research Fellow, University of Deusto, Spain

David Banister
Emeritus Professor of Transport Studies, School of Geography and the Environment University of Oxford, UK

Manuel Benegas
Director of Operations, Ineco, Spain

Peter Calthorpe
Principal, Calthorpe Associates, Berkeley, US

Ennio Cascetta
Professor of Transportation Systems Planning, University of Naples "Federico II", Italy

Robert Cervero
Professor Emeritus of City & Regional Planning, University of California, Berkeley, US

Jason Chang
Professor of Civil Engineering, National Taiwan University, Taiwan

Minglei Chen
Urban Planner, Shanghai Municipal Urban Planning & Design Research Institute, China

Mikhail Chester
Assistant Professor, School of Sustainable Engineering and the Built Environment, Arizona State University, US

Pierluigi Coppola
Associate Professor of Transportation, "Tor Vergata" University of Rome, Italy

Yves Crozet
Professor of Economics, Institute of Political Studies, University of Lyon, France

Elizabeth Deakin
Professor Emerita of City and Regional Planning, University of California, Berkeley, US

Moshe Givoni
Head of the Transport Research Unit (TRU) and Senior Lecturer, Department of Geography and Human Environment, Tel-Aviv University, Israel

Ji Han
Associate Professor, East China Normal University, China and Executive Director, Global Institute for Urban and Regional Sustainability, China

Yoshitsugo Hayashi
Professor, Chubu University; Professor Emeritus, Nagoya University, Japan

Arpad Horvath
Professor, Department of Civil and Environmental Engineering, University of California, Berkeley, US

T.C. Kao
Research Professor and Director, High Speed Rail Systems, Railroad Transportation and Engineering Center University of Illinois at Urbana-Champaign), US

Hirokazu Kato
Associate Professor, Department of Environmental Engineering and Architecture, Nagoya University, Japan

Alain Leray
President and CEO, SNCF America, US

Anastasia Loukaitou-Sideris
Professor of Urban Planning and Dean of Luskin School of Public Affairs, UCLA

Aoto Mimuro
Research Fellow, Japan Society for the Promotion of Science, Japan

Inmaculada Mohíno
Becaria FPU, E.T.S. Arquitectura, Toledo, Spain

Jin Murakami
Assistant Professor, Department of Civil and Architectural Engineering, City University of Hong Kong, China

Chris Nash
Research Professor, Institute for Transport Studies, University of Leeds, UK

Jason Ni
Assistant Professor, City University of Hong Kong, China

Cornelius Nuworsoo
Professor of City and Regional Planning, California State Polytechnic University, San Luis Obispo, US

Michael O'Hare
Professor of Public Policy, Goldman School of Public Policy, University of California, Berkeley, US

Haixiao Pan
Professor of Urban Planning, Department of Urban Planning, Tongji University, China

Blas Luis Pérez Henríquez
Founding Director, The California – Global Energy, Water & Infrastructure Innovation Initiative, Stanford University, US

Deike Peters
Assistant Professor of Environmental Planning and Practice, Soka University, US

Jean-Pierre Pradayrol
Manager of Methods Division, Major Projects and Forecasting Department, Voyages – Société Nationale des Chemins de fer Français (SNCF), France

Werner Rothengatter
Professor Emeritus, Institute of Economic Policy Research, Karlsruhe Institute of Technology, Germany

Megan Smirti Ryerson
Assistant Professor, City and Regional Planning, University of Pennsylvania, US

Jose Maria de Ureña
Professor of City and Regional Planning, University of Castilla La Mancha, Spain

Song Ye
Planner, China Academy of Urban Planning and Design Institute, China

Introduction

Blas Luis Pérez Henríquez and Elizabeth Deakin

High-speed rail (HSR) systems have been built in a number of countries in Europe and Asia, and new HSR lines are being developed in Africa and the Middle East. While Japan and France introduced HSR technology decades ago as an innovation for rail-passenger markets, today governments around the world are deploying and upgrading HSR as part of a larger effort to make their transport infrastructure cleaner as well as more efficient. From China to California, HSR is being touted as a strategic investment for connecting people across regions, while also fostering prosperity and smart urban growth.

Even as HSR's popularity has boomed, its implementation has become increasingly contentious. Debates over HSR are nothing new: given the high costs of HSR projects, forecasts of costs, revenues, and ridership of the system have long been the subject of detailed scrutiny. More recently, however, as justifications for investments have expanded to include socioeconomic and environmental objectives, so too the debates have expanded to contest the validity of such claims. In addition, it is no longer just the experts talking about evaluation methodologies and the credibility of assumptions. Today the debates are increasingly public and extend to ideologically charged policy issues such as the desirability of pursuing asserted project objectives, who benefits and who loses if the system is implemented, and more generally, the role of government versus that of the private sector in implementing infrastructure and providing public services. In short, high-speed rail is now a case example for broader debates about public policy.

The political wrangling over massive undertakings such as HSR is understandably contentious. Megaprojects entail risk, and the choice to fund such a project almost always means that other, competing programmes will receive lower priority. HSR advocates argue that its performance makes it well worth the investment needed, with direct benefits accruing to its users and co-benefits accruing to society at large, but others worry that the risks are too high, that HSR will not compete effectively with auto and air travel, and that the project could end up being a failure.

Organizational designs that establish clear accountability and operating protocols that demand high levels of transparency, sophisticated analyses that account for uncertainty, and well-designed oversight systems can mitigate risks of fraud, waste and abuse, and can shed light on questions of social welfare. In most cases, however, they cannot resolve questions of political priorities and the weighing of incommensurables. These are issues of public policy and for such issues, political leadership matters.

This book is about the political economy of planning, designing, constructing and operating HSR systems. It highlights the complexities of long-term planning and the reality of institutional stressors in the management and development of such megaprojects. It presents a review of international experiences with HSR, with a focus on key political, technical, managerial and financial considerations that such major infrastructure projects pose. The book asks the questions: Is HSR a sustainable transportation system? Under what circumstances do its benefits outweigh its costs? Are economic and social co-benefits significant? Who stands to benefit from HSR, and are there those who will not? Ultimately, the book aims to inform policymakers, industry professionals, students and academics by bringing together a compendium of experiences with HSR, and outlining the challenges and opportunities facing future system developments.

We tackle these questions from an institutional and policy analysis perspective, first by examining the international experience with HSR, and then by assessing the prospects for California's HSR proposals. Why California? With 40 million people – 50 million expected by 2050 – and an economy that would place it in the top seventh or eighth internationally, California is an important case in its own right. It also is a place where innovations often begin. In this instance California's decision to build HSR would establish the first truly high-speed rail line in the United States. Its supporters have high hopes – not only that the project will attract sufficient ridership to justify the project's $64.2 billion price tag, but also that it will reduce the need for additional investments in highways and airports, foster regional and local economic development, support smart growth and regional transit, and reduce carbon emissions in the process. This expansive view of the project and its potential to actually deliver such benefits is controversial, and the case helps to illustrate and extract lessons on how such large infrastructure projects emerge from debates over costs and impacts. The California case also illuminates some of the challenges that arise in forecasting and evaluating the performance of new systems such as HSR, illustrates the role of leadership in project design and delivery, and exposes some of the institutional and managerial vulnerabilities that such projects engender.

We have divided the edited volume into two parts. Part I addresses the question: What have we learned so far from HSR systems around the world? We asked contributors to go beyond the conventional cost-benefit analysis and financial risk assessments traditionally used for HSR projects and instead to present their views with an expansive lens that includes key social, environmental and political considerations. The chapters, written by leading experts in the field from their respective countries, outline the context in which various investments in HSR have been made, review and illustrate the methods and criteria that have been used to evaluate HSR proposals and monitor HSR performance, and present examples drawn from the experiences of Japan, France, Italy, Spain, Germany, China and Taiwan.

In Chapter 1, Deakin provides a brief historical introduction to HSR and deployment of HSR internationally to serve as background for the more detailed chapters that follow. The chapter also introduces the contextual and political issues that have deterred implementation of HSR in the United States.

In Chapter 2, Banister and Givoni provide an overview of HSR in Europe and then present the case of the UK, where rail is experiencing a resurgence and an HSR line connecting London to the Channel Tunnel has been built. A second proposed HSR line to the Midlands and north, HS2, has become mired in controversy. As the authors explain, the debates over HS2 have led to challenges to conventional cost-benefit analysis and the role of such factors as territorial linkages and national image in infrastructure decisions.

In Chapter 3, Hayashi, Mimuro, Han and Kato present a brief history of Japan's high-speed rail system, the Tokaido-Shinkansen, which opened in 1964 as the world's first HSR. The service was an immediate success and was expanded to other corridors, and today the system carries the vast majority of passengers travelling between major cities in Japan as well as some interregional travellers in the Tokyo area. The authors present an analysis of the system's impacts on economic development and urban concentrations, showing that impacts have been positive overall but are locally dependent on urban size and industrial structure.

In Chapter 4, Crozet discusses 'HSR mania', his term for the desire to extend HSR lines to ever more locations, regardless of the demand for such expansions. In France, the initial HSR line between Paris and Lyon was highly successful and additional lines extended to other major cities also fared well. Recently, however, expansions to smaller cities with limited economic activity have required subsidies, and budget constraints have forced officials to cancel or postpone several planned lines and reassess their criteria for approving new HSR. The chapter discusses evaluation methods that inform HSR decision-making and presents findings clarifying where HSR is likely to compete best with cars and air transport, emphasizing the importance of travellers' value of time and willingness to pay as well as the geography of urban and regional development.

Cascetta and Coppola in Chapter 5 discuss the Italian HSR system, which was strictly a government enterprise until 2012, when a private operator entered the market and now competes with the national rail company. The authors find that private competition has not only expanded service, but led all operators to offer differentiated price-service options, including some that have made HSR an option for moderate income travellers. Ridership has grown, primarily attracting trips away from the auto but also from air transport on longer routes. Competition also has led to increased on-board services and amenities.

In Chapter 6, Ureña, Benegas and Mohíno discuss the socioeconomic lessons of the Spanish HSR system, which was developed as part of a larger strategy for integration of Spain into the European Union and improving its economic position. System design choices aimed to increase access to the major metropolitan areas and their resources from smaller provincial centres. The resulting system, while costly, has greatly increased rail use, reduced emissions, and helped support territorial management objectives.

Rothengatter in Chapter 7 analyzes the case of HSR in Germany and in particular, its relationship to air transport. Unlike countries that invested in independent HSR lines where the trains can operate at speeds in excess of 300 km/h, Germany has built high-speed sections that link to upgraded conventional sections. The resulting speeds are slower than on other HSR systems and accordingly, HSR in Germany has not emphasized competition with air. Instead, Germany has tested four types of complementary functions of HSR, discussed in the chapter: 1) feeder service to airports; 2) taking over service between city pairs which are less profitable for air carriers; 3) serving as a backup system in the case of disturbances; and 4) providing a feeder system for air parcel service.

Chapter 8, by Ni, Chang and Kao, examines the Taiwan HSR experience. Taiwan's HSR was developed through a public-private partnership in which government secured the right of way and built a key station and a tunnel, and the private sector delivered the rest of the project, with a Build-Operate Transfer (BOT) contract for line construction and operations. Touted at the time as an example of a cost-effective project that had successfully tapped private sector capital, managerial practices and know-how, the project's subsequent financial difficulties and the interventions necessary to prevent bankruptcy eventually led to a restructuring of the ownership. The authors examine the factors that led to crisis, including overly optimistic forecasts of ridership, a poorly structured financing scheme, questionable accounting methodologies, and inexperienced private sector partners.

In Chapter 9, Pan, Ye and Chen discuss the effects of station location on ridership, drawing evidence from the case of Shanghai. China has tended to locate its HSR stations at the urban periphery to facilitate rapid line construction with lower costs. The authors show that this planning approach increases access trip length and decreases convenience for the majority of urban passengers using the system, most of whom are urban dwellers travelling for distances under 500km. The authors propose serving city centres with several smaller stations to reduce station costs while reducing connection times to the HSR system.

In Chapter 10, Pradayrol and Leray present the multifaceted and iterative analysis approach that is used in France to design and evaluate HSR proposals and reduce investment risks. A variety of models are employed and the models are continually improved by testing their results against observed data and making adjustments as necessary. Forecasts are subjected to 'stress tests' that reveal the likely consequences of potential disruptive occurrences. Operators are involved in the early design stages and multiple forecasts are carried out to test the effects of alternative designs and operations plans.

In Chapter 11, Nash discusses ways to improve the cost-benefit ratios of HSR projects. Based on a review of published studies, he concludes that revenues and travel time savings make up the largest part of HSR benefits; and fixed infrastructure costs are the largest part of costs, so designing a route that captures high ridership is the way to maximize benefits. Other important benefits of HSR are safety, reliability, and released capacity for freight and conventional passenger rail services; Nash finds that in comparison, economic development and environmental benefits are often small and context-specific.

Part II of this book turns to the California case, considering the promise of HSR in California, as well as the political, environmental and social challenges ahead.

In Chapter 12, Deakin introduces California's decision to proceed with HSR system development and the basic elements of the current plan to implement this project. From the start, HSR in California was intended not only to serve as an alternative to highway and airport expansion but also to help shift the state towards a more transit-oriented development model. Backers present the HSR system as the network that knits together the state's many urban areas and links their transport systems, facilitating seamless intercity transport and supporting sustainable growth. Critics charge that the system is too costly, that its ridership potential has been oversold, that its community impacts will be harmful, and that it focuses limited resources on the elite, leaving many other transportation needs unmet.

In Chapter 13 Calthorpe presents a vision for HSR that is more than transport infrastructure: as he puts it, HSR can be the 'backbone of a new set of development patterns and investments throughout our cities and towns.' Arguing that changing demographics, economic circumstances, and environmental mandates call for rethinking suburban development patterns, Calthorpe presents the results of an analysis showing that 'smart growth' strategies emphasizing city and town centres, higher densities, compact development, together with transit, bike and pedestrian orientation produce liveable urban districts and suburban communities with the increased affordability and environmental improvements that California is seeking. He argues that HSR supports these strategies, adding to local and regional economic development and contributing riders to local and regional transit systems.

Chapter 14, by Pérez Henríquez and Deakin, then presents a brief history and analysis of the role of legislation, politics and gubernatorial leadership in advancing HSR in California. Legislative action established the initial institutional framework for HSR development and provided detailed direction on how it was to be developed, but it also established constraints that have become part of the project's institutional stressors. Voter endorsement of the project has both enabled HSR to proceed and, along with environmental reviews, has created opportunities for challenges to the project's legislative compliance. Gubernatorial leadership has been important in keeping the project afloat during economic downturns and in securing federal funds,

In Chapter 15, Murakami and Cervero present findings from their analysis of development potential around HSR station areas in the Northeast Corridor and proposed station locations for the California HSR, as compared to the experience around HSR stations in Japan. They conclude that HSR is likely to deliver economic benefits primarily to knowledge-intensive businesses in large, globally connected cities, possibly at the expense of small intermediate ones. They see some potential for better linking peripheral areas with major city centres and key trip attractors such as airports and large recreational areas. To capture these benefits, they recommend that public authorities should encourage station area development and aggressively pursue joint development opportunities, recouping costs by capturing a portion of the accessibility and agglomeration benefits that would be capitalized into land values.

In Chapter 16, Deakin summarizes the anticipated environmental effects of HSR. Proponents of HSR in California have argued that it will deliver superior environmental performance. While the evidence shows that HSR would have a smaller environmental footprint than airports or highways, and could produce savings in emissions compared to air or auto travel, HSR nevertheless has adverse impacts as well. Both temporary losses, such as disruptions during construction, and permanent or ongoing impacts will occur. The latter include loss of access across tracks, losses in prime farmlands and habitats, noise and vibration due to train operations, and visual impacts of elevated structures, sound walls, and stations. Positive secondary impacts may accrue from station area opportunities for infill and higher densities around HSR stations, which may shift travel patterns toward non-motorized travel and transit. The timing of HSR is important because other modes are expected to become more environmentally friendly over coming decades, potentially reducing HSR's modal advantages.

In Chapter 17, Chester, Ryerson and Horvath argue that life cycle assessments (LCAs) should be used to evaluate the cumulative impacts of HSR and its chief competitors, auto and air. They also discuss the considerable uncertainties in such evaluations, considering in particular the effects of vehicle technology choices, fuel costs, and consumer values of time. Assuming the use of average (unmitigated) construction inputs, they produce an LCA assessment of CA HSR plans. Under the assumptions that they make, they find that emissions embodied in CA HSR infrastructure could be as large as propulsion emissions, suggesting that mitigation strategies should assess design and construction as well as operation. Otherwise it would take three decades of operation for HSR to offset the construction impacts and begin to deliver emissions benefits.

Nuworsoo presents an equity analysis of long-distance travel options for California in Chapter 18. He analyzes the 2001 and 2012 California Household Travel Surveys to reveal which segments of the population make long trips, and presents a modal analysis broken down by population group and distance travelled. The analysis shows most Californians make long-distance trips infrequently if at all, and the more affluent segments of the population are the most likely to make intercity trips; if travel patterns remain the same, HSR is likely to benefit the well-off more than the poor. Nuworsoo suggests that income equity could be improved by offering lower fares for youth and seniors or discounted passes for riders who belong to lower income brackets.

In Chapter 19, O'Hare and Audikana discuss opposition to HSR from the perspective of community activist 'not in my backyard' (NIMBY) sentiments. They assess some of the costs and benefits identified through the public participation processes surrounding the California HSR planning, and why and how some of the groups got involved and operate. They conclude that 'without appropriate political leadership that both recognizes and credits good behaviour and calls out the easy retreat to "my fair share...and not a penny more" morality into which project neighbours can easily fall, the complexity of NIMBY conflicts, both in terms of participants and issues, favours paralysis and failure.'

Loukaitou-Sideris and Peters' Chapter 20 builds upon three top lessons that emerged from an earlier Delphi survey of high-speed rail experts: 1) provide good connections with urban transportation systems; 2) plan stations as intermodal nodes; and 3) integrate the station with the surrounding urban form. The authors provide examples of best practices based on a review of HSR stations in Germany and Spain, and discuss how to apply these lessons to California's stations. They recommend designing California's stations both as functional transportation nodes with good connectivity and services, and as outward-oriented, social hubs with high levels of connectivity and good integration with the surrounding city fabric.

The final chapter of the book, by Deakin and Pérez Henríquez, provides a brief summary of the lessons that can be drawn from the international examples and the California case, focusing in particular on high-speed rail's potential to increase sustainability. They conclude that high-speed rail can provide a relatively fast, convenient, efficient, safe, cost-effective and environmentally responsible mobility service and can enhance economic, cultural and social sustainability, but to achieve these outcomes, it must be implemented in a supportive context. For California, they conclude that after some difficulties, forecasts of costs, ridership and revenues are now technologically adequate and so is their oversight, but that questions of political will to proceed still remain and are the project's major challenge.

* * *

The ideas presented in the chapters were tested and refined in a series of symposia and a conference before the final versions of the chapters were prepared. These events enabled researchers to present their findings and exchange views with business leaders, consultants, developers and operators of rail and HSR systems.

We are particularly grateful to our chapter authors for their thoughtful work and responsiveness to questions as the book progressed. The authors, all busy scholars, gave generously of their time in preparing their contributions to the book.

Major support for the project was provided by the French National Rail Corporation (SNCF) and the Center for Environmental Public Policy (CEPP) at the University of California, Berkeley (UCB), with additional contributions from the Institute of Transportation Studies (ITS) and the Institute of Urban and Regional Development (IURD) at UCB. In addition, support was provided for the final stages of the project through Stanford University's California – Global Initiative on Energy, Water & Infrastructure Innovation, a project co-sponsored by the Bill Lane Center for the American West and the Precourt Institute for Energy.

We also would like to thank the many participants in project reviews and campus events whose viewpoints enhanced the work presented here. They include SNCF's President Guillaume Peppy and his colleagues Lysianne Aubertin, Frank Bernard, Michel Leboeuf, Alain Leray, Anne de Martel, Fabrice Morel, Jean-Pierre Pradayrol and Sheherazade Zekri-Chevallet, as well SNCF practitioner representatives Pierre Messulam, Alain Le Guelle and Andreas Heym. Special thanks to Stringtheory's Pierre Tilhou for being our conduit to the wealth of expert knowledge that SNCF has in terms of lessons in technological advancement, development, planning, operating and financing of the French HSR system. Among the many who shared their perspectives and contributed their expertise to the discussions held during the academic-practitioner symposia were Gabriel Ahlfeld, Donna Andrews, Maria Ayerdi-Kaplan, Michael Bernick, Eda Beyazit, Sébastien Blandin, Marlon Boarnet, Sandip Chakrabarti, Karen Chapple, Dan Chatman, Stuart Cohen, Julien Dehornoy, Rod Diridon, Sr, Mark Hansen, Robert D. Infelise, Jim Lazarus, Michael D. Lepech, Samer Madanat, Mike McCoy, Gabriel Metcalf, James L. Oberstar, Sean Randolph, Gian-Claudia Sciara, Don Sepulveda, Lisa Schweitzer, Egon Terplan, Lou Thompson, Roelof Van Ark, Paul Waddell, Joan Walker and Jim Wunderman. We are also appreciative of the several dozen experts in the field who agreed to interviews with us regarding California HSR politics. Finally, we are grateful to Bruce Cain, who reviewed critical chapters of the book.

Special thanks go to our bright, methodical and diligent principal graduate research assistants (GSRs) at UC Berkeley for their heavy lifting in assisting us in getting this manuscript in shape for publication: Leo Covis and Joshua Dimon. Also, we are thankful to additional GSRs who throughout the development of this project provided research support: Jason Barbose, Ankit Jain, Nadia Rhazi and David Richey. In addition, thanks are due to the students who volunteered to take notes at our symposia and conference: Raphael Barchman, Craig Bosman, Marie Claire Evans and Anna Scodel. While we couldn't have done it without them, we assume responsibility for any editing gaps or mistakes in the text.

Finally, we dedicate this volume to three colleagues and friends who contributed to the early development of this project but passed away before it was completed: Denis Doute, who as CEO of SNCF America was always supportive of our project; Lee Shipper, whose enthusiasm about taming the energy and environmental consequences of transportation systems was always an inspiration to his many friends and colleagues; and UC Berkeley Professor John Quigley, whose interest in HSR and its political and economic dimensions kept us focused on making its analyses useful to public sector decision makers and the broader community.

Part I
What have we learned so far from high-speed rail systems around the world?

1 Background on high-speed rail

Elizabeth Deakin

At one time intercity rail transport was the pre-eminent means of travel for long-distance trips. With the advent of the automobile, rail began to lose market share; air transport further eroded rail's position. Up through World War II, however, rail remained a major mode of intercity passenger transportation throughout the world.

Post-war, countries took different approaches to intercity travel. In Europe and Japan, aging and war-damaged railroads were rebuilt and renovated. In Japan, France, Germany and Italy, new materials and innovative designs were tested as lines were upgraded. Rail ridership remained high despite growing auto ownership and air travel. In the US, in contrast, little public investment was made in rail and the nation focused instead on upgrading highways and airports. US rail ridership plummeted as highway modes and air travel gained market share and regulations hamstrung rail's ability to compete. Bankruptcies and mergers of the private rail companies were numerous. In 1970 the federal government moved to rescue the railroads by taking over most passenger services and operating them under a government-owned corporation, Amtrak. Transport deregulation in the following decades allowed private freight rail to regain a solid footing, but public US rail passenger services remained shaky, requiring annual subsidies to continue.

Speed has always been of keen interest to the railroads. American folk hero and railroad engineer Casey Jones, who died in 1900 while trying to keep his train on schedule, reputedly was running his steam engine at speeds nearing 100 mph (160 km/h). Trains in Germany, Italy, Great Britain and the United States ran at speeds reaching that figure in the early years of the twentieth century. Trains often averaged between 40 and 65 miles per hour (64 and 105 km/h), and most railroads offered faster 'express' trains between major cities. In the 1930s, railroads developed streamlined trains which were even faster; for example, in the US, Zephyr services reached speeds over 110 mph (180 km/h) with an average speed two-thirds of that.

However, it was not until the post-war period that commercial passenger rail speeds in the 150–200 mph (240–320 km/h) range were first attained. Tests conducted by the French National Railway in the 1950s showed that speeds over 300 km/h could be achieved with powerful electric locomotives. New designs were developed to reduce oscillations and swaying at these high speeds.

Japanese railway engineers began their own extensive research and development on high-speed rail in the 1950s, aiming to improve rail transportation for the densely populated and rapidly growing Tokyo-Osaka corridor. The Shinkansen became the world's first commercial high-speed rail system, opening just in time for the 1964 Olympics. The new service operated at speeds up to 210 km/h and averaged over 110 km/h. It was an immediate success. Further system expansions and technological improvements speeded the trains up even more, to the current 320 km/h, and locked in rail's commanding lead in Japanese domestic intercity travel markets.

In Europe, a high-speed rail service opened between Rome and Florence in 1978 with a top speed of 250 km/h. The French *train à grande vitesse* (TGV) began operation a few years later, in 1981, offering a service between Paris and Lyon with a 260 km/h (162 mph) top speed. The French HSR's popularity led to lines being built to other major cities in France and beyond and to technological improvements that have increased top speeds to 320 km/h.

Germany introduced HSR with its 320 km/h ICE train in 1991, building several new lines and upgrading segments of other lines. Spain began its system of dedicated HSR lines the following year. The Spanish system today is even larger than France's. Additional new HSR lines and section upgrades have been completed in Italy and Germany and lines have been added or extended to

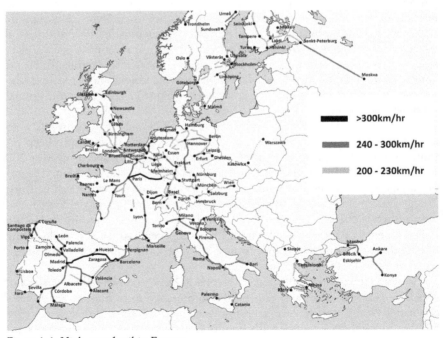

Figure 1.1 High-speed rail in Europe

cities in Belgium, the Netherlands and Great Britain. Austria, the Scandinavian countries, Poland, Turkey and Russia have also built HSR (see Figure 1.1).

Recently HSR has proliferated in Asia, with new lines in South Korea, Taiwan, and especially in China, where a massive investment in HSR has resulted in the country now having two-thirds of the world's total kilometres of high-speed rail lines (see Figure 1.2). In addition, HSR is underway or is proposed for Saudi Arabia, South Africa, and Morocco, and there are HSR plans for other countries in Eastern Europe as well as in Latin America.

The booming interest in HSR not only reflects a desire to emulate the successes of early adopters but also a desire to make intercity transportation more sustainable. Advocates for HSR enumerate a number of potential benefits, including competitive or superior door-to-door travel times, lower risks of delay due to weather or equipment problems, greater comfort on board, increased ability for travellers to make productive use of time while travelling, reduced congestion on highways and at airports, a lower level of environmental damage than from automobiles or aircraft, and higher potential for economic development due to station area development and inter-city linkages. The European Union has called HSR a sustainable transport mode and promotes it because of these broad social, economic and environmental impacts (EU 2010). Chinese leaders likewise have

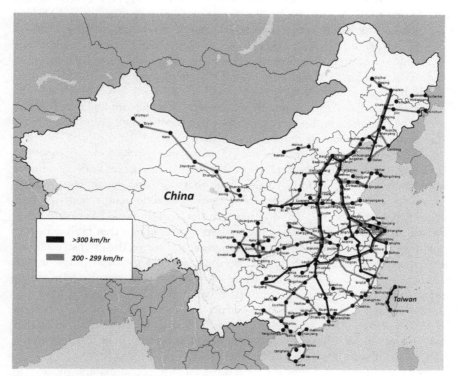

Figure 1.2 High-speed rail in China and Taiwan

cited energy independence, environmental benefits and economic development impacts as justifications for HSR.

The US, in sharp contrast, has given limited attention to high-speed rail. Amtrak has made improvements to increase passenger rail speed, comfort and reliability, but none comes close to the performance of HSR in other countries. Investments in the Northeast Corridor (Boston to Washington) have resulted in a near-high-speed service, the Acela Express. However, Acela reaches its maximum speed of about 150 mph (240 km/h) on only two sections of its route between Boston and New York and tops out at 135 mph (217 km/h) between New York and Washington. Elsewhere rail upgrades have increased train speeds, but generally to no more than about 80 mph (about 129 km/h).

Federal and state proposals for HSR operating at 150 miles per hour (240 km/h) or higher have emerged for a number of corridors across the US, but most have failed to move forward. The Passenger Railroad Rebuilding Act of 1980 led to a series of HSR corridor studies in the mid-1980s, and the Intermodal Surface Transportation Efficiency Act of 1991 (ISTEA) designated a number of HSR corridors. A lack of an obvious funding source, opposition from airlines, and concern about market risks meant that these proposals went nowhere. California, Florida, Texas and the upper Midwest are among the states and regions that have seriously considered HSR recently. The Obama Administration proposed funding HSR in ten corridors in addition to the Northeast Corridor as part of its recovery package in 2009, and the Federal Rail Administration proposed a series of projects all around the US (Figure 1.3). A few privately led proposals also have been floated, e.g., for service in Florida and between Los Angeles, CA and Las Vegas, NV. As of 2015, however, only California has moved forward toward HSR implementation. The CA project would build a network of fast passenger rail lines linking Los Angeles and the San Francisco Bay Area, eventually extending to Sacramento and San Diego as well. The first phase of this project is now under construction, even though many questions remain about route selection and financing.

HSR has been controversial in the US, and opposition has come from several directions. The high costs of HSR are a widespread concern, both in terms of construction and operations. Critics argue that the costs are simply too high, especially since for most projects a definitive funding source had not been identified. Observers question whether very much travel would be attracted away from auto and air. In addition, some analysts dispute claims that HSR generates significant environmental benefits, questioning and noting the intensive amount of energy and materials that must be used to build the new infrastructure. Comparing costs and benefits to those of other intercity travel modes, critics argue that HSR's advantage is marginal at best and is likely to decline over time as automobiles and aircraft become cleaner and more fuel efficient – especially if HSR is extended to smaller cities and areas with lower levels of economic activity, where ridership is likely to also be low (Peterman *et al.* 2013, Levinson 2013, Feigenbaum 2013, Will 2011, Grunwald 2014).

For the US case, differences between the American context and those of its international counterparts are also cited as reasons why HSR is a poor fit. In

Europe and Japan, HSR was introduced to populations that were already frequent users of rail systems. Gas prices were high; auto ownership was relatively low. Airlines had a weak presence in the short-haul market. Many trips, particularly for business, were focused on the central city, which for the most part was walkable and well served by transit. Large city pairs were several hundred kilometres apart. These conditions fit well with HSR capabilities and allowed the new system to compete effectively – and in several cases the government also helped HSR along by suspending or reducing operations on competing modes. While auto use has grown in Europe, HSR has competed effectively against most short-haul air offerings. China has likewise introduced HSR to a populace accustomed to intercity train travel, before autos or air had captured major market shares. But in the US, HSR would have to compete for riders with highway travel, available to almost everyone, and with low-cost airline fares. Relatively few Americans alive today have experience with intercity trains, fast or slow; car ownership is widespread and fuel is cheap; low cost airlines bring flying within the means of working families; cities are sprawling and multinucleated, often with more jobs in the suburbs than downtown; urban transit is spotty. These conditions make HSR a much harder sell.

Political opposition to HSR in the US has stemmed from such concerns, but it also has arisen due to localized concerns about land takings, noise, visual impacts and potential development pressures. In addition, there has been partisan opposition. In 2009, Congress appropriated $42.5 billion to help fund a variety of rail improvement projects, and the Federal Rail Administration received over $57 billion in requests for funding from thirty-four states. Funds were approved for thirty-one states and thirteen rail corridors in 2010; the projects funded

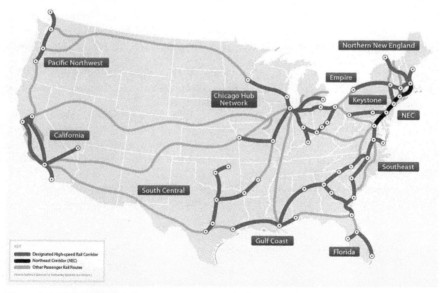

Figure 1.3 Federal Rail Administration vision for high-speed rail in America

ranged from new HSR initiatives to projects that would upgrade and straighten tracks, repair bridges and tunnels, and add sidings on existing rail lines. About $850 million was directed to projects in the heavily used Northeast Corridor. However, in 2011, newly elected Republican governors in Ohio, Wisconsin and Florida rejected federal allocations of HSR funding for their states. While that same year the Obama Administration proposed that rail improvements receive $53 billion over six years, the Republican majority in Congress have refused to appropriate any additional funds. Their reasons range from a preference for spending on highways to a belief that private investment is the better way to proceed with rail projects, with many criticizing the Administration for spreading money too thinly and supporting projects that were doomed to fail.

Meanwhile, in other parts of the world HSR construction continues. There are concerns about some of the extensions' ridership and financial performance, ongoing evaluations of social and environmental benefits vs. costs, and debates about the trip lengths and city sizes that HSR can serve well. Partnerships with the private sector have worked better in some cases than in others. Some analysts worry that HSR is overextended or is becoming so (*The Economist* 2015). Yet riders express satisfaction with the service, and many observers of the HSR systems applaud their growing reach and broader mission. The chapters that follow address these issues from a variety of perspectives, drawing upon international experience.

References

The Economist, 2015, 'High-Speed Rail in Europe: Problems Down the Line,' 10 January, 2015.

European Union (EU), 2010, *High Speed Rail: A Sustainable Link between Citizens*, Directorate General for Mobility, Publications Office of the European Union.

Feigenbaum, B, 2013, *High-Speed Rail in Europe and Asia: Lessons for the United States*, Reason Foundation.

Grunwald, M, 2014, 'The Truth About Obama's High-Speed Rail Program,' *TIME*, 11 August, 2014. At http://ec.europa.eu/transport/themes/infrastructure/studies/doc/2010_high_speed_rail_en.pdf (Accessed 1 August 2016).

Levinson, D, 2013, 'Why Covering The US In High-Speed Rail Makes No Sense At All,' *Business Insider*, 12 February 2013.

Peterman, DR, Frittelli, J and Mallett, WJ, 2013, *The Development of High Speed Rail in the United States: Issues and Recent Events*, Congressional Research Service, at http://www.fas.org/sgp/crs/misc/R42584.pdf (Accessed 1 August 2016).

US Federal Railroad Administration, 2009, High-Speed Rail Strategic Plan.

Will, GF, 2011, 'Why Liberals Love Trains,' *Newsweek*, 27 February, 2011.

2 Realising the potential of HSR
The United Kingdom experience

David Banister and Moshe Givoni

Introduction

Across the EU27,[1] travel by high-speed rail (HSR) has been the main driving force behind the recent growth in passenger rail travel. Although its overall share of travel is still modest – rail travel accounts for about 6.2 per cent of all travel in the EU27 (as measured by distance or passenger-kilometres), there has been a steady growth in the EU15 countries since 1990, about 1.5 per cent per annum. This has been seen by some as a rail renaissance or a second rail age in Europe (Givoni and Holvad 2009). However, the renaissance is not universal; the increase among the EU15 has been countered by a dramatic and continuing decline in rail travel in the newer members (EU12), where by 2011 the distance travelled by rail had fallen to one-third of its 1990 level. In addition, some observers challenge whether additional HSR is the best way forward.

In 1990, France was the only EU country that had invested in HSR, and at that time the high-speed services accounted for 23.4 per cent of France's rail passenger-kilometres (pkm). By 1995, HSR had spread to Germany, Spain and Italy, and by 2000 the main network had been established in eight of the EU27 countries. Over this 10-year period (1990–2000), the distance travelled in the EU15 by HSR had increased from about 15 billion pkm to 59 billion pkm (an increase of about 15 per cent per annum – 1990–2000). By 2011, that number had nearly doubled again in the EU27 to about 110 billion pkm (an increase of 5.2 per cent per annum), as shown in Table 2.1.

HSR currently accounts for over 27 per cent of all rail travel in the EU27, but in the individual countries that have invested heavily in new rail infrastructure, this figure is much higher. Over 41 per cent of all rail travel is by HSR in the countries that invested heavily in it, while among those that have made more limited investments in HSR, only 11 per cent of rail travel uses HSR. Considering overall rail travel, countries with no HSR experienced a modest 8 per cent increase in rail travel over the 16-year period, as compared to those with heavy investment in HSR, where rail travel increased by 26 per cent. It is worth noting that the group of countries with limited HSR investment experienced the greatest increase in rail travel – 56 per cent – but this increase may be distorted by the huge growth in rail travel in the UK, where privatisation in 1994/5 undoubtedly figured in the observed changes.

Table 2.1 HSR in EU27 (billion passenger–kilometres)

	1995	2000	2005	2010	2011
France	21.43	34.75	43.13	51.89	52.04
Germany	8.70	13.93	20.85	23.90	23.31
Spain	1.29	1.94	2.32	11.72	11.23
Italy	1.10	5.09	8.55	11.61	12.28
Sweden	0.42	2.05	2.33	2.94	2.83
Belgium	-	0.87	0.98	1.06	0.91
UK	-	-	0.45	1.01	5.98
Other	-	0.17	1.50	1.75	1.77
Total	32.94	58.80	80.11	105.88	110.35
% of all rail	9.4	15.9	21.2	26.2	27.1

Source: Author / DG TREN (2013)

Note: Other includes Czech Republic, the Netherlands, Portugal, Finland and Slovenia. HSR includes trains able to travel at more than 200 km/h, and this means that some of the Inter-City services in the UK have been reclassified as HSR so the total pkm has increased from 1.01 billion (2010) to 5.98 billion (2011).

This picture of rail travel in Europe provides the context for this chapter, which looks at the situation in the UK where rail is an important and resurgent mode of travel. Over 58 per cent of the UK population travel at least once a year by rail, and the number of journeys has doubled since 1995, from 735 million to 1,502 million in 2011 (GB DfT 2014). The distances travelled by passenger rail have also almost doubled in the past two decades, from 32 billion passenger-km (1994) to over 57.6 billion passenger-km (2013) (GB Department for Transport 2013b). Despite this substantial growth in rail use, however, rail accounted for only 7.4 per cent of the passenger-km travelled on land in the UK in 2011. This was 19 per cent higher than the average for the EU27 (6.2 per cent), but far behind Switzerland with 17.5 per cent (EU 2013).

High-speed rail to date has played a small role in the rail system in the UK. Of the increase in rail travel, the new HSR line between London and the Channel Tunnel (HS1) accounted for 18.1 million passenger journeys in 2011, or about 2.14 per cent of all rail travel in the UK. The proposal to build additional lines to the Midlands and the north (HS2) would increase availability of HSR to more of the populace, but the proposal has become embroiled in controversy.

This chapter focuses on the debate over HS2. The proposed project must be authorized by Parliament; as of Spring 2016 the authorization had been through its third reading in the House of Commons and had been forwarded to the House of Lords. The focus here is on the debate that has evolved from the more conventional cost benefit analysis and the importance of speeding up travel between UK cities, to a newer discussion over the means to provide additional capacity, connectivity, wider economic impacts, and improved national image.

The conventional economic analysis has become much more political in its approach, and this in turn has generated a range of coalitions for and against the investment. A new debate is emerging about the role of economic analysis

Table 2.2 Growth in rail travel in the EU15 (billions of passenger–kilometres)

Countries not investing in HSR				Countries with heavy investment in HSR				
	1995	2011	% change		1995	2011	% change	% all rail travel by HSR
Portugal	4.8	4.1	−15	France	55.6	89.0	+60	58.5
Denmark	4.9	6.6	+35	Germany	71.0	85.0	+20	27.4
Ireland	1.3	1.6	+23	Spain	16.6	22.8	+37	49.3
Greece	1.6	1.0	−38	Italy	46.7	43.3	−7	28.4
Austria	10.1	10.9	+8					
Finland	3.2	3.9	+22					
Luxembourg	0.3	0.3	-					
Total	26.2	28.4	+8		189.9	240.1	+26	41.2

Countries with limited investment in HSR				
	1995	2010	% change	% all rail travel by HSR
Belgium	6.8	10.4	+53	8.8
Netherlands	16.4	15.7	−4	2.0
UK	30.3	56.6	+87	10.6
Sweden	6.8	11.4	+68	24.8
Total	60.3	94.1	+56	10.7

Length of High-Speed Rail Network 2012 (km)

Countries with high levels of investment in HSR		Countries with limited investment in HSR	
Spain	2144	Belgium	209
France	2036	Netherlands	120
Germany	1334	UK	113
Italy	923	Sweden	
Total	6437 km	Total	442 km

Source: Author / DG TREN (2013)

Note: All seventeen new HSR lines currently under construction are in Spain (10), France (4) and Germany (3) – three will be in operation in 2015, and a further two in 2016 and two in 2017.

in helping to make decisions on large-scale transport infrastructure projects. In the past, the well-established methods based on cost benefit analysis had been accepted as an important part of the decision-making process, but more recently questioning of these methods has proliferated, with doubts raised about the values of time used in the analysis, the valuation of externalities, the difficulty of making demand forecasts over the longer term, the assumptions on the costs of travel by HSR, the wider economic benefits, and whether investment costs should be paid (or underwritten) by the public sector. Rather than one set of economic analyses, there are several different ones that have been produced by the different interested parties both for and against HS2 (Dudley and Banister 2014). This new form of contested realities has meant that non-contested situations where rationality has been seen as the means to resolve complex decisions (classic positivism) have been replaced by essentially untameable political problems with many different and conflicting realities (critical theory and constructivism) (Douglas and Wildavsky 1983; Martens and Van Weelden 2014).

Background on HS1 and HS2

Planning for the HSR in Southeast England began in the 1990s. As described by the National Audit Office (NAO 2012), the Department for Transport awarded a private finance initiative contract in 1996 to London & Continental Railways (LCR). LCR was to build the line and run the British arm of the Eurostar international train service (Eurostar UK). Construction began in 1998. The project was built in two sections, the first of which opened in 2003. Section 2, continuing the line to London St Pancras, opened in November 2007, bringing the total length to 108 km. The actual cost of constructing the high-speed line was £6.163 billion.

The Department had guaranteed the loans for the project but originally expected that the guarantees would not be exercised; it was anticipated that LCR would raise private sector finance against expected revenue from Eurostar UK. International travel was below expectations, however, and the government guarantees did come into play.

In 2009 the LCR was brought into public ownership and the right to run services on the high-speed line was put up for sale. The November 2010 sale price was £2,048 million for a 30-year concession to run the high-speed line. Of the 18.1 million total passenger journeys on the line in 2011, 9.7 million were international and 8.4 million were domestic. According to the NAO (2012) the international ridership figures on HS1 in 2011 were still well below the original estimates.

A second high-speed rail project, HS2, is proposed to be built in phases and would include a London to Birmingham line of about 221 km (Phase 1) and subsequent links (Phase 2) from Birmingham to Manchester (150 km) and Birmingham to Leeds (185 km). A Heathrow spur also would be built in Phase 2.

The total cost of HS2 is expected to be £40 billion or more (2011 prices). The total budget for Phase 1 has been estimated at £21.4 billion including a contingency of £5.8 billion, and Phase 2's total budget is £21.2 billion including a contingency of £8.76 billion. An additional £7.5 billion would also need to be spent on new rolling stock. If approved, construction could start as early as 2017, with Phase 1 being completed in 2026 and Phase 2 in 2033.

Table 2.3 presents some of the key findings from the studies of the proposed project. However, debate about the project's social and environmental impacts is vigorous and the economic case continues to be a matter of controversy.

Table 2.3 Selected impacts of HS2

Benefit Cost Ratio - Phase 1	1.4 – 1.7	
Benefit Cost Ratio - Phase 1+2	1.8 – 2.3	
Breakdown of the benefits of the proposed HS2 scheme	*Phase 1*	*Phase 1+2*
Time savings	17,334	45,679
Crowding benefits	4,068	7,514
Improved reliability	2,624	5,496
Car user benefits	568	1,162
Total transport user benefits	24,594	59,851
Wider economic impacts (WEIs)	4,341	13,293
Other impacts	407	788
Loss to Government of indirect tax	−1,208	−2,912
TOTAL – all prices in £M present values (2011)	28,134	71,020

Source: Author, Butcher (2014), GB DfT (2010b), GB DfT (2013a), Castles and Parish (2011)

The economic case for HS2

Five main elements seem to have dominated the economic debate over HS2 in the UK and the rationale for it: speed (or travel time), capacity, connectivity, wider economic benefits, and implicitly, image. These are discussed in turn below, along with the challenges that are arising in how each is conceptualized and measured.

Speed

Initially, the main benefits of the high-speed rail project were seen to be faster journeys, and the core of the business case was travel time savings for business users who valued their time highly and were willing to pay to save time. Overall, about 80 per cent of all user benefits were attributed to travel time savings, a level consistent with other large scale transport investment projects.

Travel time savings and speed as the means to save time have been overriding concerns of transport planning for the last 50 years. The rationale for counting travel time savings as a benefit is that travel is 'wasteful' (Hamilton 1989) and therefore travel time ought to be minimised. In this view, saved travel time can be used in other ways, among them to increase output and productivity; through the reduction of time expenditures (mainly achieved through higher speeds but also through other mechanisms such as process efficiencies, mechanisation, and other technology changes, Taylorism and Fordism) there can be a reorganisation of activities temporally and spatially which increase productive output. This perspective is complemented by a slightly weaker argument that a faster transport system provides a wider range of destinations and such greater choice is beneficial. The inevitable consequence of this thinking is to promote speed as the clear primary objective of transport systems to 'save time' and increase access. However, this has also led to longer travel distances, which results in greater use of resources, as higher speed increases energy consumption and carbon emissions. In addition, there are distributional outcomes (greater inequality).

Challenges to the view of speed as the most important objective for transport planning have come from several directions. One concern has to do with marginal benefits, both in time savings and in increased choice in spatial opportunities, versus marginal cost. Another challenge is the travel time budget argument, which reasons that if trips are speeded up, travellers will on average simply make more or longer trips. If additional travel is generated to use the 'saved time', then the motivations for speeding up travel become less clear. Still another view, backed by evidence from traveller behaviour, is that travel time is highly onerous under some conditions but far less so under others. The ability to make productive use of time while travelling by rail is an important element in this debate.

For HS2, the value of time assumed in initial analyses was challenged as too high and has subsequently been reduced by almost a third. To some extent this has been offset by an increase in the numbers of projected business travellers. The growth in rail (classic and HS2) was assumed to increase threefold, far faster than the growth rate for other forms of transport; HSR demand was expected to increase by 1.9 per cent per annum to 2043, a rise of about 96 per cent on current levels.

Castles and Parish (2011) question these forecasts, believing them to be optimistic as they were related to high economic growth rates over longer than usual time horizons. Their best estimates for HSR demand are 30 per cent lower than those used in the official demand forecasts, which on its own would reduce the benefit cost ratio (BCR) from 1.6 to 1.1, making the project marginal as an economic investment decision. Furthermore, if sensitivity analysis is carried out as part of the evaluation and the value of time is set at the commuting rate, this again would reduce the BCR, in this case from 1.6 to 1.2 (Castles and Parish 2011).

Some scholars have argued that more flexible objectives, such as 'reasonable' travel time and travel time reliability, may be more appropriate ways to determine investment priorities (Banister 2011). Such arguments draw upon alternative views of travel time as a social construct, the quality of which should be maximised and more highly valued (Cresswell 2006, 2010). The benefit of placing travel and travel time within a wider context is that it extends and enriches our understanding of the human processes behind travel, and it begins to make more explicit the real reasons for the differences in behaviour. It is not just a matter of economic uses of time that determine the value of travel, but important personal (emotional, relational and experiential), cultural (societal) and social factors that are also instrumental in everyday decisions about travel. The commodification of time has led to just one aspect of time, namely travel time savings, being emphasised over all other aspects of time.

There is a huge literature on the concept of time and its many expressions (Adam 1995). Perceptions about the pace of life speeding up are common, and technology is seen as being the main driver. But these relationships are not simply unidirectional (acceleration), as new complex linkages are being established between technological innovation and the use of time, which include finding time and having more of it, and considering how time practices change (Wajcman 2008). The concern with time savings needs to be balanced with a richer interpretation of the many different constructs of time that might begin to increase our understanding of travel decisions, the quality of time and the benefits of slower not faster movement (Banister 2011).

More generally, the traditional positivist approach to transport analysis is now being questioned, as travel can no longer only be seen as a derived demand with no real value in the activity of travel. Both the empirical and theoretical evidence challenges the continued emphasis over the need to speed up transport to 'save time' and the assertion of constant aggregate travel time budgets (Metz 2008). Travel itself has a substantial and positive value in some cases. Factors related to the quality of the experience, including ease of use, reliability and comfort, have important impacts on the perception of time during travel and travel choices. The use of time while travelling, coupled with technological advances in IT, vehicle designs and operating rules, and the economics of passenger space, can result in time being seen as productive and not wasted (at least in part) (Cairns *et al.* 2013; Lyons *et al.* 2013).

For all these reasons, the valuation of time has become a matter of contention in the HS2 debates.

Capacity

The debate in the UK has more recently concentrated on the need to develop HSR because of the lack of *capacity* on the conventional rail network. This reason was behind investment decisions in the Shinkansen in Japan and the TGV in France (Givoni 2006, and Chapters 3 and 4 of this book), and more recently the HSR in China (Fu *et al.* 2012). In the UK, the need for HS2 was accentuated by the forecast growth in the demand for rail and expected lack of peak capacity, especially on the West Coast Main Line (WCML) that runs from London, through Birmingham, Manchester and Liverpool, to Glasgow in Scotland. Part of the concern here has been with the reliability of travel, but overcrowding is also at issue, as is how these factors impact on the experience of rail travel and affect demand. This new debate broadens the concern over speed to include the reliability and crowding aspects of the travel experience.

The initial HS2 plans included eighteen train services per hour from London at peak, with each train able to provide over 1,000 seats (two sets of 200m-long trains). This capacity is intended not only to serve demand on the HS2 route, but importantly to free capacity on the conventional (slow) network due to the diversion of some demand to the HS2. It will also allow more track capacity for use by freight trains. All these factors together serve several policy goals, including shift of freight transport from road to rail, and they are expected to form the large bulk of the economic benefits of HS2. However, there are several limitations in this strategy that need to be considered, and these could significantly erode the economic case.

First, doubts have been raised whether it is technically and practically feasible to run eighteen trains per hour. In comparison, Eurostar normally operates three trains per hour and can increase this to five at peak, while in Japan and France, where there is a much longer tradition of HSR operations, twelve trains per hour is achieved. The demand for eighteen trains per hour (a maximum of about 18,000 passengers per hour) is only likely to exist at the peak, with much lower demand during the rest of the operating day. The additional costs of planning to cater for forecast peak demand needs to be carefully considered.

Diverting demand and services from the conventional network to HS2 could harm the remaining passengers on these routes in several ways. HS2 would primarily serve the main cities and the trains would bypass (not stop in) intermediate cities. These cities are likely to see the frequency of conventional train services reduced as the demand originating from these cities might not be large enough to support the same service frequency once some demand transfers to HS2. There is also the risk of a downward spiral as an initial reduction in service frequency will negatively affect demand and this will in turn lead to further reductions. The new HSR line may also require a share of the available operating and maintenance resources, and this may have a detrimental impact on the conventional network, further suppressing demand.

Investment in HS2 provides an increase in capacity on a very specific route benefiting only a few locations (stations). Many other lines in the UK are far more congested than the proposed route of HS2, and suggestions have been made about whether there are cheaper ways of providing additional capacity that would provide wider benefits. Castles and Parish (2011) have commented that the capacity of the standard class seating on the West Coast Main Line can be more than tripled from the 2008 base at a relatively low cost. Suggestions have included longer trains, reconfiguring trains, more standing room in trains, investing in signalling and other control systems, and the use of peak pricing methods (Starkie 2013).

Increased capacity is expected to reduce crowding and improve service reliability, and both of these factors are important components in passengers' experience of travelling by rail. Crowding is a problem at peak demand periods, and as indicated above, capacity could be increased in a more cost-effective way to address this issue. With the increased ability to use travelling time, the need for speed or shorter travel time is reduced, but the reliability of the service remains crucial. Passengers want to be on time, and if sufficient capacity is provided to operate a daily timetable with some slack, reliability will improve. When a rail network is operating at capacity and the maximum number of trains that can be safely operated are running, any delay or disruption to one service can have a knock-on effect on the entire timetable and the network. While high-speed trains provide the maximum capacity (more trains can be run through a station within an hour), their operation creates conflicts with other slower trains. This is one of the reasons why HS2 requires a costly dedicated track. Where slow and fast trains share part of the line, for example at stations, the complexity of operations increases, and with it the propensity for disruptions and delays. A slower train network might be more reliable.

Connectivity

A third aspect underlying the motivation to build HS2 has been the need for greater *connectivity*. Connectivity has several different aspects. One is the ease to get from origin to destination, and speed here plays a role, but it is the average speed door-to-door (not the maximum speed) and ease (or inconvenience) of transfer between modes of transport that is central. Another related aspect is the ease of access to the many (spatially distributed) destinations. Although it is the main (high-speed) part of the journey that receives most attention, and this is the part of the journey that will cost the most to provide or improve, the potential in reducing overall travel time door-to-door is most likely to be achieved by interventions at the station and in improving its accessibility to other modes of transport (Givoni and Rietveld 2007; Brons *et al.* 2009).

The nature of HSR suggests a low number of intermediate stations along the route, as each stop can 'cost' up to 15 minutes (Connor 2011). Having fewer stations makes HSR faster while also making HSR more difficult to access. HSR in this respect might be viewed like an airport, although a noticeable advantage HSR has is that its station(s) are often in the city centre. But city-centre location is costly, due not only to the size of the station (HSR trains can be 400m long) but the need to traverse densely populated areas, often requiring tunnelling. City-outskirt locations could reduce such costs, but this option will make the station less accessible for most passengers (Banister and Givoni 2013). To compensate for the low number of stations, HSR should be fully integrated with the rest of the transport network, and it is this integration that will increase connectivity, namely the ease of getting from the trip origin to many destinations.

Access to an HSR station and journey can be divided between local (urban), regional and national, and international levels. At the local level it is the integration with the rest of urban public transport that is critical – and here lies another advantage for city-centre location for the station, as this is where most of the public transport network is concentrated. Many HSR stations located in the outskirts suffer from lack of demand due to poor accessibility from the city centre (e.g. in Taiwan; Chou *et al.* 2011). At the regional level, integration with the conventional rail network is most critical, as rail will be the main feeder of traffic for HSR. An integrated rail-HSR service means that both the high- and low-speed trains need to share a station, otherwise the penalty of transferring between stations even if only a few hundred meters apart can reduce the accessibility and time savings HSR might offer. Martínez Sánchez-Mateos and Givoni (2012) demonstrate that this problem will occur in Birmingham, where the new (planned) HSR station is located about a 5-minute walk from one of the busiest conventional rail stations in the UK (Birmingham New Street Station). City-centre station location will be advantageous at the regional level for integration with public transport, but location in the outskirts will allow the provision of large parking facilities and this will favour integration with urban and regional car journeys. As HSR is a competitive mode of transport for up to 1,000 km,

HSR stations at large airports are another critical element for providing better connectivity internationally. Such airport stations will also have the advantage of substituting rail for air on some routes.

The need to integrate conventional, slow rail services with high-speed services can be overcome by designing the HSR to be fully compatible with the conventional rail network, as is the case in France with the TGV. This has not been an option that has been extensively discussed and examined in the case of HS2, although it is suggested that HS2 services could continue north to Scotland on the conventional lines. As part of planning HS2, an analysis by Network Rail (2013) suggested seamless transfer between HS2 and other rail services is the most beneficial way for integrating HS2 into the rest of the rail network, but the report concluded that further investigation is required. A recent report on HS2 (GB DfT 2014) proposes an extension of Phase 1 beyond Birmingham to a new hub station at Crewe, about 60 km to the north. This hub will allow more cities to benefit from HS2, by integrating HS2 with the conventional rail network and the road network at Crewe.

From the early days of planning HS2, a motivation for its construction was 'bringing the regions closer', that is to reduce the geographical separation and divide between South (London) and the North (Newcastle, Leeds, Manchester, Liverpool, etc.) and thus reduce the economic disparities between these regions. HS2 will no doubt bring the connected cities closer in terms of rail travel time, city centre to city centre, but the effect of this might only be further strengthening the South at the expense of the North. The question arises as to whether the better connected core city (London) benefits more than the secondary cities that are connected to it, as there might be an abstraction effect as businesses and people move or commute longer distances to the core city. The evidence is mixed, but there does seem to have been a concentration of activities in both Paris and Madrid after the HSR networks in both those countries opened, and this was at the expense of the secondary cities (WBS 2012). London is probably in a similar position as it is the dominant city in the UK in terms of population and share of the national economy, and London and the Southeast also provide the headquarters for sixty-six out of the FTSE largest companies, while the area in England north of Birmingham hosts only six such companies (GB DfT 2014). With improved connectivity to London, there is a risk that these companies will move to London, rather than some of the sixty-six companies moving their headquarters to the North.

Wider economic benefits (WEB)

Banister and Thurstain-Goodwin (2011: 213) conclude that 'transport benefits should always be the main outcome of a transport investment', but there is the question of what benefits are being sought. In addition to improved travel times and accessibility, increased capacity, and greater connectivity, investments in HSR are increasingly justified based on the wider economic benefits, including employment, regeneration and agglomeration benefits.

The Department for Transport has estimated that HS2 would create 3,100 permanent jobs in operating the new railway and around 24,600 temporary jobs (excluding the supply chain) during construction. There might also be up to 400,000 jobs in additional developments in areas close to HS2 stations (House of Commons 2013). These estimates were based on a report prepared for the Core Cities Group – the cities concerned are Birmingham, Bristol, Leeds, Liverpool, Manchester, Newcastle, Nottingham and Sheffield – by consultants (Volterra/ ARUP 2011), and they are controversial. It is not clear that investment elsewhere in the economy, for example in improving and developing the conventional rail network or investments outside the transport system (e.g., in education), would not provide similar or greater employment benefits.

A considerable amount of research has been carried out on the agglomeration effects, mainly with respect to intra-regional changes, and the key question here is whether they are also found on an inter-regional scale as well (Graham and Melo 2010). The basic argument is that improved connectivity within a city or region can compound the benefits of agglomeration by making spatial economic transactions between firms and other organisations more efficient through mechanisms such as sharing, matching and learning (Duranton and Puga 2004). There are difficulties here in the specification of the relationships and in their measurement, and in the implied causality (including the strength of the statement – whether agglomeration effects *cause* higher output or productivity). Graham and Melo (2011) examined long-distance travel flows in Britain to provide an indicative assessment of the potential order of magnitude of agglomeration benefits, resulting from travel time reductions. They draw conclusions from this analysis by making inferences as to the likely effect on HSR and conclude that 'even in the best case scenario for the improvement in long-distance travel times and the market share of classic and high-speed rail, the potential order of magnitude of the agglomeration benefits is expected to be small.' They qualify their conclusion by saying that their analysis refers to the domestic market but 'benefits could also arise from improved connections to continental Europe (Paris, Brussels, Amsterdam, etc.) by linking HS2 to HS1.' From this econometric analysis it seems that the agglomeration effects observable at the intra-regional level are either not apparent or are difficult to measure (or both) at the inter-regional level, where HS2 is likely to have the most impact.

In contrast, Chen and Hall (2011) have developed the argument that improvements in rail travel time can result in wider economic benefits, even if these are not quantifiable (or are difficult to measure). When examining the effect of introducing high-speed rail services on some trunk routes in the UK – entering into service the IC125 (intercity trains with a 125mph/200kph maximum speed) and IC225 (intercity trains with a 225 kph/140mph maximum speed) in the late 1970s and early 1990s respectively – they found that 'substantial and demonstrable effects in aiding the transition to knowledge economy within a 2-hour travel limit of London, thus helping to generate renewed economic growth, but the effects have not been automatic or universal'. Furthermore they concluded that 'Cities connected to a new HST could seize opportunities which non-HST cities will not be able to seize.' The implications for HS2 are clear. First, it cannot be assumed that HS2 will automatically bring wider economic benefits (Graham and Melo 2011), and secondly, that if it does bring such benefits it will be for a selected number of places that are probably already benefiting from economic growth, and the introduction of HSR would then enhance such growth (Chen and Hall 2011).

The final issue that has featured in the debate over HS2 has been the *image* of HSR, as promoting a modern view of transport, and that the UK was lagging behind its European neighbours and international competitors. Unlike many other countries such as Spain, Italy, Germany and France, and those outside Europe, such as Japan and China, the UK (where rail transport was invented) is lagging behind in joining the HSR era, despite one short high-speed line (HS1). The UK rail network was perceived as old, crowded, and unreliable, and this could reflect on the whole image of the country. The speed of the HSR is central in the image of an advanced, state-of-the-art rail development and technology. If high-speed rail is defined as reaching speeds of up to 350 kph (the maximum operating speed of French and Chinese HSR), but was originally considered to be 200 kph, then it should not be surprising that the HS2 is designed with a maximum operating speed of 400 kph. The issue here is whether the perceived efficiency of the rail transport system of a country influences the overall perspective of foreign investors and companies about whether they should invest in that country. This does not just relate to the HSR network, but the rail (and transport) system overall, and it is not clear whether speed is the most important determinant of that image, and even if it were, whether the high cost of HSR would be justified.

The political case for HS2

In the past, the political debate mainly stayed in the background of major decisions on infrastructure, but this is no longer the case. Many well established interests have been supplemented by a new generation of advocates, both for and against the HS2 proposals. Politicians from all parties, national and local, have been principal advocates for and against HSR, and HS2 has had a high profile in the press and in media news coverage. The politicians, from prime ministers, ministers of transport and further down the political hierarchy, have represented different sides of the debate largely based on political party affiliation, but they have often replaced support for HS2 with objections to it in the process (see Hall 2013 for illustrations of this). Other important stakeholders have been the various NGOs, largely objecting to HS2, and industry stakeholders, largely supporting it. But even here the boundaries have not been clear cut, for example the Confederation of British Industry (CBI) originally supported HS2 but later cast doubts on its business case, stating that 'Important questions need to be answered before we undertake a project of such significance, in particular about how the project would be financed and managed as well as how a new high-speed rail network would complement existing transport networks' (CBI 2010). The CBI also stated that HS2 could strengthen long term economic prospects, but that six conditions would need to be met if business support was to be guaranteed. The government must ensure commitment to the full high-speed network, promote international gateways and networks, get private sector funding agreed before construction starts, safeguard any negative effects on rail freight, safeguard spending in other areas of transport capital spending, and support climate change objectives.

The Institute of Directors (IoD), a UK business organization, has called for the government to abandon HS2, branding it as 'a grand folly' (IoD 2013). A survey of IoD members found that 27 per cent felt that HS2 represents good value for money and 70 per cent stated that the scheme would have no impact on the productivity of their business. On the other hand, the IoD survey reported that only 6 per cent of directors say they never work on the train, with 48 per cent saying that they spend at least half the journey working, a further 26 per cent work for between a quarter and half the time, and 21 per cent spend up to a quarter of the journey time working – their conclusion is that work is an essential part of travel by high-speed rail and that travel time is productively used.

Some of the NGOs have been generally in favour of investment in rail, but the HS2 proposal is not seen to be so environmentally advantageous, particularly when it passes through unique natural habitats (e.g. the Chiltern Hills). For example, Friends of the Earth state 'We support increases in rail capacity to enable modal shift from air and road to reduce carbon emissions. However, HS2 can only help if it is part of a wider policy and funding framework that ensures more urgent priorities that will cut more carbon more quickly and have wide societal benefits are adequately supported' (FOE 2011). Greengauge21 was a unique NGO in this respect, as it was established by the industry to promote (for non-profit reasons it was argued) HSR in the UK and indirectly HS2. Greengauge21 was pivotal for the promotion of HS2 from just an idea to a concrete plan which was then adopted by the government. Each of these political stakeholders was supported by research (from academia or in consultancy), and they have provided the evidence to base policy on, or the evidence to support the policy decided on. This is the nature of the contested realities, as no one group has all the expertise needed to make the decision on HS2, and it is the putting together of political, economic, business and NGO alliances that now seem to hold the key to the final decision.

There are however many difficulties with this process as complex (and often unnatural) alliances take place between the different interested parties, and all participants increasingly use the media (including social media), their own research, and lobbying to gain influence either for or against the proposal. Underlying the decision is the necessary access to finance and the overall costs of the project. This in itself carries considerable risk in terms of potential cost overruns, demand expectations not being fulfilled, and the wider economic effects not being fully realised. The inclusion of optimism bias in the estimates and large contingencies may also add to the possibility of cost overruns. Reality rarely matches up with expectations. There are also potential risks, as once decisions are made there are substantial sunk costs so that if a subsequent government decides to reverse the decision, then compensation may have to be paid. This is why political consensus is important.

Over time, the balance in the rhetoric has changed from an economic rationale to a political one that also has a range of key dimensions. It seems that the economic case has been sufficiently weakened to make it untenable, and increasingly the planning function of government (the main decision maker) has switched from economic to political. Markets no longer dictate outcomes, and expertise has become more politicised. Governments are accountable to the electorate, but major decisions like HSR seem to require cross-party support and a clear leader to push the decisions through the parliamentary processes. A recent example of this change has been from David Higgins, the new Chairman of HS2 Ltd, the executive agency charged with implementing the HS2 project. He has stated that HS2 responds to a 'national need' and that HS2 is a 'catalyst for change', as there is a lack of rail capacity south of Birmingham and a lack of connectivity in the North, both between the northern cities and to the South. He is now trying to build a strong consensus and an alliance around these overtly political and emotional objectives (GB DfT 2014).

Conclusions

The era of rational decision making has now passed, and it could be argued that it never existed, as all major infrastructure decisions are essentially political. But it does seem that decisions surrounding HS2 in the UK have become much more overtly political over time. Strategic decisions now seem to be based on their legacy value and our responsibilities to future generations. One basic question here is the extent to which analysis and expertise can help in making decisions that take more than 10 years to realise (or at least three parliaments, and where the main beneficiaries are a future generation of riders). Over 70 per cent of current rail users are between 25 and 60 years of age (GB DfT 2010a).

There is still a need for analysis, but it seems that narrow based benefit cost ratios are rather restricted in terms of what is currently offered, as they have been criticised for being overly optimistic on both the demand and cost estimates (Flyvbjerg 2007). The current debate over whether travel time, particularly by HSR where distances (and times) are long, is wasted or productive continues, but it is clear that future generations will be able to make more use of it than at present and in ways that we have not currently thought about. Analysis that depends on the wider economic impacts is also currently limited, as issues around causality, whether employment opportunities are new (and permanent) or transfers between locations, the treatment of time, and the role that external factors play (economic, social and technological), all contribute to increased uncertainty.

Perhaps future uncertainties should be explicitly included in the process, but there needs to be long term stability about strategy that can provide continuity between parliaments. This continuity is necessary to give confidence to investors and to provide the means to have clear accountability in parliament. A Royal

Commission on major infrastructure decisions might provide the means to have an open and clear debate about alternative strategies that would address all forms of transport, and think strategically about longer term futures.

We do not know what future generations will do with their time, or how much and to where they will be travelling, or the potential for new types of activities and the untapped power of technological innovation. Within this set of choices, the role for HSR might be substantial or very limited. This does not seem to have been a debate that the great Victorian railway pioneers had and we are grateful for that, but the question still remains as to whether we should do the same now.

Note

1 There are currently 28 Member states of the EU (year of entry): Austria (1995), Belgium (1952), Bulgaria (2007), Croatia (2013), Cyprus (2004), Czech Republic (2004), Denmark (1973), Estonia (2004), Finland (1995), France (1952), Germany (1952), Greece (1981), Hungary (2004), Ireland (1973), Italy (1952), Latvia (2004), Lithuania (2004), Luxembourg (1952), Malta (2004), Netherlands (1952), Poland (2004), Portugal (1986), Romania (2007), Slovakia (2004), Slovenia (2004), Spain (1986), Sweden (1995), United Kingdom (1973). EU27 refers to all these countries except Croatia. EU15 refers to all countries that were members of the EU before 2000, and EU12 covers those that joined between 2004 and 2007.

References

Adam, B 1995, *Timewatch: The Social Analysis of Time*, London: John Wiley.

Banister, D 2011, 'The trilogy of distance, speed and time', *Journal of Transport Geography*, Vol. 19, no. 4, pp. 950–9.

Banister, D and Givoni, M 2013, 'High-Speed Rail in the EU27: trends, time, accessibility and principles', *Built Environment*, vol. 39, no. 3, pp. 324–38.

Banister, D and Thurstain-Goodwin, M 2011, 'Quantification of the non-transport benefits resulting from rail investment', *Journal of Transport Geography*, vol. 19, no. 2, pp. 212–23.

Brons, M, Givoni, M and Rietveld, P 2009, 'Access to railway stations and its potential in increasing rail use', *Transportation Research Part A*, vol. 43, no. 2, pp. 136–49.

Butcher, L 2014, 'Railways: High Speed Rail (HS2)', *House of Commons Library Briefing Paper*, no. SN00316, 14 April 2014, p. 24, www.parliament.uk/briefing-papers/sn00316. pdf, Accessed 1 August 2016.

Cairns, S, Harmer, C, Hopkin, J and Skippon, S 2013, 'Sociological perspectives on travel and mobilities: a review', *Transportation Research A*, vol. 64 (May), pp. 107–17.

Castles, C and Parish, D 2011, 'Review of the economic case for HS2: economic evaluation of the London to West Midlands line', *Report for the RAC Foundation*, November, http:// www.racfoundation.org/assets/rac_foundation/content/downloadables/hs2_review-castles_parish-281111.pdf, Accessed 1 August 2016.

CBI 2010, *On the Right Track? The Business View of High Speed Rail*, London: Confederation of British Industry, http://www.cbi.org.uk/media/544779/90F4E6238662DBA180257 7FC003D2FDC__CBI%20brief%20-%20The%20business%20view%20on%20high-speed%20rail.pdf, Accessed 1 August 2016.

Chen, CL and Hall, P 2011, 'The impacts of high-speed trains on British economic geography: a study of the UK's InterCity 125/225 and its effects', *Journal of Transport Geography*, vol. 19, no. 4, pp. 689–704.

Chou, J-S, Kim, C, Kuo, Y-C, and Ou, NC 2011, 'Deploying effective service strategy in the operations stage of high-speed rail', *Transportation Research Part E: Logistics and Transportation Review*, vol. 47, no. 4, pp. 507–19.

Connor, P 2011, Rules for high speed line capacity, railway technical web pages: http://www.railway-technical.com/Infopaper%203%20High%20Speed%20Line%20 Capacity%20v3.pdf, Accessed 1 August 2016.

Cresswell, T 2006, *On the Move: Mobility in the Western World*, London: Routledge.

Cresswell, T 2010, 'Towards a politics of mobility', *Environment and Planning D*, vol. 28, no. 1, pp. 17–31.

DG TREN 2013, *EU Transport in Figures: Statistical Pocketbook 2013*, Brussels, European Union, http://ec.europa.eu/transport/facts-fundings/statistics/pocketbook-2013_ en.htm, Accessed 1 August 2016.

Douglas, M and Wildavsky, A 1983, *Risk and Culture: An Essay on the Selection of Technological and Environmental Dangers*, Los Angeles: University of California Press.

Dudley, G and Banister, D 2014, 'The economic case for HS2', *Submission to the House of Lords Committee on the Economic Case for HS2*, September, p. 7.

Duranton, G and Puga, D 2004, 'Micro-economic foundations of urban agglomeration economies', in: Henderson, V and Thisse, J-F (eds), *Handbook of Urban and Regional Economics*, Volume 4, Amsterdam: North Holland, pp. 2063–117.

EU 2013, *EU Transport in Figures – statistical pocketbook*, European Union, Luxemburg.

Flyvbjerg, B 2007, 'Policy and planning for large-infrastructure projects: problems, causes, cures', *Environment and Planning B: Planning and Design*, vol. 34, no. 4, pp. 578–97.

Friends Of The Earth 2011, *FOE Response to the Government's Consultation on HS2*, London, Richard Dyer, http://www.foe.co.uk/sites/default/files/downloads/hs2_consultation0. pdf, Accessed 1 August 2016.

Fu, X, Anming, Z, Zheng, L 2012, 'Will China's airline industry survive the entry of high-speed rail?' *Research in Transportation Economics*, vol. 35, no. 1, pp. 13–25.

GB Department For Transport 2010a, *National Rail Travel Survey: Overview Report, Update, December*, https://www.gov.uk/government/uploads/system/uploads/attachment_data/ file/73094/national-rail-travel-survey-overview-report.pdf, Accessed 1 August 2016.

GB Department For Transport 2010b, *High Speed Rail*, Cm 7827, The Stationery Office, March.

GB Department For Transport 2013a, *Strategic Case for HS2*, The Stationery Office, October.

GB Department For Transport 2013b, *Transport Statistics Great Britain*, The Stationery Office, December.

GB Department For Transport 2014, *HS2 Plus – A Report by David Higgins*, High Speed 2 (HS2) Limited, http://assets.hs2.org.uk/sites/default/files/inserts/Higgins%20 Report%20-%20HS2%20Plus.pdf, Accessed 1 August 2016.

Givoni, M 2006, 'The development and impact of the modern High Speed Train', *Transport Reviews*, vol. 26, no. 5, pp. 593–612.

Givoni, M and HOLVAD, T 2009, 'The prospects for European railways: is the second railway age still here or yet to begin?' *Built Environment*, vol. 35, no. 1, pp. 5–10.

Givoni, M and Rietveld, P 2007, 'The access journey to the railway station and its role in passengers' satisfaction with rail travel', *Transport Policy*, vol. 14, no. 4, pp. 357–65.

Graham, D and Melo, P 2010, *Advice on the Assessment of Wider Economic Impacts: A Report for HS2*, February http://webarchive.nationalarchives.gov.uk/+/http:/www.GB DfT. gov.uk/pgr/rail/pi/highspeedrail/hs2ltd/appraisalmaterial/pdf/widereconomicreport.pdf, Accessed 1 August 2016.

Graham, D and Melo, P 2011, 'Assessment of wider economic impacts of High-Speed Rail for Great Britain', *Transportation Research Record: Journal of the Transportation Research Board*, no. 2261, pp. 15–24.

Hall, P 2013, 'High Speed Two: The great divide', *Built Environment*, vol. 39, no. 3, pp. 339–54.

Hamilton, BW 1989, 'Wasteful commuting again', *Journal of Political Economy*, vol. 97, pp. 1497–504.

House Of Commons Transport Committee 2013, 'High speed rail: on track?' *Ninth Report of Session 2013–14*, HC 851, December.

Institute Of Directors 2013, *Press release*, 27 August 2013, http://www.iod.com/influencing/press-office/press-releases/institute-of-directors-calls-on-the-government-to-abandon-hs2 , Accessed 18 September 2014, no longer available.

Lyons, G, Jain, J, Susilo Y and Atkins, S 2013, 'Comparing rail passengers' travel time use in Great Britain between 2004 and 2010', *Mobilities*, vol. 8, no. 4, pp. 560–79.

Martens, K and Van Weelden, P 2014, 'Decision making on transport infrastructure and contested information: a critical analysis of three approaches', *European Planning Studies*, vol. 22, no. 3, pp. 648–66.

Martínez Sánchez-Mateos, HS and Givoni, M 2012, 'The accessibility impact of a new High-Speed Rail line in the UK – a preliminary analysis of winners and losers', *Journal of Transport Geography* 25(2), pp. 105–14.

Metz, D 2008, 'The myth of travel time saving', *Transport Reviews*, vol. 28, no. 3, pp. 321–36.

National Audit Office 2012, *Completion and Sale of High Speed 1*, *Report by the Comptroller and Auditor General, Session 2010–2012*, HC1834, March.

Network Rail 2013, 'Better connections: options for the integration of High Speed 2', *Network Rail*, July. Available from https://www.networkrail.co.uk/improvements/high-speed-rail, Accessed 1 August 2016.

Starkie, D 2013, 'Transport infrastructure: adding value', *Institute for Economic Affairs Discussion Paper*, no. 50, London, November.

Volterra/ARUP 2011, *Understanding the Transport Infrastructure Requirements to Deliver Growth in England's Core Cities*, Manchester Core Cities Group.

Wajcman, J 2008, 'Life in the fast lane? Towards a sociology of technology and time', *The British Journal of Sociology*, vol. 59, no. 1, pp. 59–77.

Warwick Business School 2012, *Warwick HS2 Forum: Final Report*, Unpublished Report from the WBS for the Warwick HS2 Forum, January.

3   The Shinkansen and its impacts

Yoshitsugu Hayashi, Aoto Mimuro, Ji Han and Hirokazu Kato

Introduction

The first line of Japan's Shinkansen high-speed rail system, Tokyo to Osaka, opened in 1964. The fast and innovative service was an immediate success. Lines were extended to other parts of Japan in a series of projects implemented in the ensuing years. Now 50 years old, the Shinkansen system has carried over 11 billion passengers and in doing so it has helped to transform the Japanese economic landscape.

This chapter presents a brief history of the Shinkansen, discussing its special features, its ridership, and its mode share over the years. The chapter then examines the impacts of the system on population concentrations and industrial location. A model of the latter is developed to distinguish the effects of the Shinkansen's accessibility improvements from other factors driving industrial growth and change. The final section of the chapter summarizes the key findings.

Development of the world's first HSR – the Shinkansen

In the mid-1950s, Japan faced a serious shortage of railway capacity due to the heavy and increasing demand for both passenger and freight transport. Demand was especially heavy in the Tokaido corridor connecting the cities of Tokyo, Nagoya and Osaka. Earlier government plans to improve the national rail systems had been developed but only small portions of the proposals had been implemented. In order to tackle the growing transport problem, in 1956 Japan National Railways established the Tokaido-Line Improvement Committee at its headquarters. Three improvement measures were discussed: (1) widen the existing narrow gauge (1,067mm) rail line, (2) construct a new dedicated line with narrow gauge, or (3) construct a new dedicated line with standard (1,435mm) gauge. After several meetings, in December 12, 1958, the new Five-Year Plan of Railway Improvement was adopted by the Transport Ministry, specifying that a new dedicated railway line with standard gauge should start construction in 1959, for completion by the opening of the Tokyo Olympic Games on October 10, 1964. The Tokaido Shinkansen connecting Tokyo and Osaka opened on October 1, 1964, just in time for the Olympics. The twelve-station, 552.6 km line connecting Tokyo and Osaka was the world's first high-speed rail service on dedicated track.

Since its debut over 50 years ago, the Shinkansen network has been extended to over five times its original length, to its current 3,407 km (as of March 2016). The various extensions and their opening dates are shown in Figure 3.1. Figures 3.2-1 and 3.2-2 show the Shinkansen in its early days and Figure 3.2-3 shows the train as it appears today.

The Shinkansen was constructed under a completely new concept with an exclusive track, almost no at-grade crossings, and extensive use of tunnels and viaducts to keep grade changes to a minimum. In addition, the Shinkansen was equipped with an Automatic Train Control (ATC) system and a Centralized Traffic Control (CTC) system, both new technologies at the time. These design innovations and technological advances, which have been updated over the years, produce the train's distinguishing features:

- **High speeds:** When service started in 1964, the Tokaido Shinkansen operated at a maximum speed of 210km/h, much faster than any other train in the world at the time. Since then, the speed of the Shinkansen has been increased step by step, to 220km/h in 1985, 270km/h in 1992, and most recently to 300km/h in the Sanyo Shinkansen and 320km/h in the Tohoku Shinkansen (see Figure 3.1). High speeds are achieved by a combination of network design, train design, and operating systems.
- **High frequencies:** The automated control system allows the trains to operate with short headways. In 2013, the system was operating 336 trains per day with over twelve trains per hour from Tokyo to Osaka.
- **High reliability:** The Shinkansen is punctual; in 2013, the average delay time was **30 seconds**. This high reliability has been achieved by the system design (in particular the separated guideway) and control features (ATC, CTC), together with highly trained operators. The CTC system was first implemented in 1964 and has been substantially expanded and improved since then, first with COMTRAC (COMputer aided TRAffic Control system) and then with COSMOS (COmputerized Safety, Maintenance and Operation System).
- **High safety:** The Shinkansen has experienced only one fatal accident (at a grade crossing) since its opening in 1964. There have been two derailments, one during an earthquake and one during a blizzard, but no deaths resulted. An earthquake detection system and anti-derailment devices have been installed to further ensure safe travel.

In addition, the Shinkansen provides high capacity transport. The Shinkansen was designed at a time when rail was the major transport mode for the Japanese populace, with heavy and dense demand. The system was accordingly designed to carry a large number of passengers per train as well as to operate frequently. A Tokaido Shinkansen trainset consists of sixteen cars, providing 1,323 passenger seats.

Figure 3.1 High-speed rail network in Japan (2016)

Figure 3.2 The Shinkansen, then and now

Shinkansen ridership

In its first year of operation, the Shinkansen attracted 30.97 million annual passengers (MAP), or about 87,000 passengers per day. Ridership nearly tripled between 1965 and 1970, and topped 160 MAP by 1974. Ridership then grew more slowly on the Tokaido-Sanyo Shinkansen, with added growth system-wide largely due to the opening of additional lines and stations (Figure 3.3).

The growth in Shinkansen ridership tracks economic conditions in Japan (Figure 3.4). Ridership boomed in the 1960s along with the Japanese economy, which was growing by 10.13 per cent per annum in that period. Ridership declined during the economic downturns caused by the oil crises of 1973–75 and 1980–83, but picked up again with economic recovery. During the 'bubble economy' of the late 1980s, ridership grew by 8.2 per cent per annum; with the collapse of the bubble, ridership levelled off. Ridership on the Tokaido-Sanyo

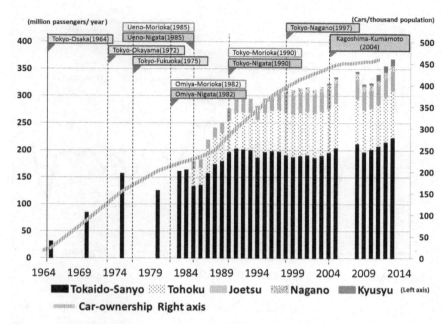

Figure 3.3 Annual passenger volume on all Shinkansen networks

line has remained just under 200 million passengers per year; it accounts for over 60 per cent of total ridership on the network of Shinkansen lines.

Ridership increases have resulted from the addition of lines and extensions, particularly the 1985 Tohoku Shinkansen connecting Tokyo and northern Japan. Like its predecessor, the Tohoku Shinkansen immediately attracted a high ridership, starting with 31 million passengers per annum – almost the same volume that the Tokaido-Sanyo Shinkansen achieved in its first year. Ridership on the northern line increased by a factor of 2.6 before levelling off in the 1990s. The line has been the system's second highest performer despite the fact that there are no big metropolises along the route.

The Joetsu Shinkansen, connecting Tokyo with Nigata, opened in 1982 with 16 million passengers in its first year. It experienced solid growth in use and currently carries about 50 million passengers annually. However, more recent lines have been less productive. The Nagano Shinkansen, opened in 1997, started with 5.1 million passengers per annum and carries somewhat less than twice that number currently. The Kyushu Shinkansen, extending from Fukuoka to Kagoshima on Kyushu Island in the south, opened in 2004 with 2.8 million passengers per year.

High ridership was achieved on the Shinkansen and has been maintained over five decades despite the fact that Japan was rapidly increasing its auto ownership and building expressways during the same period. Figure 3.3 traces car ownership from 1964 to 2013. Car ownership grew from only eighteen passenger cars per 1,000 in 1964 to about 225 per 1,000 by 1984, and to over 400 per 1,000 by the

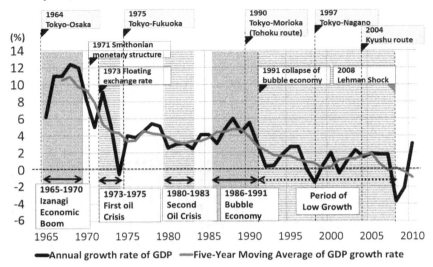

Figure 3.4 Annual growth rate of GDP (1965–2010)

end of the century. Freeway building during this period included the Meishin Expressway (Nagoya-Kobe), which opened in 1964, and the Tomei Expressway (Tokyo-Nagoya) which opened in 1969. However, the Shinkansen's top speed of 210km/h was double the expressways' top speed of 100 km/h, and with high petroleum prices, auto use was three times more expensive per person-km than the train.

Two other factors helped confirm preferences for travel by Shinkansen. One was that it was made available at a time when conventional trains were the dominant travel mode, at the beginning of Japan's motorization era, before driving habits were established. A second move that helped to cement the train's position was the political decision to abolish the air route between Tokyo and Nagoya at the start of operation of the Shinkansen in 1964. The result has been a commanding lead for high-speed rail for intercity trips over 200 km, as discussed in detail in the following section.

Shinkansen's share of intercity travel

Figure 3.5 shows mode share data for travel from Tokyo to other major cities in Japan in 2010. The data are based on averages including weekdays, weekends, and holidays. They show that the Shinkansen has captured over 70 per cent of the intercity trips under 900 km. However, for travel from Tokyo to Fukuoka (1,175km), Shinkansen's share is only 15.1 per cent.

Inter-city mode share is affected not only by line-haul travel time and distance but also the time it takes to get to and from the business districts and residential areas where the trips start and end. Comparison of these factors to those for other intercity modes (air, auto) reveals where modal advantages and disadvantages lie.

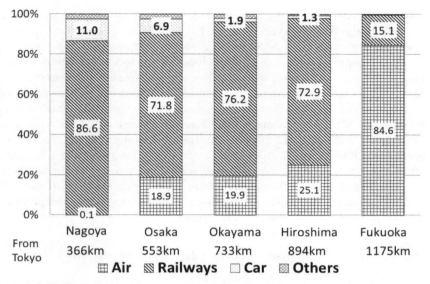

Figure 3.5 Mode share, intercity travel from Tokyo (2010)

Line-haul time on the Shinkansen is always faster than by car, but access time to and from stations can reduce the train's competitive edge, especially for shorter trips. This shows up in the data for Nagoya, where 11 per cent of travellers from Tokyo drive the 366 km. (Other factors such as travel party size and the desire to have a car at the destination end of the trip also enter into the auto mode choice decision.)

Line-haul time by Shinkansen is almost always slower than on-board flight time, but long airport access times and long wait times in the air terminals can reduce the apparent advantage of flying. Airport access is more likely to require transfers than when Shinkansen is used, and scheduling can be less convenient because flights are less frequent than train departures. Since travellers care about door-to-door travel times and schedules, these other factors can weigh heavily in their travel decisions. For example, between Tokyo and Hiroshima, it takes 3 hours 55 minutes to travel by Shinkansen between the city pairs' main stations, whereas it takes only 3 hours 30 minutes to make the same trip by air including access times. However, air attracts far fewer trips than the Shinkansen, reflecting the inconvenience of airport access (45 minutes by bus) and the relatively low frequency of air service (seventeen flights per day vs. seventy Shinkansen departures).

Air transport is more competitive and Shinkansen's mode share is lower for trips between Tokyo and Osaka than for trips to Hiroshima, even though Osaka is closer to Tokyo. This is largely due to the high level of air service between Tokyo and the three airports in the Osaka metropolitan area (Itami, Kansai and Kobe).

Between Tokyo and Fukuoka, 1,175 km along the Shinkansen track, air carries 84.6 per cent of the trips, and Shinkansen just 15.1 per cent. By air, it takes 3 hours 30 minutes door to door, 1.5 hours less than by Shinkansen. In addition, travel from the Fukuoka Airport to the Fukuoka main station in the centre of town takes only 6 minutes by subway. It is very convenient for passengers.

These examples indicate that station location and local accessibility are very important factors for high-speed rail. They also suggest that air could capture a higher share of the trips currently made by HSR if airport access were improved.

The case of the Yokohama station underscores the importance of local accessibility. While Yokohama is Japan's second largest city, with 3.7 million inhabitants, and is located adjacent to Tokyo, it is not well situated on the Shinkansen line, as the Shin-Yokohama station is 5 km away from Yokohama's central rail station. As a result, it is relatively inconvenient for Shinkansen passengers to access Yokohama city centre. The effects show up in the city's employment data, which show it capturing a smaller share of service employment than its size and prime location would suggest.

Impacts of the Shinkansen on urban development patterns

Impacts on population and the economy

In 1964, the population of the Tokyo metropolitan area had already reached 22.4 million, making it one of the world's largest urban agglomerations. Tokyo was also the capital city and the nation's chief financial and cultural centre. At that time, the populations of the Nagoya and Osaka metropolitan areas were 7.9 million and 14.4 million respectively. The two cities were important manufacturing hubs and Osaka was a leading regional centre. The opening of the Tokaido-Sanyo Shinkansen meant that these major cities were connected at three times the previous speed, and with much improved reliability. This transformation of the physical connections supported extraordinary changes in other dimensions of urban geography.

By 2009, the population of the Tokyo metropolitan area had increased by 170 per cent to 38 million, while the Nagoya metropolitan area had reached 11 million and the Osaka metro area topped 20 million. The three major metropolises today constitute half of the nation's population and a similar share of the employment. However, Tokyo had strengthened its dominant position among Japan's largest cites, and indeed as one of the leading metropolises in the world. Osaka has remained an important city but has lost some of its role as a centre of commerce.

The Shinkansen played a role not only in the overall economic development of the served areas but also in the positional growth of Tokyo. From the beginning, because of its substantial impact on the accessibility of various cities, the Shinkansen contributed to urban growth and development. The impacts were differential across the three major cities along the original line because of their relative locations and economic roles. The main cities were also affected by the subsequent Shinkansen extensions, which brought smaller cities into the high-speed rail network and in so doing changed their relationships to the main cities and their roles in the Japanese economy.

The Shinkansen's impact must be viewed in the context of international as well as interregional competition. During the period in which the Shinkansen was introduced, Japan was losing international market share in light manufacturing, though it was capturing market share for automobiles. Leading service industries, meanwhile, were increasingly seeking locations with excellent access to financial and legal services and a highly skilled professional workforce as well as high levels of amenity. The net result was to increase the attractiveness of world cities such as Tokyo and to reduce the appeal of secondary cities. The greater access provided by the Shinkansen underscored these economic trends.

Looking at the economic effect of the Shinkansen, we can see that Tokyo has benefited and the effects on Japan's secondary cities have varied. All three of the large metro areas connected by the first Shinkansen line have grown substantially, but their specific experiences have differed.

First let's consider Osaka. In 1964, the Osaka metropolitan area, also known as the Kansai region, had 14.4 million population within a 50 km radius, including cities such as Kyoto, Kobe and Nara. Osaka had long been the dominant gateway for West Japan and an international centre for manufacturing, trade and commerce.

Economic competition hit hard at key manufacturing enterprises in the Kansai region in the 1970s and 1980s. In the 1970s the region's textile industries lost market share to lower-cost countries such as Taiwan and Korea. In the 1980s the region's electronics industries such as Panasonic and Sanyo declined for similar reasons.

High-speed rail was unable to address the factors causing manufacturing decline. However, by increasing the relative accessibility of Tokyo, it reduced some of Osaka's regional advantage over the larger capital city. Some company headquarters moved to Tokyo once the Tokaido Shinkansen had greatly improved interregional accessibility. In addition, with extensions from Osaka to Okayama, Hiroshima, and Fukuoka, these cities gained in relative accessibility as well, and were better able to compete with Osaka for regional employment that might otherwise have been located in Osaka.

The Nagoya metropolitan area's industrial base was different from that of Osaka and its economic trajectory was different as well. In Nagoya, manufacturing employment had stagnated through the 1970s because, as in Osaka, Nagoya's textile industry had moved offshore. But Nagoya's manufacturing sector recovered because of the rapid growth of its automotive industry. Toyota, headquartered in Nagoya, became a major employer and stimulated the development of a wide range of parts industries. This industrial base was well anchored in the region and was linked to international markets, and therefore could not be swallowed up by Tokyo. Nagoya was also able to attract tertiary industries to service the industrial base.

The various regions and their hinterlands and the populations of the cities along the key Shinkansen routes are shown in Figure 3.6. Changes in regional population 1964–2014 are shown in Figure 3.7.

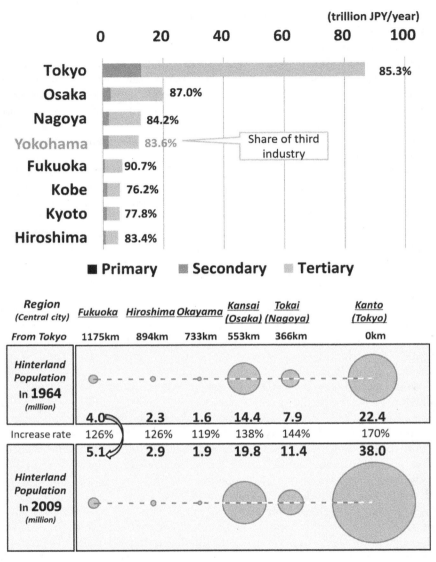

Figure 3.6 Major cities and their hinterlands; 2009 populations

The implications are that secondary cities both grow and lose position as a result of vastly increased interregional accessibility. They can resist these trends and protect their regional economies if they have unique assets – less so if the industries they host are not firmly anchored in place and can be lured elsewhere by lower wages, larger markets, higher level services, more amenities.

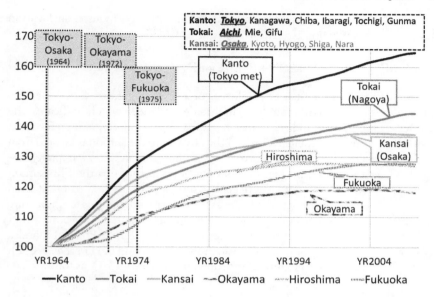

Figure 3.7 Population change, 1964–2004 (1964=100)

A deeper look: modelling the Shinkansen's impacts on industrial and business location

Large economic trends have brought about population and employment changes in Japan (and other nations as well) over the last 50 years. Some of these changes, it has been argued, have been supported and even accelerated by the Shinkansen, but for other changes the Shinkansen most likely had little effect. To more firmly identify the Shinkansen's role in economic transformations, and especially its impacts on industrial location and related population shift, several relationships were tested in a formal model.

We used the work of previous studies (e.g. Nakamura *et al.* 1983; Sumitomo Trust Business Research Institute 1991) as a base since the authors had already explored the role of broad economic factors affecting industrial location choice. We add to the analysis by incorporating the local accessibility to the Shinkansen network as another potentially important driving force. Good access to interregional passenger services is likely to be of great value to some industries and of relatively little importance to others.

A logarithm-type multivariable stepwise regression model is used to analyze the Shinkansen's impacts on eleven industries' location choice in forty-seven Japanese prefectures for 1990 and 2000. The major industries are: 1) agriculture, forestry and fishery, 2) mining, 3) manufacturing, 4) construction, 5) electric power, gas and water supply, 6) transport and communication, 7) commerce, 8) finance and insurance, 9) real estate, 10) services, 11) public administration. The number of employees is used to represent the size of each industry in location choice. The specification is as shown in Eq. (3.1):

$$\ln(EMPL_i^k) = \alpha^k \ln\left(InterD_i^k\right) + \beta^k \ln\left(ConsD_{ik}\right) - \gamma^k \ln\left(AT_i\right) + C^k \tag{3.1}$$

where $EMPL_i^k$ is the number of employees of a specific industry k in prefecture i; $InterD_i^k$ is a function of industrial interdependence, which indicates the interaction influence of industries in other areas on the industry k in prefecture i; $ConsD_i^k$ is consumption demand only in the city where the station is located from neighbouring areas on the products or services offered by industry k in prefecture i; and AT_i is a weighted average access time of prefecture i to the Shinkansen network, which to some extent reflects the difficulty of an area to profit from Shinkansen. It is assumed that the larger AT_i the more difficult it is for prefecture i to attract employees from other industries and areas. Finally, C^k is a constant.

A detailed description of the variables ConsD and AT in Eq. (3.1), and a discussion of the data employed for the analysis can be found in Han *et al.* (2012).

The explanatory variable InterD is defined by Eq. (3.2)–(3.4), as follows:

$$InterD_i^k = \sum_m \theta^{mk} (\sum_j EMPL_j^m \cdot PL_{ji}^{mk}) \tag{3.2}$$

where θ^{mk} denotes the employment correlation between industry m and k; $EMPL_j^m$ is the number of employees of k's relevant industry m in neighbouring prefecture j; PL_{ji}^{mk} is the probability of industry m in prefecture j in choosing prefecture i to trade with industry k, which is further defined by the model in Eq. (3):

$$PL_{ji}^{mk} = \frac{EMPL_i^k \exp(\lambda^{mk} \cdot GC_{ji})}{\sum_j EMPL_i^k \exp(\lambda^{mk} \cdot GC_{ji})} \tag{3.3}$$

where λ^{mk} is a distance decay parameter when industry m trades with k. Here we set the value of λ at 1.0, which is consistent with previous work on accessibility (Frost and Spence 1995; Gutiérrez 2001). GC_{ji} is the weighted average generalized transport cost from prefecture j to i, which is measured by

$$GC_{ji} = \sum_{n \in N} s_{ji}^n \cdot (F_{ji}^n + \omega^n \cdot t_{ji}^n) \tag{3.4}$$

where n denotes transport mode, which means airway, highway and railway (conventional railways and Shinkansens) in this study; s_{ji}^n is the modal share of n in the total transport from prefecture j to i; F_{ji}^n is transport fare of mode n from j to i in JPY; t_{ji}^n is travel time of mode n from j to i in minutes; ω^n is time value of mode n in JPY/min.

The probability of industries' choices among different prefectures is illustrated in Figure 3.8.

Figure 3.9 shows the interdependence among the eleven industries. Taking construction as an example, it is found that real estate and electric power, gas and water supply rely heavily on the construction industry, whereas construction is mainly dependent on the inputs of commerce, services, manufacturing, transportation and communication. Such a strong correlation suggests that industrial interdependence may play an important role in construction's location choice.

The model results are shown in Table 3.1. It is found that in 1990, the dominant variable that influenced industrial location was industrial interdependence (InterD). In eight out of eleven industries, including construction, finance and insurance, and public administration, their elasticity is as high as 0.70–

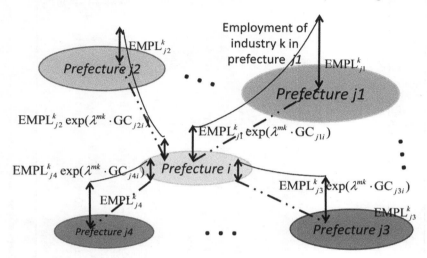

Figure 3.8 Probability of industries' choices among prefectures

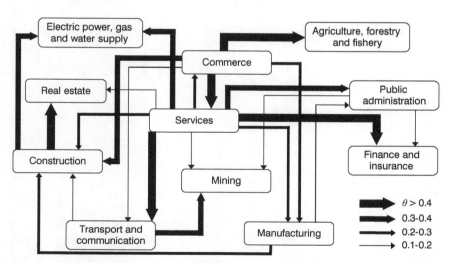

Figure 3.9 Interdependence mechanism among eleven industries in 2000

Note: only the value of θ larger than 0.1 is mapped

Table 3.1 Estimates with cross-section data for 1990 and 2000

Industry	1990					2000				
	InterD	ConsD	AT	C	R2	InterD	ConsD	AT	C	R2
Agriculture, forestry and fishery		0.35** (2.53)		4.86*** (3.19)	0.29		0.41*** (3.58)		2.27*** (4.95)	0.20
Mining	0.25* (1.92)	0.21* (1.77)		0.33 (0.18)	0.35	0.16* (1.93)	0.29*** (3.25)		0.47 (0.39)	0.40
Manufacturing	0.44** (2.58)	0.40** (2.49)	-0.04* (-1.69)	0.32 (0.49)	0.96	0.19** (2.04)	0.56*** (5.36)	-0.05* (-1.89)	1.05* (1.73)	0.97
Construction	0.89*** (15.66)		-0.07** (-2.37)	1.93** (2.27)	0.90	0.79*** (12.52)		-0.09* (-1.79)	2.89** (2.97)	0.87
Electric power, gas and water supply	0.50** (2.48)	0.35* (1.70)	-0.07** (-2.56)	-1.99** (-2.43)	0.93	0.44* (1.97)	0.38* (1.80)	-0.06* (-1.69)	-1.89** (-2.17)	0.91
Transport and communication	0.39* (1.82)	0.56** (2.47)	-0.11*** (-4.43)	-1.44** (-2.67)	0.98	0.34* (1.98)	0.73*** (4.25)	-0.08* (-1.80)	-3.53*** (-5.21)	0.97
Commerce	0.59*** (3.62)	0.31* (1.84)	-0.09*** (-4.15)	1.34** (2.42)	0.98	0.45** (1.96)	0.49** (2.15)	-0.13** (-2.46)	0.15 (0.20)	0.98
Finance and insurance	0.72*** (8.24)	0.17** (2.27)	-0.04** (-2.48)	-0.35 (-0.86)	0.96	0.50** (2.19)	0.37* (1.62)	-0.04 (-1.32)	-2.68*** (-3.52)	0.97
Real estate	0.25* (1.76)	0.77*** (4.09)	-0.15*** (-2.72)	-3.73*** (-2.47)	0.89	0.18* (1.86)	0.85*** (5.58)	-0.21*** (-3.53)	-4.45*** (-3.04)	0.90
Services	0.52*** (3.05)	0.38** (2.15)	-0.08* (-1.69)	0.63 (0.96)	0.98	0.49** (2.05)	0.47** (2.05)	-0.11* (-2.38)	-0.30 (-0.40)	0.97
Public administration	0.70*** (13.82)		-0.09* (-1.98)	2.26** (3.09)	0.89	0.57*** (3.78)		-0.14** (-1.84)	5.14** (2.36)	0.84

Source: Author

Note: *significance: 10%, **significance: 5%, ***significance: 1%. Figure in parentheses is t-value.

0.89, which indicates that a 100 per cent increase in employment in said industry would result in 70–89 per cent growth in the number of employees in the corresponding industry. However in 2000, the most important variable affecting industrial location was consumption demand from neighbouring areas (ConsD), a finding applicable to over half of the industries including real estate, transport and communication, and manufacturing, with elasticities ranging from 0.29 to 0.85.

The effect of access time to Shinkansen (AT) on industrial location is relatively small compared to that of the other two explanatory variables, suggesting that interregional passenger accessibility matters but does not dominate location decisions. Location elasticity with respect to AT was in the range of −0.04 to −0.21 for most industries and showed a slight increase from 1990 to 2000. The increase is consistent with expectations that the more the Shinkansen network is expanded, the more significant its impact will be on the regional economy, including industrial location.

To illustrate the model results, consider the change in employment for eleven industries in the Nagano prefecture 1990–2000, shortly after the Hokuriku line opened. Passenger access time to the Nagano prefecture decreased significantly as a result. The model predicts and the data show that employment has increased in industries such as real estate, services, commerce and public administration, for which the importance of Shinkansen interregional access time is relatively high.

In sum, industrial location choice is driven by many variables including industrial interdependence and consumption demand in neighbouring areas; accessibility to Shinkansen plays a relatively minor role but one that has become somewhat more important over time as the system has expanded. The Shinkansen appears to be more important in location decisions of industries like real estate, commerce and services, and public administration, and hence is likely to have a greater affect on the location decisions of enterprises in those fields.

Conclusions

The analyses presented in this chapter show that Japan's Shinkansen network has provided a fast, safe, efficient intercity transport service for trips in the range of 100–900 km. The system has attracted high mode shares in this distance range, dominating both auto and air transport. Introduction of the system at a time when automobile use was low and rail was the dominant intercity mode may have helped to establish the Shinkansen as the preferred mode for intercity travel, but its competitive door-to-door travel times and convenient station locations have helped to keep it in heavy use despite widespread auto ownership, prosperous income levels, and competitive air transport in many city pair markets including Tokyo-Osaka. The analysis also shows that while many factors affect economic growth and location choices, the added connectivity of high-speed rail may have affected population and industrial urbanization patterns, especially for service industries and their workers, who have increasingly concentrated in the cities served by the Shinkansen, and especially in Tokyo.

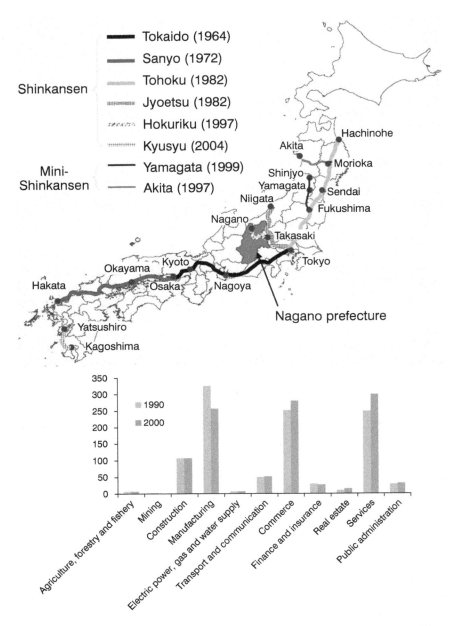

Figure 3.10 Number of employees for eleven industries in Nagano prefecture 1990–2000

References

Frost, M E, Spence, N A, 1995, 'The rediscovery of accessibility and economic potential: the critical issue of self-potential,' *Environment and Planning A*, vol. 27, pp. 1833–1848.

Gutiérrez, J, 2001, 'Location, economic potential and daily accessibility: an analysis of the accessibility impact of the high-speed line,' *Journal of Transport Geography*, vol. 9, no. 4, pp. 229–242.

Han, J, Hayashi, Y, Jia, P, Yuan, Q, 2012, 'High speed rail's economic effect: empirical analysis of Shinkansen's impact on industrial location,' *Journal of Transportation Engineering*, vol. 138, no. 12, pp. 1551–1557.

Nakamura, H, Hayashi, Y, Miyamoto, K, 1983, 'A land use-transport model for metropolitan areas,' *Papers in Regional Science*, vol. 51, no. 1, pp. 43–63.

Sumitomo Trust Business Research Institute, 1991. *Survey report on land use plan of megacities*. Tokyo, Japan.

4 Where high-speed rail is relevant
The French case study

Yves Crozet

Introduction

Since the 1980s, high-speed rail (HSR) has spread rapidly. The first line of the Japanese Shinkansen was inaugurated in 1964 and the initial line of the French *Train á Grande Vitesse* (TGV) began operations in 1981. Both countries subsequently expanded their networks and other countries have followed suit. Today, HSR projects are numerous, not only in Europe and in Asia, but in Africa and in the United States.

Enthusiasm for HSR runs high. However, HSR projects also raise numerous questions because they are often very expensive and the observed results are not always what were expected. Thus, we must set aside any 'HSR mania' – a desire to extend it everywhere – and ask where HSR is relevant. Why and when is it appropriate to build HSR? Conversely, why and when is it inappropriate (Nash 2009)? This chapter addresses these questions by drawing lessons from the French experience. France is the country with the highest HSR traffic in Europe and has four new high-speed lines under construction. However, many proposed projects have recently been postponed or even abandoned, suggesting that France is probably close to the end of its period of expansion of the national HSR network.

The chapter begins with an overview of the development of HSR in France, including its period of system growth and its recent decision to delay most additional expansions. It then turns to the relationship of mobility to economic growth and the standard of living and the apparent need for higher speed. The growing value of time is shown to be a key factor in determining the potential of HSR; however, access times, station times, and transfer times must be considered in weighing modal competitiveness. Both network design and urban and regional geography are then discussed as factors affecting the market for HSR. Finally, the chapter discusses the implications of these market factors on the demand for HSR, both in France and elsewhere.

The French HSR network and the limit to 'HSR mania'

France was the first European country to undertake construction of a high-speed rail system. Approved in 1975, the first high-speed line, between Paris and Lyon

(450 km), began operation in September 1981. The Paris-Lyon line's success soon became the basis for a series of network extensions. The system in France currently stretches more than 2,000 km (Crozet 2014). Table 4.1 shows key milestones in the system's development.

This expansive HSR network has supported a high volume of passenger traffic. In 2012, French HSR services carried 54 billion passenger-kilometres, more than four times the passenger-kilometres of domestic air transport. The French HSR was able to capture this substantial modal share and take a position between cars and air travel due to some unique properties:

- The French HSR offers passengers average door-to-door speeds that are faster than driving and sometimes as fast as or faster than flying, especially since security controls have increased access time at airports.
- The French HSR integrates the use of high-speed and standard rail lines, enabling service to be offered in less-populated areas. There are HSR stops in more than 200 French cities, even though some are far from high-speed lines.
- The French HSR can stop at older train stations in city centres where employment and population densities are often the highest.
- The French HSR offers frequent service, better matching travellers' needs. Currently there are twenty-three Paris-Lyon or Paris-Nantes round trips per day, for example.

Table 4.1 HSR network extension milestones in France

1981:	Opening of Paris-Lyon line (South-East service)
1989:	Opening of Paris-Tours line (South-West and Brittany service)
1993:	Opening of Paris-Lille line (Northern France, Brussels and London service)
2001:	Opening of the Lyon-Marseille line (Mediterranean service)
2007:	Opening of the Paris-East line (Lorrain, Alsace, Luxembourg and Germany service)
2007–2010:	Development of National Scheme for Transport Infrastructure which included proposals to add 4,000 km of HSR by 2040
2011:	Opening of the first section of Rhine-Rhône line (first line not directly connected to Paris)
2011–2012:	Launch of construction of four new lines: Tours-Bordeaux (South-West), Brittany-Loire Valley (West), extension of Eastern HSR to Strasbourg, Nîmes and Montpellier bypasses
2013:	Ministerial commission, composed of Members of Parliament and experts, recommended to postpone or abandon numerous HSR projects. Only the Bordeaux-Toulouse line would be opened by 2030

Source: Author

During the last decade, HSR traffic increased by 3.2 per cent per year in France, whereas all modes of transport only increased by 0.5 per cent. Since 2008, the increase in HSR traffic has been less dynamic at +0.5 per cent per year.

Buoyed by the successes of the first quarter-century of HSR, French passengers and public decision makers developed a passion for HSR and another round of investments was proposed. Between 2007 and 2010, France developed a National Scheme for Transport Infrastructure in which it planned to add 2,000 km of HSR by 2020 and 2,000 km more in the following two decades. In this context of 'HSR mania', four line-building projects were launched:

- 'BPL' (Bretagne-Pays de Loire): construction and maintenance of a 182 km new high-speed track between Le Mans and Brittany (a 25-year, €3.4 billion Public-Private Partnership)
- 'CNM' Bypass (Nîmes-Montpellier): construction and maintenance of a new 80 km high-speed track (25 years, €1.8 billion)
- SEA (Sud-Europe Atlantique): concession to a private operator of a new 300 km high-speed track between Tours and Bordeaux (50 years, €7 billion)
- End of HSR East, towards Strasbourg: 100 km financed by direct public subsidies (€1.8 billion).

But it seems that the HSR network may have grown too fast. Financial burdens pushed the Ministry of Transport to appoint a commission charged with the reconsideration of the proposed projects. The commission's recommendations, announced in June 2013, were to delay or drop many of the proposed HSR projects. The recommendations were accepted by the French government, and after the opening of the four lines that are under construction, only one additional project will be launched, between Bordeaux and Toulouse (anticipated start date 2017). No other new line will be opened until 2030.

It is important to understand this as a change in investment priorities. The questioning of 'HSR mania' does not mainly come from the passenger side, as the desire for speedy travel is still very high. But the intensity of demand weakens as the network spreads, and growing subsidy costs have led public officials to question the affordability of future expansions.

Economic growth, mobility, and the need for speed

The factors affecting demand for HSR can be viewed from the framework of economic growth and mobility studies. Research has shown that the level of personal mobility is closely correlated with gross domestic product (GDP). This has given rise to the proposition that mobility is coupled to the standard of living at both the macroeconomic and the microeconomic levels (i.e. for both nations and individuals). The basis for this coupling highlights the key factors of transportation demand, especially passenger demand for inter-urban and high-speed mobility.

Figure 4.1, from Schäfer *et al.* (2009), graphs person-kilometres of travel versus GDP per capita in constant 2000 US dollars, presenting data from various world regions for the period 1960 to 2000. The graph reveals a strong relationship between GDP and personal mobility. One could almost say, 'Tell me a country's per capita GDP and I will tell you the average distance travelled over a year: one kilometre per dollar of GDP per inhabitant'! Furthermore, the analysis shows that over the twentieth century the distance travelled/GDP elasticity was close to one. In other words, per capita GDP growth was highly correlated with per capita distance travelled year by year.

In reality, however, it was not only distance but also speed that increased with income. Insofar as travel time budgets are relatively constant, or have increased only slightly (Zahavi and Talvitie 1980, Crozet 2005), in order to cover increased distance, average travel speed must increase. There may be limits; Schäfer *et al.* (2009) note that for travel to continue to increase with an elasticity close to one, in a few decades the average speed of daily travel would have to exceed 600 km/h. As a point of comparison, currently the average door-to-door travel speed for air travel in the United States is slightly over 200 km/h.

The key variable in continued mobility growth is therefore transport speed, and this can be accomplished by speeding up the modes or by changing mode shares to the faster modes. Figure 4.2, from Ausabel *et al.* (1998), shows how travel changed in the US over the period 1880–2000. The figure shows a steady rise in personal mobility from about 4 km/person/day in 1880 to nearly 80 km/person/day in 2000. This is a mobility increase of about 2.7 per cent a year, which tracks the rise in GDP per inhabitant over the same period. However, not all transportation systems contributed to this mobility increase; some modes surged in use while others declined. Overall, the average daily distance travelled by an American rose because fast modes of transportation replaced slow modes, allowing the average distance travelled by a person in a year to increase twentyfold.

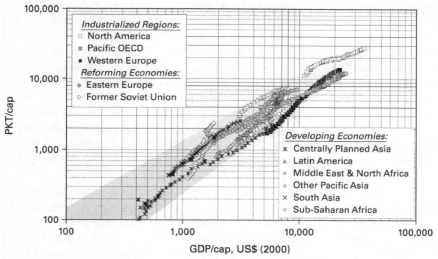

Figure 4.1 Passenger mobility per year and per country (data 1960–2000)

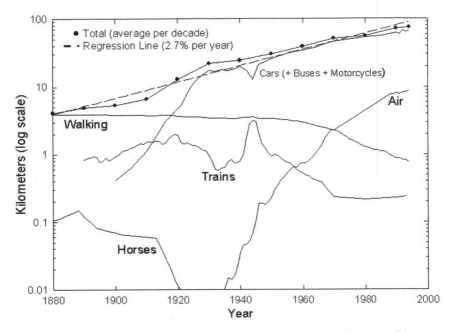

Figure 4.2 Distance travelled in km per person per day since 1800 in the United States

The question to be considered is whether fast modes of transportation can continue to replace slower modes, so that mobility continues to track GDP. Today the relative obsolescence that hit the railways in the early twentieth century may be affecting the automobile. In many developed countries, distances travelled by car are no longer increasing and there is debate over the causes. Some view the slowdown in VKT as an effect of economic downturn; others have argued that this represents an attainment of 'peak travel,' and still others focus mainly on 'Peak Car' and not a decline in overall mobility (Goodwin and Van Dender 2013, Madre *et al.* 2012). The 'peak car' view is that the flattening or reduction in VKT is not evidence that total mobility has decreased but rather is the result of a portion of travel shifting to faster modes like high-speed trains and aircraft. This appears to be the case in France, whereas in other countries there has been a large and positive relationship between standard of living and travel demand in person-kilometres, but over the past 10 years automobile passenger traffic has been nearly unchanged in comparison with a 3.2 per cent growth of HSR traffic.

An important question, for environmental as well as mobility reasons, has been how long mobility growth can continue through shifts to faster modes. In research financed by the French Agency of Environment, Lopez-Ruiz and Crozet (2010) developed passenger traffic forecasts for the year 2050 (Figure 4.3). At the start of the year 2000, each French person travelled slightly over 14,000 kilometres per year, i.e. more than 40 kilometres a day. To create a scenario for

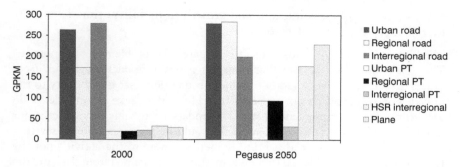

Figure 4.3 Passenger traffic in France, 2000 and 2050 (forecast) in billions of passenger-km

2050 travel, two assumptions were made to investigate the impact of the country's hypothesized traffic growth rate of 1.5 per cent per year:

- The first assumption is that there will be continued demand for speed, which will change the structure of transport demand. Relatively slow modes such as the car will lose part of their market to rapid modes such as air and high-speed rail.
- The second assumption is that there will be no increase in the absolute speed of individual modes (Crozet 2009). This is tantamount to assuming that there will be no major speed-related technological breakthroughs, or at least none that are widely implemented in the market by 2050. In order to take account of saturation phenomena, and resultant mode switching, it was assumed that speed/GDP has an elasticity of 0.33, which is relatively low.

Based on these assumptions, and using 2008 official forecasts of GDP and population growth for the nation, the overall growth in travel distance in France between 2000 and 2050 is forecast to be 40 per cent. With travel increasing from slightly less than 1,000 billion passenger-kilometres in 2000 to approximately 1,400 billion passenger-kilometres per year in 2050, the French, who will have increased slightly in number (67 million in 2050 compared to 60 million in 2000) are predicted to travel approximately 21,000 kilometres per capita a year, i.e. slightly under 60 km a day. But what is interesting is not the overall result but the change in the travel structure: almost one-third of this travel (400 P-km out of 1,400 billion P-km) is projected to be carried out in high-speed modes (HSR or plane). In other words, with continued GDP growth, unless the preference for speed declines, or other technological breakthroughs enter the market rapidly, auto transport will be less and less used for long-distance travel, and high-speed rail and air will grow in market shares.

Intensification of consumption and growth in mobility: time is increasingly the scarcest resource

Mobility and mobility-related choices pose particular problems for economists. The first is linked to the fact that transport is not a product sought for itself. Travel demand is derived, a form of joint consumption that is secondary to the linked activity. People do not generally travel for travel's sake but in order to do something else. However, calling travel secondary is probably too reductive for an understanding of transport demand. It would be more accurate to say that travel is subsidiary, insofar as it brings something more to the activity, not the least by making it possible. So there is something to be gained from studying the demand for travel in itself, taking into account among other things the costs it generates compared to the utility it procures.

Travel can be regarded in two ways. From the traditional microeconomic standpoint of consumer choice, it is customary to draw a distinction between inferior, normal and superior goods. These categories help to describe the most commonly observed preferences. When income increases, consumption of inferior goods declines relative to the other categories. Similarly, the proportion of superior goods purchased will increase. This applies, for example, to spending on healthcare or education, which ultimately grows faster than income, in contrast with spending on food, which increases much more slowly. Spending on mobility traditionally lies between these two extremes and tends to fall into the 'normal' category, where consumption rises more or less in line with income. That is precisely what Schäfer's chart tells us: demand for mobility increases at the same pace as income, and is thus a normal good.

As we have already noted, however, this trend poses a problem if we extend the microeconomic reasoning to the scarce resource of time (Becker 1965). If time's value increases with income, the time component of the overall cost of transport also increases with income. This cost increase should militate against a rise in mobility unless it brings utility gains that exceed the cost increase. We must therefore take a look at the utility gains resulting from increased mobility.

For Linder (1970), the 'leisure class' is not the indolent and unproductive one described by Veblen (1899). In Linder's analysis, the affluent, to a greater extent than their less wealthy counterparts, are confronted with the need to constantly choose between a variety of different consumption opportunities, and the relative scarcity of time compared to the amount of available income is their chief concern. General affluence has extended this 'problem' to a large proportion of the developed world's population, including the working population, to the point where time has become the scarcest resource. Average income increased eight- to tenfold during the twentieth century, and even more in many industrialized countries, so that many goods and services are financially available: but using many goods and services takes time, and life expectancy has only risen by a third. As consumers, we therefore face the dilemma of de facto competition between goods and services made accessible by higher incomes. An increase in the quantity of goods and services used (or activities engaged in) in the time available to us is one resolution to this dilemma, but it means moving towards increasingly time-intensive lifestyles (Crozet 2005).

From this standpoint, means of transport, especially fast modes, become a powerful way of intensifying consumption, not only because transport itself is a service but also because it gives access to a much wider range of goods and services. This is the case for long-distance mobility. Intensification processes are at work in both business and leisure trips. The intensification of activities (doing more in less time) becomes the result of intensification of business activity in its classic form of higher productivity (Crozet 2009).

So it is not surprising that mobility should increase more or less in line with income, since it is merely the condition that allows the variety economy to develop (Vickerman 1980, Gronau and Hamermesh 2001). Greater mobility is thus a logical sub-product of higher income together with a preference for variety. Higher speed is a coherent response to the quest for increasingly varied and intensive consumption. However, intensification in turn imposes particular constraints on activity schedules linked to the rising trend in the value of time. When income rises faster than the amount of time available, the value of time also increases, which means that the time budget we are willing to devote to each activity is potentially smaller. The result is a growing pressure on our agenda in terms of mobility: further, faster, more often and for shorter periods!

Those, in a nutshell, are the trends that underlie long-distance mobility. People travel farther and more frequently but for shorter periods. How can we explain this paradox, this diversification coupled with a reduction in the length of stays? The distinguishing feature of modern lifestyles, and what makes them more attractive than previous forms, is the incredible variety of goods and services available. But faced with this variety, our choices result from the simple combination of a few key variables. The income level and the value of time combined with the speeds offered by different transport modes are shown in Figure 4.4.

Each axis corresponds to a key variable:

- the south axis represents the level of income,
- the west axis represents the value of time,
- the east axis represents the average distance travelled,
- the north axis represents the length of stay.

At the intersection of the axis pairs, each quadrant indicates the typical relations between the variables.

- The south-west quadrant assumes that the value of time increases exponentially with income. In other words, the richer we are, the scarcer and more valuable time becomes.
- The north-west quadrant follows logically from the previous one. If income and the value of time both increase, the time budget we devote to each activity (in this case each leisure trip) will tend to decrease since the competition between the range of potential activities will cause the marginal utility of each activity taken separately to diminish more rapidly.

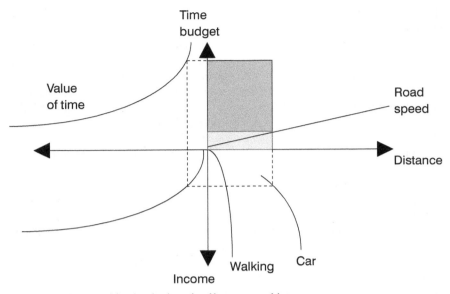

Figure 4.4 Key variables for the length of business and leisure stays

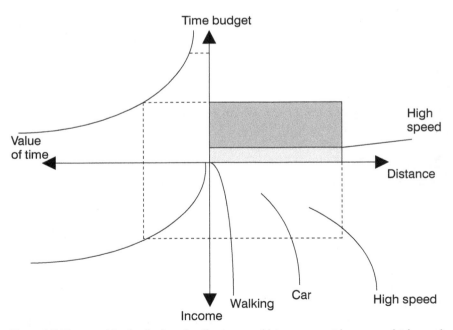

Figure 4.5 Key variables for the length of business and leisure stays with access to high speed

- The south-east quadrant shows the average speed offered by each transport mode, represented here by the average distance of possible journeys with a given mode. Walking offers few possibilities at whatever income level. In contrast, rising income progressively gives access to increasingly expensive but increasingly rapid modes, such as road, high-speed rail and air travel.
- The north-east quadrant shows schematically the outcome of the interaction between the different variables, giving an average length of stay determined by the level of income, the value of time and speed (the distance of accessible journeys). All of these are linked to a ratio that reveals that transport time represents a certain part of the total length of stay.

The rise in incomes and the value of time, combined with new, rapid transport modes, would gradually change this situation, as shown in Figure 4.5. Given increased utility drawn from a long-distance journey, a higher transport cost is accepted and the transport time budget is pushed up. It is one more reason why time scarcity becomes more acute with the increase in speed and income.

To sum up, the introduction of high-speed travel along with rising incomes allows travellers to make more trips but devote less total time to each trip. The implications are that faster modes are likely to enable an increase in total trip-making.

Estimating intercity traffic: attractions vs. costs

In order to estimate the potential traffic between two cities, a gravity-type model is typically used, whereby the volume of traffic between two urban areas can be estimated on the basis of the level of attraction between them (commonly based on their populations, although other measures of attraction can be used) and the time-distance between them. The term 'gravity' comes from the model structure, in that traffic is proportional to the attractions between the two cities and inversely proportional to the generalized costs of travel between them. A gain of speed reduces the time-distance and leads to higher traffic.

Although there are some exceptions, notably when two urban areas are separated by an international border, gravity models are a reasonably good method to predict potential traffic levels. However, in measuring the distance between two urban areas, what matters is transport time in relation to its cost rather than the actual number of kilometres. Distance is therefore measured by the generalized cost of the trip, which may be expressed as follows:

$$C_g = p + hT_g \tag{4.1}$$

where:
p = monetary price of the trip between location i and location j;
T_g = generalized time between i and j;
h = monetary parameter representing the average value of time in the eyes of travellers.

It is important for the generalized cost to reflect the different ways in which transport time is perceived. The aim here is to take into account the frequency of services in the case of public transport, number of transfers required to reach the destination, etc., which empirically have been found to be more onerous for most travellers than the time spent on board the transport vehicle. There is therefore a qualitative dimension in giving travel time a value. To take this qualitative dimension into account, the Tg parameter can be constructed in greater detail to include not only travel time on board the vehicle (car, train, plane, etc.) but also the access time upstream and downstream for each mode. In addition, performance and quality measures can be included for each mode. In the case of a trip by rail or by air, for example, the following parameters could be considered:

- Average access time to get from the trip origin to terminal *i* and to the trip destination from terminal *j*;
- Average travel time between the terminals in zones *i* and *j*;
- The number of transfers (train or plane) the traveller is required to make and the time required for the transfers;
- Frequency of trains or planes on the route;
- On-time performance and length of delays;
- Time to pass through the terminal at each end of the trip, including time through security, luggage checking and retrieval, and in-terminal wait times.

Thus, returning to the gravity model, the volume of traffic between two zones *i* and *j* can be expressed as follows:

$$T_{ij} = K \frac{P_i P_j}{C_{g_{ij}}^{\gamma}} \qquad (4.2)$$

where:
T_{ij} = traffic between zones i and j;
P_i and P_j = respective population of zones *i* and *j* (or other measure of attraction);
$C_{g_{ij}}$ = generalized cost of the transport in question between zones *i* and *j*;
γ = elasticity of traffic to the generalized cost;
K = adjustment parameter.

Depending on the type of transport and the type of activity the transport is serving, demand will respond more or less strongly to a variation in the generalized cost, e.g., sensitivity to travel time may be higher for some trip purposes than for others. A decrease in the generalized cost of transport, made possible by higher speeds and/or lower monetary costs, will fuel traffic growth; the higher the level of utility of the transport 'good', the higher the likely demand response.

The gravity model helps us think about the factors that affect traffic flows between cities and to evaluate some of the claims about HSR. When HSR projects are being proposed, promoters typically underscore the positive effects of higher speed in reducing generalized cost: they argue that cities will become closer in time with HSR, so traffic will be higher. The gravity model, and indeed other formulations of travel destination choice, also assumes that traffic will increase as speed declines, all else being equal. However, as the gravity model illustrates, it is also necessary to consider the level and type of attraction between the cities to be served. For the most part, cities generate traffic volumes that reflect their size. The largest city pairs will generate the highest traffic levels; smaller cities are likely to produce and attract relatively few trips.

System designs, geography, and mode choice

The previous two sections have argued, based on theory and empirical evidence, that with rising GDP and incomes, travel is likely to increase, as is demand for higher speed transport; also, significant improvements in travel times between two cities can lead to more trips between those cities, though sensitivity to travel time depends in part on the types of trips served. Trip volumes are likely to be proportional to the attraction between the cities. Door-to-door speeds matter, so access times at both ends of the trip, wait time, schedule frequency, and number of transfers, should be reflected in the travel time metrics used.

The question of what mode of travel the traveller will choose is partly a function of traveller characteristics (such as income), partly a function of trip purpose (e.g., business travel v. social-recreational travel) and partly a function of the travel options available. Monetary costs for each mode enter into the decision along with travel time. Thus, in estimating how many trips will be by car, how many by HSR, and how many by air, system designs and geography matter.

System designs matter not only because of operating speeds but also because of access times. In air and rail systems the number of terminals or stations and their locations are important determinants of access time. If a region has only one airport, access time will tend to be longer than if it has several; likewise the number and location of rail stations strongly affects access time. If rail stations are located or tracks are designed so that there are potential conflicts with urban uses, slower speeds may be required along urban segments. System designs also affect costs, which if reflected in fares will in turn affect demand.

City population is usually a good indicator of market size (though tourist cities can attract outsize numbers of visitors); market size matters because the cost of HSR is high. Typically, construction and maintenance costs of HSR are much greater than those for a highway. Thus, unless HSR can attract more traffic than a highway, it may not be able to deliver more social benefits than a highway, even after accounting for HSR users' time savings and HSR's (usually) lower environmental impact.

City size/population also matters because an extension to an additional city or even a stop along the line at an additional city imposes schedule time and monetary costs on the operations which need to be justified.

Distance between cities matters because if cities are close together, driving or conventional rail may be just as fast as HSR, accounting for access and wait times. At the other end of the distance spectrum, if cities are too far apart, HSR cannot compete with air's faster speeds. This is clearly illustrated by the French experience. For the trip from Paris to Lyon, about 450 km, the drive is tediously long and while flight time is short, access and terminal time at either end of the trip add considerably to the total 'length' of the journey. In these circumstances HSR is faster than the car and can compete with air because of its easier access and lower terminal times. In contrast, from Paris to Lille (200 km), cars have maintained a significant share of traffic (more than 50 per cent), and from Paris to Nice (1,000 km), air transport remains the main mode (75 per cent).

Today, it is widely agreed that HSR is most relevant for distances in the 400–800 km range, which translates to HSR travel times of 1.5 hours to 3 hours with the HSR technology in use. In that range, HSR is the dominant mode of transport in France. For shorter trips the automobile is preferred and for longer trips air travel dominates. French geography matches well with HSR's technological performance, since the HSR-relevant distance range matches the distances between Paris and Lyon, Nantes, Rennes, Strasburg and Marseille, as well as Brussels and London.

Lessons from the French experience

The French HSR system has been both a popular success and a financial success because the system has served large and dense travel markets in the 400–800 km, 1.5–3 hour range. This is the 'relevancy zone' for HSR, the markets in which HSR is most competitive. For shorter trips the auto continues to dominate and for longer trips air becomes the preferred mode.

From a strictly financial point of view, the French HSR network is already over-extended, because the recently built lines (TGV East, Rhine-Rhône) and all lines under construction require significant public subsidies. A study assessing the French HSR programme (Paix and Vilmart 2019) concluded that the public subsidies to the built lines are justified by net socioeconomic benefits, including user time savings as well as benefits to the environment. But the same does not apply for future investments.

The French projects that have been postponed have high costs and were likely to have had low ridership. For example, Marseille-Nice, and Paris-Orléans-Clermont-Lyon would serve short to medium length trips for which there is limited willingness to pay for higher speed, while building costs would be enormous (20 billion euros each). The Lyon-Turin line crosses through mountains and over a national border, both very high cost endeavours, while ridership levels were projected to be much lower than on existing lines, especially because of the 'border effect' mainly related to a lower potential of traffic.

In addition, community and environmental costs of the postponed projects would have been substantial. A recent carbon-balance analysis for the eastern section of the Rhine-Rhone HSR (RFF 2010) showed that 12 years of traffic would be necessary to offset the emissions produced during construction alone; additional years of traffic would be necessary to offset the emissions produced in the manufacture of construction materials such as concrete and steel. Some of the proposals had train stations built in suburban areas; access to the stations could actually promote driving.

The Paris-Nice experience indicates that for longer trips air can out-compete HSR and this suggests that HSR will not necessarily replace air traffic on intra-Europe trips, while there are no other interventions to alter the competitive balance. Lines are already in place or planned that within a few years would make it possible to travel by HSR from London to Madrid, Brussels to Barcelona, Rome to Paris, or Amsterdam to Geneva. But travel time, even supported by high-speed, will be 5 or 6 hours, or even more. Air travel, in comparison, would take half as much time including access and wait times. Thus air travel seems likely to remain dominant for the longer distance trips, especially if low-cost airlines continue to operate. The increase of constraints that burden airports and airways will possibly move the share line between the two modes of transport, but most likely quite modestly.

Likewise it is not necessarily possible to duplicate the French HSR experience by simply building a large and dense HSR network in another country. A fundamental lesson from the French case is that in addition to system design, geography matters. What made HSR work so well in France is that city spacing is a good match for the distance range in which HSR technology competes best (between 400 and 800 km), and the cities are of sufficient size to generate ridership justifying fifteen to twenty round trips per day. In addition, the riders are solvent and willing to pay for speed, given the distances to be covered. HSR success in France hugely depends on the fact that national geography enables links such as Paris-Lyon, Paris-Nantes/Rennes, and Paris-Marseille to offer high quality, high frequency service and generate public benefits, even considering the amount of public subsidies involved.

Planners would do well to avoid applying the French system to a set of stations and stops concerned with daily commuting. The infrastructure is expensive, having closely spaced stops would reduce speeds, and willingness to pay may be limited. To cope with the demand for daily mobility, conventional commuter trains with high frequency are the better option; rather than maximizing speed, for commute trips what matters is balancing the number of users (and seats) and the frequency of the trains. Generally what is needed is investment in the existing network (track renewal, signalling systems, control systems), complemented in some cases by new train equipment, and with investments in station facilities and their access and egress services.

There is a need for careful consideration of local needs and financial issues, and different HSR designs may be appropriate. It is important to note that with a different geography, Germany has developed a different HSR model. German cities being smaller and closer together, German HSR stops are more frequent and the average speed is much slower (180– 200 km/h instead of 300–

320 km/h). Conventional rail is linked to high-speed segments where such segments make operational sense.

To sum up, the French model of high-speed rail has its own relevancy zone (400 to 800 km), where it competes best with both car and air travel. It does not cope with all demands for travel. France has built a successful network reflecting its particular geography and may have reached the point where further extensions will not perform as well.

Belgium announced in 2009 that all HSR investments in the country would be stopped. Perhaps France will also one day stop the extension of its HSR network. Extensions that attempt to serve either shorter or longer trips or to provide service to smaller cities are questionable because they are not likely to attract enough riders to justify HSR's high costs. Extensions that attempt to serve small to medium sized cities are likely to fall short on ridership. For the origin-destination pairs for which HSR could be a real substitute to air travel, HSR lines have been already built in France, or are under construction.

References

Ausubel, JH, Marchetti, C, and Meyer, PS, 1998, 'Toward Green Mobility: The Evolution of Transport', *European Review*, vol. 6, no. 2, pp. 137–156.

Becker, G, 1965, 'Time and Household Production: A Theory of the Allocation of Time', *Economic Journal*, vol. 75, September, pp. 493–517.

Crozet, Y, 2005, *Time and Passengers Transport*, 127ème Round Table of ECMT, Time and Transport, OECD, Paris, pp. 27–69.

Crozet, Y, 2009, *The Prospect for Inter-Urban Travel Demand*, 18th Symposium of International Transport Forum, OECD, Madrid 16–18/11/2009, 28 pages, available from www.internationaltransportforum.org Accessed 1 August 2016.

Crozet Y, 2014, 'High Speed Rail Performance in France: From Appraisal Methodologies To Ex-post Evaluations,' in *The economics of Investment in High Speed Rail, Round table report #155*, ITF-OCDE, pp. 73–105.

Goodwin, P and Van Dender, K, 2013, '"Peak car" – themes and issues,' *Transport Reviews*, vol. 33, no. 3, pp. 243–254.

Gronau, R and Hamermesh D, 2001, 'The Demand for Variety: A Household Production Perspective', *National Bureau of Economic Research working paper*, no. 8509.

Linder, S, 1970, *The Harried Class of Leisure*, New York: Columbia University Press.

Lopez-Ruiz, H and Crozet, Y, 2010, 'Sustainable Transport in France: Is a 75% Reduction in Carbon Dioxide Emissions Attainable?', *Journal of the Transportation Research Board*, vol. 2163, pp. 124–132.

Madre, JL, Bussière, YD, Collet, R, Villareal, I, 2012, *Are We Heading Towards a Reversal of the Trend for Ever-Greater Mobility?* No. 2012/16. OECD Publishing.

Nash, C, 2009, 'When to Invest in High Speed Rail Links and Networks?', *Discussion paper, International Transport Forum (ITF-OECD) 18th Symposium*, Madrid, 16–18 November, p. 24. Available from www.internationaltransportforum.org Accessed 1 August 2016.

Paix, JF and Vilmart, C, 2010, 'La LGV Méditerranée: Bientôt dix ans: Bilan et retour d'expérience,' *Revue générale des chemins de fer*, vol. 193, pp. 20–34.

RFF, 2010, *Bilan Carbone®, 1er Bilan Carbone ® ferroviaire global, la ligne à grande vitesse Rhin-Rhône au service du développement durable*, 8 pages.

Schäfer, A, Heywood J, Jacoby, H and Waitz, I, 2009, *Transportation in a Climate-Constrained World*, MIT Press, 329pp.

Veblen, T, 1899, *Theory of the Leisure Class*, Penguin edition, 1994.

Vickerman, R, 1980, 'The New Leisure Society, an Economic Analysis', *Future*, June, IPC press, pp. 191–200.

Zahavi, Y and Talvitie, A, 1980, 'Regularities in Travel Time and Money', *Transportation Research Record*, vol. 750, pp. 13–19.

5 Evidence from the Italian high-speed rail market

Competition between modes and between HSR operators

Ennio Cascetta and Pierluigi Coppola

Introduction

From Europe to the US and to Asia, governments and public-private partnership (PPP) entrepreneurs are investing in developing high-speed rail (HSR) networks. HSR is widely acknowledged to be a sustainable and efficient transportation mode for medium-haul intercity trips in the range of 400–800 km. Empirical evidence shows it is also attractive for trips as short as 150–200 km (Cascetta *et al.* 2013). In Italy major investments in HSR have been carried out in recent decades, resulting in a current network of approximately 1,300 km. The HSR service, begun in 2005 between Rome and Naples, now includes several city pairs. The level of service is expected to be further improved with the completion of new stations. The design has been to avoid urban penetration in dense areas, allowing trains to run at speeds up to 360 km/h.

The Italian expansion of HSR is in line with the general trend in Europe, where starting with the *Train* à Grande *Vitesse* (TGV) launched in the early 1980s between Paris and Lyon (420 km), HSR services have been extended throughout France and have also been constructed in Spain (AVE), Germany (ICE), Benelux (Thalys) and Italy (TAV) for a total of about 6,500 km in the EU. In addition, new projects are under discussion or are in progress in Sweden, the UK, Portugal, Russia and Turkey. Asia also has seen considerable diffusion of HSR. In Japan, the pioneer Tokaido-Shinkansen HSR line (launched in 1964 between Tokyo and Osaka) has been joined by five additional HSR lines for a total network of about 2,300 km and 353 million annual passengers. HSR has also been built in Taiwan and in China. Today China has the longest HSR network in service, with about 9,300 km of rail lines operating at speeds up to 300 km/h, and plans further expansion of the network in the near future.

Different HSR operational models have been implemented (Campos and de Rus 2009), distinguished by the use, exclusive or mixed, of the rail infrastructure. The Japanese case, for instance, is an example of 'exclusive' HSR infrastructure. HSR is entirely separated from the rest of the railway network and only high-speed (HS) trains run on HSR tracks. In contrast, the French operation model is characterized by HS trains using both HSR and non-HSR (duly potentiated) infrastructure. Institutionally operations also differ. Some countries use a single operator in charge of infrastructure and operations, e.g., in Spain there is a single national operator in charge of HSR infrastructure and services. In Japan the six Shinkansen lines' infrastructure and service are managed by different private operators. In Germany, Italy and Benelux the owner is distinct from the operator. In the Benelux case the HS trains (Thalys) run on the HS infrastructure of different national railways (Netherlands, Belgium, and France).

In Italy, anticipating the European open access regulatory framework in the fourth railway package proposed by the European Commission in 2013, starting in April 2012 the new HSR private operator 'Nuovo Trasporto Viaggiatori' (NTV) entered the HSR market, and began competing with the incumbent publicly-owned Trenitalia. This is the first case in the world of pure competition between non-subsidized HSR operators on the same line (i.e. a single infrastructure managed by the state-owned company RFI).

This chapter presents an overview of the short-term effects of opening new HSR lines in Italy with a single operator from 2009 to 2012, and with multiple competing HSR operators since 2012. Effects on supply, demand and prices are presented, allowing a first evaluation of competition in a typically monopolistic market.

The chapter is organized as follows. After a brief review of the regulatory framework of rail transport in Italy, the Italian HSR infrastructure and service are presented. Next, evidence of the effects of competition in the HSR market on prices and service quality are presented. The chapter then describes the methodological framework developed to forecast the effects of competition on inter-province travel demand. Data for the period 2009–2012 are also presented, showing travel demand growth, modal shares and traveller characteristics before and after HSR. Finally, conclusions and current research areas are discussed.

The regulatory framework of rail transport in Italy

Since the early 1990s, Europe's rail transport has been characterized by a slow process of liberalization aimed at introducing competition into a sector traditionally characterized by monopolies and a strong presence of public incumbents. The policies of the European Commission (EC) are intended to rationalize the market and increase patronage and environmental benefits.

Three EC Directives set out policy for railways: EU Directive 91/440; Directive 2004/51/EC; and Directive 2007/58/EC. In January 2013 a fourth railway package was proposed by the European Commission (COM-2013 28 final, 2013/0028) which would give open access for all international passenger services across the railways of the European Union.

While EC directives must be followed, they allow member countries a certain flexibility as to specifics. As a result, each country has embarked on its own path towards the liberalization of the rail market, achieving different degrees of openness. In Italy, the European Directives and the legislation that ensued led to the separation of the various branches of activity previously within the purview of a single agency, specifically the Ferrovie dello Stato (FS). Separation of functions followed a horizontal (or 'decoupling') scheme, i.e. responsibility for lines was separated from responsibility for service (Sanchez *et al.* 2008). Management of passenger service was given to Trenitalia, while management of the railway lines was assigned to the infrastructure manager, Rete Ferroviaria Italiana (RFI). RFI has among its main tasks the maintenance of infrastructure, traffic management, the allocation of rail capacity (in terms of train paths or time slots), the collection of right-of-way revenues, and circulation safety. However, while Trenitalia and RFI are two separate companies, both are 100 per cent owned by the public holding company FSI (Ferrovie dello Stato Italiane).

Trenitalia and other national or regional rail service companies operating on the rail sections are required to pay charges for the use of lines and services to RFI, the infrastructure manager. A body of the Ministry of Infrastructure and Transport, the Office for the Regulation of Rail Services, is in charge of overseeing competition and resolving any disputes.

What makes the Italian case stand out is that a few years after HSR service began, another company, Nuovo Trasporto Viaggiatori (http://www.ntvspa.it), was authorized to provide HSR services in competition with the incumbent Trenitalia (http://www.trenitalia.com), using the same tracks and stations. Thus Italy became the first country which allowed competitive HSR services on its HSR infrastructure. Trenitalia and NTV services are not regulated under the tariff profile and are not subsidized.

The Italian HSR network: infrastructure and services

In Italy, the first HSR service was launched in 1992 between Florence and Rome with the so-called 'direttissima', which allowed trains to run at 230 km/h, covering the 257 km distance in about 2 hours. The project had been a long time in planning, dating back to 1970. The new-generation HSR (i.e. with trains running currently at 300 km/h maximum speed and 360 km/h expected in the near future) was launched in December 2005 between Rome and Naples (205 km) and Milan and Bologna (182 km). The project progressed further in December 2009 when the Milan-Turin (125 km), the Bologna-Florence (79 km) and the Naples-Salerno (55 km) lines were completed. HSR urban extensions of approximately 20 km penetrating into the cities of Rome and Naples were also completed, allowing travel time reductions of 15 to 20 minutes in entering and leaving the central stations of the two cities.

Since 2010 the backbone of the Italian HSR network from Turin to Naples has been fully operative. Excluding the urban links into Milan, Rome, Florence and Bologna, the cost of the whole 830 km network was about €40.5 billion, or €48.9 m/km. Excluding the link from Rome to Florence, whose costs are related to the out-dated technology of the 1980s, the total investment cost is about €35.8 billion and the cost is €60.7 million/km.

Today the service includes several city pairs at distances between 100–250 km such as Rome-Naples (205 km in 1 hour 10 minutes) and Milan-Turin (125 km in 54 minutes), as well as city pairs over 400 km apart, such as Rome-Milan (515 kilometres in 3 hours 30 minutes and with a direct service in 2 hours and 45 minutes). The HSR service frequency on the HSR network ranges from one train per hour to four or five trains per hour in the peak period on sections between Rome, Florence and Bologna (Figure 5.1).

The Italian HSR project is still under development. Since the opening of the first lines, station-to-station travel times have been reduced by 20–40 per cent (Cascetta *et al.* 2013). These times are expected to be further reduced with the completion of the new underground by-pass stations in Florence that will speed up the service. Moreover, Trenitalia has announced the launch of new-generation HS trains running at 360 km/h as of 2015, which would reduce the travel time from Rome to Milan by 20–30 minutes. Several extensions of the current network are also in progress, such as the Milan-Venice and the Turin-Lyon lines, or in the design stage (e.g. the Naples-Bari and the Milan-Genoa sections).

Between 2009 and 2012, the supply of HSR services in Italy saw a sharp increase both in terms of frequency (number of trains per day) and accessibility (number of cities and stations served). On the one hand, thanks to the completion of the infrastructure, HSR services have been increased between Naples, Rome and Milan with extensions to and from Turin and Salerno (Figure 5.1). On the other hand, the entry of the new operator NTV into the HSR market has led to increases in HSR services to Venice and Padua, new services to Rimini and Ancona (along the Adriatic corridor), and to Rome and Milan (particularly in the secondary stations of Roma-Tiburtina, Milano-Rogoredo and Milano-Porta Garibaldi).

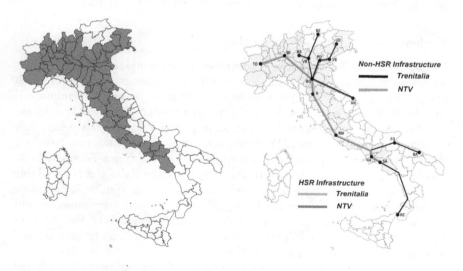

Figure 5.1 Italian HSR "Core area" (in dark grey) and rail infrastructure and services

Table 5.1 HSR daily runs and trains-kilometre growth between 2009 and 2012

Line	Trenitalia								NTV	
	2009		2010		2011		2012		2012	
	No. runs/ day	Trains-km/day (000)	No. runs/ day	Trains-km/day (000)	No. runs/ day	Trains-km/day (000)	No. runs/ day	Trains-km/day (000)	No. runs/ day	Trains-km/day (000)
TO-MI-RM-NA-(SA)	71	41	86	57	91	61	89	62	38	28
(NA)-RM-VE	24	14	26	14	29	15	37	19	6	3
Total	95	55	112	71	120	76	126	81	44	31

Source: Author

Along the Milan-Rome-Naples main line, the number of Trenitalia trains has increased from seventy-one daily departures in 2009, to eighty-nine in 2012 (Table 5.1).

In terms of train-kilometres, thanks to the service extensions to Salerno and Turin, the increase is even more significant: from 40,800 train-kilometres per day in 2009 to 61,850 train-kilometres per day in 2012, growth of about 50 per cent in 4 years. In 2012 with the entrance of the NTV operator, the number of daily trains has further increased by 44 and 31,000 train-kilometres, bringing the total to 170 runs per day (growth of 79 per cent from 2009), equivalent to 113,000 train-kilometres per day (105 per cent growth from 2009).

Evidence of price and service quality

Originally Trenitalia offered two classes of service (first and second), with trains set up accordingly. The Trenitalia train layout was revamped in 2011, with trains offering up to four different classes (Executive, Business, Premium and Standard), in anticipation of the marketing strategy of NTV, whose trains were going to offer three levels of accommodation (iClub, Prima, Smart) when they commenced operations in 2012. Moreover, a new pricing structure based on three different fare typologies (i.e. Base, Economy and Super-Economy/Low-cost) for each class, have been introduced by both Trenitalia and NTV (Table 5.2). This added up to nine tiers for NTV and twelve for Trenitalia, providing travellers with wider choice (including different physical arrangements/tariff combinations). The different fares relate to different levels of flexibility in the use of the trains, and different price points within each tariff, managed according to yield management schemes.

The new pricing structure and availability of promotional offers has led to a substantial reduction in the average price per passenger of about 30 per cent. The average price in 2011 was calculated by averaging first and second

Table 5.2 Evolution of tariff structure and ambience of travel induced by HSR competition

	2009–2010	2011	2012
HSR tariffs	BASE	BASE mini	BASE Economy Super-Economy/Low-Cost
Classes	1st class 2nd class		Executive/Club Business/Prima Premium/Smart Standard

Source: Author

class tickets according to traffic volumes, and after 2011 by averaging different price-points weighted by estimated users. The price levels increased slightly from 2009 to 2011 while showing a very strong decrease in the next year, very likely as a consequence of competition for attracting travellers initiated by the two operators.

Post-2011 the 'gap' between tariffs has also expanded substantially, and for the first time low-income travellers had access to HSR services. The effect is similar to that which resulted from the introduction of low-cost flights in the air market.

Competition also triggered an overall increase in services offered to customers. These include a range of ancillary services on board (entertainment, Wi-Fi, etc.) and on local access-egress transport (parking facilities at the station, parking reservation, integrated local public transport tickets, etc.), as well as in the form of agreements with local museums, hotels and other tourism attractions which were not available before 2012 (Table 5.3).

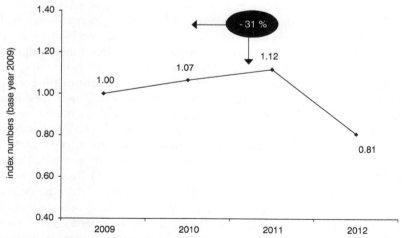

Figure 5.2 Evolution of average single ticket price by HSR from 2009 to 2012

Table 5.3 New services induced by competition in HSR market

On-board	Entertainment (cinema, news)
	Silence area
Local transport	Limousine service at station
	Reserved parking at station
	Integrated local transport and HSR ticket
Tourism	Deals and discounts with hotels, museums, other local providers

Source: Author

Methodology for the assessment of HSR impacts on travel demand and modal competition

The methodology for the assessment of HSR impacts on travel demand and modal competition is depicted in Figure 5.3. The methodology is based on integrated demand and supply models, estimated and validated through revealed preference-stated preference (RP-SP) surveys and traffic counts (Ben-Akiva *et al.* 2010).

The first step is the estimation of origin-destination (OD) matrices for intercity rail (conventional and HSR), auto and air. These OD matrices are updated every year based on current traffic counts (Cascetta 2009).

The second step consists of setting up the current multi-modal national transport network as well as future network scenarios, and to compute the related OD level of service (LOS) attributes by road, air and rail. To this aim, transport infrastructure and service supply models have been developed through a diachronic network of about 126,500 nodes and 330,000 links. Individual runs of HSR and other rail services, as well as planes, are included in the service supply model.

In the third step, given the total OD demand flows for future scenarios, a schedule-based mode choice model is used to estimate the market share of different inter-province transport modes based on level of service attributes, including alternative modes, alternative rail services (Intercity and HSR), different travel classes, and HSR operators (i.e., Trenitalia and NTV) (Cascetta and Coppola 2012). The schedule-based mode-service choice model allows for simulating the competition between transport modes and HSR operators based not only on travel times and costs, but also on the actual departure time of trains and flights (i.e. timetables) as compared to desired departure times for different market segments (Cascetta and Coppola 2016). The model is a nested-logit (see Ben-Akiva and Lerman 1985) with a nesting structure to capture higher degrees of substitutions among specific subsets of modal alternatives, particularly the HSR alternatives provided on the same route by different operators. Demand models have been estimated (Cascetta and Coppola 2012) based on two RP-SP surveys carried out in May 2009 and October 2010. Within the proposed modelling forecasting framework, the schedule-based mode choice model is applied at a first level to the current supply scenario in order to reproduce the current mode-service share by fine tuning the mode/service alternative specific

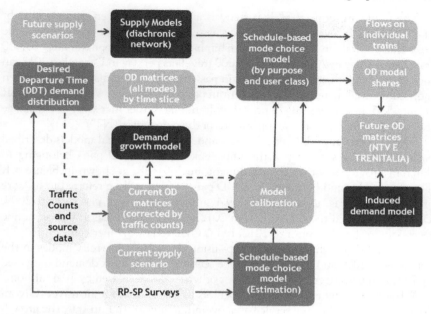

Figure 5.3 The HSR demand forecasting methodology

constants (i.e. model calibration). For the second step the model, fed by future level of service attributes computed by the supply model, forecasts the OD modal share in the future scenarios.

Finally, the induced demand model estimates the additional HSR demand generated by changes in trip-frequency due to the improvement of HSR generalized travel cost given by the weighted sum of travel times, prices and frequencies (Cascetta and Coppola 2013). All of the OD flows on the HSR services are then assigned to individual trains using a stochastic network loading model with no capacity constraints, forecasting occupancies on each train and each station-to-station link of the HSR network.

Evidence of HSR demand and modal competition

Since 2009, numerous on-board counts and surveys have been carried out to monitor the evolution of national demand for passenger transport in response to HSR. The counts and surveys have gathered information on total trips, long-distance trip frequency, modal split among the long-distance transport modes, travellers' daily routine, socioeconomic characteristics of the respondents and their households, and life-styles. The counts were used to update out-dated OD matrices of trips by Eurostar and conventional intercity trains, and to estimate the total province-to-province OD flows on HSR. In addition OD matrices were acquired on highways and between airports to evaluate the effects of HSR on competing modes.

The results in terms of HSR passengers are impressive, even more so in light of the decline in overall long-distance passenger demand due to the economic crisis that hit Italy in 2009. HSR ridership has grown from approximately 55,500 travellers per day in 2009 to about 85,000 travellers per day in December 2012, an increase of 52 per cent. The increase in passengers has been matched by an even more substantial increase of 79 per cent in passenger-kilometres travelled by HSR (Figure 5.4). It is interesting to note that Trenitalia further increased its patronage in 2012, despite the entry into operations of the competitor (NTV 2013).

The integration of different datasets and the mathematical models described earlier allowed assessment of the impacts of HSR on OD pairs belonging to different provinces within the catchment area of HSR, as shown in Figure 5.1. The overall demand between these OD pairs, which will be referred to as 'core area' demand, was approximately 69.4 million passengers per year in 2009. Demand decreased to 66.1 million in 2012 (−5 per cent) due to the economic recession: in the years prior to 2012, Italy's GDP fell by 5.9 per cent.

Table 5.4 shows the number of trips using the various intercity modes in the core area in 2009 and in 2012. It can be seen that while HSR demand increased by 7 million passengers, the demand for other modes decreased by 10.4 million.

While other studies have described HSR as a substitute for air travel (Givoni 2006), looking at the core service area overall, it appears that in Italy the growth in HSR ridership came primarily from cars (Figure 5.5a). This can be explained by the configuration of the Italian HSR network. Italian HSR connects several cities that are 100–250 km apart, OD pairs for which air demand is negligible.

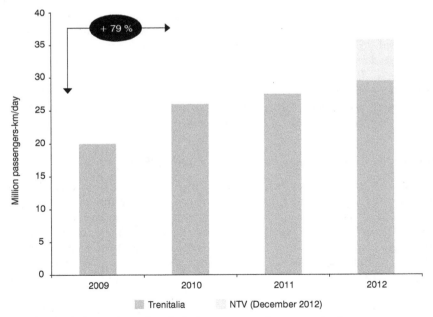

Figure 5.4 HSR demand trends in Italy (passengers and passenger-km)

On the other hand, air transport has lost share for the relatively small share of trips within Italy that are above 400 km, such as the Rome-Milan. For that OD pair, we see that the HSR modal share has increased from 45 per cent in 2009 to 68 per cent in 2012, with a substantial loss of air travel share and a negligible decrease of highway modal share (Figure 5.5b). The increase in HSR in this instance is a function of reduced travel times by HSR compared to both air and conventional intercity rail modes.

Thus, even though during the period analyzed Italy saw a general decrease in intercity passenger travel demand due to the economic crisis, HSR services grew in use and diverted trips from slower modes of travel.

The availability of HSR services also appears to have induced demand. The size of this effect was estimated by comparing the variation of travel demand by mode in the core area, with those for the whole of Italy. Figure 5.6 shows intercity travel demand by mode with respect to 2009 values, both for the whole country and the core area.

It can be deduced that the diverging trajectories exhibited in Figure 5.6 after 2010 are mostly due to the introduction of HSR. Based on this assumption, the variation in the number of passengers lost by highways, air and rail (HSR + Intercity trains) was computed as the difference between the traffic resulting by applying, mode by mode, national trends to 2009 core area traffic, and the number of trips observed in 2012. Under the above assumption, results (Figure 5.7) showed that 2.1 million trips diverted from air to HSR and 2.8 million from highways. Total rail demand (HSR + Intercity rail) increased by 6.9 million trips over the expected value resulting from projecting 2009 values to 2012. Since trips by intercity rail in the core area decreased by 2.0 million between 2009 and 2012 (Table 5.4), the incremental number of trips on HSR was estimated at 8.9 million trips per year (6.9 + 2.0) with respect to the 'no-HSR' scenario.

As a result, the demand induced by HSR can be estimated as 2.0 million trips per year (8.9 − 2.0 − 2.1 − 2.8). This figure can be compared with that obtained independently by direct surveys (Pragma 2012) in which 8 per cent of HSR travellers stated that they 'likely' or 'most likely' would not have made the

Table 5.4 Number of trips and modal shares of the core area demand for years 2009 and 2012

	2009		2012		Difference, 2009–12	
	Mil. Trips	%	Mil. Trips	%	Mil. Trips	%
Highway	38.7	55.7	31.8	48.2	−6.9	−18
Air	7.1	10.2	5.6	8.5	−1.5	−21
HSR	18.9	27.2	25.9	39.3	7	37
Intercity Rail	4.7	6.8	2.7	4.1	−2	−43
Total Rail	23.6	34	28.6	43.3	5	21
Total	69.4	100	66.1	100	−3.4	−5

Source: Author

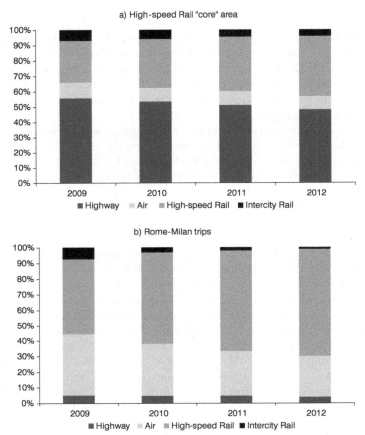

Figure 5.5 Modal shares in terms of passengers in HSR core area and on the Rome-Milan OD pair

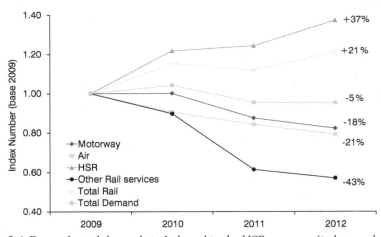

Figure 5.6 Demand trends by mode in Italy and in the HSR core area (index numbers)

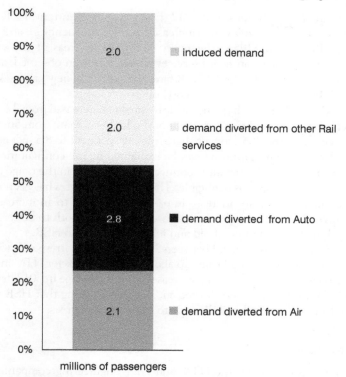

Figure 5.7 Segmentation of generated demand on HSR between 2009 and 2012

surveyed trip if the HSR service was not available. Applying these values to total HSR trips, induced demand would result in 2.1 million trips in 2012.

In the short- to mid-term, the range of induced demand can depend on changes in generalized travel cost, including direct time and money costs as well as changes in amenity values (e.g. additional trips are made because travelling on HSR is faster, cheaper and/or more comfortable). In the long-term this range of induced demand can further reflect changes in travellers' mobility or lifestyle choices (e.g. travellers start making more frequent trips due to a change of residence or of the workplace, made possible due to the better service offered by HSR). Evidence from the Customer Satisfaction Survey carried out by NTV in 2012 shows that about 23 per cent of NTV passengers changed their zone of residence in the previous 2 years and 7 per cent linked this change to the introduction of the new HSR services.

Conclusion

Empirical evidence from the Italian HSR market shows a large increase in the number of HSR passengers between 2009 and 2012. This is partly due to the opening of the new HSR lines and partly due to the effects of a new operator,

NTV, entering the HSR market in 2012. Due to the new entrant, HSR services expanded over the rail network (increased service frequencies) and in new stations in Rome and Milan (the main metropolitan areas of the country). Moreover, an increase of on-board services offered has been observed, as well as a 31 per cent overall reduction of HSR fares thanks to the new pricing structure and availability of promotional (low-cost) offers.

As a result, HSR modal share in the HSR core area increased from 27 per cent to 39 per cent, compared to a reduction of the highway share from 56 per cent to 48 per cent and the domestic air share from 10 per cent to 8.5 per cent. The greater reduction from motorways can be explained by the configuration of the Italian HSR network, which mainly connects several cities in the range of 100 to 250 km, where air demand is negligible. The rise in passengers has been matched by an even more significant increase in passenger-km, due to an increase in the average travel distance as well as to induced demand due both to better levels of service and to changes in household and job location due to HSR.

The increase of HSR demand between 2009 and 2012 corresponds to about 5 million more trips for Trenitalia, and to about 2 million trips for NTV in 2012. It is interesting to note that Trenitalia increased HSR patronage in 2012 despite the entry of NTV in the same year. Moreover, it is worth noting that HSR use grew despite a decline in overall mobility due to the economic crisis.

Acknowledgements

The authors wish to thank the NTV and NET-Engineering companies in the persons of Dr Giuseppe Bonollo and Ing. Vito Velardi for providing access to the data on which the analyses presented in this paper are based.

References

Ben-Akiva, M, and Lerman, S, 1985, *Discrete Choice Analysis*, MIT Press.
Ben-Akiva, M, Cascetta, E, Coppola, P, Papola, A, and Velardi, V, 2010, 'High Speed Rail demand forecasting in a competitive market: the Italian case study,' *Proceedings of the World Conference of Transportation Research (WCTR)*, Lisbon, Portugal.
Campos, J, and de Rus, G, 2009, 'Some stylized facts about high-speed rail: a review of HSR experiences around the world,' *Transport Policy*, vol. 16, pp. 19–28.
Cascetta, E, 2009, *Transportation Systems Analysis: Models and Applications*, 2nd ed. Springer.
Cascetta, E, Coppola, P, 2012, 'An elastic demand schedule-based multimodal assignment model for the simulation of high-speed rail (HSR) systems,' *Euro Journal on Transportation and Logistics*, vol. 1, pp. 3–27.
Cascetta, E, Coppola, P, 2013, 'High-Speed Rail induced demand models,' *Procedia – Social and Behavioral Sciences*, vol. 111, no. 5, pp. 147–156.
Cascetta E, Coppola P, 2016, 'Assessment of schedule-based and frequency-based assignment models for strategic and operational planning of high-speed rail services,' *Transportation Research Part A: Policy and Practice*, vol. 84, pp. 93–108.
Cascetta, E, Coppola, P, and Velardi, V, 2013, 'High-speed rail demand: before and after evidence from the Italian market', *disP – The Planning Review*, vol. 49, no. 2, pp. 51–59.

Givoni, M, 2006, 'Development and impact of the modern high-speed train: a review', *Transport Reviews*, vol. 26, no. 5, pp. 593–611.

NTV – Nuovo Trasporto Viaggiatori, 2013, *From Zero to Italo: So Competition was Born*, Skira Publisher, Italy.

Pragma, 2012, *Mo.Vi.*, *Monitor Viaggiatori*, Rome, Italy.

Sánchez, PC, Monsálvez, JMP, Martínez, LS, 2008, 'Vertical and horizontal separation in the European railways market: effects on productivity,' *Fundación BBVA*, Valencia.

6 High-speed rail in Spain

Territorial management and sustainable urban development

José M. de Ureña, Manuel Benegas and Inmaculada Mohíno

Introduction

High-speed rail (HSR) first began operation in Spain in 1992. The first HSR line, between Madrid and Seville, offered commercial speeds of 300–350 km/h, double those of conventional rail services (Ureña 2012a). Additional lines were built in subsequent years and today the HSR system connects with other major metropolitan areas in Spain (Madrid, Barcelona, Valencia, Bilbao and Málaga) as well as with many midsized and smaller cities. The system extends for 3,100 km, making it the largest HSR system in Europe.

HSR systems differ in the way they connect new HSR with the pre-existing, conventional rail lines. Most HSR systems in Europe have the ability to operate at lower speeds along conventional tracks (Menerault 1998). However, the French system operates primarily on dedicated HSR lines that meet conventional lines in stations, whereas the German system includes stretches of high-speed operation together with improved, but slower speed, conventional operation along the same lines. The Spanish HSR system is principally operated on dedicated lines that coordinate at stations with slower conventional rail services. There are a few cases in Spain of conventional services using the new HSR infrastructure, for example near the French frontier where new HSR tracks are being prepared for conventional French freight trains towards the Barcelona and Bilbao harbours. However, because of the use of three rail gauges in Spain, interoperability is not complete and happens at fewer places, though it is becoming easier with improved gauge-changing mechanisms (Ureña 2012a).

HSR systems also differ with regard to station spacing and service to smaller cities. In its initial deployments the French HSR system emphasized service between large cities that are relatively far apart, 200 km or more, and established stations only in major cities (whereas conventional rail networks have them approximately every 15 to 30 km). This led to HSR not serving many intermediate places, creating a 'tunnel' effect (Plassard 1991) and reinforcing urban growth poles. The German stations, reflecting the mixed system design as well as German urban geography, are more closely spaced and appear to have had less impact on growth patterns. The Spanish system design uses separate guideways but offers service to long-distance, mid-distance, and short-distance travellers, with stations spaced accordingly.

Over the years, HSR system designs have changed somewhat, and HSR is now being used in Europe for four travel time thresholds: 2–3 hours, where competition with air is a factor; 1 hour, for long commutes; shorter (half hour) trips, also for commutes; and trips of four hours or more in special cases (Ureña 2012a), the latter mostly for personal reasons and occasional trip purposes (Charlton and Vowles 2008). While debate continues about what time and distance ranges are most appropriate for HSR, increasing evidence suggests that this depends not only on the technology and its operation but also on the implementation context.

This chapter presents findings from research on the impacts of the Spanish HSR and in particular its effects on territorial management – urban growth and the relationships among cities of various sizes. While some of the studies cited were conducted before the economic crisis that began in 2008, and two new lines were added since some of the work reported here was completed (Barcelona-French frontier and Albacete-Alicante), the conclusions remain valid today; the economic crisis slightly reduced the number of passengers on the HSR lines and slowed growth somewhat, but did not alter the underlying factors affecting HSR performance.

The chapter begins by providing an overview of the HSR services provided in Spain and their prices. It then summarizes socioeconomic lessons to date, and goes on to present findings on urban and regional impact. Next the chapter summarizes evidence on environmental impacts, and finally it presents brief conclusions.

High-speed rail services

The first HSR line in Spain, between Madrid and Seville, was designed for use by professionals (business travellers) for trips that could be served with 2–3 hour one-way travel times, allowing for same-day round trip travel. The service succeeded in capturing between 50 and 80 per cent of business travel formerly made by air (Figure 6.1, Ureña *et al.* 2009c). It also induced new trips. With 2–3 h travel times, HSR could compete with air on door-to-door travel time and (for the most part) it also competed on price. HSR offered other favourable characteristics as well, including better accessibility, reliability, comfort and use of time during travel.

The Madrid-Seville HSR line succeeded for a number of reasons. It is more accessible than air because the HSR stations are located in the urban centres, where most business travel in Spain still occurs (Ureña *et al.* 2009c; Ureña 2012a, 2012b). The HSR services proved to be more reliable than air services. In addition, comparing total travel time, including access and egress time, check-in, security controls, waiting for departure, and on-board travel, HSR had a higher percentage of usable time than did air travel; travelling by HSR typically allows more time for working or relaxing.

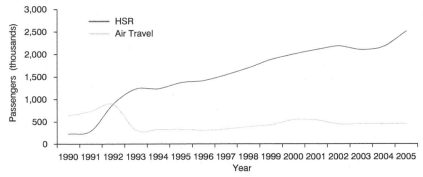

Figure 6.1 Madrid-Seville HSR line 2.5 hours (150 minutes)

Several types of HSR services are offered in Spain. Most of these services are pure long-distance HSR with a maximum speed of 300 km/h or more and with average speeds around 200 to 250 km/h. They exclusively use the new HSR infrastructure and connect major cities with €0.19/km (2010) single-ticket fares, twice the cost of conventional rail services. About one-third stop at medium-sized cities, more at larger ones, and there are frequent services between major cities, with about 15 to 24 per day per direction.

To date, new Spanish HSR lines and conventional lines operate along the same corridors. Nevertheless, several conventional lines are being upgraded to 200–220 km/h or even greater speeds, using the Iberian gauge (a wider-than-standard 1668 mm) to extend the HSR infrastructure to destinations with less demand.

On the trains, several classes of service with different prices are offered. The major difference is the space per seat. All service classes require reserved seats and provide amenities such as Wi-Fi and access to refreshments.

A second type of 'mixed' service uses both the HSR and the conventional networks to reach cities that are not directly connected to HSR. Most provincial capitals are connected in this fashion; by 2014 all but eight of the forty-seven provincial mainland capitals had some type of long-distance HSR services but only seventeen had pure HSR services to/from Madrid. The mixed service trains operate at lower maximum speeds than the HSR trains, even when using the HSR network (200 to 250 km/h). They stop at most stations on the HSR network, but only a few trains serve each final destination; the small and medium-sized cities are served by between two and seven trains per day in each direction. With added stops, the mixed service trains are less punctual than pure HSR services. Single-ticket fares are between those of conventional and pure HSR services at around €0.12/km (2010).

The use of HSR for trips of about one hour was first experienced along the Madrid-Seville line, between Madrid, Ciudad Real and Puertollano. The HSR service captured between 50 and 80 per cent of commuters in this distance range from rail and road. This opened up labour opportunities over 200 km distances (Ureña *et al.* 2005, 2006, 2009b, 2009c). At the same time, some people who had travelled on conventional rail services switched instead to bus services, due to the substantially higher HSR fares and the cancellation of many conventional rail services when HSR services were established. This phenomenon, which came as a surprise, changed the initial HSR network model, and layout decisions have since favoured the integration of more small cities to the HSR network (Garmendia *et al.* 2012a).

Recently some use of HSR has been observed over distances even shorter than 100 km, about half an hour in metropolitan environments. Short-trip use has begun to appear as a new suburban transportation mode for the outer parts of metropolitan Madrid, and also appears in London (Ureña *et al.* 2010; Menendez *et al.* 2012; Garmendia *et al.* 2012b). In addition, demand for HSR travel has begun to develop for trips over 4 hours long, both for business purposes and for personal and leisure purposes, in the Barcelona-Seville corridor. Long trips are also a portion of the Paris-Marseille market (Zembri 2005).

The medium and short distance HSR services connect a few regional city systems and some small and medium cities with metropolitan areas. They use slower and cheaper HSR trains (260 km/h maximum speed) and run frequently, between six and twelve services per day/direction – much less frequent than conventional suburban rail (Ureña *et al.* 2010; Garmendia *et al.* 2012b). In Spain they carry many metropolitan passengers (i.e. Madrid-Ciudad Real or Madrid-Toledo, around 1 million passengers per year, see Garmendia *et al.* 2012b and Ureña *et al.* 2009b) but attract far smaller numbers between small and medium-sized cities (i.e. Córdoba-Seville, around half a million passengers per year; Lérida/Lleida-Tarragona or Seville-Puente Genil, around 30,000 passengers a year, see Martínez *et al.* 2010). Single-ticket fares are about €0.10/km (2010), almost half of long-distance pure HSR services and similar to medium-distance conventional rail service fares. In addition, similar to conventional suburban rail services, they provide 20 to 50 per cent fare reductions for frequent travellers.

Overall, in addition to attracting passengers from other transport modes, air and car, HSR has induced new travel in Spain. For the system as a whole, induced travel appears to be between 10 and 30 per cent of the ridership. Some reports (e.g. Benegas 2011) have estimated that induced traffic accounts for up to 45 per cent of the total, but this refers to specific HSR stretches and not for the overall HSR network. For instance, the HSR Ciudad Real-Madrid has produced a tremendous increase in traffic, nearly all of it induced: the conventional services carried a few thousand passengers each year while HSR now carries around 800,000 passengers per year.

Socioeconomic lessons

Socioeconomic lessons from the Spanish experience with HSR can be summarized as follows:

- HSR barely meets economic investment criteria, yet Spaniards consider it an excellent investment;
- Co-financing with EU funds has been crucial;

- Upgraded conventional lines are as expensive as new HSR lines;
- Territorial HSR effects have more than marginal economic relevance; and
- HSR investments require accompanying local strategies.

Spanish HSR barely meets economic investment criteria

HSR traffic in Spain is moderate compared to other countries and this holds for all of the lines to date. However, the Spanish lines have very moderate building costs compared to those in other countries, especially considering the country's complex terrain, which increases infrastructure costs (Table 6.1 and Figure 6.2).

Most analyses have concluded that the Spanish HSR lines would require 6 to 9 million passengers a year, each passenger travelling the entire length

Table 6.1 Costs, building periods and passengers of HSR lines in Spain

Service	Year	Length (km)	Years to build	Building cost (mil. €)	Building cost (mil. €2010)	Building cost/km (mil. €2010)	Equivalent total length passengers (mil 2010)	Travel time saving
Madrid-Córdoba-Sevilla	1992	471	6	2,704	4,626	9.8	5.993	55%
Córdoba-Málaga	2007	155	7	2,672	2,825	18.2	2.137	64%
Madrid-Valladolid	2007	184	4	4,429	4,681	25.4	2.069	61%
Madrid-Barcelona	2008	664	13	9,018	9,934	15.0	5.392	62%
Madrid-Lérida	2003	442	8	4,408	5,273	11.9	5.649	45%
Lérida-Barcelona	2008	179	5	4,610	4,661	26.0	4.800	45%
Madrid-Valencia	2010	365	4	6,629	6,629	18.2	–	54%

Source: Adif, La Gaceta (31-Enero-2011), Renfe, Observatorio del Ferrocarril Fundación de los Ferrocarriles Españoles and Authors.

* Not considering Madrid-Valencia passengers

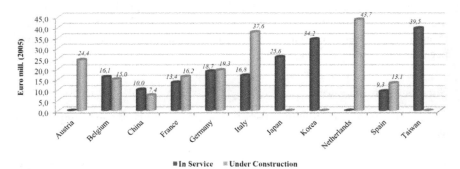

■ In Service   ▩ Under Construction

Figure 6.2 Average per km HSR line cost comparison in several countries up to 2005 (excluding cost of land purchase)

of the line, to pass public investment profitability evaluations (Inglada *et al.* 2012). However, other than the Madrid-Valencia line, the only HSR stretches that were used in 2010 by more than 6 million passengers were Madrid-La Sagra-Ciudad Real-Puertollano and Zaragoza-Lérida/Lleida (Figure 6.3). The Madrid-Barcelona line comes close, with 5.4 million equivalent total length passengers. The Madrid-Seville-Málaga line not as profitable with 5.1 million (almost 6 million without considering the Córdoba-Málaga stretch). Nevertheless, governments continue building new lines and networks that will not reach this traffic figure. In Spain, even as the economic crisis tremendously

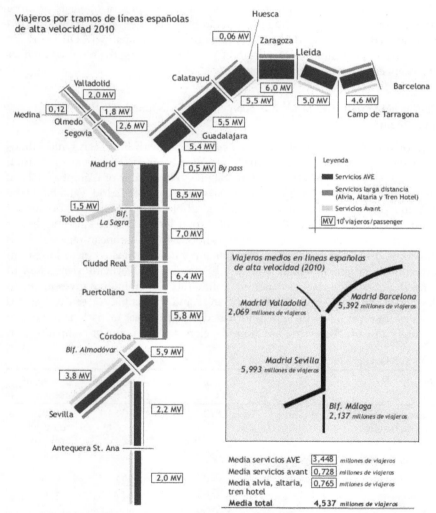

Figure 6.3 Passengers using each stretch of the HSR network (2010, before Madrid-Valencia, Barcelona-Girona-French Frontier and Orense-Santiago-La Coruña lines)

reduced investment in transportation infrastructure, the Spanish government decided to maintain investment in HSR, a sign of its acceptance by society. HSR investments should be considered impulsion public investments, rather than accompanying ones, and thus economic investment profitability should not be the only evaluation argument.

One factor in the marginal economic performance of the lines is that public investments are economically assessed using short useful lifetimes (MOPT 1991). As an average of the various categories and sites, a value of 45 years has been estimated for the entire set of infrastructure types (Inglada *et al.* 2012). However, most infrastructure has a much longer lifetime – consider the famous Alcántara or Mérida Roman bridges in Spain – and useful lifetimes of 60 years or more are increasingly being suggested and used in Spain by the railway transportation company (RENFE), by the railway infrastructure company (ADIF) and by transportation consultants (such as INECO), thus reducing the required number of passengers for investment evaluation.

Co-financing with EU funds has been crucial for Spanish HSR investments

Investment in Spanish HSR has been co-financed with European Union funds (provided to improve less developed areas) for around 30 per cent of its total costs: 10 per cent of Madrid-Córdoba-Seville, 32 per cent of Córdoba-Málaga, 38 per cent of Madrid-Zaragoza-Barcelona, 42 per cent of Madrid-Valladolid (the first and very expensive stretch of the Madrid-North of Spain lines, because of two tunnels of 28 km and 8 km out of a total length of 184 km) and 30 per cent of Madrid-Valencia. It is debatable whether these European regional funds should be dedicated to short-run profitable public investments or to long-term structural investments which may only become profitable many years later. In general, public investment economic profitability tests reinforce investments in developed areas or between developed areas and their adjacent territories; this strategy however offers little help for less developed areas or nations to be able to catch up with those that are more developed. As a point of comparison, in

Table 6.2 Envisaged HSR lines finance

Project	Country	Total investment (mil)	Public funds (mil)	Public funds percentage
Campinas-Sao Paulo-Rio de Janeiro	Brazil	19,870 $	0 $	65% lent by public Brazil bank
Perpignan-Figueres	Spain-France	1,085 €	626 €	58%
Tours-Bordeaux	France	7,000 €	4,446 €	64%
Caia-Poceirao	Portugal	1,360 €	694 €	51%
Mecca-Medina	Saudi Arabia	5,370 €	5,370 €	100%

Source: Benegas (2011) and Authors

the US during the Great Depression, New Deal economic policies provided federal funds to support diverse public infrastructure investments in every state, significantly modernizing the country. This historic precedent has influenced how the European Union currently co-finances infrastructure in its member countries. It could be debated which major New Deal public investments would have passed a public investment economic profitability evaluation, however.

In any case, public funding has been common in past HSR projects in most countries (including France and Germany) and continues to be used in projects being planned today. Table 6.2 lists some examples of proposed HSR lines that include substantial shares of public financial support, which may take the form of a direct public funds contribution, a government-backed loan, or a pledge of public payment for a minimum number of passengers and services.

In Spain, upgrading conventional lines to 200–250 km/h is as expensive as building new HSR lines

In Spain, HSR operates primarily on new rail lines built specifically for that purpose and only a few stretches are based on conventional lines upgraded for higher speed. This is in contrast to the German system, where most HSR trains operate along conventional upgraded lines with speeds ranging from 160 km/h to 200 km/h, and new lines supporting speeds of 280–300 km/h (e.g., Mannheim-Stuttgart and Hannover-Würzburg) are only about a quarter of the system. Deciding whether to upgrade existing lines or build new ones is not straightforward and depends on the design and condition of the existing conventional rail infrastructure, the urban pattern, and the terrain. The better the conventional infrastructure (electrification, signalling, security, crossings, etc.) and its commercial speed (a function of slopes, curve radii, etc.), and the flatter the topography, the easier to improve the speeds to reach 200–250 km/h. The reverse is also true: where the present speed is low and the terrain is rough, reaching 200–250 km/h design speeds would require extensive alterations (sometimes to the point of total reconstruction). In addition, maintaining services during construction complicates and prolongs the improvement process. As a result, upgrading can result in costs similar to those of building a new line for higher design speeds (300/350 km/h). Another important factor is the urbanization level of the areas to be traversed, to determine whether purchase of new land to introduce the new line would be easier and less expensive than redesign.

Cost figures are normally reliable for new lines since the costs are all assigned to a single project which is managed by one institution. However, cost data for upgrading particular lines are much less reliable since in many cases they combine many projects along various stretches of track, and are often carried out by different organizations.

In Germany, with rather good and technically advanced double track electrified conventional rail lines and a very urbanized countryside, the cost of upgrading lines has in general been lower than that of building new ones. It has

Table 6.3 Costs and time required to upgrade conventional lines in Spain

Upgraded lines	Length km	Design speed km/h	Upgrading period until operation years	Building cost mil €	Building cost/km mil € 2010
Santiago-Coruña From single track no-electrified to double track	61.7	250	10 (2001–2011) and still lacks appropriate security system (ERTMS)	800 + ERTMS	16.4
Vigo-Santiago Under construction from single track not-electrified to double track	94.0	250	14 (expected to operate in 2016)	2297 + ERMTS	25.9
Vigo-Santiago-Coruña	155.7	250	14 (approximate)		22.2

Source: Authors, RENFE and INECO (www.adif.es)

been reported for example, that the costs of upgrades were €33.3M/km for the new Köln-Frankfurt line (around 150 km) versus €18.5M/km for the upgraded Berlin-Hamburg line (around 250 km) (see Ferropedia es 2016).

In Spain, the average costs of new 300–350 km/h lines have been €15.7M/km. The available public information on improving conventional lines to 200 km/h only refers to two short stretches on very flat terrain, making them unrepresentative, but data were not available at the time of writing for the other line upgrade projects in Spain. Comparing the costs of these two upgraded conventional lines (Table 6.3) to the new lines (see Table 6.1), the lesson is that improving conventional lines in Spain has required similar or greater costs than building completely new HSR lines (€15.7M for new lines and €22.2M for upgraded lines). In addition, the stretches of 150 or more km of new HSR lines have taken around 5 years to build while upgraded ones have taken around 15 years (see Tables 6.1 and 6.3).

The costs of upgrading a conventional line will affect not only HSR passengers but also conventional rail passengers and freight services, thus extending the usefulness of the public investments. On the other hand, HSR services on upgraded conventional lines will not be as efficient and will reduce the number of attracted and induced passengers, thus reducing the efficiency of public investments. In addition, a new line will result in two lines along the same corridor, providing more opportunities but also increasing maintenance costs.

Territorial HSR effects have more than marginal economic relevance

Without undertaking specific project evaluations, most economic literature has viewed the spatial benefits of HSR as marginal, and thus adding very little to the traffic evaluations (Albalate and Bel 2011; Inglada et al. 2012). To the contrary, the Spanish example shows that spatial impacts of HSR at the interurban and urban scales are important economically as well as politically. Work by Ureña (2012b) suggests that the balance between HSR upfront investments, running costs, and usefulness cannot be analyzed without considering both the transportation and the spatial planning perspectives, and shows that spatial benefits of HSR and a longer period of return may transform a negative socio-economic HSR investment profitability into a positive one.

In particular the following spatial HSR implications should be taken into consideration:

- Incorporating distant small cities into metropolitan processes, medium-sized cities into inter-metropolitan flows, increasing relations among small distance cities, and opening up possibilities of balancing national spatial development;
- Producing more sustainable territorial structures and facilitating a more sustainable travel demand;
- Improving overall urban efficiency and growth possibilities; improving efficiency, modernity, and size of central CBDs; facilitating urban renewal; and solving inherited rail related and non-related urban problems and barriers; and
- Establishing newly envisaged sub-regional structures to promote bigger agglomerations in small city environments (with peripheral HSR stations).

The need for local strategies

The HSR is seen in Spain not only as a great improvement over the deteriorated railways that were the only rail option previously, but also as a powerful instrument for local economic development. However, though HSR provides important comparative advantages (Gutiérrez 2004; Ureña *et al.* 2006), it is widely acknowledged that HSR is only capable of affecting activities sensitive to the improved accessibility, and the mere existence of HSR is not enough, in itself, for places to mechanically and substantially improve local economic dynamics (Plassard 1991; Klein 2001; Bellet *et al.* 2012; Vickerman 1997; Bellet *et al.* 2010a; Offner 1993; Givoni 2006; Ribalaygua 2006).

To generate economic growth and substantially revitalize city structures (Plassard 1997; Fariña *et al.* 2000), local agents must develop strategies that ensure the integration of HSR within the local socioeconomic and physical environment and take advantage of new HSR service opportunities (Bellet *et al.* 2012; Van den Berg and Pol 1997; Bazin *et al.* 2006; de Meer *et al.* 2012). Even then, French and Spanish experiences suggest that it can take over 20 years before the socioeconomic dynamics and spatial impact of HSR will be fully felt (Serrano *et al.* 2006).

The strategies that local agents (public and private) can adopt include planning, management, and promotional measures (Van den Berg and Pol 1998; Ribalaygua 2004; Bellet *et al.* 2012):

Planning measures, preferably proposed before the HSR arrival, seek to integrate HSR with the local environment. They include ensuring coordination with urban and territorial planning, alleviating the possible negative impacts of its physical location, and promoting added value associated with development in the area around the station. Zaragoza and Lérida/Lleida are two interesting *a priori* examples and Segovia an *a posteriori* one (Bellet *et al.* 2010b; Bellet 2010; Bellet *et al.* 2012).

Management measures take advantage of the station's central location, providing new intermodal connections and developing land and/or redeveloping areas around the station. Segovia and Ciudad Real are good examples of urban mobility reorganization, and Zaragoza and Córdoba of regional intermodal reorganization.

Promotional measures are aimed at improving the local and external urban image, attracting potential tourists, recruiting economic activity and investments, and linking the image of the city to modernity (Bellet *et al.* 2012). A good example is Lérida/Lleida (Bellet *et al.* 2010a).

Territorial lessons

In Spain strong local and regional pressure has resulted in the HSR network being extended to serve medium-sized and small cities; examples include Albacete, Cuenca, Segovia and Tarragona (Gutiérrez 2004; Bellet and Gutiérrez 2011). The creation of abundant intermediate stations along HSR lines demonstrates a major sensitivity to local concerns in what could be called the second generation of HSR in Europe. After the French experience, whose first HSR network was structured by connecting the great metropolitan centres, a modified vision seemed to emerge, with the introduction of more intermediate stops (Troin 1995; Ureña *et al.* 2006).This regional and territorial vision seems to have prevailed in the planning of the railway network undertaken in Spain (Ureña *et al.* 2009b; Bellet *et al.* 2012).

Spain has achieved mostly positive results by balancing HSR national layout criteria with local ones. However, they must be considered cautiously in countries with different spatial models (settlement system and demographic density) and travel patterns (commuting distances), because HSR is most useful in polarized urban networks.

HSR effects on accessibility, mobility and local economic development have long-term implications for territorial development, potentially giving rise to changes in functional integration of HSR cities, spatial and urban hierarchy reorganization, and city re-structuring (SETEC 2004).

Inter-urban implications of high-speed rail station locations

HSR has created new relations between big and small cities that force them to start competing in a common market. When the connection between places is improved by transport, some people and firms may relocate to either of the places.

Table 6.4 HSR station locations in Spanish cities (more than 10,000 inhabitants)

City	Agglomeration inhabitants (2011)	HSR station	Rail between traditional and HSR stations	Type
Madrid	6,052,000	Two Central	Same station	Renovated
Barcelona	5,031,000	Central	Same station	Renovated
Valencia	1,552,000	Central	Same station	Semi-new
Seville	1,295,000	Central	Same station	New
Malaga	953,000	Central	Same station	Renovated
Zaragoza	746,000	Edge of centre	Same station	New
Coruña	410,000	Central	Same station	To renovate
Valladolid	409,000	Central	Same station	Renovated
Tarragona-Reus	382,000	10 km from cities	Unconnected	New
Córdoba	330,000	Central	Same station	Semi-new
Albacete	171,000	Edge of centre	Same station	Renovated
Lérida	167,000	Central	Same station	Renovated
Guadalajara	155,000	8 km from city	Unconnected	New
Gerona	152,000	Central	Same station	To renovate
Santiago	142,000	Edge of centre	Same station	To renovate
Orense	132,000	Edge of centre	Same station	Being renovated
Toledo	118,000	Edge of centre	No traditional rail	Renovated
Ciudad Real	89,000	Edge of centre	Same station	New
Segovia	72,000	6 km from city	Unconnected	New
Cuenca	57,000	3.5 km from city	Unconnected	New
Puertollano	52,000	Central	Same station	Semi-new
Figueras	45,000	Edge of city	Unconnected, same station in future	New
Antequera	41,000	17 km from city	Unconnected	New
Puente Genil	30,000	6 km from city	Unconnected	New
Requena	21,000	6 km from city	Unconnected	New
Calatayud	21,000	Edge of centre	Same station	Renovated

Source: Authors based on 'Atlas Digital de la Áreas Urbanas' for agglomeration inhabitants.

Peripheral HSR stations have generally led to new sub-regional agglomeration initiatives. When an association between municipalities existed prior to the HSR, it increases its activity; when it did not exist prior to the HSR, it led to its creation. In general, their activities are directed at three territorial themes: sub-regional public transport (including the HSR station), technology parks (mainly located by HSR stations), and tourist developments (Colin and Zembri 1992; Troin 1995).

When differently sized places become connected, people and activities flow and/ or relocate in both directions, but generally the changes are imbalanced. Small cities may lose high-level economic activities to the big cities and gain low-level ones or vice versa. The imbalance may manifest in terms of quantity or in terms of quality, so the differences between the two places may increase or decrease. For example, between Ciudad Real and Madrid, commuting profiles are unbalanced, with about three times as many commuters travelling to Madrid, but these commuters are less educated than those travelling towards Ciudad Real (Menéndez et al. 2006).

The location of the HSR station is not neutral in this competition. Station locations are usually the result of tradeoffs between national infrastructure/ service benefits versus urban/social local benefits. A desire to establish the shortest and least expensive HSR lines between metropolises typically gives rise to peripheral stations whereas a desire to reach central districts to provide greater access to destinations gives rise to longer and usually more costly HSR lines. The pros and cons of these choices have been strongly debated (Vickerman and Norman 1999; Menerault 1996). The HSR station locations in Spain are conditioned by pre-existing infrastructure in big cities and by national criteria in small ones (Table 6.4).

In Spain, whether they are central or peripheral, all HSR station locations are reasonably accessible for trips beginning at home. Central locations are easily accessible on foot or by public transport. Peripheral stations in small cities with fewer passengers often lack good public transport, but most HSR passengers have cars and can use park-and-ride. Nevertheless, recognizing that this is a deficiency, recent peripheral Spanish stations have tended to be located near other transportation means and in denser residential areas.

The situation is different when travelling towards an HSR city, since in most Spanish cities (and especially in small ones) the majority of destinations, such as offices, have central locations. Therefore, a central station is better for professionals and for business attraction, and the Spanish experience indicates that central locations in small cities help their competitiveness, although other factors are also important.

Inter-urban lessons

HSR increases accessibility of the places it serves, but the results are not evenly shared. HSR access points (stations) gain large communication possibilities while the rest of the territory gains less (due to the 'tunnel effect') and may even become less attractive than before. Nevertheless, accessibility has to be understood in relation to the combination of all transport networks and not only to one of them.

In cases where pre-existing transport infrastructure is dismantled to build HSR, the result is likely to be less beneficial to accessibility than in cases where new services are added. For the Madrid-Seville and the Madrid-Toledo lines, two conventional rail tracks were dismantled to introduce the two HSR lines along the same paths. The consequence was twofold: first, accessibility was reduced for many places since the traditional lines had many more stations than the new HSR (Mohíno *et al.* 2012), and second, access options were reduced since from many places it was no longer feasible to get to the station by walking or public transit. The net impacts of these positive and negative consequences are not simple to evaluate. Nevertheless, it can be said that HSR is facilitating, in general, a more concentrated urban system.

The Spanish city system is appropriate for HSR efficiency, being composed of a populated geographical centre, a populated band by the coast at distances of 400 to 700 km, and an emptier area in between with abundant small and few big cities. HSR can efficiently connect the centre and the coast and open up new opportunities in the emptier in-between area (Garmendia *et al.* 2008; Ureña *et al.* 2006, 2009c, 2009b).[1]

The most important HSR territorial effects in Spain are not derived from changes in transport modes reinforcing existing inter-metropolitan relations but from new relations between cities where HSR has produced major transportation changes (Ureña *et al.* 2012c), many of them in the emptier Spanish areas. In particular, two types are especially important: new contacts between distant cities (Garmendia *et al.* 2008) and involvement in metropolitan flows (Ureña *et al.* 2009c).

Increased metropolitan processes at distant small cities

In Spain, HSR is facilitating two metropolitan processes (Ureña *et al.* 2005, 2009c, 2012c) around dense historical small provincial cities:

• Non-contiguous expansion into areas about one hour's HSR travel time from the city centres, with surrounding areas not necessarily being integrated into the metropolis (Ureña *et al.* 2005); and
• Reinforcement of the integration of areas within around half an hour's HSR travel time, within areas already integrated into the metropolises (Ureña *et al.* 2009b; Garmendia *et al.* 2012; Mohíno *et al.* 2014).

In the case of non-contiguous expansion, HSR brings together two types of areas that have different and complementary characteristics: metropolises with high living cost, abundant professionals and high-quality services, and historic, dense, small provincial cities that are comparatively less expensive and have plenty of available land, but a relatively small number of highly qualified professionals. With HSR, these now-accessible cities become investment attractions and commuting origin/destination points. Two directional flows do occur, but the flows are imbalanced both in terms of commuter characteristics and business locations (Menéndez *et al.* 2002, 2012). Ureña *et al.* (2012c) have found that previously important administrative and service activities in these small cities improve their integration with those of the larger cities. The small cities also can attract new activities that seek to locate in the metropolitan area but require large development parcels and fewer environmental restrictions than can be found in the central areas. The activities most likely to locate in the small cities use low levels of professional labour, the need for which can met by professionals commuting from the metropolis (Ureña *et al.* 2005). However, this requires HSR travel times of an hour or less, frequent services, cheap fares and a high level of comfort.

Lessons from the reinforcement of continuous metropolitan integration to facilitate the generation of metropolitan sub-centres are discussed in Ureña *et al.* (2009b, 2009c, 2010, 2012c) and Mohíno *et al.* (2014). These authors find that HSR's effects are stronger in cities that already have a good image and high-quality public services, as well as those in locations already used for high-quality office and housing developments. In addition, cities do better with HSR and conventional rail services connecting to several parts of the metropolis, not only to the centre. Studies of Guadalajara, Segovia, Tarragona and Toledo suggest that an inappropriate metropolitan HSR station location and a heavy emphasis on long-distance travel (Bellet *et al.* 2008; Ureña *et al.* 2009b) diminishes the possibilities of creating metropolitan sub-centres.

Re-articulation of medium-sized cities to the system of metropolises

Most large Spanish cities have been located within major transportation corridors over history, with many important economic and personal transactions passing through them. The twentieth century changed their transport connections in two ways: motorways strengthened inter-metropolitan links, while contrarily, air transport resulted in most inter-metropolitan business trips bypassing the small and mid-sized cities, weakening their connectivity.

Ureña *et al.* (2009c) showed that air and HSR transport have similar advantages for the major metropolises while rather different ones for HSR cities located in between them. Inter-metropolitan air services entirely bypass and therefore do not add benefits to intermediate cities, while between 20 and 70 per cent of inter-metropolitan HSR services stop at them, offering these intermediate cities new and improved accessibilities.

Studies undertaken shortly after the construction of the first HSR lines suggested a small capacity to facilitate the distribution of activities from metropolises to big cities (Mannone 1997; Burmeister and Colletis-Wahl 1996; SETEC 2004). However, Ureña *et al.*'s (2009c, 2012d) studies of several HSR lines demonstrated that intermediate cities' connection to the HSR network brings major accessibility changes, which in turn improve these cities' relations with intercity business passengers. The percentage of HSR services stopping at the intermediate cities is a key factor. Here Spanish urban geography works in favour of stopping at the intermediate cities. For HSR services to be competitive with air transport, HSR travel time must be below 2.5–3 hours, and the Spanish network layout and the travel time between Spain's major metropolises allow for intermediate stops within this time limit (see Ureña *et al.* 2009c).

Ureña *et al.* (2009c and 2012d) also showed that large or medium-sized intermediate cities are starting to attract more metropolitan activities than previous scientific literature had suggested. Professional meetings, congresses, scientific meetings, seminars and related events that used to take place in metropolises are now being held more frequently in the intermediate cities, and urban tourism to these cities has increased. In addition, mid-sized businesses and technical consultancy firms carrying out metropolis-related work are increasingly locating in the intermediate cities.

Collaboration between small distant cities

Prior to HSR, one-day round-trip travel was feasible between distant national metropolises through air transport and between most small cities and some distant national metropolises through a combination of ground and air transport. However, it was not feasible between most distant small cities. With HSR stations in a greater number of small Spanish cities, this is changing. For example, among small Spanish cities with HSR service, in about 50 per cent of the cases same-day round trips are possible with more than 6 hours at the destination. This has led to signs of new exchanges (Ureña and Coronado 2009a; Ureña *et al.* 2012c; Coronado *et al.* 2012). The Madrid and Barcelona HSR stations are being transformed to allow more services between small cities.

These long-distance small-to-small relations depend on connection options and HSR configurations. End-of-line cities will only have as many services as local demand will support, while services in and through junction stations could be more numerous than what is locally demanded (Ureña *et al.* 2006).

Prior to HSR and the internet, most relations were polarized from territorial, social and economic points of view, almost always with dominance by the largest entities (metropolises or large firms); thus, activities located in small cities tended to relocate to metropolises. Today, however, electronic communications are nearly ubiquitous and allow direct small-to-small connections and equal-to-equal economic relations (Dupuy and Geneau 2007). With HSR, the argument is similar: there is less need to use the metropolises for the relations between small distant cities, and thus the territory could become less polarized and more decentralized. In addition, some of these small HSR cities are becoming '*villes en mouvement*' in which their inhabitants are travelling as an everyday or routine activity, more so than in other small provincial cities. This happens even more where HSR services are more frequent and cheaper.

Urban/agglomeration project lessons

Prior to the HSR, railway integration within Spanish cities was not satisfactory (Capel 2007; Santos 2007): degraded station neighbourhoods, tracks acting as urban barriers, and railway spaces without use were common.

European studies show that HSR is usually accompanied by actions for attracting activities to areas surrounding HSR stations (Díaz *et al.* 2012), including significant local urban development projects (Van den Berg and Pol 1998; Bruinsma *et al.* 2008; Bellet *et al.* 2012) designed to increase urban concentrations around stations (transport nodes and central places (Bertolini and Spit 1998)). According to Pol (2002) and Bellet *et al.* (2012), in these urban developments, local agents tend to invest in four main elements: the transport node itself, the station and its environs as a place, spatial quality, and image. The Spanish experience is consistent with these findings, but there are differences based on specific context.

Bellet and Gutiérrez (2011) and Bellet *et al.* (2012) classify the ways in which HSR has been introduced in Spain into three types:

- Construction of a new railway system mainly with new peripheral or occasionally new city-edge HSR stations;
- Transformation of the railway system as a driver for major urban redevelopment projects mainly at central stations; and
- Minimal transformation of the railway system with urban redevelopment centred on the station area within pre-existing central or city edge stations.

When it was deemed possible to use the existing railway infrastructure in central locations, Spanish cities have used HSR as an occasion to redevelop the whole station area, improving its intermodal connections and underscoring its centrality. This has occurred in large city centres as well as at mixed stations serving both HSR and conventional trains, usually located at the edge of cities. The redevelopments have often been based on powerful architectural designs and have included abundant dense apartment buildings (for co-financing). In Spain it is only in the largest metropolitan agglomerations (Madrid and Barcelona) and some of the major cities (particularly Zaragoza and Valladolid) where there are plans to locate major office buildings around HSR stations. In smaller cities residential uses dominate the redevelopment plans; however, studies in Spain show that HSR stations in small cities are an attractive residential location only for immigrants, while locals prefer to locate close to their families, friends and other amenities away from the stations (Garmendia *et al.* 2008).

To integrate HSR into the urban fabric in cases where the existing railway infrastructure was found wanting, 'hard solutions', i.e., capital-intensive solutions, were widely pursued in big and medium-sized Spanish cities when the economy was in an expansionist phase. Actions included covering the tracks, relocating railway facilities out of the city (Bellet and Gutiérrez 2011) and redeveloping the former railway land hoping to attract advanced tertiary (service) activities (Van den Berg and Pol 1998; Bruinsma *et al.* 2008). In addition, cities occasionally used the HSR as an opportunity to solve problems not directly related to railway infrastructure or rail properties (Bellet *et al.* 2012; Bellet and Gutiérrez 2011). Typically, an effort was made to cover most project costs by selling the former railway areas, and local authorities were often asked to participate in joint ventures and co-finance them. However these costly solutions are less attractive under current economic realities and lower-cost 'soft' approaches appear to be the wave of the future.

Urban improvements in Spain have been more rapid and substantial when stations are central or urban centre edge. In comparison, the efficacy of attracting activities around peripheral stations has been very small. Peripheral stations have faced several difficulties. First, the peripheral location is difficult to reconcile with a means of passenger transport that bases its efficiency in large part on the accessibility of its stations (Troin 1995). Most peripheral stations simply have less local transport access. In addition, in the case of Spain, peripheral location reduces the possibilities of attracting professional and tourism activities, especially around the stations in ex-urban locations (Ureña *et al.* 2012c). Instead of attracting urban development, the abundant land around the peripheral stations is used to facilitate parking and attract passengers. Indeed, in small urban areas attempts to attract development have been failures, as projects in Guadalajara and Tarragona have illustrated.

To sum up, the HSR urban/agglomeration implications depend on both the station plan and the urban renewal or expansion projects around it. In evaluating the benefits of these improvements, some broad conclusions are warranted by the evidence to date. First, in big cities, most of them with central stations, HSR is substantially extending their CBDs and making them more efficient, improving the station's surroundings for new central mixed housing and tertiary developments. HSR in most medium-sized cities with central or city centre edge stations has affected not only their station surroundings but also their overall city structures, for example in Lérida/Lleida (Bellet *et al.* 2012), Córdoba (Ureña *et al.* 2009c), Zaragoza and Valladolid (Bellet *et al.* 2012; Ureña *et al.* 2009c, 2012d; Díaz *et al.* 2012). HSR has reinforced their historic centres; the station acts as a revitalizing element and motor for major urban redevelopment projects, providing the station or its surroundings with new activities and key public amenities such as conference centres and city services such as bus lines. In peripheral areas, station locations have had much weaker impacts.

Sustainability lessons

Transport represents a large part of total emissions and energy consumption in Europe. In 1998, it was responsible for 20 per cent of all CO_2 emissions in Europe and for 63 per cent of all NOx emissions (van Essen *et al.* 2003). In the Spanish case, between 1990 and 2006, total emissions have increased by 48 per cent, while transport emissions have increased more rapidly, by 89 per cent from 19.41 per cent of total emissions in 1990 to 24.09 per cent in 2006 (Rodríguez 2010). Despite the overall growth in Spanish emissions, RENFE (the Spanish railway operator) reduced the emissions from each transported unit by almost half between 1990 and 2009, despite an increase of 7.5 per cent of all railway services (conventional and HSR) during the same period. This reduction has been caused by greater traction efficiency and substitution of electric engines for petrol.

The issues to be considered when analyzing environmental impacts in terms of CO_2 emissions are (Marsden 2011[2]):

- Emissions resulting from the construction, maintenance and decommissioning of rolling stock and infrastructure;
- Energy consumption for the movement of the HSR and conventional rail rolling stock and, indirectly, occupancy levels and service frequency;
- Energy consumption and emissions savings resulting from changes in the modal shift due to HSR; and
- Emissions from electricity production.

Different analyses have produced different results in terms of estimated emissions and comparative efficiencies.

Network Rail (2009) presented a comparative assessment of the relative environmental performance of conventional electric and HSR services in the context of new line developments. Although conventional (electric powered) rail uses less energy and produces fewer greenhouse gas (GHG) emissions per vehicle kilometre than HSR, HSR produces significantly lower emissions per passenger than conventional rail, due to higher occupancy levels. For the year 2025, high-speed rail would be expected to result in around 9.3 per cent more GHG emissions per seat-mile on average, at 12.8 g CO_2eq/seat-km versus conventional rail's 11.7 g CO_2eq/seat-km, but in emissions per passenger km, HSR is the superior performer, with around 15 per cent less GHG emissions on average (at 30.3 g CO_2eq/passenger-km vs. 35.7 g CO_2eq/passenger-km for conventional rail).

García and Martín (2007) compared CO_2 emissions for five Spanish routes with HSR and other transport modes, showing that the lowest emissions are produced by HSR, followed by conventional rail and bus services; planes showed the highest levels. For long distances, HSR produces five times less kg of CO_2/

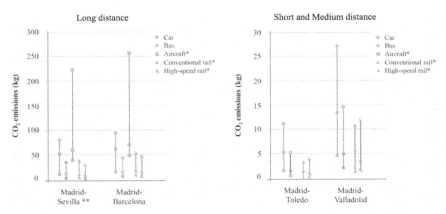

Figure 6.4 CO_2 emissions/passenger for four Spanish HSR connections with full, high and low level occupancies*

*The aircraft, conventional rail and HSR emissions include travel to the initial airport/station and from those at destination to the real end of the journey.

** The Madrid-Malaga line has similar features to the Madrid-Seville one.

passenger-km than the private car, six times less than planes, and approximately the same as buses and conventional trains (García 2007). Automobiles with full occupancy (five passengers) could reach the same level of emissions as the HSR, the conventional train, or the bus if the occupancy levels of the latter three are very low. However, planes never reach similar emissions even when flying at full occupancy levels (see Figure 6.4).

Other analyses have reached somewhat different conclusions. For example, the study conducted by van Essen *et al.* (2003) on CO_2 emissions per passenger-kilometre comparison for several transport modes and distance categories (short – less than 10km, medium – 10/250 km, and long – more than 250km) concludes that for long-distance passenger transport, the highest levels of CO_2 emissions are produced by aircraft. However, in their analysis, inter-city trains show the lowest average CO_2 emissions/passenger-km, followed by buses, electric local trains and HSR trains.

Both technology and operating decisions enter into the calculus. Comparing the energy consumption per kilometre of HSR, conventional rail and upgraded conventional rail in Spain, García (2005), García and Martín (2007) and Andersson and Lukaszewicz (2006) conclude that consumption is lower for high-speed trains, because of their better aerodynamics, fewer stops, better line path requiring less energy consumption, and a reduction in length for the same origin-destination (conventional lines have greater circuity). Fuel consumption due to aerodynamic drag is much higher (+71.6 per cent) in the high-speed train, but all the other consumption addends are lower: mechanical resistances (–30.4 per cent), auxiliary services (–28.9 per cent), losses in the locomotive and in the network (–30.7 per cent) and, most of all, energy dissipated in the brake (–57.29 per cent), this being the addend with the biggest reduction in consumption (García 2010).

Comparing the modal distribution along the Madrid-Seville and Madrid-Barcelona routes before and after the HSR (Figure 6.5), the share of HSR has increased considerably and air and auto modes have declined. For the Madrid-Seville line the HSR share is now almost four times that of air while for Madrid-Barcelona it is almost double. Taking into consideration the greater environmental efficiency of HSR as compared to air and car travel, the increase in HSR market share (and reduction of air and car travel) has had a positive environmental impact in terms of lower CO_2 emissions (Sánchez-Borrás *et al.* 2011).

Therefore, the effect of the new HSR service along a corridor should consider the difference in consumption and emissions due to the traffic transfer from other transport modes, as well as increased emissions due to induced demand. The simulation carried out by García (2008) for different Spanish HSR lines demonstrates that for long-distance routes, the avoided emissions by those passengers travelling by conventional train prior to HSR varies from 6.5 per cent to 15 per cent. This figure is larger considering the avoided emissions by car and plane users, because of the outstanding number of passengers transferred from plane to HSR and because of the lower emissions (kg of CO_2/passenger) HST generates compared to cars and planes. For example, for the Madrid-Barcelona

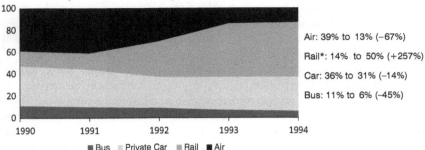

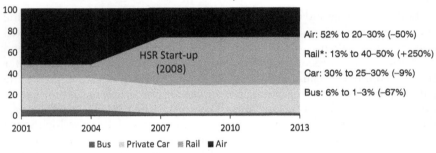

Figure 6.5 Modal share evolution in two Spanish HSR routes

route, the total number of kgCO$_2$ avoided per HSR/HST passenger is 40.42 (adding 0.54kgCO$_2$/HSTpass transferred from the conventional train, 36.18kgCO$_2$/HSTpass from plane travelers, 5.09kgCO$_2$/HSTpass from cars, and subtracting 1.39kgCO$_2$/pass corresponding to the induced travellers (García 2008)).

Finally, HSR (as well as the conventional train) consumes less primary fossil energy than cars and planes. As a result, HSR has contributed to an improvement in the environmental impact of transport regarding emission levels. An improvement in the environmental consequences of electricity generation mix has also occurred due to the increased use of renewable energy sources (which produce lower levels of CO$_2$ emissions), which means that electric-powered transport such as HSR is cleaner than before. Furthermore, RENFE (the Spanish railway operator), unlike other transport modes, uses a significant amount of renewable energy in traction rolling stock (29 per cent in 2009) (Rodríguez 2010).

Conclusions

The Spanish experience with HSR reflects the context in which HSR was implemented – Spain's particular urbanization patterns, infrastructure options, economic conditions, social preferences and political situation. The HSR implementation process in Spain cannot be understood without considering the fact that investment in HSR infrastructure was part of a larger strategy for integration of Spain into the European Union and improving its economic outlook, which is why Spanish HSR lines have been partially financed with European funds. It also is important to note that conventional long-distance rail infrastructure in Spain was not in very good shape, which made upgrade options almost as costly as new high-speed infrastructure. System design choices reflected both national and local/regional criteria and included the objective of increasing access to the major metropolitan areas and their resources from provincial centres. The resulting system has greatly increased rail use, reduced emissions, and helped support territorial management objectives. Public opinion in Spain has been highly in favour of the enormous expenditure required, and the only opponents are small groups of economists who are concerned about the costs. However, HSR benefits need to consider not only the direct time saving benefits to users but also the positive spatial implications for many cities, and the emissions reductions that accrue over time. These last two benefits take time to show their importance.

Notes

1 Ureña *et al.* (2012) also described the appearance of new isolated transportation poles but the present economic crisis is stopping these initiatives and may be cancelling them.
2 For a full HSR sustainability analysis see Chapter 7 of this book 'Life-cycle Analysis of High-Speed Rail in California' by Chester, Horvath and Ryerson.

References

Albalate, D and Bel, G, 2011, 'Cuando la economía no importa: auge y fulgor de la alta velocidad en España', *Revista de Economía Aplicada*, Vol. 55, No. XIX, pp. 171–190.
Andersson, E and Lukaszewicz, P, 2006, *Energy consumption and related air pollution for Scandinavian electric passenger trains.* Report KTJ/AVE 2006:46, Stockholm (Sweden).
Bazin, S, Beckerich, C and Delaplace, M, 2006, 'La LGV Est-Européenne en Champagne-Ardenne: quels effets sur la cohésion territoriale champ ardennaise?', *Revue d'Économie Régionale and Urbaine*, Vol. 2, pp. 245–261.
Bellet, C, 2010, 'Nuevas tecnologías de transporte y metropolización discontínua del territorio. El tren de alta velocidad en Segovia', ACE-Arquitectura, Ciudad y Entorno [Online: CPSV Polytechnic University of Barcelona], Vol. 12, pp. 27–41.
Bellet, C, and Gutiérrez, A, 2011, 'Ciudad y ferrocarril en la España del siglo XXI. La integración de la alta velocidad ferroviaria en el medio urbano'. *Boletín de la Asociación de Geógrafos Españoles*, Vol. 55, pp. 251–279.
Bellet, C, Alonso, MP and Casellas, A, 2010a, 'Infraestructuras de transporte y territorio. Los efectos estructurantes de la llegada del tren de alta velocidad en España', *Boletín de la Asociación de Geógrafos Españoles*, Vol. 52, pp. 143–163.
Bellet, C, Alonso, MP and Casellas, A, 2010b, 'La integración del ferrocarril de alta velocidad en el medio urbano. El caso de Segovia-Guiomar', *Anales de Geografía de la Universidad Complutense de Madrid*, Vol. 30, No. 1, pp. 9–26.

Bellet, C, Alonso, MP and Gutiérrez, A, 2012, 'The High-Speed Rail in Spanish Cities: Urban Integration and Local Strategies for Socioeconomic Development', in Ureña, JM de ed. 2012, *Territorial implications of High-Speed rail: A Spanish perspective*, Aldershot: Ashgate, pp. 163–196.

Bellet, C (dir.), Alonso, P, Casellas, A, Morell, R and Gil, E, 2008, *Los efectos Socioeconómicos y Territoriales de la llegada del Tren de Alta Velocidad a Segovia*. Segovia: Ed. Caja Segovia.

Benegas, M, 2011, 'High Speed Infrastructures: the Spanish Case', *California-Spain Conference on High Speed Rail*, California High-Speed Rail Authority and Spanish Trade Commission, San Francisco June 3, Unpublished presentation.

Bertolini, L and Spit, T, 1998, *Cities on Rails. The Redevelopment of Railway Station Areas*. London: Spon Press.

Bruinsma, F, Pels, E, Priemus, H, Rietveld, P and Van Wee, B, 2008, *Railway development Impact on Urban Dynamics*. Amsterdam: Physica-Verlag.

Burmeister, A and Colletis-Wahl, K, 1996, 'TGV et fonctions tertiaires: grande vitesse et entreprises de service à Lille et Valenciennes', *Transports Urbaines*, Vol. 93, pp. 11–16.

Campos, J, de Rus, G and Barrón, I, 2006, 'Some stylized facts about high speed rail around the world: an empirical approach'. *4th Annual Conference on Railroad Industry Structure, Competition and Investment*, October 19–21, Universidad Carlos III, Madrid.

Capel, H, 2007, 'Ferrocarril, territorio y ciudades'. *Biblio 3w, Revista Bibliográfica de Geografía y Ciencias Sociales* [Online], XII(717). http://www.ub.es/geocrit/b3w-717.htm Accessed 1 August 2016.

Charlton, C and Vowles, T, 2008, 'Inter-Urban and Regional Transport', in Knowles, R, Shaw, J and Docherty, I (eds) *Transport Geographies: Mobilities, Flows and Spaces*, Oxford: Blackwell.

Colin, R and Zembri, P, 1992, 'Vendôme et le TGV: un mariage surréaliste?', *Transports Urbains*, Vol. 75, pp. 19–24.

Coronado, JM, Garmendia, M, Moyano, A and Ureña, JM de, 2012, 'Measuring High Speed Rail Usefulness for Tourism in Spain', *49 Colloque de la Association de Science Régionale de Langue Française*, 9–11 July, Belfort (France).

De Meer, A, Ribalaygua, C and Martín, E, 2012, 'High-Speed Rail and Regional Accessibility', in Ureña, JM de (ed.) 2012, *Territorial Implications of High-Speed Rail: A Spanish Perspective*. Aldershot: Ashgate, pp. 197–216.

Díaz, SE, Ureña, JM and Ribalaygua, C, 2012, 'Transport Interchanges Effects on their Surroundings in Tunja (Colombia) and Córdoba (Spain): A Comparative Approach', *The Open Geography Journal*, Vol. 5, pp. 38–47.

Dupuy, G and Geneau, I, 2007, *Nouvelles échelles des firmes et des réseaux. Un défi pour l'aménagement*. Itinéraires Géographiques. Paris: L'Harmattan.

Fariña, J, Lamíquiz, F and Pozueta, J, 2000, 'Efectos territoriales de las infraestructuras de transporte de acceso controlado', *Cuadernos de Investigación Urbanística-CIUr*, Vol. 29.

Ferropedia ES, 2016, 'Costos de construcción de infraestructura,' http://www.ferropedia.es/wiki/Costos_de_construcción_de_infraestructura Accessed 1 August 2016.

García, A, 2010, *High speed, energy consumption and emissions. Study and Research Group for Railway Energy and emissions*, International Union of Railways (UIC): Paris, FR.

García Álvarez, A, 2005, 'El tren de alta velocidad no es un depredador de energía', Dyna. http://www.revistadyna.com/Documentos/pdfs%5C2005%5C200505jun%5C891DYNAINDEX.pdf Accessed 1 August 2016.

García Álvarez, A, 2007, 'Consumo de energía y emisiones del tren de alta velocidad en comparación con otros modos', extended and updated version of the paper published in *Anales de Mecánica y Electricidad*, LXXXIV (V).

García Álvarez, A and Martín Cañizares, P, 2007, 'Más velocidad, menos consumo', *Vía Libre*, Vol. 511, pp. 23–25.

García Álvarez, A, 2008, *Normalización de los consumos energéticos de los trenes de viajeros*, *ponencia presentada en el III Congreso de Innovación Ferroviaria* (Tenerife, mayo 2007).

Garmendia, M, Ureña, JM, Ribalaygua, C, Leal, J and Coronado, JM, 2008, 'Urban Residential Development in Isolated Small Cities that are Partially Integrated in Metropolitan Areas by High Speed Train', *European Urban and Regional Studies*, Vol. 15, No. 3, pp. 249–264.

Garmendia, M, Ribalaygua, C and Ureña, JM, 2012a, 'High speed rail implications for cities', *CITIES*, Vol. 29 (Sup 2), S26–S31.

Garmendia, M, Romero, V, Ureña, JM de, Coronado, JM and Vickerman, R, 2012b, 'High-speed Rail Opportunities around Metropolitan Regions: The Cases of Madrid and London,' *Journal of Infrastructure Systems (ASCE)*, Vol. 18, No. 4, pp. 305–313.

Givoni, M, 2006, 'Development and Impact of the Modern High-speed Train: A Review', *Transport Reviews*, Vol. 26, No. 5, pp. 593–611.

Gutiérrez, J, 2004, 'El tren de alta velocidad y sus efectos espaciales', *Investigaciones Regionales*, Vol. 5, pp. 199–221.

Inglada, V *et al.*, 2012, 'Economic Assessment of High-Speed Rail in Spain', in Ureña, JM de (ed.) 2012. *Territorial Implications of High Speed Rail: A Spanish Perspective.* Aldershot: Ashgate, pp. 217–239.

Klein, O, 2001, *Les horizons de la grande vitesse: le TGV, une innovation lue à travers les mutations de son époque.* PhD-thesis. Université Lumière, Lyon 2. November 2001.

Mannone, V, 1997, 'Gares TGV et nouvelles dynamiques urbaines en centre ville: le cas des villes desservies par le TGV Sud-Est', *Les Cahiers Scientifiques du Transport*, Vol. 31, pp. 71–97.

Marsden, G, 2011, 'Review of CO_2 Emission Studies of High-Speed Rail in Europe', *TRB 90th Annual Meeting – Workshop*, January 23–27, Washington, DC. http://cta.ornl.gov/TRBenergy/trb_documents/2011_presentations/Marsden%20Review%20of%20CO2%20-%20Session%20118.pdf, Accessed 1 August 2016.

Martínez, H, Ureña, JM, Coronado, JM, Garmendia, M, Romero, V and Solís, E, 2010, 'Regional High-Speed Rail Services Typology, Demand and Spatial Implications'. Paper to the *ERSA L Conference: High-Speed Rail as a new transport network. Sustainable Regional Growth and Development in the creative knowledge Economy*, Jonkoping, August 2010.

Menéndez, JM, Coronado, JM and Rivas, A, 2002, 'El AVE en Ciudad Real y Puertollano: notas sobre su incidencia en la movilidad y el territorio', *Cuadernos de Ingeniería y Territorio*, 2. Ciudad Real: Universidad Castilla-La Mancha.

Menéndez, JM, Rivas, A and Gallego, I, 2012, 'Mobility Characteristics of Medium-Distance High-Speed Rail Services', in Ureña, JM de (ed.) 2012, *Territorial Implications of High Speed Rail: A Spanish Perspective.* Aldershot: Ashgate, pp. 105–127.

Menéndez, JM, Coronado, JM, Guirao, B, Ribalaygua, C, Rodríguez, J, Rivas, A and Ureña, JM, 2006, 'Diseño, dimensión óptima y emplazamiento de estaciones de alta velocidad en ciudades de tamaño pequeño'. *Cuadernos de Ingeniería y Territorio*, 7, Ciudad Real: E.T.S.I. Caminos, Canales y Puertos, UCLM.

Menerault, P, 1996, 'TGV et transports ferrés régionaux dans le Nord-Pas-de-Calais: analyse d'une politique publique locale', *Annales Les Pays-Bas Français*, Vol. 21, pp. 45–62.

Menerault, P, 1998, 'Processus de territorialisation des réseaux: analyse de la grande vitesse ferroviaire à l'échelle régionale', *Networks and Communication Studies NETCOM*, Vol. 12, Nos. 1, 2 and 3, pp. 161–184.

Ministerio de Obras Públicas y Transportes (MOPT), 1991, *Manual de Evaluación de Inversiones en Ferrocarril de Vía Ancha*. Madrid: Ministerio de Obras Públicas y Transportes.

Mohíno, I, Loukaitou-Sideris, A and Ureña, JM, 2014, 'Impacts of High-speed Rail on Metropolitan Integration: An Examination of London, Madrid and Paris', *International Planning Studies*, In Print (DOI: 10.1080/13563475.2014.950638).

Mohíno, I, Ureña, JM de, Solís, E and Martínez, H, 2012, 'Radial versus tangential transport networks and services and their role in metropolitan spatial structures: The central area of Spain as a case study', *EURA Conference 2012 – Urban Europe – Challenges to meet the Urban Future*, 20–22 September, Vienna.

Network Rail, 2009, Comparing environmental impact of conventional and high speed rail, New Lines Programme, available from http://www.networkrail.co.uk/newlinesprogramme/ Accessed 1 August 2016.

Offner, JM, 1993, 'Les 'effets structurants' du transport: mythe politique, mystification scientifique', *L'Espace Géographique*, Vol. 3, pp. 233–242.

Plassard, F, 1991, 'Le train à grande vitesse et le réseau des villes', *Transports*, Vol. 345, pp. 14–23.

Plassard, F, 1997, 'Les effets des infrastructures de transport, modèles et paradigmes', in Burmeister, A and Joinaux, G (eds) *Infrastructures de Transport et Territoires*. Paris: L'Harmattan, pp. 39–54.

Pol, PMJ, 2002, *A renaissance of stations, railways and cities: economic effects, development strategies and organisational issues of European High-Speed-Train stations*. PhD-thesis. Delft: Delft University Press.

Ribalaygua, C, 2004, *Evolución de las estrategias de incorporación de la alta velocidad ferroviaria y sus efectos urbanísticos en ciudades medias francesas. Aplicación a los casos españoles*. PhD-thesis. Madrid: Universidad Politécnica de Madrid.

Ribalaygua, C, 2006, 'Nuevas estaciones periféricas de alta velocidad ferroviaria: estrategias para su incorporación a las ciudades españolas', *Colección Cuadernos de Ingeniería y Territorio*, Vol. 5. Universidad de Castilla-La Mancha, Ciudad Real.

Rodríguez, A, 2010, 'La contribución de Renfe a la sostenibilidad'. *Seminario de transporte y cambio climático en la Argentina*. Vol. 22, septiembre 2010. Buenos Aires.

Sánchez-Borrás, M et al., 2011, 'High-Speed Railways in Spain. Example of Success?' *Transportation Research Record: Journal of the Transportation Research Board*, Vol. 2261, pp. 39–48.

Santos, L, 2007, *Urbanismo y ferrocarril. La Construcción del Espacio Ferroviario en las Ciudades medias españolas*. Madrid: Fundación de los Ferrocarriles Españoles.

Serrano, R, Garmendia, M, Coronado, JM, Pillet, F and Ureña, JM, 2006, 'Análisis de las consecuencias territoriales del AVE en ciudades pequeñas: Ciudad Real y Puertollano'. *Estudios Geográficos*, Vol. LXVII, No. 260, pp. 199–229.

SETEC, 2004, *LGV PACA Etude relative aux effets socio-économique et en terme d'aménagement: Volet 1, Analyse bibliographique des effets des LGV, Synthèse du fonds documentaire*. SETEC Organisation.

Troin, JF, 1995, *Rail et aménagement du Territoire. Des héritages aux nouveaux Défis*. Paris: Edisud.

Ureña, JM and Coronado JM, 2009a, *Changing Territorial Implications of High Speed Rail in Spain: From Individual Lines, Stations and Services to Networks*. Paper to the International Congress City Futures in a Globalising World, Madrid, 4–6 June 2009.

Ureña, JM, Garmendia, M and Coronado, JM, 2009b, 'Nuevos procesos de metropolización facilitados por la Alta Velocidad Ferroviaria', *Ciudad y Territorio Estudios Territoriales*, Vol. XLI, No. 160, pp. 213–232.

Ureña, JM, Menerault, P and Garmendia, M, 2009c, 'The high-speed rail challenge for big intermediate cities: a national, regional and local perspective', *Cities*, Vol. 26, pp. 266–279.

Ureña, JM, Coronado, JM, Escobedo, F, Ribalaygua, C and Garmendia, M, 2006, 'Situaciones y retos territoriales de la Alta Velocidad Ferroviaria en España', *Ciudad y Territorio Estudios Territoriales (CyTET)*, Vol. XXXVIII, No. 148, pp. 397–424.

Ureña, JM, Garmendia, M, Coronado, JM, Vickerman, R and Romero, V, 2010, 'New metropolitan processes encouraged by High-Speed Rail: the cases of London and Madrid'. *WCTR Congress*, Lisbon, July 2010.

Ureña, JM, Menéndez, JM, Guirao, B, Escobedo, F, Rodríguez, FJ, Coronado, JM, Ribalaygua, C, Rivas, A and Martínez, A, 2005, 'Alta velocidad ferroviaria e integración metropolitana en España: el caso de Ciudad Real y Puertollano', *EURE Revista Latinoamericana de Estudios Urbano Regionales*, Vol. 92, pp. 87–104.

Ureña, JM de, 2012a, 'High-Speed Rail and its Evolution in Spain', in Ureña, JM de (ed.) 2012, *Territorial Implications of High Speed Rail: A Spanish Perspective*. Aldershot: Ashgate, pp. 1–15.

Ureña, JM de, 2012b, 'Afterthoughts: High-Speed rail Planning Issues and Perspectives', in Ureña, JM de (ed.) 2012, *Territorial Implications of High Speed Rail: A Spanish Perspective*. Aldershot: Ashgate, pp. 241–250.

Ureña, JM de, Coronado, JM, Garmendia, M and Romero, V, 2012c, 'Territorial Implications at National and Regional Scales of High-Speed Rail', in Ureña, JM de (ed.) 2012, *Territorial Implications of High Speed Rail: A Spanish Perspective*. Aldershot: Ashgate, pp. 130–161.

Ureña, JM de, Garmendia, M, Coronado, JM and Santos, L, 2012d, 'El análisis de red en las ciudades intermedias sobre líneas de Alta Velocidad Ferroviaria', *Ciudad y Territorio Estudios Territoriales*, In Print.

Van den Berg, L and Pol, P, 1997, *The European High-Speed Train-Network and Urban Development. European Regional Science Association*. Paper to the XXXVII European Congress, Rome, 26–29 August 1997.

Van den Berg, L and Pol, P, 1998, *The European High-Speed Train and Urban Development. Experiences in Fourteen European Urban Regions*. Aldershot: Ashgate.

Van Essen, H *et al.*, 2003, *To shift or not to shift, that's the question. The environmental performance of the principal modes of freight and passenger transport in the policy-making context*. Report 03.4360.09. Delft. CE Solutions for environment, economy and technology.

Vickerman, R, 1997, 'High-speed rail in Europe: experience and issues for future development', *The Annals of Regional Science*, Vol. 31, pp. 21–38.

Vickerman, R and Norman, C, 1999, 'Local and Regional Implications of Trans-European Transport Networks: the Channel Tunnel Rail Link', *Environment and Planning A*, Vol. 31, pp. 705–718.

Zembri, P, 2005, 'El TGV, la red ferroviaria y el territorio en Francia', *Ingeniería y Territorio*, Vol. 70, pp. 12–19.

7 High-speed rail and air travel complementarity

The case of Germany

Werner Rothengatter

Introduction

High-speed rail (HSR) and air travel are generally considered to be competitors for distances between 400 and 1,000 km. There are only a few city pairs more than 1,000 km apart in which HSR can compete successfully with air, e.g. Beijing-Shanghai in China or Barcelona-Madrid-Seville in Spain. Even within the competitive distance range, low-cost airlines are powerful competitors. As long as there is capacity to add flights at the airports, the landside investments needed to provide air transport between city pairs are much lower than for the cost of providing HSR, and short-haul airlines can construct a network between agglomeration centres easily, while the construction of an HSR connection is extremely expensive and risky. Therefore HSR is a reasonable option primarily in busy corridors which link major urban agglomerations with high population density. Extending HSR networks to smaller urban agglomerations with numerous stops along the way can result in major financial problems, as the Spanish example shows.

It follows that HSR can substitute for only a modest part of total air travel. It cannot compete on long flight distances and can only compete on short- to medium-flight distances when market conditions are favourable. But the relationships between HSR and air travel are not only substitutive, they can also be complementary. Four types of complementarity are possible:

- HSR can serve as a feeder to airports for medium- and long-distance flights;
- HSR can provide short- to medium-distance travel services to city pairs in which the airlines are not much interested;
- HSR can be used as a backup system if air connections have to be cancelled because of weather conditions or other problems;
- HSR can be used as a feeder system for freight parcel service.

This chapter discusses the competitive relationships between HSR and air travel using examples from the EU and in particular from Germany. Germany provides an interesting case because it has chosen to develop a mixed system with some high-speed links integrated with the conventional train system, offering an important contrast to the experiences in France and Spain. In addition, Germany has had experience with using HSR as a complementary service and continues to look for such complements to extend HSR's market reach.

The chapter first presents some background on HSR in the EU and provides a brief overview of different approaches to the development of HSR that have been taken in EU countries. It then goes on to discuss the air transport system in the EU and its competitive position with respect to HSR. Next the chapter examines modes of complementarity between air and HSR and Germany's experience with them, and finally it concludes with lessons learned from the German experience.

Background on HSR in the EU

Figure 7.1 illustrates HSR ridership in Germany (DE), Spain (ES), France (FR) and Italy (IT) for the period 1995–2010. The figure shows that HSR ridership has grown throughout this period, though at different rates in different countries and with a slowing of growth in Germany and France after the economic crisis hit in 2008. Total rail passenger travel in the EU increased only modestly over this same period, while air transport increased dynamically until the economic downturn hit it hard. Thus it appears that HSR has helped to stabilize the modal share of rail transport in the four major HSR countries in the EU.

The different growth rates in HSR use shown in Figure 7.1 reflect differences in the timing and nature of the HSR networks delivered in each country. Network characteristics also affect the share of rail travel that is made by HSR, as shown in Figure 7.2. HSR first emerged as an intercity travel option in the EU with the opening of the first *Train á Grande Vitesse* (TGV) line between Paris and Lyon in the early 1980s. Since then, the French HSR system has been extended to the West (TGV Atlantique), North (Lille, Brussels, Channel Tunnel) and East (Strasbourg). TGV trains operated about 52 billion passenger kilometres (pkm) in 2010 and currently make up about 60 per cent of the French rail patronage. In Spain, the first HSR link opened between Madrid and Seville in 1992 but the share of travel by HSR remained modest until the opening of Madrid-Barcelona service in the 2003–2008 period. It then increased rapidly. Follow-up investments to the South (Valencia), North (Valladolid) and East (Barcelona-Perpignan) completed the framework of the ambitious HSR plan. The expanded service has boosted HSR patronage and the HSR share of total rail passenger transport in Spain from 10 per cent in 2001 to more than 50 per cent in 2010.

In Germany and Italy the HSR networks developed more slowly and according to different philosophies. HSR in these countries was offered link by link such that the railway lines connecting most city pairs included both high-speed and conventional tracks. As a consequence, the service has not been as fast, and up to the end of 2010 the share of rail travel on HSR remained smaller than in France and Spain.

The EU has plans for future expansions of HSR as well as increased coordination of the existing services, developed in the context of the Trans-European Network – Transport (TEN-T), the European Commission's policy framework for system integration. The concept is for HSR lines of category I (faster than 250 km/h) and category II (200–250 km/h) to grow from 9,693 km in 2008 to 22,140 km in 2020 and 30,750 km in 2030 (European Commission, 2010). It remains to be seen if this concept is financially viable because of the extremely high investment costs in hilly areas and the decreasing marginal revenues per HSR kilometre when extending the network to less busy corridors. In addition, a number of countries are planning to expand their own HSR systems. For example, France and Spain have plans to significantly extend their HSR networks in the future; Italy also had ambitious plans before the economic crisis, which are presently under revision.

In Germany some projects are underway which will close missing links (e.g. Berlin-Erfurt-Nuremberg) or expand and improve HSR services (Stuttgart-Ulm, Stuttgart 21 central station project). The projects will reduce the fragmentation of the German HSR network, but are unlikely to dramatically affect its attractiveness overall. The new generation of rolling stock will not attempt to achieve the highest possible speeds (i.e., will be for speeds of not more than 250 km/h) in favour of

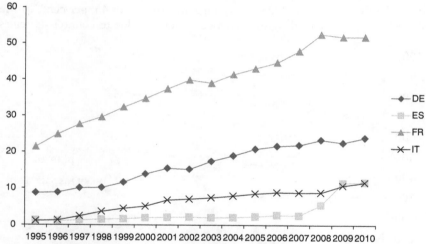

Figure 7.1 Growth in HSR ridership in four EU countries (billion pkm)

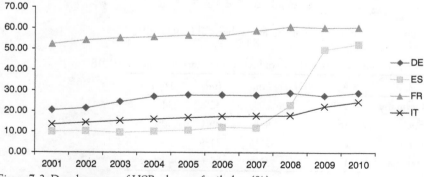

Figure 7.2 Development of HSR: shares of rail pkm (%)

energy savings. Instead, the German policy objective is to make intelligent use of high speed where it is justified and to use a well maintained conventional rail network elsewhere, in both cases responsive to passenger demand.

Air travel in the EU: HSR's competition?

Air passenger travel grew dynamically in the EU until the beginning of the world economic crisis in 2008 (Figure 7.3). In the following years air travel was hit by the crisis more than other transport modes, shrinking from 572 billion pkm (2007) to 522 billion pkm (2009), a loss of 9 per cent. By 2010 the air travel volume had again reached 2005 levels, but up to the end of 2018 Eurocontrol (2012) predicts only modest growth of air traffic for most EU countries, for instance for Germany, France, Italy and Spain growth is forecast to be on the order of 2 per cent or less.

Low-cost carriers (LCC) entered into competition in the EU in the late 1990s and achieved rapid growth from 13 million passengers in 1999 to more than 100 million passengers in 2005, an average growth rate of 45 per cent. In the following years the growth rates decreased somewhat, due to counter-strategies

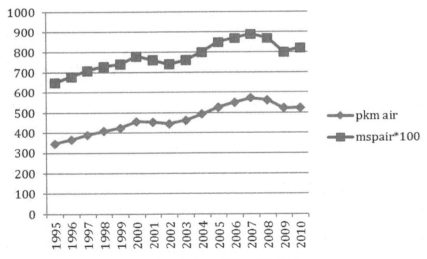

Figure 7.3 Air passenger km and mode share, EU, 1995–2010

Table 7.1 Actual market shares of low-cost carriers and forecasts 2018

Country	Actual 2011	Low	Base	High
Germany	29%	29%	32%	34%
Spain	46%	41%	46%	50%
France	18%	18%	21%	24%
Italy	37%	36%	40%	42%

Source: Eurocontrol 2012

of the regular air carriers and, from 2008 onward, due to the economic downturn as well. Market shares for LCC are expected to grow only modestly until 2018 (Table 7.1) and may even decrease (low scenario) (Eurocontrol, 2012).

The competitive situation between HSR and air transport on the supply side is affected by network considerations. While HSR expansions are planned and integration is to be improved, the HSR network will still be restricted to busy corridors. In contrast, airlines are able to avail themselves of a great many airports located throughout Europe, especially if small regional airports are used (Figure 7.4).

The current situation gives several advantages to air transport, in particular the LCCs. Air carriers can serve numerous markets from regional airports, offering flight schedules that can be adjusted relatively quickly to reflect demand. In many cases they have low landside costs – especially when operating from regional airports that receive government subsidies. In addition, LCCs have had favourable labour

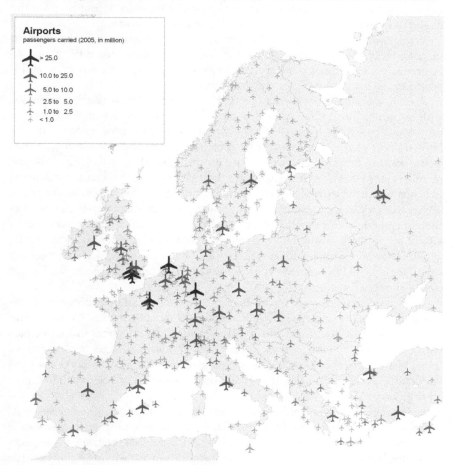

Figure 7.4 Distribution of airports in Europe

agreements. In contrast, HSR services have typically been constrained by policy to operate with fixed stops and schedules even when demand is low. HSR labour costs have been high, reflecting the power of the rail trade unions. HSR also continues to face disadvantages stemming from the high costs of border crossing services, exacerbated by heterogeneous HSR technologies reflecting national preferences and country-specific regulations. Finally, HSR stations in the large cities have been costly to build and operate. While recent directives to cap regional airport subsidies and harmonize HSR regulations and technologies are moving forward, it remains to be seen how quickly these moves will be implemented.

Attempts to increase the attractiveness of HSR by expanding its network runs the risk of tremendously high investment costs and the need for subsidization of operations. Spain is a stark example. The Spanish HSR network is the largest in Europe and it serves many urban regions of only moderate size. Except for the main corridors Madrid-Barcelona, Madrid-Seville and Madrid-Valencia, the HSR network has not been economically profitable even accounting for the public (national and EU) co-finance for the investment costs.

While attempting to compete by serving many cities may not work, efforts to increase HSR attractiveness by competing on time, cost and amenities appear to be promising. HSR already has certain time use features that are attractive and is beginning to compete on costs and amenities.

A main motivation for users to prefer HSR to air transport is its performance with respect to travel time, and in this regard HSR has some advantages, because total travel time from door to door counts and not only the time spent within the HSR train or plane. In the case of air travel the access and egress times, as well as the waiting times in the airports, are much higher than with HSR. Business travellers may also value the better opportunities for working and communication in trains compared with planes and therefore may be willing to accept somewhat higher train travel times. Tourists might prefer the train because they can use it as their only mode of travel, whereas air travel will in most cases require a transfer to a local access mode (train, bus, taxi, auto). A further reason for preferring HSR, which holds for Germany at least, is the flexibility of time choice for travelling by rail including HSR, while in contrast travellers are bound to the booked travel time if they choose air travel.

The competitiveness of travel fares is not easy to analyze because of the manifold discounts and special tariffs offered by the companies. Certainly the lowest of the LCC tariffs on small and medium flight distances in Europe can hardly be beaten by HSR. On the other hand, various surcharges applying to air travel as well as the costs of access and parking increase air transport's door-to-door costs. Overall, it is likely that HSR and air costs will not be much different, all things considered.

It appears that there are some longer-distance markets where HSR will compete well. The plans of Deutsche Bahn AG to extend their long-distance connections (e.g., Frankfurt-London, 763 km) indicate that the company expects a growing market for rail travel over long rail distances. The experiment with opening an HSR connection from Frankfurt to Marseille via Lyon – operated by TGV – has proven unexpectedly successful (150,000 passengers in the first year for the 1,000 km trip). Pricing policy has contributed to this result (39 EUR for second class and 69 EUR for first class) and made HSR competitive with low-cost airlines. German HSR may also be able to capture a significant market share for international transport to Amsterdam and Brussels, as well as for longer-distance domestic trips. Sprinters between Munich-Hamburg: railway distance 765 kilometres, and Munich-Berlin: 620 kilometres, are planned; these city pairs are sizeable travel markets for which non-stop HSR services would serve the needs of business travellers, running in the morning and late afternoon.

Opening up HSR operations to competition also may open up more price options and a wider variety of amenities, as has been the case in Italy. However, most EU HSR services remain in the hands of government, and the proposal to increase competitive bidding (tendering) for operations has been highly controversial. Nevertheless, the reduction of airport subsidies, expanded route coverage and increased services in major markets, improved interoperability among HSR systems, greater use of pricing incentives, and improved customer information systems all seem likely to improve the prospects for EU HSR in competition with short-haul air services.

Complementarity of HSR and air transport

While, as the previous section has discussed, HSR competes with air transport for passengers, it also may serve as a complement to air transport. As noted, four types of complementarity are possible:

- HSR can serve as a feeder to airports for medium- and long-distance flights;
- HSR can deliver services to city pairs which the airlines are not much interested in, serving in particular the regular air carriers;
- HSR can be used as a backup system if air connections have to be cancelled because of weather conditions or other problems; and
- HSR can be used as a feeder system for freight parcel service.

HSR as a feeder service to airports

On long flight distances HSR is not competing with air transport; but it can make air transport chains more efficient and comfortable for customers, thus increasing demand for air transport. The Frankfurt/Main Airport station for long-distance trains provides an outstanding example of HSR trains connecting southern (Munich, Basel) and northern agglomerations (Cologne, Dortmund, Amsterdam) with the Rhine/Main area and the main German airport. Passengers using rail lines connecting to Frankfurt central station (e.g. from Hamburg/Berlin/Hanover or Würzburg/Nuremberg) can easily change from regional and local airport lines to the regional train station at the airport which is only 15 km, or 12 minutes, away. In 1999, the year the airport railway station opened, 9,000 travellers used this service each day; today there are about 25,000 passengers per day. The station building was expanded in 2011 through an investment of 1.2 billion EUR to include a large centre of commerce, retail businesses, restaurants, hotels and conference facilities.

The success of the Frankfurt Airport rail station, and that of Paris-Roissy (Charles de Gaulle Airport) has led the EU Commission to suggest that major airports should be connected to the long-distance rail network (EU White Paper on Common Transport Policy 2011). In Germany additional airport stations were built in Düsseldorf, Cologne/Bonn and Leipzig. The Düsseldorf Airport station, opened in 2000, is served by the hourly Intercity Express (ICE) line as well as by conventional train services, and is integrated with the regional public transit network connected by a people mover ('Sky Train') to the air terminals. For the Cologne/Bonn Airport station, opened in 2004, the travel demand was lower than expected and the number of ICE trains was reduced to six pairs per day in 2007. The Leipzig Airport station is served by one ICE train per day and two other trains at 2-hour time intervals. The number of passengers is less than 1,000 per day.

The planned HSR link between Ulm and Stuttgart, for which construction has started, will connect the airport to the ICE service every 2 hours. Furthermore ICE trains and regional trains will offer attractive travel times from regional origins to Stuttgart Airport. ICE service and the use of the HSR link by intercity and regional trains dramatically reduces the travel time in the catchment area of Stuttgart Airport. For instance, the forthcoming HSR link can cut the rail travel time from Friedrichshafen (Lake of Konstanz) to Stuttgart Airport by half, from 190 minutes to 91 minutes.

Among the German airport rail stations that have been operating for some time, only Frankfurt can be called a success and Düsseldorf a reasonable investment, justifiable based on total social benefits. The main reason is simple: Frankfurt (about 58 million annual passengers) and Düsseldorf (21 million annual passengers) have a much higher volume of air and rail travellers compared with the smaller airports of Leipzig (2.3 million pax) or Cologne/Bonn (9.3 million pax), all data for the year 2012. Stuttgart Airport counted 9.7 million pax in 2012, and given its modest size, it is unlikely that the large investments for the new underground station at the airport and its links to the new underground HSR central station and the regional rail networks, will be cost-effective.

One can conclude that airport-railway stations can be economically successful or at least reasonable investments if the air passenger volume is high enough and the station has additional functionality in the regional and intercity network. In other cases an improvement of feeder services from the existing central stations to the airport might be economically much more reasonable. This also holds for larger airports, like Munich Airport, which are not located along busy railway corridors. For Munich an express S-Bahn (rapid transit) is planned, which could already have been established if the state of Bavaria had not invested inordinate time and political effort into a maglev connection (37 km) between the Munich central station and the airport. This project was cancelled in 2008 because of drastic increases in cost estimations and the planning of an express S-Bahn had to start from scratch.

HSR as a substitute for short-distance air transport

Regular air carriers like Lufthansa or Air France have long been interested in substituting train service for some of their short-distance air connections. The reasons are two-fold: first, short-distance flights are costly because of high fuel consumption during take-off and landing, and second, the carriers worry that a shortage of capacity will eventually develop at major airports and lead to restrictions on flights. Figure 7.5 shows the principal idea: air carriers would focus on the hub-to-hub connections between large airports, and rail services would substitute for the feeder flights from small airports to the hubs.

As early as 1982 Lufthansa introduced the LH Airport Express service between Düsseldorf and Frankfurt airports, using its own rolling stock. In 1990 a second connection to Stuttgart was opened such that the Frankfurt-Düsseldorf, Frankfurt-Stuttgart and Stuttgart-Düsseldorf/Cologne-Bonn flights could be substantially reduced. Passengers could check in at Düsseldorf or Stuttgart for flights from Frankfurt. However, the first leg of their service was on rail.

The Lufthansa Airport Express service was cancelled in 1993. Instead, LH and DB offer two joint services. The first service, called Rail&Fly, can be booked at all of the 5,600 railway stations in Germany and to or from all German airports and Basel, Switzerland. The railway connections include direct rides to airport stations in Frankfurt, Düsseldorf, Leipzig and Cologne/Bonn. Passengers receive one integrated ticket for the complete round trip travel chain at a special ticket price. The second service, called AIRail service, is the direct successor to the LH Airport Express service. The central stations of Cologne, Siegburg/Bonn, and Stuttgart are linked to Frankfurt airport station by HSR, with code-sharing, integrated ticketing, and reservation of compartments on ICE trains for rail/air passengers.

In 2007 LH discontinued flights between Frankfurt and Cologne/Bonn. In 2011 the rail service between the two cities was used by more than 200,000 customers. Beginning in July 2013 the Düsseldorf Airport station was included in the AIRail connections.

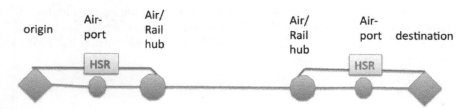

Figure 7.5 Air/rail hubbing

HSR as a backup system for air transport

Air traffic is occasionally disturbed by weather conditions, catastrophic events, or employee strikes.

For example, from March 20 to April 12, 2010, the Icelandic volcano Eyjafjallajökull ejected ash clouds which drifted in the air over Europe until mid-May and caused about 100,000 flight cancellations. Short-distance flights could partially be shifted to the railways. Deutsche Bahn's HSR passenger transport profited from this catastrophic event and increased from 22.5 million passengers in 2009 to 23.9 million passengers in 2010 (+6.2 per cent).

And in September 2012 the cabin personnel of LH went on strike. Deutsche Bahn provided extra train capacity and carried about 10,000 air passengers on September 7. Likewise on April 22 and 23, 2013, almost 2,000 LH flights had to be cancelled because of a strike by the ground personnel, and rail took up a portion of the travel.

While the examples show rail providing backup service for air, the reverse is also possible. DB is also exposed to a risk of strike, which might shift travellers from HSR to air transport. Furthermore, weather can cause delays on the rail system, as happened in winter 2010 when DB was not well prepared for uncommonly low temperatures and high snowfall. Freezing rain affects electric train operations much more than aircraft because a train's frozen pantographs (the arms that draw power from overhead wires) cannot function, while aircraft can prepare for flights by de-icing. In short, the complementarity of the HSR and air systems is two-directional and dependent on the nature of the disturbance.

HSR as a feeder system for parcel delivery services

Big parcel service companies such as UPS, FedEx and DHL usually locate their distribution centres close to airports. They are interested in fast feeder services from other airports to the distribution centre. DHL, for instance, operates three hubs worldwide and moved its distribution hub for Europe from Brussels to Leipzig Airport in 2008. At the Leipzig facility up to fifty-two planes can be processed in parallel.

As the air cargo centre of Leipzig Airport is connected to the railway network and Leipzig Airport station can be served by ICE, it has been proposed to operate parcel trains by night between Frankfurt and Leipzig airports for DHL. The financial and economic crisis led to a postponement of this idea, but it remains an option to be reconsidered as parcel services are growing again. The use of HSR for parcel services is already well advanced in France, where the Société nationale des chemins de fer français (SNCF) and business partners like FedEx started parcel TGV operations in 2011.

Lessons from the German experience with HSR

When the first German HSR links were opened in 1991, 10 years after opening the first TGV line, it turned out that the costs of the German HSR infrastructure were six times the French figures. Reasons were the topography (hilly regions in Germany, flat area with a minimum of bridges and no tunnels in France) and the German policy at the time to use the HSR links for night freight, which required lower gradients and the construction of by-pass tracks for the freight trains. This dampened the enthusiasm for HSR and fostered the hope that the maglev development (of Thyssen and Siemens) might offer better chances for German high-speed technology. Also, the German political system, in which the federal states have a powerful position, led to fragmented development of the HSR network, in contrast to the experience in countries like France or Spain where the HSR links were built in long corridors between urban agglomerations. The length of the German HSR network is modest compared to those of France or Spain, and the fragmented allocation of HSR links as well as the low distances between HSR stations do not allow for very high average speeds. For instance, the fastest track, Frankfurt-Cologne, allows for a maximum speed of 300 km/h while the average speed between Frankfurt and Cologne central stations is about 170 km/h.

In addition, because for many city pairs the German system combines HSR lines with conventional rail lines, transfers are required for many trips. As it is important for passengers to catch the connecting trains, buffer times are integrated in the timetables and HSR trains wait up to 10 minutes at important connecting stations for corresponding trains. As a result, the speed performance of the German system is much lower than in France or Spain. The integration of HSR into the overall railway service, which has advantages in some ways, also imposes costs.

As the distances between HSR stations are relatively short and the reliability of train connections at points of interchange are most important, the further development of HSR and rolling stock does not aim at highest speeds. The links connecting Frankfurt to Cologne and Nuremberg to Munich will remain the only sections which allow for a maximum speed of 300 km/h. Other HSR sections under construction or planned (Nuremberg-Erfurt, Stuttgart-Ulm, Karlsruhe-Basel, Hanover-Hamburg, Hanover-Bremen) are designed for a maximum speed of 250 km/h. The new generation of rolling stock will be adjusted to this speed design and focus on energy savings, modular composition of train sets, and flexible operations on HSR and conventional sections. Emphasis will be on design and scheduling that support the efficiency of operations.

Lower speeds do not necessarily mean longer travel times for passengers. Assuming a stop at stations every 50 kilometres, a 300 km/h fast train would only be about 3 minutes faster on a 100 km journey than a 250 km/h train. The buffer time at important connection stations is presently 9–11 minutes. This provides a big window within which trains can arrive and transfers can be made. Therefore intelligent train scheduling and control schemes can contribute to timesaving without investing in higher-speed trains that use more energy.

The German example shows that a dual HSR-conventional train system can capture an important share of the intercity market, but this requires careful attention to operations. For many trips in the 100–800 km range, door-to-door travel times on HSR can compete with those by air; and HSR can compete with a more comfortable and productive ride, even if it has no monetary cost advantage for users. HSR also can capture a share of longer trips by offering express services. HSR may be able to serve as a feeder mode to airports, though this is likely to be cost-effective only for the largest airports. Finally, HSR may be able to substitute for some short-haul flights, but how far this can go will depend on many factors including airport subsidy policies and airline operating costs relative to HSR costs. In short, it is necessary to make full use of HSR advantages as well as potential synergies with other modes to improve the economic and environmental efficiency of the overall transport system.

References

Eurocontrol, 2012, *Medium-term forecast: flight movements 2012–2018*, Brussels.
European Commission, 2010, *High-speed Europe: a sustainable link between cities*, Brussels.
European Commission, 2012, *EU transport in figures*, Brussels.
NEA, 2004, *NEA Transport Research and Training: Final Report: Scenarios, Traffic Forecasts and Analysis of Traffic Flows Including Countries Neighbouring the European Union*, Rijswijk, Netherlands.

8 Taiwan's HSR and the financial crises of the Taiwan High Speed Rail Corporation

Jason Ni, Jason Chang, T.C. Kao

Background

Taiwan's high-speed rail system (HSR), which began operation in 2007, runs at speeds up to 300 km/h over 345 km of track from Taipei, the national capital, to Kaohshiung in the south. While it initially was planned as a government project, in the mid-1990s the Taiwan HSR project was reconceived in order to tap into private capital and private sector know-how. The project became a public-private partnership (PPP) in which the government handled land acquisition, the construction of one main tunnel and the Taipei Main Station, and agreed not to build a competing line. A build-operate-transfer (BOT) scheme was set up to build and run the new system under a 35-year concession to the private operator. The US $18 billion project, managed and operated by the Taiwan High Speed Rail Corporation (THSRC), was at the time of construction one of the largest build-operate-transfer projects in the world.

Ridership on the system, which serves a substantial portion of the Taiwanese population, was initially disappointingly low, but grew to over 130,000 passengers a day by 2014. However, the THSRC was accumulating debt, which reached crisis levels by 2008–2009. The THSRC turned first to the private sector and then to the government for relief. The government responded with a restructuring plan.

This chapter examines the financial difficulties that accompanied the building of Taiwan's HSR and the factors that led to those difficulties, including overly optimistic forecasts of ridership, questionably structured financing and accounting approaches, and inexperienced partners.

The roots of the crisis

The Taiwan HSR project had been proudly touted as a successful public-private partnership operation by the Taiwanese government, and to many it came as a shock to find that it was in financial trouble. However, looking back it is possible to uncover the roots of the crisis that eventually burst into public view. A mega-project, Taiwan's HSR carried with it risks that have previously been associated with other mega-projects – optimism bias that leads to exaggerated estimations of benefits and understatement of costs, public and private sector boosterism, and a tendency to look for 'painless' forms of finance (see, e.g., Flyvbjerg *et al.* 2003, Altshuler and Luberoff 2003). Many of these elements can be seen in the Taiwan project. For example, the financial plan was based on passenger revenue streams resulting from the government's forecasts of traffic volume and a re-estimate conducted by THSRC. However, both ridership forecasts were seriously over-estimated. While the government provided a range of ridership estimates, five in total, the actual ridership was the same as the most conservative of these government estimates and only half of the estimate conducted by THSRC itself – initial ridership was only 50,000 riders a day compared to the 100,000 riders forecast. Indeed, ridership has only now grown to levels approximating those initially predicted. Figure 8.1 shows the curve of HSR demand forecast, and a large gap between the predicted and the real ridership in 2012.

In hindsight the initial bid itself looks questionable. During the bidding process in 1997, the THSRC, competing against the Chunghwa High Speed Rail Consortium, won the bid by promising zero government funding, repaying the public sector's investments of US $3.5 billion and utilizing all private capital going forward. Based on international historical precedents in HSR development, this promise was unrealistic.

Another major problem was that the THSRC financial plan was based on unsecured loans with relatively long terms for payback, negotiated at a time when the economic outlook was promising. Consequently, interest rates were high. In addition, the initial accounting used straight line depreciation and assumed asset lives equal to the 35-year life of the concession. These accounting practices resulted in much higher liabilities than would otherwise have been on the books, especially in the early years, and added to the financial difficulties of the THSRC when the early operation revenues fell short of expectations.

Initially the government had emphasized that the basic spirit of BOT project financing is 'Bankable or Terminate' (i.e., if finance institutions had no wish to

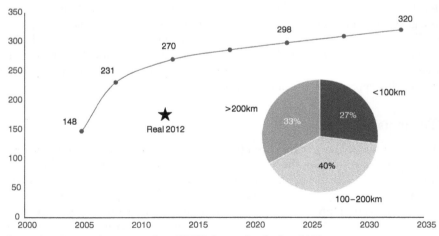

Figure 8.1 Demand estimates from THSRC v. real ridership 2012

provide the capital, the project should not be implemented). The government asserted that it was not in a position to step in and that indeed, if it were to do so, social welfare would suffer. The government also quoted the famous example of the Channel Tunnel: when that BOT project's construction cost increased substantially, the French and British governments stuck to the rule of 'no funding, no guarantee and no clean up job'. Nevertheless, the Taiwan government did offer its financial support during the construction period when THSRC was facing difficulty in securing international funds due to the worldwide economic recession. Eventually, the Taiwanese government promised to assist the THSRC with their financing by guaranteeing its loans, and then by investing in the THSRC through several publicly-owned companies as well as through the Aviation Development Fund and Postal Service Development Fund, both managed by the Ministry of Transportation and Communications (MOTC). Preference shares were issued as an investment incentive for these public companies and funds.

Some of the difficulties encountered appear to be due to a lack of experience not only with projects of such a magnitude but with BOT as a financing technique, and even with expectations for government-backed loans. According to staff from MOTC's Bureau of High Speed Rail, not only were the government agencies inexperienced, but so were the banks. In the agreement signed jointly by MOTC, the THSRC and representatives of the financing banks, loans guaranteed by the government totalling NT$308.3 billion carried interest rates between 7 per cent and 8 per cent. Such interest rates are surprisingly high given that the loans were backed with a government guarantee and are more in keeping with rates for short-term construction loans than with long-term financing, but the need to refinance once construction was completed was apparently not part of the agreement. The high interest rates were simply assumed to be acceptable under the 'good-economy' scenario which prevailed and under which the HSR plans and forecasts were prepared; it was assumed that there would be substantial growth in HSR revenues and therefore no need for adjusting the interest rate downward. When revenues were lower than expected and growth more sluggish, the high interest rate was the fundamental reason for THSRC's heavy debts.

The financial crisis comes to a head

Although ridership increased substantially year by year in the first years of operation, costs exceeded revenues (taking depreciation into account) and within a few years of commencing operation, the THSRC was having difficulty securing capital and was seeking relief. The Taiwanese government responded with a restructuring plan designed to reduce costs, re-raise capital, and extend the concession period from 35 to 75 years. The plan was proposed jointly by MOTC and THSRC in mid-2013, and the government started seeking public consensus. However, on January 8, 2015, the Transportation Committee of Taiwan's Legislative Yuan voted to postpone the restructuring plan. Reasons given for the postponement included the following: (1) the proposal to extend the concession period was deemed to need clarification, (2) the question of whether the new plan should be open to investment by members of the general public had not been resolved, (3) other alternatives were available, and (4) there did not seem to be an urgent need for action. The postponement decision prompted Dr Yeh Kuang-shih, Minister of Transportation and Communications, to resign shortly thereafter.

Yeh blamed the failure to proceed on the refusal of Continental Engineering Corporation (CEC), one of the five main founding shareholders of THSRC, to accept the new conditions. According to Chapter 15 of the 'Agreement on Construction and Operation of Taiwan High Speed Rail' signed by MOTC and THSRC, in the case of unavoidable factors affecting the business operation of THSRC, the company would be entitled to compensation by the government in ways both parties found appropriate and would be willing to accept. Ms Nita Ing, chair of CEC and original chair of THSRC, proposed to resolve the numerous unexpected problems that had occurred during the process of construction and operation in accordance with this provision of the original contract, engaging in commercial arbitration before negotiating a new financial plan.

With the breakdown in negotiations, it became publicly known that THSRC had been struggling with finances from the start. According to the company's financial statements for the third quarter of 2014, THSRC had total assets of NT$501 billion and total liabilities of NT$452.8 billion, or net assets of almost NT$50 billion (about US$1.7B) – a debt:equity ratio that is highly troublesome from a risk perspective. As documented in the next sections, this precarious financial position resulted from a number of problems, but two in particular stand out: the issuance of preference shares that came due only a few years after operation had commenced, and the use of asset lives and depreciation methods that resulted in high depreciation costs.

The preference share problem

The figures shown on the 2014 financial statements, if not satisfactory, were still enough for the THSRC to remain solvent – though securing additional loans clearly becomes more difficult and costly when a company is so highly leveraged. However, what drove the company to a state of near-crisis was the impending redemption date for preference shares.

Preference shares had been issued between 2003 and 2006 at a 5 per cent annual interest rate with full principal redemption at the end of the sixth year, i.e., 2009–2012. As of the third quarter of 2014, the THSRC had outstanding ordinary shares of NT$65.1 billion plus preference shares of NT$40 billion.

The initial agreement establishing the THSRC called for shareholding by the company's founders to be maintained at or above 25 per cent. In 2000 and 2001, the Taiwan Sugar Corp and the National Development Fund of the Executive Yuan invested NT$5 billion and NT$3 billion respectively in ordinary shares, pushing close to the limit of what could be sold under the initial agreement. To further facilitate capital raising for the company, the Ministry of Finance issued

'Directions Governing Limitations on Types and Amounts of the Securities in which a Commercial Bank may Invest', a ruling which allowed commercial banks to invest in 'fixed income preference shares'. Investments in the company's preference shares boomed as a result, with new investments totalling NT$40 billion, of which NT$5.7 billion came from the China Steel Corp, NT$4.5 billion from the China Aviation Development Foundation, NT$3 billion from the CTCI Foundation, and the rest from a group of domestic commercial banks.

While the preference shares provided much-needed revenue, they also carried with them payment obligations that portended coming difficulties. By some interpretations of international accounting standards, the NT$40 billion of preference shares could be classified as a liability instead of equity, which would mean that the company was virtually without net value.

By 2008, the THSRC's debt ratio had reached 90 per cent and the THSRC was urgently seeking a way to deal with its growing financial problems. Redemption of preference shares was coming due the next year. At that point Lehman Brothers stepped forward. THSRC announced that Lehman Brothers was offering to provide capital of NT$300 billion; in addition, Lehman Brothers proposed to provide new loans at an interest rate below 0.5 per cent for the first 3 years. This deal would have allowed THSRC to pay off its outstanding debts. However, an earlier agreement with the government and lenders, signed in 2000, specified that any termination of the original financial contracts would be subject to the government's approval. This posed a dilemma for the government, which was caught between the desire of THSRC to escape the burden of high-interest loans and the desire of the banking group to retain such loans (favourable to their interests as long as they were government-guaranteed). Ultimately the government blocked the deal and the company's 'easy way out'.

In 2009, the term of the first preference shares expired, and holders expected the THSRC to redeem the shares. However, the company quoted Art. 158 of the Company Ordinance, which provided that 'preference shares issued by the company shall be redeemed by using profit or issuing new shares'. Claiming that no profit was made, the THSRC 'postponed' the redemption.

In June 2011, the Legislative Yuan revised Art. 158 to state simply that the preference stocks 'shall be redeemed' without specifying the mechanism or conditioning repayment on profitability. The change in law triggered lawsuits filed by the company's preference shareholders, including the China Development Industrial Bank and the Continental Engineering Corporation (CEC), accusing the THSRC of unlawful postponement of the preference share redemption (due to lack of profit on its balance sheet). The first two preference shareholders won the case in the first trial. Additional preference shareholders were expected to file similar law suits against THSRC for the purpose of getting preference share redemption, and the fear was that this could put the THSRC at risk once it could no longer postpone preference share redemption, possibly to the point of bankruptcy.

Guan Bi-ling, a legislator of the Democratic Progressive Party, proposed to arrange a meeting inviting eight government-backed institutions to discuss the feasibility of deploying NT$43.2 billion from the government's credit guarantee account to solve the short-term financing problem. However, the banking group contended that they would not approve the proposal given that the government guarantee limit was not being raised.

The intervention of Wu Tang-Chieh, Deputy Minister of the Ministry of Finance, finally led the banking group to agree, albeit reluctantly, that the balance in the credit guarantee account could be used to redeem the preference shares. The bankers insisted on two conditions: that the restructuring plan gained approval from the Legislative Yuan, and that future operations of the THSRC be guaranteed. Moreover, the banks remained concerned that if the credit guarantee account were not paid back, the affected banks could experience significant losses.

Some of the experts who had been assessing the crisis suggested that the government could intervene and require that banks' preference shares be converted to ordinary shares. However, that proposal was vigorously opposed by the bankers, because each preference share had a par value of NT$10 compared to less than NT$4 per share for ordinary shares. From the bankers' perspective, there is no way that their board of directors could approve the proposal equivalent to an unconditional loss of more than 60 per cent of the book value.

Thus, a restructuring of the debt of the THSRC, precipitated to crisis levels by preference stocks coming due, proved to be a highly complex and contentious matter and government actions may have exacerbated the problems rather than mitigating them.

The asset depreciation problem

A second major source of financial problems for THSRC stems from the depreciation of its assets. Depreciation costs are rising steadily from NT$15.1 billion in 2013 to NT$28.4 billion at peak in 2017, and will remain above NT$26 billion for the subsequent 5 years. Consequently, by 2017 or thereabouts, total liabilities may exceed total assets.

The problem with depreciation costs is tied to the terms of the initial BOT agreement, as well as to the method of depreciation chosen. According to the initial agreement, the period of concession was set at 35 years with all facilities to be transferred to the government at the concession's expiration. Although this 35-year period is shorter than the useful life of key rail system assets, it was reasoned that for the corporation, the value of the agreement expires in 35 years and therefore total assets should also be depreciated over 35 years, reflecting zero to the company at the time of the transfer. With such an assumption, using the straight line method, the company's revenue couldn't even cover its annual depreciation cost in the first years of operation. Even with the operational profit of recent years, it is not enough to cover all depreciation costs with the original straight line depreciation method and an assumed 35-year life.

In 2009, THSRC changed its depreciation method from straight line to the unit of production method, based on passenger volumes. This move initially saved the company over NT$10 billion of depreciation cost. However, the depreciation schedule assumed that passenger volumes would increase in future years, and accordingly, depreciation amounts are scheduled to become commensurately higher. If revenues do not increase enough to offset these increasing depreciation costs, a deficit will appear and grow in the days to come.

Resolution of the problem

It was apparent that if the THSRC were to declare bankruptcy, the government would be obliged to pay off guaranteed loans, redeem the assets and take over future operations. Under such circumstances it would have been likely that the 3,500 shareholders' equity would become worthless. It would also have been likely that the government would re-evaluate its assets and re-consign HSR operation to another company. No one could foretell what the impacts might be on costs and service quality, but few expected that they would constitute an improvement. As one expert put it, such a situation would create a buyer's market; the government might not be in a position to insist on the same levels of service that riders had enjoyed.

The restructuring plan was finally accepted with minor revisions in September 2015. Basically, the restructuring plan is composed of two elements, capital restructuring and an extension of the concession period. Under the capital restructuring element, THSRC will first undertake a capital reduction of NT$39 billion by retiring 60 per cent of its NT$65 billion in shareholders' equity, and then raise NT$30 billion as new capital. To raise new capital, in phase one, the government will guide the government-backed banks and legal entities who held preference shares to invest another NT$13 billion. An amount of NT$7 billion will be reserved for subscription by existing shareholders and employees. In phase two, NT$10 billion of new shares will be sold in its initial public offering.

The extension of the concession period will postpone transfer of assets back to the government for 35 years, until 2068. As a result, the annual depreciation cost can be recalculated and will drop dramatically.

The Ministry of Transportation and Communications has re-evaluated expected traffic volumes and operation costs with the new plan's provisions and estimates that investors could obtain a rate of return between 5.9 per cent and 6.1 per cent. In response to this estimate, some observers have suggested that subscription by the Civil Servant Pension Fund, the Labour Pension and the Labour Insurance Fund could be considered, so that the projected rate of return of 5.9 per cent promised in the restructuring plan could be shared among the whole of society. However, there remain serious doubts about the validity of the estimate. Asked how extending the concession period by 40 years could generate a large profit of NT$800 billion, the former president of Nomura Securities in Taiwan, who was also the financial advisor for THSRC, commented that the number is probably derived from Earnings Before Interest, Taxes, Depreciation and Amortization (EBITDA) multiplying by 40 years. Since costs would have to be covered first, the amount available for return to investors would be significantly reduced.

There is a divergence of opinions among the founding shareholders of THSRC regarding the desirability of the restructuring plan. The Chairman of Fubon Financial Corp., Daniel Tsai, has been very supportive of the financial restructuring plan. On the other hand, Nita Ing, chair of CEC, and other original shareholders, think there is still a need to resolve additional issues. In their view, these issues include: 1) costs incurred due to inaccurate estimates of future traffic volume provided by the government in the bidding process; 2) unanticipated construction costs due to earthquakes; and, 3) concessionary fares for the elderly that are mandated but were not part of the original agreement. Proponents have estimated that NT$300 billion is owed to THSRC by the government due to these three items. The original shareholders continue to insist that the parties should proceed to commercial arbitration over these issues.

Commentary

The case of the Taiwan HSR points to the sorts of problems that can arise when large, risky projects are undertaken. Despite rhetoric about build-operate-transfer allowing the government to tap private sector know-how as well as resources, in this case it appears that neither the government nor the private sector had sufficient expertise and experience to manage the process without problems. Furthermore, the government was expected to step in when the HSR system finances reached crisis stage.

Overly optimistic ridership forecasts, questionable financing strategies, and dubious depreciation methods all contributed to financial difficulties, as did unforeseen events such as earthquakes. Government interventions had unintended consequences. The disagreement among the founding shareholders, witnessed by the public, added to uncertainties about how to proceed.

References

Altshuler, AA, and Luberoff, D, 2003, *Mega-projects: The changing politics of urban public investment*, Brookings Institution Press.

Flyvbjerg, B, Bruzelius, N, and Rothengatter, W, 2003, *Megaprojects and risk: An anatomy of ambition*, Cambridge University Press.

9 The influence of high-speed rail station site selection on travel efficiency

The case of the Shanghai Hongqiao Hub

Haixiao Pan, Song Ye, Minglei Chen

Introduction

China is a large country, and with its recent rapid economic development, there is massive demand for land transport between different regions. Rail transportation plays a very important role in this development. Since the 1990s, the rail share of the intercity passenger market has declined because of the development of highways and aviation. But there is growing recognition that excessive reliance on these transport modes would cause a number of environmental, energy and safety problems. Weather factors (e.g., fog) and congestion can sharply reduce the efficiency and reliability of these modes as well (Börjesson 2014). Therefore, how to provide a fast and reliable inter-regional rail service – which is somewhat less affected by weather and can avoid congestion – has become an important issue for government.

While intercity transport in China has grown rapidly since 1978, the use of rail, as measured in rail passenger-kilometres, has grown far less than the other modes, especially the highway mode. To provide a better rail option, China began experimenting with high-speed rail in the late 1990s, and began building a national HSR network in the early years of this century with four 'vertical' (north-south) and four 'horizontal' (east-west) passenger corridors, eventually totalling over 16,000 km (NDRC 2008). Design and technology advances have allowed the running speed of HSR to increase from its initial 200 km/h to its current maximum of 350 km/h. In addition, coastal regions like the Yangtze River Delta and the Pearl River Delta are developing dense regional high-speed rail networks.

Many researchers believe that HSR can bring economic, environmental and social benefits to the regions and cities it serves (Xiao 2011, Feng 2009). Researchers have also asserted that areas situated outside the HSR network but efficiently linked to it could benefit from the diffuse effects of major urban agglomerations (Gutiérrez et al. 1996). US researchers have argued that in addition, HSR can enable big cities to connect further into the hinterland where housing and commercial space is more affordable (Tierney 2012). However, capturing these benefits requires attention to station location and design (Yu et al. 2014).

Chen and Hall (2011) found that China's HSR services have had substantial and demonstrable effects in aiding the economic transition of cities that are now within 2 hours of the country's major urban regions, helping to generate renewed economic growth. The important point here is the time factor. In this regard both in-vehicle and access times must be considered, and if access time is too long or is unreliable, it will reduce door-to-door travel efficiency. This can affect not only the mode used to get to the station but the decision on whether to use HSR or a different mode altogether (Martín *et al.* 2014).

However, in order to accelerate the construction of China's high-speed rail network and reduce the difficulty of land acquisition for HSR construction, many new station sites in China are located in suburbs distant from large urban centres. This means that access to the stations can require a long trip from the city centre where many activities are located. If station locations are inconvenient for passengers, they are more likely to consider an alternative mode of intercity travel if one is available.

In the study presented here, the authors investigate the effects of station location on HSR passenger travel behaviour. To establish the context for the analysis, the discussion begins with a review of intercity transport in China, the growth of the Chinese HSR system, and the reasons why many HSR stations are located in the suburbs or at the urban periphery. The chapter then presents research that uses the Shanghai Hongqiao Station as a case example. It explores the origin points of HSR passengers, their mode of travel access to the Hongqiao HSR Station, door-to-door transit time for HSR travel, and changes in access time before and after the opening of the Hongqiao HSR Station. The results show that the station's long distance from the city centre requires long access times for the majority of passengers, even when significant investments in new rail and highway links to the HSR station have been made. These long access trips partly offset the fast speeds of the HSR and thus reduce overall transport efficiency. The final section of the chapter discusses the implications for the continuing development of China's HSR system, suggesting that direct HSR links to the major population centres be considered in the future.

Multi-modal intercity transport in China

China's railway network grew from 51,700 km in 1978 to 93,200 km in 2011. The number of rail passengers also increased, reaching 1.862 billion trips in 2011. This was a 128.52 per cent increase in passengers over 1978 levels, with an average annual growth rate of 4.55 per cent. Between 2003 and 2011, the average annual growth rate in passengers accelerated, reaching 8.51 per cent by 2008 (Yang and Wang 2009). In 2011, the growth rate was over 11.0 per cent.

Passenger intensity (the number of passengers carried per km of railway) has also grown quickly, to levels of nearly 20,000 passengers/km. This is almost 2.5 times highway passenger intensity. Total passenger-kilometres by rail has grown from 1,093 billion passenger-kilometres in 1978 to 9,612 billion passenger-kilometres in 2011, an increase of 779 per cent (Figure 9.1). By 2011, passenger-kilometres were growing by 12.52 per cent per year (Fan 2011). As more HSR comes on line, the passenger-kilometre volume of rail transportation is expected to keep growing.

However, despite the remarkable growth in rail service and use, the rail share of intercity travel has been dropping. As Figure 9.1 indicates, both highway and aviation volumes have increased. The growth rate of the highway sector is particularly notable. Between 1978 and 2001, the rail share of the intercity passenger market dropped from over 30 per cent to around 5 per cent (National Bureau of Statistics of China 2012).

The loss of rail market share reflects the tremendous developments in the road transport network (and associated increases in auto ownership) that have occurred over the last few decades. China's highway network grew from 890,200 km in 1978 to 4,106,400 km in 2011. Today, in the intercity passenger transport market, highway travel has displaced train transport as the dominant means of travel. This is true even for travel distances over 300 km, where rail should be highly competitive.

Rail is a more efficient use of land for transportation than highways and has less associated pollution than does the automobile. Because of scarce land resources and high population densities, China seeks to make efficient use of land and reduce pollution emissions and exposures by promoting rail use. Since early signs suggested that rail would have to become more attractive to compete with air and the auto as incomes rose and the economy developed, China has been planning the construction of HSR since the 1990s.

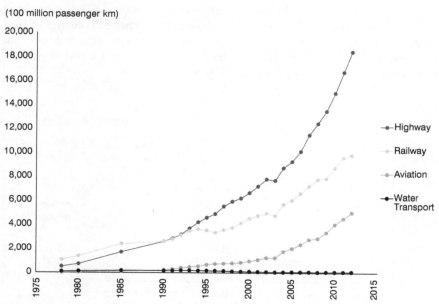

Figure 9.1 Passenger-kilometres by different transport modes, 1978–2011, China

High-speed rail network planning and construction in China

In China the construction of high-speed rail started with the opening of the Qinhuangdao-Shenyang line, with a top speed of 200 km/h, in October 2003. In order to accelerate rail development, the state council executive meeting discussed and passed the 'Mid-term and Long-term Railway Network Plan' in January 2004. The State Council again adjusted the HSR planning programme in 2008, expanding the programme to produce over 120,000 km of national railway by 2020, with over 16,000 km of HSR. By September 2012, China had built over half of the planned HSR, 8,257 km.

Figure 9.2 illustrates how fast the HSR system expanded after 2007. While there was some slowdown after 2011 due to economic circumstances, the commitment to continue expanding the HSR system remains strong.

Also in 2008, a decision was made that extensive networks of intercity HSR should cover the main cities in economically developed and densely populated areas, such as the Yangtze River Delta, the Pearl River Delta and the Shandong Peninsula. The Yangtze River Delta is one of the most developed areas in China, with 20 per cent of national GDP output, an area of 109,600 km², and a high urbanization rate. The regional HSR network will serve four major cities: Shanghai, Nanjing, Hangzhou and Hefei, as well as the smaller cities in the region. The system design is for a 12-hour 'traffic circle' between the major cities, with transfers allowing passengers to arrive at other cities in the Yangtze River Delta within 3 hours. Such a network could allow the four cities and their smaller counterparts to function as a single integrated urban mega-region. The rail network proposed for the Pearl River Delta Region is even more extensive. It consists of twenty lines, the total length of which is about 1,670 km, reaching a network density of 4.5 kilometres of rail per million square kilometres of land area. The network design consists of three rings and eight axes and will link the nine cities of the Pearl River Delta Region and extend to other parts of Guangdong province, Hong Kong and Macao.

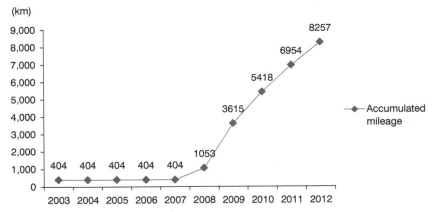

Figure 9.2 Expansion of HSR in China

In order to allow for the fast construction of this extensive HSR system, many HSR stations are planned for suburban locations away from city centres. This raises questions about the impact of the station location on overall travel time and also on the choice of HSR vs. air and highway modes.

China's high-speed rail station site location

In China, most of the new HSR station sites are located in suburbs or exurbs, distant from the large urban centres. The hope is that the HSR stations will spark the development of 'new towns' at these peripheral locations. (In Western terms, these 'towns' would be major metropolitan sub-centres or districts.) The intent is to stimulate local economic development by offering an attractive, accessible alternative location to the crowded city centres.

The Beijing-Shanghai HSR line is an example. The total length of this line is 1,318 km. Of the twenty-four cities connected by the line, eighteen cities built their HSR stations in the suburbs. Table 9.1 shows the location of some major HSR stations in China. The reasons for suburban site selection included lower costs, hope of capturing rising land values, and a desire to relieve pressure on the central areas of the cities. Since there is less densely developed land in the suburbs, the cost of land acquisition is greatly reduced compared to city centres. Suburban station development may also generate land value increment profits due to positive spill-over effects of the railway station. Finally, many cities are interested in promoting the transformation of their urban spatial structure from a single centre to a polycentric form in order to alleviate the pressures of high population density and intense commercial activity in the central cities, and they hope that a suburban HSR station could become a high-value sub-centre.

The railway authority also wants to locate HSR stations in the suburbs. This simplifies HSR track alignment, allowing straight lines which reduce project construction costs as well as operation costs in the future. Their preference for the suburbs may be compounded by the fact that the railway authority is not responsible for the connecting transport for passengers accessing the rail station.

It should also be noted that the location of HSR stations varies according to the influence of local government in the cities through which rail passes or provides a station. Because of China's hierarchical administrative system, large cities are better able to control the discourse in the negotiations between local government and the railway authority than are smaller cities. As a result, most HSR sites are located in the suburban areas of large cities, while in most medium and small cities the new stations are located in the exurban fringe, where it is even easier to provide a station but far more difficult to provide good public transport service. The smaller cities thus have greater local car traffic associated with the stations.

Shanghai's Hongqiao HSR Station provides a typical example. The station is part of the Hongqiao Integrated Transport Hub, which includes a regional airport, and the Hongqiao Business Plan, which is intended to guide development in the vicinity of the transport hub. The station is located 15 km from Shanghai

Table 9.1 China's major HSR station site locations and rail line plans

Names of HSR way stations	Number of metro lines	Location of station	Distance from the city centre	Operation situation of metro lines	Operation time of high-speed railway stations
North Xi 'an Station	1	Suburban	13km	Line4: not opened	2011.1
East Zhengzhou Station	-	Suburban	8km	——	2012.9
East Hangzhou Station	2	Suburban	13km	Line1: 2012.11 Line4: not opened	2013.6
Shanghai Hongqiao Station	2	Suburban	15km	Line2: 2000.6 Line10: 2010.4	2010.7
South Guangzhou Station	4	Suburban	18km	Line2: 2010.9 Line7, Line20, Foshan Line2: not opened	2010.1
South Nanjing Station	3	Suburban	10km	Line1: 2011.6 Line3, Line6: not opened	2011.6
South Beijing Station	4	City centre	5km	Line4: 2010.12 Line14: not opened	2008.8
Wuhan Station	2	Suburban	12km	Line4, Line5: not opened	2009.12
Tianjin Station	3	City centre	0	Line2: 2013 Line3: 2012.10 Line9: 2012.10	2008.8
South Changsha Station	2	Suburban	9.5km	Line2, Line3: not opened	2009.12

Source: China Urban Transport Planning and Development Report 2010

city centre and links the Beijing-Shanghai HSR with the Beijing-Shanghai railway and Shanghai-Nanjing intercity railway to the north, and the Shanghai-Kunming railway, Shanghai-Hangzhou-Ningbo passenger dedicated line and Shanghai-Hangzhou intercity railway to the south. It began operation on July 1, 2010, with a predicted yearly passenger dispatch of 52,720,000 in 2020 and a planned capacity of 78,380,000 passengers.

To enhance the connection between Shanghai city centre and the Yangtze River Delta Region through the station, both expressways and rail transit lines have been constructed. So far, rail transit lines 2 and 10, which provide seamless transfer from Shanghai city centre, have been extended to the station. Additional rail transit lines are planned which will link the Hongqiao HSR Station with other parts of Shanghai.

Research questions and survey

At present, national HSR station construction is in full swing. Relevant international and domestic research indicates that large-scale HSR construction creates new opportunities for the region and spurs urban development. Site selection for HSR stations will have an enormous impact on urban and regional spatial structure transformation, especially for stations located close to city centres. However, as noted earlier, many HSR stations are located quite far away from city centres in China, so empirical data is needed to analyze the impact of HSR station location on travel characteristics of passengers and urban spatial structure, including travel distance distribution, changes in travel time and HSR passenger distribution in different geographic locations. This information will be useful in improving the travel efficiency of intercity HSR service through station location or connecting transport service options, as well as the design of stations.

To investigate the effects of station location on travel behaviour, we conducted a survey of 1,834 respondents from February 27, 2012 to March 3, 2012 within the Hongqiao HSR Station. We randomly selected passengers in the waiting hall to conduct face-to-face interviews. We questioned passengers regarding their trip origin and destination, on-board high-speed train travel time, mode of travel to the HSR station and time station, and demographic characteristics.

From this survey we know the social and economic attributes of passengers. We also have the information for each segment of their travel from origin to destination, and travel characteristics before and after the opening of the HSR station. Based on these data, we can analyze the impact of the location of HSR stations on train users and evaluate the impact of the connections to the HSR system in terms of time and cost. We also can compare the findings to the forecasts that were made by transit planners in preparing for the development of the HSR service and station. We cannot, however, determine how many travellers may have been deterred from using HSR because the service is less attractive than competing modes or the station location is a deterrent.

The following research questions are explored in this study:

1 How far will the passenger travel by HSR and what factors influence passenger volume between Shanghai and a destination city?
2 Where do the passengers come from in Shanghai? As the location of the station is closer to the neighbouring provinces of Zejiang and Jiangsu, how many passengers are from regions outside of Shanghai?
3 What is the proportion of time spent in each segment of travel and how can we improve their travel efficiency?

High-speed train passenger travel distance

China covers a vast geographical territory, and the construction of a national HSR network will facilitate interregional connection. How are passengers distributed from the Hongqiao Station to their destination city? Conducting a regression analysis based on the variables of number of passengers, population of the destination city and the distance between Shanghai and the city, we show that the number of passengers is in direct proportion to the destination city's population, while in inverse proportion to the distance between Shanghai and the city (Table 9.2). In other words, the larger the population of the destination city, the more passengers travel from Shanghai to the destination city, and the shorter the distance to the destination city, the more passengers travel via HSR.

The research reveals that the average passenger travel distance is 377.4 km, which is not as far as was expected before the opening of HSR. The data show that short- and medium-distance passengers still comprise a majority of all HSR travel, with 58 per cent of them travelling less than 300 km, and 71 per cent of all passengers travelling less than 500 km (Figure 9.3).

Table 9.2 Number of passengers as a function of city population and distance

Model		B	t	Sig.
1	(constant)	67.832	2.71	.015
	City Population (0,000)	.086	2.76	.013
	Distance(km)	−0.125	−3.01	.008

Figure 9.3 Cumulative percentage of travellers

The origination points of high-speed train passengers

From Table 9.3 we see that that 88 per cent of the passengers surveyed are from different districts in Shanghai, with 4.1 per cent of passengers transferring from the nearby Hongqiao Airport and 7.8 per cent of passengers from outside of Shanghai.

To analyze the geographic location of passengers from Shanghai, we divided the sixteen districts and one county in Shanghai into three major categories, the central urban area, city outskirts and outer suburban districts (Table 9.4 and Figure 9.4).

Figure 9.5 reveals that approximately half of the HSR passengers come from the central urban area of Shanghai, 40 per cent are from the city outskirts, and only about 10 per cent of the passengers are from the outer suburban areas.

Table 9.3 The origin of surveyed passengers in Hongqiao HSR station

	Passengers	Percentage
Hongqiao airport transfer	75	4.1%
Within Shanghai	1,595	88.1%
Outside of Shanghai	141	7.8%

Table 9.4 Administrative districts distribution in Shanghai

Location	District name
The central urban area	Hunagpu district
	Zhabei district
	Jing'an district
	Xuhui district
	Hongkou district
	Changning district
	Yangpu district
	Putuo district
The city outskirts	Baoshan district
	Jiading district
	Pudong new area
	Minhang district
Outer suburban districts	Chongming county
	Fengxian district
	Jinshan district
	Songjiang district
	Qingpu district

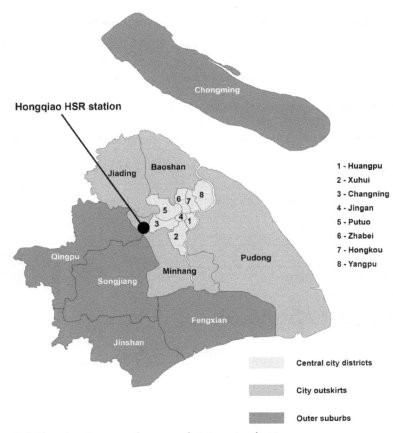

Figure 9.4 Shanghai district and county administrative divisions

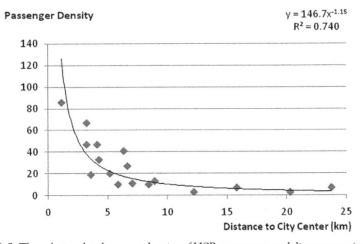

Figure 9.5 The relationship between density of HSR passengers and distance to city centre

Further analysis of passenger intensity from various administrative districts of Shanghai (where intensity is the number of passengers divided by the population of the district) shows that passenger intensity is in inverse proportion to the distance to the central urban area. In other words, the majority of passengers come primarily from the dense central urban area and adjacent districts. Thus, an HSR station located in the suburbs will require a majority of passengers to travel extra distance.

Mode of travel access to Hongqiao HSR Station

Because the Hongqiao HSR Station is located a considerable distance from Shanghai's city centre where there is a high demand for travel by HSR, much effort was given to improving transport between the station and the city centre, with the extension of rail transit lines, expansion of the conventional bus system, and construction of an elevated motorway as well as 3,000 parking spaces for cars, available for RMB 50/day (approx. US $7.70/day). There are also 2,826 parking spaces at the east end of the hub close to the regional airport terminal. We found that 60.4 per cent of passengers accessed HSR by urban rail transit, an additional 7.9 per cent used the conventional bus system, and the remaining 6.6 per cent used other public transport modes, bringing the total percentage using public transport to access HSR to 74.9 per cent. This is far in excess of the planning forecast share for transit, which was 50 per cent. Of the private transit modes, only 7.6 per cent of passengers take a personal car to Hongqiao Station, while 14.5 per cent take a taxi. The forecasts for the project predicted considerably higher private transport access at around 50 per cent. As a result, the elevated motorway to Hongqiao Station may have been over-supplied.

Figure 9.5b shows mode of access to the HSR station by car owners and those without a car. Even among HSR users who possess a private car, only 13.6 per cent drove to Hongqiao Station. These private car-owning passengers showed a preference for the metro, with 53.9 per cent of them using the metro to get to the station. However, private car-owning passengers use conventional bus transit much less than passengers who do not have cars. These results clearly show the importance of provision of high quality public transport in connecting city centres and HSR stations in order to attract people to public transport and reduce the demand for car travel. The investment in metro to HSR stations undoubtedly reduced car travel to the HSR stations located far away from city centres – a boon from a traffic and air pollution perspective.

Comparing mode choice to the HSR station from the various districts of Shanghai, we find that 76.5 per cent of the passengers from the central urban area take urban rail to the HSR station, while only 7 per cent take cars to the station. For passengers from the suburban areas, which are less well served by the urban rail network, people rely more on conventional bus transit, with 38 per cent of passengers taking buses to the station and only 27.7 per cent taking urban rail. From suburban areas, demand for travel to the HSR station by car is 15.1 per cent, double that of the central urban area (Figure 9.6).

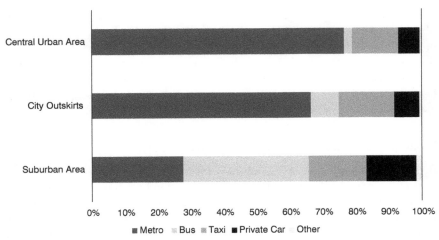

Figure 9.6 Modal split of transit to the HSR station from different regions of Shanghai city

Analysis of door-to-door transit time for HSR travel

The total door-to-door travel time for HSR is composed of four parts: time from origin to the Hongqiao HSR Station, waiting time in the station, travel time on board the high-speed train, and finally time from the destination HSR station to the point of destination.

As the speed of high-speed trains is so high, the on-board time between two stations is greatly reduced from that of traditional rail or highway travel. However, if people travel a relatively short distance, the on-board time may comprise only a small portion of their total travel time. Thus during the planning and construction of HSR, we have to pay attention to the access modes serving the HSR stations. HSR can provide large improvements in travel efficiency only when the connecting travel time from the origin to the HSR station and the egress time to the travel end point can be kept down in proportion to overall travel time. If this is not done, increasing train speed may make a limited contribution to total travel efficiency.

Figures 9.7 and 9.8 show the composition of passenger door-to-door travel time and the off-train time as a percentage of total travel time as reported in our survey. For the reported origin-destination pairs, the average on-board HSR travel time is 192 minutes. The survey respondents' travel time to the Hongqiao HSR station averages 56 minutes, and waiting time for the HSR train averages 61 minutes. For the shorter trips under 300 km, on-board travel time for HSR accounts for only 25 per cent of total travel time. Therefore, for the shorter trips, the higher train speed will produce less benefit to improved travel efficiency, and efforts during HSR planning to reduce the off-train time are key.

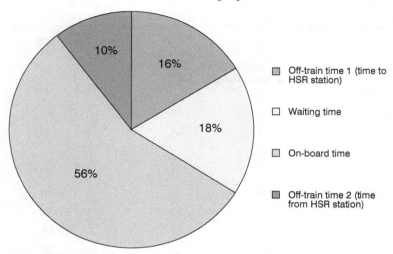

Figure 9.7 Total passengers' door-to-door time composition

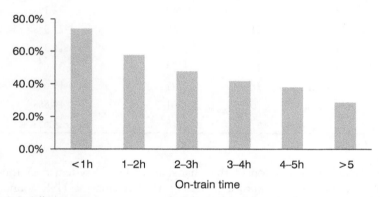

Figure 9.8 Off-train time as percentage of total travel time compared to on-train travel times

Changes in access time before and after the opening of the station

Before the opening of the Hongqiao HSR Station, people could take traditional or high-speed trains in either the Shanghai Railway Station or the Shanghai South Railway Station, both of which are located quite close to the city centre. Comparing passenger average access time to those two stations to the average access time to the newly established Hongqiao HSR Station, we find that average access time increased by about 2%, from 57 minutes to 58 minutes (Table 9.5). The passengers whose access time increased the most are those whose origin is the central urban district. Passengers in the suburban south part of Shanghai benefit from the location of Hongqiao HSR Station in the form of reduced access times to the station, but passenger intensity is relatively low there.

Table 9.5 Access time changes in different districts of Shanghai

	District	Average access time to Hongqiao HSR Station (min)	Average access time to Shanghai or Shanghai South Railway Stations (min)	% Change
Central urban area	Jingan	40	36	11.1%
	Huangpu	46	37	24.3%
	Hongkou	46	40	15.0%
	Yangpu	70	54	29.6%
	Zhabei	50	33	51.5%
	Putuo	44	43	2.3%
	Xuhui	40	41	−2.4%
	Changning	27	41	−34.1%
City outskirts	Baoshan	66	52	26.9%
	Pudong	61	49	24.5%
	Minhang	46	47	−2.1%
	Jiading	51	67	−23.9%
Outer suburban area	Songjiang	61	72	−15.3%
	Qingpu	47	73	−35.6%
	Jinshan	78	97	−19.6%
	Fengxian	70	61	14.8%
	Chongming	147	118	24.6%

The large-scale expansion of the Shanghai urban rail system over the past several years has partially mitigated the effects of having the HSR connection located farther away, and it appears that the travel time increase is acceptable to most passengers. However, the investment in rail expansions needed to serve the station are costly and even though the railway authority does not bear these costs, the costs must be considered in evaluating overall impacts of the station location. In addition, it is not known how many potential passengers may have been deterred from using HSR because the station is too far away from them to be convenient.

Conclusion

Since 2003, the China Railway Authority has been implementing the national strategic plan for a massive increase in rail construction, with high-speed rail a major priority. China's network of high-speed rail services is now the largest in the world.

HSR is a well-suited transport mode for China's rapidly growing demand for intercity passenger travel. Its high speeds, high capacity, and modest land and resource requirements are a good match for a country with a large territory and many large cities, a dense and increasingly urban population, and serious resource and environmental constraints. Operating at speeds of up to 350 km/h, China's HSR is far faster than auto travel and is competitive with domestic air travel for the majority of intercity trips, and is even competing with air travel for trips of over 1,000 km.

In Shanghai and many other Chinese cities, suburban and exurban HSR station locations have been chosen because they are less expensive to build, may stimulate sub-centre growth, and permit straighter alignments and faster rail service. However, our survey, conducted in Shanghai's Hongqiao Station which is fairly typical of the new HSR stations, shows that over 70 per cent of the passengers travel on HSR for distances under 500 km. and over half travel less than 300 km. For these travellers, the amount of time it takes to access the HSR station is a major consideration; higher train speed has a decreasing contribution to total travel efficiency the shorter the total travel distance. Therefore, the challenge is how to balance location of HSR stations with the provision of improved urban centre transit connections where there are higher HSR passenger intensities.

The Shanghai case shows that extending connections, especially rail transit connections, to the HSR station can attract many passengers. However, this comes at a high cost and HSR access still takes more time from the customer than the earlier, in-city station locations required. In addition, it is not known how many travellers may have been deterred from using HSR because the station location is not as convenient as other modes of travel; that would require a survey of all intercity travellers rather than just the HSR station.

The investigation presented here suggests that planners should broaden their investigations when planning for HSR. Instead of constructing a large HSR station in a distant suburb, planners should consider the direct connection of HSR to existing traditional rail stations, where the HSR train can be more easily accessed from the passenger-intensive urban areas. While the HSR line to the centre may be costly, it will simultaneously decrease the need for costly new metro construction to connect the HSR to its user base. In addition, a central location is likely to reduce or eliminate the need for road transportation, and thus air pollution and road infrastructure costs. The overall efficiency and benefit to society may be greater.

References

Börjesson M, 2014, 'Forecasting demand for high speed rail,' *Transportation Research Part A: Policy and Practice*, vol. 70, pp. 81–92.

Chen CL, Hall P, 2011, 'The impacts of high-speed trains on British economic geography: a study of the UK's InterCity 125/225 and its effects,' *Journal of Transport Geography*, vol. 19, pp. 689–704.

Chinese Society for Urban Studies, 2012, *China Urban Transport Planning and Development Report 2010*. China City Press.

Fan YJ, 2011, 'The importance of China's high-speed railway development: from a strategic perspective,' *Integrated Transport*, vol. 10, pp. 34–36 (in Chinese).

Feng CA, 2009, 'Impact analysis of high-speed rail construction on urban development,' *China Urban Planning Annual Conference, Tianjin 2009.* Beijing: Urban Planning Society of China, pp. 175–184 (in Chinese).

Gutiérrez J, González R, Gómez G, 1996, 'The European high-speed train network: predicted effects on accessibility patterns,' *Journal of Transport Geography*, vol. 4, pp. 227–238.

Martín JC, Román C, García-Palomares JC, Gutiérrez J, 2014, 'Spatial analysis of the competitiveness of the high-speed train and air transport: the role of access to terminals in the Madrid–Barcelona corridor,' *Transportation Research Part A: Policy and Practice*, vol. 69, pp. 392–408.

National Bureau of Statistics of China, 2012, *China Statistical Year Book*, Beijing: China Statistics Press.

NDRC, 2008, *Mid-term and Long-term Railway Network Planning (Revision)*.

Tierney S, 2012, 'High-speed rail, the knowledge economy and the next growth wave,' *Journal of Transport Geography*, vol. 22, pp. 285–287.

Xiao SS, 2011, 'Impact analysis of improving integrated transport system though high-speed rail development,' *Integrated Transport*, vol. 9, pp. 9–13 (in Chinese).

Yang Y, Wang, HX, 2009, 'Study on calculating the comprehensive cost of transportation for High-Speed Railway,' *Journal of Railway Engineering Society*, vol. 1, pp. 102–105 (in Chinese).

Yu S, de Abreu e Silva J, Martínez LM, 2014, 'Assessing High-Speed Rail's impacts on land cover change in large urban areas based on spatial mixed logit methods: a case study of Madrid Atocha railway station from 1990 to 2006,' *Journal of Transport Geography*, vol. 41, pp.184–196.

10 Forecasting for high-speed rail

An operator's perspective on risk reduction through informed use of forecasting

Jean-Pierre Pradayrol and Alan Leray

Introduction

The *Société nationale des chemins de fer français* (National Society of French Railways, SNCF) operates national and international rail services, including the *Train à Grande Vitesse* (TGV) on France's and Western Europe's high-speed rail network. Divisions of SNCF also provide urban and regional rail services, freight and logistics services, infrastructure design, construction and maintenance, and station management. Four million passengers take SNCF trains every day; long-distance and high-speed rail services account for over 130 million passengers a year and include almost 500 high speed French and international trains. Since 1981, more than 2 billion passengers have travelled on the TGV.

SNCF started developing methodologies for traffic forecasting in the late 1960s when its first high-speed rail (HSR) project between Paris and Lyon took off. Since then, SNCF has forecast traffic and revenues on hundreds of different city-pairs, and (as required by French law) has compared these forecasts with the actual traffic and revenue observed after HSR was implemented. The comparisons have been used to corroborate and calibrate the forecasting tools.

This chapter discusses approaches for reducing the risk of HSR through the informed use of forecasting and strategic planning and operations, based on the experience of the SNCF over the past three and a half decades. SNCF teams have based their work on several well-known forecasting methods as well as on advanced modelling techniques including probability theories and Monte-Carlo methods, and have also used bootstrapping, back-casting and scenario testing approaches. SNCF partnered with Institut de Statistiques de l'Université de Paris (ISUP) to build the econometric models used in its various forecasts and to implement probabilistic approaches (Champeaux and Pradayrol 2007). However, SNCF has also used its practical operating experience to adjust forecasts.

The chapter is organised as follows. It first discusses the context in which forecasting is carried out. The chapter then describes methods for forecasting with a focus on SNCF's forecasting process as it has evolved. Next it covers limitations of forecasts and then goes on to discusses ways to limit risk. The concluding section presents recommendations for improving forecasts.

Background: the contested realm of demand forecasting for HSR

The combination of three factors makes funding decisions for large infrastructure projects such as HSR difficult: the magnitude of the investment required, the lengthy period for construction and for return on investment, and the multiplicity (and divergence) of traffic and costs/revenue forecasts (Leboeuf 2014, Ni and Pradayrol 2013). When public funding is involved, the high cost of these projects creates high stakes for decision-makers due to the potential impact on long-term resource allocation. In the case of private funding, a large infrastructure investment translates into a high level of exposure for the investors.

The lengthy period for construction means that conditions can change between the time that the decisions are made and the time that the project actually comes on line (David and Talbi 2011). Conditions can in some cases become more favourable for the project, for example rising petroleum prices can make high-speed rail more desirable compared to automobile or air travel. However, changing conditions could also reduce HSR attractiveness, e.g., a slowing of growth in population between key city pairs or reduced economic activity in one of the regions served. The lengthy period for construction also means investors must be willing to wait years for their return and therefore are likely to insist on a higher rate of return, or other compensating benefits, than otherwise might be acceptable.

French law specifies how the consultation process should be implemented and a national framework guideline explains how to assess a major infrastructure project (such as high-speed lines), including risk aspects. Elsewhere this is not always the case and it has become increasingly common for stakeholders to critique the official forecasts and sometimes to produce or commission their own analyses and forecasts based on different assumptions about future conditions – population and economic growth rates, prices for competing modes, technological performance, etc. As a result, in addition to the uncertainty inherent in long-range forecasts, there may also be competing forecasts produced by various stakeholders with diverging interests. This has been the case in California, for example, where official forecasts prepared by the consulting firm Cambridge Systematics for the California High-Speed Rail Authority have been challenged twice, in 2008 (Cox and Vranich) and again in 2013 (Vranich, Cox and Moore), in 'due diligence' reports prepared by a libertarian think tank – the first of which led to a response by a US planning organization aiming to refute the criticisms (APTA 2012). In addition, at the request of a legislative committee, researchers at the Institute of Transportation Studies at the University of California critiqued the Cambridge Systematics models and identified a number of problems, recommending additional work to improve the models and quantify error bounds (Brownstone *et al.* 2010).

Such challenges can vary greatly in their sophistication and in their relevance to the issues at hand, but regardless, the very fact that there are challenges can create doubts about the credibility of the official forecasts, and hence increase the perception of risk associated with a proposed project – especially in cases where there is no local experience to help ground the discussion. Contested forecasts can also lead to increased polarization of the public debate, which can become a fight between various interest groups and their political patrons, rather than staying focused on the project and its potential benefits and costs.

In this context, the SNCF has worked to reduce the discrepancy between forecasts and observed reality, through a three-step process:

1   Measuring the intrinsic reliability of forecasts through a history-based probabilistic approach;
2   Understanding the dynamics of the HSR system – potential changes over time – in order to design it in a way that optimizes its risk/profitability profile; and
3   Using 'stress tests' (rupture scenarios) to evaluate the system's resilience to 'out of known range' events.

This process is iterative, and includes feedback loops. Every time the system is redesigned, new forecasts are generated that will shed light on specific areas of risk, which will in turn lead to incremental improvements not only in the design of the system but also in the forecasting process itself.

Methods for traffic forecasting

To understand the issues involved in preparing useful forecasts, it is worthwhile to first review what we mean by forecasts, what methods we use, and what their limitations are.

What is a forecast and what is it used for?

In the transportation field, a forecast is a prediction of future traffic (global or for one specific mode), revenue, or cost. It generally spans 20 to 30 years, though it can be for a shorter time frame, e.g., 5 years, and in some cases may be for a longer time period, as has been the case for large infrastructure projects like HSR, which can have a life cycle of well over half a century. Forecasts are based on econometric models, expressed as equations that specify how various factors affect the outcomes. Transportation models typically include such variables as traveller socioeconomic characteristics, journey time, frequency, and costs. The relative importance of the variables is determined by the coefficients associated with each variable (which are computed by the modeller using data inputs). The resulting models are often calibrated (adjusted) to match observed results. They are then used to predict future traffic levels (or mode choices, for example) based on anticipated conditions in the future, e.g., income levels, journey times that can be offered, fares, etc.

Public authorities tend to produce general mobility forecasts in order to anticipate the need for infrastructure development or new operating regulations. These forecasts are used to inform policymaking and feed the preliminary public debate over such questions as: Do we need additional transport infrastructure? If so, what sorts of infrastructure would be pertinent?

Various projects' proponents will then produce forecasts of traffic, revenues, and costs for the projects they propose. These forecasts will be used by policymakers in order to feed their own models and understand whether a specific project can help them meet their policy objectives (for example, reduce oil dependency or carbon emissions) and therefore qualify for public funding. Private funding agents will also use these forecasts to evaluate the potential return on investments in the projects, as well as the risks attached.

For a project such as HSR, the forecasts for intercity travel, the share of that travel that HSR can capture, and its potential revenue and costs are used together to address key questions about project feasibility and desirability, including: Is HSR a pertinent solution? If so, what kind of service should be delivered by the HSR system (in terms of capacity, journey time, cost of travel, comfort, and other factors)? What is the expected business case of HSR operations? What implementation strategy should therefore be decided for an HSR system (funding, operations, etc.)? In France, the 2014 Framework Guideline updates the methodology to implement in order to assess the economic and socioeconomic interests of a major investment project. These recommendations are based on the work of a high-level reflection group chaired by Emile Quinet. New French high-speed lines are all assessed in France according to the recommendations of the current Framework Guideline. There were two previous versions of this guideline in the past (1995 and 2004).

Since the late 1960s, SNCF has used mostly aggregate models that consider the entirety of the market without segmenting it according to different demographics. As required by French law since 1983 (LOTI, *Loi d'Orientation des Transports Intérieurs* or Domestic Transportation Bill), these forecasts have been systematically compared with observed traffic after a few years of operation for the high-speed lines being built. This systematic feedback has allowed SNCF to better calibrate the model: the margin of error was 0.8 per cent (in 2004) for the Mediterranean TGV launched in 2001 (Paris to Marseille and beyond, 11.5 million travellers) and 0.7 per cent (in 2010) for the East European TGV launched in 2007 (Paris to Strasbourg and Germany, 8.15 million travellers).

Main methodologies used by SNCF

SNCF focuses on simple, aggregate models based on revealed preferences, i.e., what can be observed from statistics on actual travel behaviour, real-life experience, rather than extrapolated through questionnaires? (As is done in stated preference or behavioural intention surveys.)

The models used by SNCF are based on the concept of transportation generalized cost (TGC). TGC is the sum of the actual cost of the ticket and the value of the time spent in transit. Time spent in transit is a function of journey time, frequency (or wait time), access and egress times, and transfers, as applicable. Various time components are evaluated differently; SNCF has found that transfers in particular represent a significant inconvenience for the traveller. The inconvenience of a connection reduces the attractiveness of a service for the traveller, even if the time required is short; the longer it takes to make the connection, the more onerous the impact. This finding has been incorporated into SNCF modelling, using the actual (experienced) transfer times on the system.

For personal vehicle operating costs, we focus on fuel prices rather than full vehicle operating and ownership costs because numerous studies as well as SNCF's own model estimations show that the perceived price, i.e., the out-of-pocket cost, is a stronger determining factor in consumer transportation decisions than the real (full) cost. Most travellers own a car, for instance, and few will consider the depreciation of their vehicle or insurance in thinking about the cost of one specific journey: they will consider marginal costs instead, and marginal costs of the journey are mostly fuel costs. The price of fuel is thus a proxy for the way that consumers think about cost of transport.

Price/time models, gravity models, and logit models are all used in SNCF forecasting. Each type of model is discussed briefly in the paragraphs following.

Price/time model

Value of time varies between individuals and so understanding the value of time and the distribution of values of time in the population helps us to forecast market shares. A simple price/time model compares the TGC of air and HSR options (in its simplest form: ticket price + value of time spent in transit). Let us take the example of an air journey that lasts 1 hour, and is priced at $200, compared to a journey by HSR that takes 2 hours and is priced at $100. The TGC for air in this case is: 200 + 1VoT (ticket price plus 1 hour of Value of Time). For HSR the figure is 100 + 2VoT. It is then simple to find the value of time that creates iso-utility between two modes:

$$200 + 1VoT = 100 + 2VoT$$
$$\rightarrow VoT = \$100 \text{ /hour}$$

In this case, anyone who values their time above $100 per hour will prefer flying (spend an extra $100 to save 1 hour).

As we know the distribution of the population according to their values of time (it follows the same distribution as available revenue for spending), we can easily derive the market share of HSR. (In our example, it is the proportion of people who value their time below $100 per hour.)

Gravity models

Gravity models – so called because their formulation is similar to Newtonian models of gravity with attractions offset by distance – stipulate that the traffic between two cities is determined by some measure of 'attractions' between the city pair offset by the resistance or impediments to travel between the two. A common formulation estimates the travel between the city pair as a function of the ratio between the product of their populations P and p, weighted by two coefficients α and β to reflect the wealth of their populations, and the transportation generalized cost between the two cities to the power γ:

$$T = k\, P^{\alpha} \times p^{\beta} / TGC^{\gamma}$$

Logit models

Logit models consider the utility of a mode i (described by a vector of attributes $\mathbf{X}_i$) versus other modes j (described by $\mathbf{X}_j$) for an individual t, described by a vector $\mathbf{S}_t$. By comparing the various utilities of all modes of transport for all individuals, and taking into account the socioeconomic characteristics of individual travellers, we can derive the probability that an individual will prefer one mode of transport over another one, and therefore the various market shares. From a sample of travellers we can project to the general population or can study the behaviour of particular market segments.

We derive utility from the inverse function of TGC. In addition, logit methods allow the analyst to compare any number of modes and to take into account factors such as car ownership, household or individual income, and differences that may result from travel purpose (business travel, leisure travel, for example). An interesting property is the link between various utilities and the modal share, as the modal share for mode i among n competing modes equals:

$$MarketShare_i = \frac{e^{U_i}}{\displaystyle\sum_{k=1}^{n} e^{U_k}}$$

Logit models are well established in the literature and are widely used in a variety of applications. For further details, see Train (2002).

Limitations of forecasts

While forecasts are key tools for the planning of infrastructure, including HSR, they face several limitations, some of which are inherent and some of which are a function of the way forecasts are sometimes applied.

First, forecasts can be difficult to understand by those who have limited training in advanced mathematics. This can be compounded by secrecy regarding forecasts which may result from the use of proprietary data or models. Simply presenting forecasts as 'best expert assessments' is not likely to be convincing, nor will it adequately communicate the factors and assumptions that have been utilized in making the forecasts (such as anticipated growth rates, level of investment in competing modes, etc.), even though these factors might be very important determinants of the results and ought to be part of the public discussion.

Second, forecasts must inevitably rely on assumptions about future conditions, and the magnitude of the interests at stake in megaprojects such as HSR is an incentive for all parties to provide their own forecasts. The resulting forecasts can be based on more or less rigorous techniques, and in some cases have simply been based on an example from another project that will help carry a point in the public debate (regardless of its relevance). While project sponsors, public or private, must consider how the project will affect their finances, project opponents do not necessarily need to build accurate models; often, simply challenging the forecasts or producing alternative forecasts will suffice to generate doubts and raise questions about the validity of the project itself. Thus while forecasts are intended to help reduce risk, the presence of competing forecasts can be a significant distraction and may divert attention from critical issues, actually exacerbating risk.

Third, forecasts are sometimes treated as 'the answer' whereas a more accurate depiction would be that the forecast is a starting point. While models are generally run for a particular target year, the projection of total expected benefits and costs in a particular target year (e.g., 5 or 20 years after opening) is not necessarily very useful. A single traffic forecast that does not take into account the fact that traffic is likely to build up over time may overstate benefits that will be delivered in early years. By the same token, it may understate or ignore benefits that appear in later years. For example, some kinds of environmental benefits will not be realized until traffic reaches a particular threshold.

The French 'Rhine Rhone' high-speed line is a significant example of limitations of forecasts: since the forecasts were carried out 7 years before the completion of the line in Eastern France, they did not take into account the economic crisis which occurred a few years later and which significantly changed results at the opening in 2011. They also did not take into account the more recent development of car-pooling, which was not anticipated 10 years ago, and regulatory changes for intramodal competition.

Strategies for improving forecasts

Given the limitations of forecasts, transparency is paramount for project developers so they can build trust. Transparency can come from explaining the models being used, but also from giving more information about and making improvements to several key elements of the planning process:

- Lessons that can be drawn from past margins of error in forecasts and the distribution of various values of the forecasts depending on their probability;
- The dynamic and temporal nature of demand and its interaction with operations;
- Accounting for internal and external costs and regulatory factors;
- Transferability of experience from other cases; and
- Risks due to 'game-changers' or 'rupture scenarios'.

A clear and forthright discussion of these elements can properly inform the public debate and thus the policymaking decisions.

Considering margins of error and probabilistic distributions of traffic forecasts

A first step in the process of maximizing the utility of forecasts is to move away from a single point and to instead propose a range of possible forecasts, with a probability attached to each of these values. This can be instrumental in pricing access to capital for funding agents. It also can be critical in evaluating all benefits and inconveniences of the new infrastructure.

Let us take a simple example. Suppose a new HSR system is projected to carry 25 million passengers a year, and will have a favourable impact on global carbon emissions provided the HSR system carries more than 20 million passengers a year (with significant transfers from air and road required to offset the massive emissions caused by construction). Policymakers would have to know the probability that actual traffic would not reach 20 million in order to determine the risk of the project not having a positive carbon impact. If the risk can be managed, the project should continue, but policymakers might request that project developers redesign the project to further reduce emissions (and therefore bring the passenger threshold down to a lower level).

SNCF has developed its own method to define the probability distribution of forecasts based on Monte Carlo and bootstrapping methods. The traffic forecast is expressed as an econometric equation, which includes inputs (journey time, GDP growth, competition offering, etc.) and coefficients (obtained through the calibration of the model based on historical data):

$$Traffic = N + \sum_{i=1}^{n} \alpha_i X_i^{k_i}$$

where N is a constant, X_i are inputs (such as GDP growth or travel time), and α_i and k_i are coefficients.

Traditional methods would simply run the equation, selecting the most likely inputs, and using fixed coefficients. We proceed a bit differently. The objective is to be in a position to measure the confidence intervals around future forecasts (and possible extreme values), rather than generating one single numeric value.

First, we compare the predicted inputs (like journey time or GDP growth) with observed data to define the margin of error of these forecasts. We can then list these forecasts in ascending order to get a table of errors. For example, we may say the first five forecasts underestimated actual traffic by 5 per cent, the next twelve by 4 per cent, and all the way up to the last five, which may have overestimated traffic by 5 per cent.

Then, we consider the coefficients. We use a sample of city-pairs for which forecasts were produced and can be compared with real traffic at the time HSR was implemented. We run the model using real values for the various inputs of the equation, and adjust coefficients in order to best calibrate the model (i.e. minimize the squared difference between the forecast and observed reality). From a modelling perspective the problem is the relatively limited size of the sample: we need additional samples (for example 10,000), each of them of the same size of the original population of observation, which we will generate using a draw with replacement (therefore, one city-pair can be drawn multiple times). For each set of coefficients, we now have 10,000 possible sets of values in this example. At this stage, we can produce new forecasts.

To clarify, let us consider the case where there is only one input and one coefficient. We know we have 100 observations of past forecasts of this input and we have established a table of errors for this input. We also know we have 10,000 possible values for this coefficient, which we will name $\alpha_1, \ldots, \alpha_i, \ldots, \alpha_{10,000}$. We will randomly select two numbers: one between 1 and 100, and the other between 1 and 10,000 – say 3 and 587. Using the table of errors, we know that the third observation underestimates reality by 5 per cent. We therefore adjust the value of the input to reflect this error (adding 5/95, or 5.26 per cent), and use it along with coefficient a_{587} to generate a first forecast value. We can repeat this operation by again drawing two other values between 1 and 100 and between 1 and 10,000.

The case of a more complex equation (with more inputs and coefficients) is similar: we simply draw more random numbers to match the higher number of terms that can vary. Eventually, we end up with a multiplicity of possible values for the forecast. The probability distribution is derived from the frequency distribution of values generated by the model, under the condition that a large number of possible values are generated. This helps explain why in spite of the relatively low number of variables, the method requires massive computing power.

Using this method, we obtain the two results that are of interest: extreme values of the forecast (say, the maximal error in 99 per cent of cases) and the distribution of potential values within this interval. Combined with the previous steps, these results allow us to identify those inputs that are the most difficult to forecast and the coefficients that are the most difficult to calibrate, and evaluate

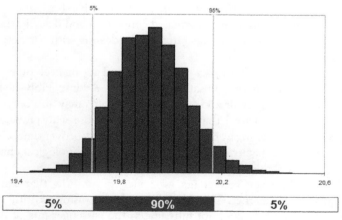

Figure 10.1 Probability distribution of total rail traffic

their contribution to overall risk. The forecasts generated in this fashion have demonstrated their accuracy, especially as we can quantify their reliability through probabilistic calculus.

The dynamic nature of demand and its interaction with operations

The next step is to get a better understanding of the drivers of costs and revenues and how they unfold over time. We consider these forecasts through an operator lens, digging into them to inform long-, medium-, and short-term strategies. Complementing forecasts with operator experience, expressed in terms of business plans, is a key step to further reduce the discrepancy between forecasts and reality.

Traffic is traditionally forecast using one or more of the methods presented earlier, calculating traffic as a function of price and other elements of the utility of the offered HSR versus alternative modes of transport. Price is very important because in very broad terms, SNCF has found that regardless of the specific method used, the travel mode's overall performance (journey time, frequency, comfort, convenience, etc.) and its price weigh equally in customers' minds.

To prepare forecasts, the modeller will select a price that makes sense in the market. For HSR routes with heavy air competition, the average price is usually positioned slightly below the bottom-end of air fare range, excluding deeply discounted promotional offers. A reference forecast, where all else is considered to be as in today's market, is then prepared.

The resulting forecast of traffic is only a starting point, however. It does not suffice for several reasons.

- The operator will need to adjust its service offer based on demand that varies by time of day, day of week and season.
- The service levels provided by other modes (air, road) are likely to change over time due to a variety of factors, both positive (e.g., improved fuel economy) and negative (e.g., increased congestion and delay in the air and road networks) and thus the operator will be dealing with competition that varies over time.
- The current supply of transport may be saturated during peak times, creating difficulties in estimating unsatisfied demand. Adding HSR is likely to shift some traffic from air and road and in so doing may also open up some capacity on air and road that can be used by those who previously were deterred from travelling by congested conditions. Also, over time, competing modes may add capacity through new services or technological changes not contemplated in the original (baseline) forecasts.
- HSR will induce new behaviours, as it offers possibilities that currently do not exist in the market. Thus the passenger mix using existing modes of transport quite likely does not fully match the passenger mix of the future HSR system.

A single forecast for a single future year cannot capture these subtleties. Yet ignoring them can result in a forecast that lacks credibility and may well miss important opportunities for cost savings and revenue capture.

SNCF has empirical evidence based on historical data that HSR service can induce new behaviours that are not captured in typical models. For instance, train journeys taking 10 to 12 hours are typically taken using night trains (so demand is expressed in the evening). When HSR is introduced and journey time is shortened to between 3 and 7 hours, the time of departure shifts, peaking in the late morning. For shorter trips, there are two peaks (morning and evenings), which denotes day trips for business travellers and commuters and new habits for other travellers, who provision only half a day for their travel instead of a full day as they may have done in the past.

In addition, there is evidence supporting the potential for the emergence of new travel markets. This is travel demand that is induced by the new transport service, and by new services offered by competitors who adapt their services to cope with the new competition and attempt to capture a share of new markets.

In SNCF's view, it is important to recognize forecasts as starting points for the analysis rather than final results, and to involve an operator in the discussions of traffic, revenue, and cost forecasting. An operator has the experience required to understand the fluidity of demand, and the potential level of flexibility in operations, to help manage demand as it changes over time.

In actual operations, it is crucial to consider traffic, revenue, and cost forecasts through the lens of operations and not rely on simple demand forecasts that assume a single service level and price for a typical day or week. An operator will calibrate services to best satisfy the potential demand, and implement the necessary adjustments (such as revenue management, fleet management, etc.) that will make the system more sustainable. Drawing upon this expertise in refining demand forecasts is advisable because doing so will result in far more sophisticated estimates of revenues and costs. In particular, operators can provide experienced assessments on such questions as: How can operations (e.g. number of cars per train, number of trains per hour) be adjusted to minimize capital costs while maintaining peak capacity of the HSR system? How and to what extent can demand be dynamically managed through pricing, reducing the capacity needed in peak times, making better use of capacity off peak, and producing overall increased profitability?

As an example, consider the impact of temporal variation. Traffic is not evenly produced throughout the year; there is variation based on the time of day, the day of the week, and the season. This temporal variation is widely acknowledged and can be empirically estimated by measuring the usage of existing modes of transport, through quantitative research and data analysis. However, this is not done in most modelling exercises, where the usual rule of thumb is to consider a typical week, sizing peak capacity considering the trade-off between unused capacity off peak (and the fixed costs having that capacity entails) v. potentially lost customers if demand in peak exceeds capacity. (For rail forecasts, in situations when demand exceeds supply of seats (typically Friday evenings), the modeller may state that the load factor will reach 100 per cent about once a week. The reality, of course, is that demand may exceed supply at other times, and it most likely will not exceed supply every Friday. How should this be considered in planning the system?

Understanding capacity management is key. Capacity is defined as the maximum number of passengers transported in a specific time (say, 1 hour) at a particular level of service (which depends on space allowance per passenger in the train cars, among other things).

The specific time over which capacity is measured must be relevant in the context of the travel demand. For example, if 10,000 people want to travel between 5:00pm and 6:00pm on a Friday night but the system can only carry 2,000 people per hour, it would require at least 5 hours to cope with the demand. From a user point-of-view, this would mean waiting up to 5 hours to travel, i.e. adding 5 hours to her travel time (and massively increasing the subsequent transportation generalized cost). She will then almost certainly prefer to fly or drive to her destination. Note that a trip lost to the system at 5 pm on a Friday will likely mean the loss as well of the other half of a round trip: for example, if the passenger cannot make a Friday early evening trip, she may choose to drive, and the return trip Sunday morning that she wanted to make on the train will also be lost to driving. If such deterred trips become common, the result may well be that traffic will never reach its full forecast potential.

Capacity management strategies aim to match demand and supply sufficiently well to avoid such problems. For this, we need to profile the demand by time of day (generally hourly for an intercity project). SCNF has built up considerable experience in responding to capacity issues through operations and pricing strategies. It is often possible to add cars to trains during the peak period to increase capacity for a few hours and to take other steps to handle peak demand through operations optimization. In addition, the demand can be managed dynamically through revenue management strategies, i.e., by making prices vary to entice people to trade time for money (which can be analyzed using the transportation generalized cost measures described earlier). This means that prices will be higher in peak times (hours of the day, days of the week, seasons) and lower off peak. Because travellers *do* respond to price, the resulting shifts in the times that they choose to travel result in a higher and more constant load factor through peak and off-peak periods, and overall higher revenue than would be forecast using a single price assumption.

Other elements of operations can be optimized to better cope with peak demand. Maintenance of trains during off-peak periods avoids producing too much capacity during peak periods. Preventive maintenance is an up-front cost but will result in a lower risk of incidents and a better predictability of equipment availability (maintenance being scheduled before the incidents happen, the operator can choose to program it off peak). This will also result in a better availability of trains during peak hours (for instance, 100 per cent of SNCF's fleet is available during peak periods such as Friday and Sunday evenings). More trains available during peak demand lead to a higher return on assets (revenue per train).

Accounting for internal and external costs and regulatory risks

While demand forecasts are often the most publicly debated of the forecasts for major infrastructure projects such as HSR, forecasts also need to be prepared for costs, which will move from top-line or gross revenue forecasts to bottom-line or net revenue forecasts. These costs can be categorized as internal costs (labour, reservations and ticketing services, communication, etc.) and external costs (meaning here expenses such as energy, insurance, taxes, etc.). In addition, planners should carefully consider regulatory aspects, which may deeply affect the long-term business case.

Internal costs

Fleet acquisition, maintenance and labour are the primary internal costs of HSR operations once construction costs (or depreciation of capital investments) are accounted for. Fleet acquisition and maintenance strategies should be incorporated in the fine-tuned cost forecasts, as they will greatly impact the financial profile of the project in terms of capital requirements and operating costs, as well as quality of service (reliability of service, comfort of equipment, etc.). Maintenance strategy should be considered dynamically, as it will impact not only maintenance costs but also availability in peak (and therefore condition the sizing of the fleet) and durability of assets (which may vary between 15 and 40 years depending on the selected strategy). Furthermore, the operator may choose to lease the fleet (including the maintenance) from a rolling stock operating company, such as ROSCO, or another entity, or subcontract the maintenance, rather than handle it internally. In these cases, the upside is that the risk of non-availability can be transferred to the partner, the downside being that this risk transfer is generally costly.

In terms of labour, SNCF's experience shows that productivity sharply improves after a few years of operation. First, the operator accumulates feedback and can adjust its operations (supply of seats) according to the actual demand and how it is expressed in time (seasonality). In addition, various processes improve and staff get better at what they do, resulting in higher productivity. Last, it is good practice to overstaff customer service operations in the ramp-up period to better attend to first-time customers. As the proportion of first-timers decreases with time and repeat travellers become more autonomous, fewer employees are required to provide travellers with the same quality of service. Statistical approaches to measure the margin of error in labour cost forecasts can also be used.

External costs

Energy costs are the primary external costs, followed by taxes (depending on local regulations) and marketing, reservations and ticketing services.

While many models make the assumption of a fixed price for energy, we contend that the price should be dynamically adjusted based on available forecasts. Additionally, planners should measure the margin of error attached to these forecasts in order to reflect the risk posed by energy price evolution in the overall business case. While this adds complexity to the modelling process, the price of energy is pivotal information, which affects many other variables (such as air and car costs).

Taxes are less volatile than energy prices, yet it is worth reviewing historic trends and the most likely evolutions of the tax policy in order to anticipate a potential increase. Marketing and distribution costs are a mix of external costs (media purchase, third-party commissions, IT procurement) and internal costs (direct channel maintenance). Costs for reservations and ticketing services typically amount to between 6 per cent and 20 per cent depending on key strategic choices in terms of customer experience (compulsory reservation, seat allocation, etc.) and strategy (e.g. push towards proprietary channels). Other factors will also influence these costs, such as the share of first-timers or international visitors, who typically need more assistance in the planning and buying process.

The total cost of acquisition of a customer (including distribution and marketing) may vary up to five-fold depending on the customer's frequency, paid fare, and other variables. This is common in the travel industry, as evidenced by the efforts carriers make to secure their high-contribution clientele's loyalty. A careful review of passenger profiles and the subsequent marketing and distribution strategies is therefore another necessary step in the process of refining the cost and revenue forecasts.

Regulatory risks

Regulatory instability is the second largest risk for investors after traffic forecasts. As an example, consider the experience of the French HSR system. In recent years, infrastructure and management operations have been dissociated, with operators paying tolls to the infrastructure manager on a per train basis, regardless of the occupancy of the train. The effect of per train tolls is that operators may be enticed to operate fewer trains, simply servicing peak demand, in order to maximize their profit – and therefore leaving ample infrastructure capacity unused. Conversely, should tolls be calculated on a per traveller basis (as is under discussion), the operator would have incentive to maximize the utility of its service by increasing its frequency, as the cost of running additional services is not prohibitive. The operator, the infrastructure manager, the travelling population, and potentially taxpayers benefit from a system that maximizes usage of assets and profitability of the entire system, but even a favourable change in regulation in the course of operations can be severely disruptive. In this case, it would have a significant effect on fleet dimensioning.

It may be beneficial to run simulations to demonstrate the impact of changing regulations on the business case in order to negotiate shielding clauses with the authority that prevent radical modifications of the regulatory context, especially in the case of public-private partnerships or concessions. A careful review of existing policy options is helpful. Even though politics can change swiftly, major policy shifts tend to follow much longer cycles when it comes to infrastructure. The authority will have to balance its desire to keep freedom to modify the operating rules, especially if it becomes dissatisfied with the service rendered by the operator, or the share of revenue paid to the authority, with the level of stability necessary to reassure investors and allow the project to proceed.

Transferability of experience from other cases

While the discussion thus far has focused on econometric approaches to forecasting demand and calculating costs, in many instances experiences from other cases are also introduced as evidence when major new infrastructure projects such as HSR are being considered. The utility of such case evidence is worth examining and may in fact be pivotal when a new project is developed in a country without previous experience of high-speed rail travel, as in the USA. Proponents (or opponents) of an HSR project might hastily jump to conclusions by deriving numbers from experience in other countries that turn out to be only weakly comparable to the proposed project. However, advocates for the use of international experience argue that even the most sophisticated of forecasting models could also prove weak: how could consumers express preference towards a mode of travel they have never experienced, or have experienced only in very different conditions (for example, in regions of higher population and employment density, stronger local transit services feeding intercity transport hubs, and higher costs for air and auto)?

Based on SNCF's experience with numerous projects, we posit that although we cannot directly derive figures from experience in other countries, this experience can shed some light on critical aspects of the forecasts, and help once again reduce the discrepancy between what is forecast and what is observed. SNCF experts have drawn on this experience to contribute to HSR project assessments around the world, for instance, in evaluating the market potential and its reaction to the introduction of HSR in Taiwan, South Korea, and Morocco.

The most common comment when considering HSR in a new region is that attitudes towards modes of travel vary immensely from one country to another. Based on extensive market research conducted by SNCF in various countries across the world, we believe that this is only partially true. Market research in numerous countries, including the USA, shows that perceptions of various modes of transportation are very similar both in practical terms (e.g., time and cost considerations) and symbolic terms (e.g., emotional attachment to autos, social status associated with personal autos). This most likely reflects the fact that air travel and car travel are two of the most standardized transport modes worldwide, and hence reactions to them do not differ much. Where high-speed rail travel has been introduced, it has also been met with quite consistent consumer responses across many countries.

On the other hand, how modes are viewed can change over time. A study conducted by the marketing consulting firm TNS Sofres in eight European countries (Cetelem 2014) reveals that twenty years ago, individual cars were a symbol of social success (52 per cent) and luxury (48 per cent), whereas cars are today related to freedom (52 per cent) and time-saving (49 per cent). Observers also are watching the reaction of today's young adults, who seem to be less interested in cars than previous generations (TNS Global 2013).

Yet, there are differences in context which need to be considered and accounted for in forecasts. Access to different modes of transportation (proportion of car ownership, air service levels, prices) and real travel times, a reflection of urban density as well as quality and congestion of the road network, are the most salient elements from a supply perspective. Income differences are another factor to consider. All of these factors can be incorporated into the econometric equations that constitute forecasting models. Experience shows that when properly calibrated to take into account local characteristics of a market, such models can deliver accurate forecasts.

Costs and revenues likewise can be informed by carefully contextualized use of evidence from other cases. While the specifics may not be consistent from one country to another, it is possible to analyze the key elements of cost and identify what will drive them up or down in a particular context. For example, labour policies and costs may differ significantly from country to country and this can affect construction and operation costs in a large way. It also is possible to anticipate a certain level of costs based on the expected clientele profile. The experience of an operator is therefore useful in the sense that it allows a better understanding of the determination of the cost and how it is derived from objective factors (usually market-based). Forecasts gain in accuracy through a more careful identification of cost and revenue drivers.

Predicting the unpredictable: how should we improve the resilience of the system when confronted with game-changing events?

Game-changing events or 'rupture scenarios' – so called because they represent a drastic change from the past – might include events such as a massive rise in energy prices, rapid demographic changes such as large migrations from coastal areas to inland areas, breakthroughs in transportation technologies such as driverless cars or ultra-fast surface transport systems, or a radical increase in the price for car use. The purpose of considering such events is not to review all possible scenarios and devise contingency plans for each of them, but instead to try to identify a few key events and their likely effects on HSR operations. For each event, the analysts can briefly evaluate its likelihood and operations experts can consider how they would respond to the event.

For instance, a shift towards a higher cost per car use would certainly benefit the HSR option, as customers would compare that higher cost against the costs of HSR. With increased demand, HSR operators might face crowding, the need for additional capital improvements, etc. On the other hand, the emergence of driverless cars might make it possible to make a multi-hour, long-distance road trip without the stress of driving and that could reduce HSR demand. Such scenarios could have differential affects based on trip purpose (business or leisure) as well as the specific origin and destination of the trips being made.

Not every new technology would necessarily be a game-changer. For example, consider a new, very high-speed land option such as maglev or the Hyperloop project. Such an option would create competition in the intercity transport market, and would likely lead to a shift in HSR focus, with more emphasis on network coverage and mass accessibility than pure speed performance between a limited number of stations. A situation like this will occur in Japan when the new Chuo Shinkansen line, using maglev technology, begins competing with existing Shinkansen services between Tokyo and Osaka around 2040. The new, faster infrastructure will service new areas inland, and will double as a backup for the existing infrastructure in case of natural disaster along the Pacific coast. It will capture a large share of the long-distance market thanks to dramatically reduced journey times. However this could still leave some competitive space for the older technology which can be repurposed to better service intermediate cities or offer a lower-cost alternative for long-distance travel. Thus the new technology could significantly change the market for HSR as we know it today without necessarily making HSR obsolete. On the contrary, some complementarities could arise.

A massive demographic movement would be much more critical, as rail infrastructure is not very mobile by nature. Thorough analysis would need to consider where those people would migrate to and how that would affect businesses, among many other factors.

The methods used to analyze such scenarios can be quantitative or qualitative. The likelihood is that most disruptive events would be challenging to run using most forecasting models, since a radical change in the variables (generalized costs, travel times, fares, origin-destination pairs, etc.) may bring the models out of their range of proven reliability. Thus one option is to simply consider a scenario using a more qualitative approach, potentially informed by travellers' interviews or analysis of historically comparable phenomena in other instances. Alternatively, we could simply apply 'stress tests'; for instance, we could imagine that a new mode of transport (regardless of what it could be) will capture one-third of the market, and measure the impact of this market shift on HSR revenues and costs. We could combine that assessment with a form of 'back-casting', to strategize a reasonable path to maintain the profitability of the project should such a loss of market share occur. For example, should a new mode of transport dominate the market in 2070 after being introduced in 2050, how can we right-size the supply of seats and price them in a way that keeps the HSR system profitable?

Conclusions

To sum up, the risk associated with HSR falls into three categories:

• Risks that can be predicted using conventional models if the necessary information is assembled and assessed;

- Risks such as future changes in income, energy costs, etc. that can be evaluated through probabilistic approaches; and
- Risks that are likely to go beyond the range reliably covered by available models, such as drastic shifts in location, price, or technology.

SNCF approaches these three families of risks with three different methods:

- We make it a priority to acquire enough data to run a variety of models and we improve our forecasts by regularly testing them against real data;
- We use Monte-Carlo methods to investigate the second category of risk – for traffic and revenue forecasts, as well as capital and operating expenditures; and
- We use qualitative approaches as well as stress tests and back-casting approaches to assess the potential impact of risks that are plausible but beyond the range of forecasting models.

SNCF has found that operating experience offers additional insight through a more granular understanding of various costs, traffic, and revenue drivers, such as the temporal profile of demand and ways to manage it. This in-depth understanding allows strategies to be developed for the dynamic adjustment of the system to improve its profitability and mitigate risk factors. Thus rather than treat operations as something that is only considered after planning is finished, SNCF believes that operations needs to be considered to refine demand forecasts and plan the system. This in turn results in the need for iterative demand forecasts testing the strategies.

In addition, SNCF has found that by measuring the deviation between past forecasts and observed reality, we can identify the main factors of deviation, and focus our attention on the domains where we know forecasts are less robust. Models should be regularly readjusted as a result of the regulatory changes and IT advances in terms of access to information and reservation services. For instance, in France, the opening of domestic markets to coach competition and the car-pooling development make a difference.

One should not rely on another operator's experience to predict ridership or costs, as situations vary substantially from one market to another. However, experience elsewhere can help identify factors that need to be considered in the case at hand. It is also possible to draw upon international experience to deconstruct the cost and revenue structure into more basic elements, which are more comparable across markets and can be quantified using available data. Additionally, a probabilistic approach provides an overview of these forecasts and helps refine them.

The main lesson learned from operating in various contexts is the need to articulate long-, medium-, and short-term strategies, from policy level to daily operations, and properly inform these strategies with the right forecasts. Long-term strategies include the design of the entire system, and are based on long-term, traffic, revenue, capital expense and operating expense forecasts. Middle-term strategies include fleet management, labour contracts, staff training and similar processes. Short-term strategies include day-to-day or real-time adjustments to supply or pricing through capacity and revenue management, for instance. As we have shown here, it is problematic to treat traffic, revenue and cost forecasts as static results. A knowledgeable operator can use these forecasts to develop strategies for system design and operation that can often result in acceptable service levels and profitability.

What form of project organization will ensure the capacity to develop such forecasts and the various short-, middle-, and long-term strategies that respond to them? Three steps can go a long way toward making this possible. First, early operator involvement is key and can be facilitated by pre-selecting an operator early in the project, or alternatively by working with a panel of potential operators, or an industry body that will be in a position to share information while protecting the interests of its members. Second, operators must structure their experience in a way that makes it easy to share and is beneficial to the policy-makers. It is essential to move beyond empirical or anecdotal evidence towards identifying underlying patterns. That is the purpose of the work undertaken by SNCF in terms of data analysis. Third, policy-makers should ensure not only long-term stability of the regulatory context, but also instil some flexibility in the project, leaving room for future operators to optimize operations on a short-term basis. Using industry standards, for instance, will allow competition between more suppliers. Additionally, the specifications of the project should leave room for the operator to propose improvements and innovate over the lifetime of the system.

References

American Public Transportation Association (APTA), 2012, *An Inventory of the Criticisms of High-Speed Rail With Suggested Responses and Counterpoints*. http://www.apta.com/resources/reportsandpublications/Documents/HSR-Defense.pdf Accessed 1 August 2016.

Brownstone, D, Hansen, M, and Madanat, SM, 2010, *Review of Bay Area/California High-Speed Rail Ridership and Revenue Forecasting Study*. Institute of Transportation Studies, University of California.

Cetelem, 2014, *L'Observatoire Cetelem 2014*, http://observatoirecetelem.com/publications/2014/observatoire-cetelem-automobile-2014.pdf Accessed 1 August 2016.

Champeaux, J, Pradayrol, J-P, 2007, 'Études de dessertes Intercités à Grande Vitesse', *Revue Générale des Chemins de Fer*, November.

Cox, W, and Vranich, J, 2008, *The California High Speed Rail Proposal: A Due Diligence Report*, Reason Foundation: 27.

David, G, Talbi, N, 2011, 'Determining the opportunity of new railway stations', *World Congress in Railway Research*.

Leboeuf, M, 2014, *High Speed Rail*, Paris: Editions du Cherche-Midi.

Loi d'Orientation des Transports Intérieurs 1983 (Fr).

Ni, J, Pradayrol, J-P, 2013, 'La tarification et la rentabilité des projets d'infrastructure', *Variances*, vol. 47(May 2013).

TNS Global, 2013, 'Generation Y is "out of love" with cars,' http://www.tnsglobal.com/blog/automotive/generation-y-is-out-of-love-with-cars Accessed 1 August 2016.

Train, K, 2002, *Discrete Choice Methods with Simulation*, http://elsa.berkeley.edu/books/train1201.pdf Accessed 1 August 2016.

Vranich, J, Cox, W, and Moore, AT, 2013, *California High Speed Rail: An Updated Due Diligence Report*, Reason Foundation.

11 Enhancing the cost-benefit analysis of high-speed rail

Chris Nash

Introduction

The aim of this chapter is to consider the costs and benefits of high-speed rail in the light of worldwide experience, and thus to contribute towards an understanding of in what circumstances it is an appropriate technology to use. The emphasis is on those elements of a cost-benefit analysis which may be missed, or incorrectly handled, by a typical cost-benefit analysis. In the next section we provide some background information about the development of high-speed rail worldwide to date. We then consider in turn its costs (capital, operating and environmental) and its benefits (revenue, time savings, reliability, accident savings, increased rail capacity, relief of congestion and capacity constraints on other modes, reduced environmental costs on other modes, generated traffic and wider economic benefits). Finally we consider the implications of the foregoing discussion for the appropriate circumstances for the introduction of high-speed rail.

Background

Definitions of high-speed rail (HSR) differ, but a common one is rail systems which are designed for a maximum speed in excess of 250 km/h (UIC 2012). These speeds invariably involve the construction of new track, although trains used on them can also use existing tracks at reduced speeds.

The first country in the world to build a dedicated line for new high-speed trains (originally at 210 km/h) was Japan. The background to this was that the original Tokaido line was narrow gauge and unsuitable for high speeds. It was also at capacity. The twin desire for a big increase in capacity in one of the most densely used corridors in the world, and for a major improvement in journey time to be competitive with air, led to the approval of the construction of a new high-speed line at standard gauge. The Tokaido Shinkansen started running between Tokyo and Osaka in 1964, and was an immediate success, carrying 23m passengers in its first year and leading to demands for its extension countrywide (Matsuda, in Whitelegg *et al.* 1993). Wider considerations such as regional development and equality led to Shinkansen investment on progressively less busy and less profitable routes (see Chapter 3).

The success of the Japanese high-speed system, particularly in gaining market share from air, was undoubtedly a major factor inspiring European railways to follow the same path. The next country in line was France, where intensive economic and technical research led to the proposal to build a new high-speed line from Paris to Lyon. Again the background was a shortage of capacity on the route in question plus the growing threat of competition from air (Beltran, in Whitelegg *et al.* 1993). From this beginning plans were developed for a network of lines, with the justification being largely in transport cost-benefit analysis terms, although hopes were also raised for wider regional economic impacts (Polino, in Whitelegg *et al.* 1993) (see Chapter 4).

The background to the introduction of high-speed rail in Germany was somewhat similar: a perceived shortage of capacity in the face of growing demand, accentuated by particular bottlenecks on north-south routes which had become more important following partition. However, the geography of Germany did not lend itself to development of a single key route; instead new sections of track were built where particular bottlenecks occurred. The geography in Spain is more like that of France, with long distances between the major cities and even less intermediate population. Given the relatively low quality of the inherited infrastructure, Spanish Railways were rapidly losing market share to air and the car. High speed was seen as a way of enabling rail to compete, as well as promoting regional economic development (Gómez-Mendoza, in Whitelegg *et al.* 1993), and, starting with Madrid-Seville, a network of new lines linking all the major cities is under construction. Italy took its first steps towards construction of dedicated high-speed lines early with the Rome-Florence Direttissima, work on which started in 1966 and the first section of which opened in 1976 (Giuntini, in Whitelegg *et al.* 1993); but it was not until 1985 that a team was set up explicitly to study high-speed rail, leading ultimately to plans for a network of completely new north-south and east-west high-speed lines.

With the opening of the Channel Tunnel, Britain started with a high-speed line from the Channel to London, forming part of a network of international routes linking Paris, Brussels, Koln, London and Amsterdam. The British government has now committed itself to building a new high-speed line from London to Birmingham, with probable extensions to Manchester and Leeds.

By 2010, high-speed trains worldwide were carrying 250b passenger km per annum (UIC 2012). In Europe, approaching half was in France. In the meantime, high-speed rail has been extended to more countries in Asia, including Korea, Taiwan and China. China built so many lines and grew its ridership so quickly that in 2013, China HSR lines carried slightly more HSR passenger-km than the rest of the world combined (Bullock *et al.* 2014).

All the above high-speed lines use conventional steel wheel on steel rail technology. The only other form of high-speed rail that has been implemented is maglev, which currently operates in limited applications (e.g., from Pudong International Airport into Shanghai and at Incheon National Airport in South Korea). Construction began in 2014 on the first intercity maglev line, between Tokyo and Nagoya, which is anticipated to open in 2027, and there are plans for further extension to Osaka. It has been argued that maglev could be built at a similar cost to conventional high-speed rail; would permit much higher speeds, although at the cost of increased energy consumption (Kluhspies 2010). However, maglev trains are not able to transfer to existing tracks to finish their journey. Such inter-operability is a feature of most new high-speed rail systems worldwide, even where – as in Japan and Spain – the new lines are built to a different track gauge from the existing lines. (Spain uses bogies capable of adjustment to the different gauge, whilst Japan has undertaken installation of limited sections of multi-gauge track.) Thus maglev technology has its greatest chance in intercity transport where either there is effectively no existing rail infrastructure or there is sufficient traffic to justify both HSR and a new dedicated route, a requirement that the Tokyo-Nagoya-Osaka corridor in Japan is deemed to satisfy.

Costs of high-speed rail

Table 11.1 summarizes European experience of the costs of building, maintaining and operating high-speed rail and presents typical costs for a 500 km line in Europe. Construction costs vary enormously from case to case with Spain having the lowest costs and Britain the highest. (At £70m per km the British link to the Channel Tunnel is outside the range covered by Table 11.1; Steer Davies Gleave 2004.) Some of these cost differences are inevitable, as a result for instance of land prices, although these do not usually account for more than around 5 per cent of the costs of an HSR project. A very major contributor to costs is the amount of tunnelling involved, and generally the costs of entering large cities are high. The British high-speed link to the Channel Tunnel is the most expensive high-speed line ever built, largely because of the lengthy tunnelling at the approach to the London terminal to avoid environmental objections. If these costs can be avoided, for instance by using existing under- or un-utilized rail infrastructure, then the case can be considerably improved, even if this means a compromise regarding speeds.

Table 11.1 Estimated costs of a 500 km HSR line in Europe (2004)

	Cost per unit (€ thousand)	Units	Total cost (€ million)
Capital costs			
Infrastructure construction (km)	12,000–40,000	500	6,000–20,000
Rolling stock (trains)	15,000	40	600.0
Running costs (p.a.)			
Infrastructure maintenance (km)	65	500	32.5
Rolling stock maintenance (trains)	900	40	36.0
Energy (trains)	892	40	35.7
Labor (employees)	36	550	19.8

Source: de Rus and Nash (2009)

With respect to operating costs, the overall cost per train km depends of course on the utilization of resources achieved. In general, high speeds mean high utilization in terms of kilometres per train and per member of staff, and for that reason the cost per train km of high-speed operation is often below the cost for conventional trains.

Regarding accident costs there has never been a fatal accident on a purpose-built high-speed railway; no doubt the fact that such lines invariably have state of the art cab signalling and complete grade separation from roads and footpaths contributes to this excellent record. Even the fact that trains were travelling at high speed when earthquakes shifted the tracks in incidents in Japan and Taiwan did not cause injuries – such is the stability of the rolling stock, that the trains came to a stand safely.

More of an issue is the environmental cost of HSR. Noise, land take and visual intrusion are significant issues, although these can be minimized by careful design including the use of noise barriers. High speeds also require higher energy use than conventional trains. One of the few studies to break down emissions in detail by type of train, as well as type of air and car transport is C E Delft (2003). They produce the following results:

Because they generally travel long distances without intermediate stops, most countries apply compulsory seat reservations to high-speed rail and use yield management systems to maximize revenue whilst achieving high load factors. Thus both the French TGV network and Eurostar between London, Paris and Brussels achieve average load factors of 70 per cent or more. This helps offset the higher energy consumption of high-speed rail. Because high-speed rail uses electric traction, the implications for carbon and other emissions depend on the primary fuel used to produce the electricity. It is an advantage of rail that it can readily utilize electricity, which offers possibilities for low carbon production using nuclear, carbon capture coal or a variety of renewable sources of power.

Table 11.2 only considers energy used for traction. A further relevant issue is the carbon and other emissions resulting from energy use in construction and maintenance of the infrastructure, which is obviously much more extensive

Table 11.2 Energy consumption by mode 2010

	Intercity train	High-speed train	Air (500km)	Diesel car on motorway
Seating capacity	434	377	99	5
Load factor	44%	49%	70%	0.36
Primary energy (MJ per seat km)	0.22	0.53	1.8	0.34
(MJ per passenger km)	0.5	1.08 (0.76*)	2.57	0.94

Source: CE Delft (2003)

*At 70% load factor

than the infrastructure needed for air transport. Recent work for Network Rail suggests that on a heavily used new high-speed line from London to Manchester, energy embodied in the infrastructure might add some 15 per cent to these figures; obviously for a less well used line the increase could be substantially more (Network Rail 2009a).

Benefits of high-speed rail – revenue, time savings and reliability

If in considering the costs of high-speed rail we evaluate them net of any cost saving in the operation of conventional trains, then obviously we should also only consider net revenue – i.e. revenue over and above that earned by the previous service. This revenue may come because high-speed trains are charged at a premium over previous fares, because traffic is attracted from other modes or because new trips are generated. If it assumed that on other modes cost savings from reduced traffic compensate for loss of revenue, then the net revenue generated by high-speed rail may be regarded as a genuine benefit, reflecting part of the willingness to pay of users to use the service. In this case, benefits to users from time savings or increased comfort and reliability must be valued net of any increase in money costs that they pay.

The most obvious benefit of high-speed rail is that it saves time for its users. For former users of conventional rail, estimating these savings is typically straightforward, although attention must be paid to the possibility that some users have longer access journeys as a result of the high-speed service having fewer stops. For car and air journeys access times are of greater importance. Thus it is the change in door-to-door journey time that matters. For car and even more for air travellers, this will depend very much on their precise origins and destinations; if they are remote from the railway station and close to the airport, then air will obviously be favoured (unless there is a cost advantage that offsets this) and vice versa. There is also good evidence that travellers prefer not to change mode, so for both rail and air, an interchange penalty will apply, as well as the time actually taken in changing between modes, which for air given the current security situation may be substantial. Finally there is evidence that walking and waiting time are typically valued more highly than in-vehicle time (Wardman 2004). The author has been unable to find any studies specifically of the value of time spent waiting at airports, although at least for time spent queuing to check in and pass through security, it is reasonable to assume that the higher value of waiting time applies.

Time savings are generally split into business, commuter and leisure. There has been extensive research into the value of time savings for commuter and leisure travel, but rather less in the case of business travel (Wardman 2004). For business travel, the argument is often used that this is travel in the employer's time, and that its value is therefore the cost of employing labour (the wage rate plus overheads), as this is what the employer will save if less time is spent travelling. This gives a much higher value for business travel time than for leisure (for the values currently in use in Britain, see Table 11.3).

A relatively high proportion of HSR traffic (30–40 per cent in European conditions) is likely to be travelling on business, and with the higher value of business travel time, this means that the value of business travel time is absolutely crucial to the case for high-speed rail. For instance, in the case of the proposed British high-speed line from London to the North (HS2), business travel time savings are 55 per cent of all the benefits (HS2 Ltd. 2009).

Questions have been raised on whether the full business value of time should be applied to all this traffic (Hensher 1977). According to a recent survey, a third of rail business passengers in Britain state that they spend most of their travel time working (Lyons *et al.* 2007); if a faster journey results in less time spent on work during the journey, then it is only the greater productivity of the time spent working in a location other than the train that is relevant. Also, many long-distance business trips start and end outside normal working hours; part of the time saving may be used for leisure activities rather than work. However, empirical research does suggest much higher values of business travel time than leisure, with values of time being much higher for first class travel than economy (Wardman 2004). Whilst in some cases it is unclear whether the studies are assessing the value of time of the individual or the organization they work for, in others (e.g. Marks, Fowkes and Nash 1986) this is clear. According to this study, firms appear to be willing to pay something like the full business value of time even in these circumstances, presumably because of the benefits they perceive in shortening long working days and having staff less tired, or because it becomes possible to fit in more meetings in a day and therefore to remove the need to stay overnight or to make a second trip.

Wardman (2004) also noted that values of time may vary by mode (according to comfort) and by users of the mode (according to income and other factors which lead particular groups to be more likely to use one mode than another). HSR offers a comfortable environment in which passengers can work, relax, eat or drink without the interruption of needing to change mode or move from

Table 11.3 Values of time (£2,002 per hour in market prices)

In working time	
Car driver	26.43
Car passenger	18.94
Rail passenger	36.96
Bus passenger	20.22
Walker	29.64
Cyclist	17.00
Out of working time	
Commuting	5.04
Leisure	4.46

Source: DfT: WEBTAG Unit 3.5.6 (www.webtag.org.uk)

terminal to aircraft. According to Lyons *et al.* (2007) more than 40 per cent of rail users work or read for most of the journey, and only 18 per cent regard time spent on the train as totally wasted. A recent review of the evidence finds that car users value time spent on an aircraft at some 80 per cent more than that in a car, but time spent on a train at 13 per cent less than time in a car (Abrantes and Wardman 2011). This suggests that there may be substantial benefits from diverting passengers from air to rail even where there are not significant time savings, and that passengers may choose rail on grounds of comfort even if it is not the quickest mode. Car users presumably find other benefits of car use, such as privacy, ability to listen to music, etc., largely offset the advantages of rail in respect to the ability to work or read.

Passengers also value frequency of service and again the car has the advantage of a lack of schedule delay. To the extent that aircraft have smaller capacity than high-speed trains, air may offer higher frequency than HSR; however, the fact that trains can serve intermediate points with a small time penalty compared with aircraft means that on a corridor with a number of well-spaced cities, rail frequencies may be higher than air.

A further important aspect of journey time is its reliability. A self-contained high-speed rail system devoted solely to high-speed passenger services can achieve much higher levels of reliability than can conventional rail, where there are conflicts between fast and stopping passenger trains and between passenger and freight. It is also higher than is usually found on road and air transport. For instance, in 2009, Eurostar (the operator of high-speed trains on the dedicated high-speed line between London, Paris and Brussels via the Channel Tunnel) achieved a 95 per cent record of arrivals within 10 minutes of the scheduled time. For conventional long distance rail operators in Britain, the equivalent figure averaged 89 per cent, still better than typical figures for air. Evidence suggests that passengers value time spent in delays at something like three times the level of scheduled travel time (Wardman 2001).

In terms of the impact on mode split, early results on market shares are available for the Paris-Lyon and Madrid-Seville lines. TGV Sud-Est between Paris and Lyon was opened in two stages between 1981 and 1983. The train journey time was first reduced by around 30 per cent, after the opening of the Northern section, and the implied journey time elasticity was around −1.6. However, the time elasticity was around −1.1 for a journey time reduction of around 25 per cent on the opening of the Southern section of the route. The cause of this lower elasticity was because the transfer from air had been largely completed in the first phase when rail was fast enough to provide effective competition. The Spanish AVE service introduced in April 1992 reduced rail journey times between Madrid and Seville from around 6½ hours to 2½ hours.

Table 11.4 indicates the market shares of plane, train and road before and after the introduction of high-speed rail on these two routes. The impact on rail market share is very large, particularly in Spain where the improvement in rail journey time was larger. Much more traffic is extracted from air than road. It should be noted that the figures include a significant amount of newly generated traffic.

Table 11.4 Before and after high-speed market shares

	TGV Sud-Est		AVE Madrid-Seville	
	Before	After	Before	After
Plane	31%	7%	40%	13%
Train	40%	72%	16%	51%
Car and bus	29%	21%	44%	36%

Source: COST 318 (1998)

Wilken (2000) reports that surveys of AVE passengers indicated that 15 per cent of the additional rail traffic was newly generated; according to Bonnafous (1987) no less than 49 per cent of the additional traffic on Paris-Lyon in the first 4 years was generated traffic. In other words, while there was indeed a substantial transfer from air, the reduction in road mode share was largely caused by the generation of additional rail traffic, rather than direct transfer.

Figures quoted by Steer Davies Gleave (2006) and Campos and Gagnepain (2009) for the air–rail mode split, showing that where rail journey times are reduced below 4 hours, rail share of the rail–air market increases rapidly with further journey time reductions, and rail tends to have a market share of at least 60 per cent and sometimes effectively drives air out of the market when rail journey times are below 3 hours. Future trends are found to depend on a wide variety of factors including the introduction of environmental charges on air transport and trends in air and rail costs.

It should be stressed that this evidence is from countries where for most people a city centre rail station is more convenient than an airport, so that – allowing for time spent at the airport – door-to-door journey times are similar by air and rail even where the actual rail journey time is 3 hours. Where development is low density with weak city centres and poor public transport this may not be the case, and a shorter rail journey time may be necessary to compete with air.

Kroes (2000) also points out that the available evidence concerning modal shift relates to traffic that is not transferring at the airport to another plane. There is very little evidence on the transfer market. However, the increasing integration of rail with air with high-speed rail stations at airports such as Paris, Brussels, Frankfurt and Amsterdam offers the prospect of much greater rail penetration into this market, especially if ticketing and baggage handling is better integrated.

Benefits of high-speed rail – capacity and diversion from other modes

Laird, Nellthorp and Mackie (2005) demonstrate how network effects may take place within the transport sector, leading to costs and benefits beyond the project being considered, as a result of the presence of one or more of the properties of economies of scale, scope or density, congestibility and consumption externalities. How far do such benefits improve the case for high-speed rail?

First, it may be argued that there is a network effect from extending existing high-speed rail schemes. Essentially the argument is that once one stretch of high-speed rail has been built, extending it further will add to traffic on the existing stretch, reducing unit costs and increasing revenues and benefits. At the same time, the high-speed lines affect existing conventional rail networks. By relieving conventional lines of fast passenger trains, capacity may be released which enables other services, passenger or freight, to be improved, although, at the same time, the finances of the conventional network may be seriously weakened by taking away their most profitable traffic (Atkins 2002). If capacity is available, the high-speed line may also be used by other services such as commuter trains or even freight over some or all of its length (for instance the high-speed line from London to the Channel Tunnel is already used by commuter services into London and a small amount of freight use has now started), although shared use with freight significantly raises costs and reduces capacity unless confined to slack times such as night. Of course, other options exist for increasing capacity, including building new capacity not for high-speed passenger traffic but for regional passenger or freight traffic. But there is evidence (Network Rail 2009b) that if new capacity is required, the incremental cost of building it for high speeds is relatively small, and given adequate volumes of traffic the benefits may be large.

There is also clear evidence (Gibson *et al.* 2002) that running rail infrastructure less close to capacity benefits reliability; it may also lead to less overcrowding on trains. Both of these features are highly valued by rail travellers and especially business travellers (Wardman 2001). There will also be benefits from diverting traffic from other modes. Typically, as illustrated in the previous section, a substantial proportion, but not all, of the new traffic attracted to rail will be diverted from other modes – mainly car and air. To the extent that the costs of carrying this traffic by high-speed rail are included on the costs side of the analysis, the cost savings from no longer needing to carry it by road and air should be added as a benefit (as noted above, this may be done by including the revenue diverted from these modes to rail as a benefit of high-speed rail if this is seen as a reasonable approximation for costs). Furthermore, to the extent that infrastructure charging on these modes does not cover the marginal social cost of the traffic concerned, there will be further benefits from such diversion.

Table 11.2 shows that high-speed rail has a substantial advantage over air transport, is similar to the car and substantially worse than conventional rail in terms of energy consumption. If low carbon electricity is used, the implications for global warming will be much more favourable than this, with HSR offering substantial advantages over conventionally fuelled cars as well as over air. However, while the load factor given for high-speed rail of 49 per cent may be typical of Germany, where high-speed trains spend a lot of their time running at conventional speeds on traditional track, and seat reservations are not compulsory, both the French TGV and Eurostar, with long non-stop runs, compulsory seat reservations and sophisticated yield management systems, claim load factors similar to the 70 per cent shown for air, reinforcing the advantage over air. For Britain, the savings and costs tend to cancel out and the introduction of high-speed rail cannot lead to a substantial energy saving; where there is little diversion from air, it will undoubtedly lead to an increase. So the claim of HSR to reduce greenhouse gases must rest on a non-fossil fuel source of electricity generation, as is currently the case in some countries (e.g. France, with a high share of nuclear, and Switzerland, with a lot of hydropower). Of course, where there is currently little conventional rail traffic and air dominates the market, as in most corridors in the US, the advantages of introducing HSR in terms of greenhouse gases will be greater.

Diverting traffic from road does not simply affect greenhouse gases, but also reduces road noise, accidents, air pollution and congestion. Table 11.5 presents the unit values for these costs for a petroleum car, as estimated for a major European corridor in the European research project GRACE (GRACE 2005). While the off-peak costs are quite similar between routes, the peak costs are

Table 11.5 Marginal social cost and prices for long distance car transport (Euros per vehicle km)

Milano-Chiasso				Chiasso-Basilea			
Interurban petrol GRACE car petrol EV				*Interurban petrol GRACE car petrol EV*			
	Peak	*Off-Peak*	*Night*		*Peak*	*Off-Peak*	*Night*
Noise	0.007	0.011	0.035	Noise	0.004	0.007	0.021
Congestion	0.147	0.002	0.001	Congestion	0.194	0.003	0.001
Accident	0.015	0.015	0.015	Accident	0.008	0.008	0.008
Air pollution	0.001	0.001	0.001	Air pollution	0.001	0.001	0.001
Climate change	0.005	0.005	0.005	Climate change	0.005	0.005	0.005
W&T	0.016	0.016	0.016	W&T	0.032	0.032	0.032
TOTAL	0.191	0.050	0.073	TOTAL	0.244	0.056	0.068

Basel-Duisburg				Duisburg-Rotterdam			
Interurban petrol GRACE car petrol EV				*Interurban petrol GRACE car petrol EV*			
	Peak	*Off-Peak*	*Night*		*Peak*	*Off-Peak*	*Night*
Noise	0.005	0.009	0.027	Noise	0.009	0.014	0.043
Congestion	0.123	0.002	0.001	Congestion	0.122	0.002	0.001
Accident	0.008	0.008	0.008	Accident	0.006	0.006	0.006
Air pollution	0.001	0.001	0.001	Air pollution	0.001	0.001	0.001
Climate change	0.005	0.005	0.005	Climate change	0.005	0.005	0.005
W&T	0.019	0.019	0.019	W&T	0.020	0.020	0.020
TOTAL	0.161	0.044	0.061	TOTAL	0.163	0.048	0.076

much larger and more variable, being dominated by congestion costs which vary greatly from route to route.

Table 11.6 shows what motorists pay for these routes. (It is doubtful whether vehicle excise duty should be included here, as it is a fixed cost of car ownership and is unlikely to influence the decision to drive on a particular journey.) It is found that in the peak there is a significant benefit of up to 10 eurocents per kilometre from removing cars from untolled roads; while in the off-peak, cars pay around their marginal social cost on untolled roads and more than that where a toll is payable. A higher shadow price of carbon would affect this comparison, but greenhouse gas costs still would not be a large part of the total. In other words, for road transport, the biggest issue concerns congestion. But it is unlikely that there will be a large net benefit from relief of road congestion unless the road is congested in the off peak as well as the peak.

Table 11.7 shows similar estimates for social costs of air transport, taken from the IMPACT study which is based on EU data (CE Delft 2008). In the case of air, the absence of fuel tax means that there is normally no charge for environmental externalities, although this is crudely allowed for in some countries (including Britain) by a departure tax. In the absence of a departure tax there is an uncovered cost of perhaps 1.5 eurocents per passenger km on a 500 km flight, or a total of 7.5 euros. In other words, diversion of 1 million passengers from air might give a benefit of 7.5m euros. The diversion of 1 million passengers from congested untolled roads over this distance might yield a similar figure. Even if we had a very successful HSR project, diverting maybe five times this figure from both modes, and even if the valuation of environmental costs were doubled, this only gives a total benefit of 150m euros. Compared with capital costs of 10–20b euros, this is not a very great contribution to the justification of HSR. In other words, the biggest external benefits of HSR are likely to come where road or air are highly congested and expansion on those modes difficult and expensive, including in terms of environmental costs.

For the Channel Tunnel rail link in Britain, benefit and cost data are presented in Table 11.8. Benefits from reduced external costs on other modes were not considered to be of great magnitude, as the data show. Most benefits came from time savings for travellers.

Table 11.6 Road transport prices (euros per vehicle km) petrol car

Corridor segment	Km	Toll	Fuel tax gasoline €km	Vehicle excise duty per km car gasoline	Total price
A8-A9 Milano–Chiasso (I)	50	0.055	0.064	0.013	0.132
E35 Chiasso–Basilea (CH)	279	0.093	0.053	0.010	0.156
A5-E35 Basel–Duisburg (D)	584	0.046	0.056	0.012	0.114
E35-A25 Duisburg–Rotterdam (NL)	204	-	0.058	0.020	0.078

Source: GRACE (2005)

Table 11.7 Externalities air (2000 Euro cents per passenger-km)

	Air pollution	Climate change	
Flight distance (km)	Direct emissions	Direct emissions	Indirect emissions
<500 km	0.21	0.62	0.71
500–1,000	0.12	0.46	0.53
1,000–1,500	0.08	0.35	0.40
1,500–2,000	0.06	0.33	0.38
>2,000	0.03	0.35	0.40

Noise costs per landing or take off (Schiphol)

	40 seater	100 seater	200 seater	400 seater
Fleet average	180	300	600	1,200
State of art	90	150	300	600

Source: CE Delft (2008)

Table 11.8 Cost-benefit analysis of the Channel Tunnel rail link (£m)

Benefits	(1998 Appraisal)
International services	1,800
Domestic services	1,000
Road congestion	30
Environmental benefits	90
Regeneration	500
Total benefit	3,420
Costs	1,990
Net present value (NPV)	1,430
Benefit-cost ratio (BCR)	1.72
BCR excluding regeneration benefits	1.5

Source: National Audit Office (2001)

On the other hand, where air has a high market share over short distances, the external costs would likely be different. External costs for short-haul air are largely related to take-offs and landings and thus external costs are much higher on a passenger-kilometre basis. In a market where short-haul air currently dominates the intercity market and rail has a very small mode share, as appears to be the case for the proposed high-speed rail system in California, benefits to users of other modes from reduced congestion are almost as great as those to users of high-speed rail themselves (Brand *et al.* 2001).

Benefits from high-speed rail – generated traffic and wider economic benefits

Generated traffic leads directly to benefits to users. In the EU these benefits are generally valued at half the benefit to existing users using a linear approximation to the demand curve; where the change is large, and an explicit demand curve is used for forecasting, a more accurate measure of consumer surplus may be calculated. But there has been much debate as to whether these generated trips reflect wider economic benefits that are not captured in a traditional cost-benefit analysis. Leisure trips may benefit the destination by bringing in tourist spending, commuter and business trips reflect expansion or relocation of jobs or homes or additional economic activity in the area concerned. The debate on these issues centres on whether these changes really are additional economic activity at the national level or whether it is simply relocated. In a perfectly competitive economy with no involuntary unemployment, theory tells us that there would be no net benefit (Mohring 1976). In practice, there are reasons why there may be additional benefits. For instance, if the investment relocated jobs to depressed areas, it may reduce involuntary unemployment. As noted in Table 11.8, regeneration in East London was included as part of the benefits in the Channel Tunnel Rail Link study, although these benefits were very controversial (National Audit Office 2001). However, in this case, the area in need of regeneration was close to the largest city. It is common for high-speed rail to favour central locations, and if the depressed areas are at the periphery, the effect may be for the peripheral areas to further lose activity to the central ones, the opposite of what is desired.

Agglomeration benefits are relevant in two respects. There is evidence that labour productivity is higher in locations with high accessibility than where it is lower. It is hypothesized that this happens for a variety of reasons – better allocation of workforce skills between jobs, economies of scale in the provision of specialized services (e.g. financial and legal services) in the immediate area, and increased opportunities for innovation to diffuse throughout the workforce. HSR may encourage centralization of jobs in cities where productivity is higher than in their current location and also increase accessibility for jobs in their existing locations. However one would think that these impacts would be strongest in the commuting market. While high-speed rail is used for substantial commuting in some cases (e.g. into Madrid from Ciudad Real, and into London from Kent), this is not usually the major use of HSR. In Britain, in the study of the proposed high-speed line from London to Birmingham (HS2), it has been estimated that such wider economic benefits from expansion of output under imperfect competition and from agglomeration effects within conurbation areas would account for only a little over 10 per cent of the total benefits. The latter arise from improved services on the conventional railway as a result of capacity released by diverting long-distance trains to the high-speed line, and by reduced road congestion (HS2 Ltd 2009).

Graham and Melo (2010) provide evidence that the agglomeration benefits of longer distance travel on the high-speed rail may be very small. However, they based this finding on the distance delay of commuting and business travel as a whole and on the low average share rail has of passenger kilometres in Britain (6.7 per cent), which mean that high-speed rail will not raise average accessibility of employment or population very much. To the extent that rail has a higher share of commuting and business travel, and particularly among those sections of the population which one might speculate were more important for agglomeration effects, namely professional and managerial employees, this could be a considerable underestimate, although the results would have to be orders of bigger magnitude before they had a significant effect on the case for high-speed rail.

SACTRA (1999) suggested that wider economic benefits of schemes would not generally exceed 10–20 per cent of measured benefits, whilst a specific study of investment in the European Network as planned by the European Commission suggested that it would not change regional GDP by more than 2 per cent (Brocker 2004). On the other hand there may be specific cases where effects are much larger. A study of a proposed high-speed route in the Netherlands found wider economic benefits to add 40 per cent to direct benefits (Oosterhaven and Elhorst 2003), but this was in the context of a relatively short route specifically designed to integrate the labour markets of the north of the country with that of Amsterdam. Ahlfeldt and Fedderson (2009) found that smaller towns on the Koln-Frankfurt high-speed route gained substantially in terms of GDP compared with other local towns, whilst it has been suggested that the remarkable development of cities such as Lille, and of the areas surrounding the HSR station in Lyon, is due to HSR (Harman 2006). In both cases, it is not clear whether this is a net benefit or a relocation of economic activity. Summing up the evidence, Vickerman (2009) concludes that whilst high-speed rail may have major wider economic benefits, the impact varies greatly from case to case and is difficult to predict.

Finally there is evidence that property prices rise in the vicinity of HSR terminals. Cascetta et al. (2010) found that the high-speed line from London to the Channel Tunnel raised house prices around stations (a finding confirmed by Pagliara et al. 2010). Preston and Wall (2008) also found a small impact around Ashford. By contrast Ahlfeldt (2009) found no impact with respect to the new intercity station in Berlin. Again, a key issue is how far these benefits are genuinely additional as opposed to the reallocation of economic growth, or the capitalization of other benefits in the form of higher property prices.

In what circumstances is HSR worthwhile?

There are relatively few published ex post cost-benefit analyses of specific high-speed rail projects. Two of the few published studies are for Madrid-Seville, which opened with less than 3m trips per annum and is still carrying only of the order of 5m trips per annum, and Madrid-Barcelona, which opened with 5.5m trips a year. A summary of the appraisals is given in Tables 11.9 and 11.10. In both cases, it is seen that benefits fall well short of costs, with reduced external costs on other modes contributing little.

Table 11.9 CBA of Madrid-Seville high-speed rail (billions of 2010 euros)

Costs	6.8
Benefits	4.5
Of which time savings	1.6
Generated traffic	0.8
Costs saved on other modes	1.9
External costs saved	0.2
Net present value of HST	−2.3

Source: de Rus (2012)

Table 11.10 CBA of Madrid-Barcelona high-speed rail (billions of 2010 euros)

Costs	12.4
Benefits	7.2
Of which time savings	2.8
Generated traffic	1.1
Costs saved on other modes	2.9
External costs saved	0.4
Net present value of HSR	−5.2

Source: de Rus (2012)

As mentioned above, France is one of the countries with the most experience of HSR, and it is also a country which is systematic in conducting cost-benefit analyses of all transport projects. More recently, an ex post evaluation of French HSR projects has been undertaken and compared with the ex-ante appraisals (Table 11.11). It will be seen that all the lines considered were expected to have acceptable financial and social rates of return, and to carry at least 15m passengers per annum. In practice, the out turn rates of return are generally lower, mainly because of higher infrastructure costs and lower traffic levels than forecast in some cases, although these cases of optimism bias are not as dramatic as has been found in some cases (Flyvbjerg *et al.* 2003). However, the only line for which the social case turned out to be marginal was the TGV Nord, where the major shortfall in traffic was mainly due to extreme over-estimation of Eurostar traffic through the Channel Tunnel.

De Rus and Nombela (2007) and de Rus and Nash (2009) have explored the key parameters determining the social viability of high-speed rail, and in particular the breakeven volume of traffic under alternative scenarios. They built a simple model to compute capital costs, operating costs and value of time savings for a new self-contained 500 km line at different traffic volumes. Typical costs were estimated using the database compiled by UIC. A range of time savings from half an hour to one and a half hours was taken, and a range of average values of time from 15 to 30 euros per hour. Other key assumptions are the proportion of traffic that is generated, and the rate of traffic growth.

Table 11.12 shows the breakeven volume in terms of millions of passengers per annum in the first year, assuming all travel the full length of the line, under a variety of assumptions about other key factors. For example, if on average passengers travel half the length of the line, then the required number is doubled. Note that benefit growth may occur because of rising real values of time as incomes rise, as well as traffic growth. With exceptionally cheap construction, a low discount rate of 3 per cent, very valuable time savings and high values both for the proportion of generated traffic and for benefit growth, it is possible to find a breakeven volume as low as 3 million trips per annum, but it is doubtful whether such a favourable combination of circumstances has ever existed. Construction costs of 30 million euros per km will increase the breakeven volume to 7 million.

Table 11.11 Ex post appraisal of French high speed line construction

		Sud Est	Atlantique	Nord	Inter Connection	Rhone Alpes	Mediterranean
Length (km)		419	291	346	104	259	
Infrastructure cost (m euros 2003)	Ex ante	1,662*	2,118	2,666	1,204	1,037	4,334
	Ex post	1,676	2,630	3,334	1,397	1,261	4,272
	% change	+1	+24	+25	+16	+22	−1
Traffic (m pass)	Ex ante	14.7	30.3	38.7	25.3	19.3	21.7
	Ex post	15.8	26.7	19.2	16.6	18.6	19.2
	% change	+7.5	−12	−50	−34	−4	−11.5
Financial return (%)	Ex ante	15	12	12.9	10.8	10.4	8
	Ex post	15	7	2,9	6.5	n.a.	n.a.
Social return (%)	Ex ante	28	23.6	20.3	18.5	15.4	12.2
	Ex post	30	12	5	13.8	n.a.	n.a.

Source: Conseil Général des Pont et Chaussées (2006) Annex 1

Table 11.12 Breakeven demand volumes in the first year (m passengers) under varying assumptions

Construction cost (£k per km)	Rate of interest (%)	Value of time saved (euros)	% generated traffic (%)	Rate of benefit growth (%)	Breakeven volume (m passengers)
12	3	45	50	4	3.0
12	3	30	50	4	4.5
30	3	45	50	4	7.1
12	3	45	30	3	4.3
12	5	45	50	4	4.4
30	5	30	30	3	19.2
20	5	45	30	3	8.8

A reduction of the value of time savings to a more typical level will increase the breakeven volume to 4.5 million; lower benefit growth and levels of generated traffic will take the result to 4.3 million; an increase in the rate of discount to 5 per cent would take the value to 4.4 million. In other words, it appears to be the construction cost that is the key determinant of the breakeven volume of traffic; all the other adjustments considered have similar, smaller, impacts. All of these adjustments together would increase the breakeven volume to 19.2 million trips per annum, and even worse scenarios can of course be identified. On the other hand, a more modest increase of capital costs to 20 million euros, with a high value of time savings but a discount rate of 5 per cent, 30 per cent generated traffic and a 3 per cent annual growth in benefits leads to a breakeven volume of 9m. This represents a realistic breakeven volume for a completely new self-contained high-speed line under reasonably favourable circumstances.

These representative breakeven volumes ignore any net environmental benefits, but as explained previously, there are reasons to expect these to be small. The numbers also ignore any network benefits in terms of reduced congestion on road and air, and also within the rail sector, and wider economic benefits. These can be small under some circumstances and larger under others. If these effects are significant then HSR may be justified at lower volumes.

Conclusions

Investment in HSR is expensive. The key benefits are typically revenue, time savings for business and leisure travel, better reliability, more comfortable journeys with the ability to use the time spent travelling and increased rail capacity. Most successful applications of high-speed rail seem to arise when there is both a need for more rail capacity and a commercial need for higher speeds. It seems difficult to justify building a new line solely for purposes of increased speed unless traffic volumes are very large, but when a new line is to be built, the marginal cost of higher speed may be justified; conversely the benefits of higher speed may help to make the case for more capacity. It follows from the above that appraisal of HSR will need to include assessment of the released capacity benefits for freight, local and regional passenger services and the changes in service levels on the conventional lines. It also follows that the case for HSR is often heavily dependent both on future economic growth and on the assumption that demand for long-distance passenger and freight transport will continue to increase. If long-run economic recession, or environmental constraints prevent this from occurring then far less new HSR will be justified than in a 'business as usual' scenario. Already the current recession will have at least delayed the case for some new lines, although increased government spending in some countries to reflate the economy may have the opposite effect.

It is important to consider network effects. The benefits of a high-speed line may be maximized by locating it where it may carry traffic to a wide number of destinations using existing tracks beyond the end of the high-speed line, whilst extensions to an existing network lead to greater benefits than isolated new lines by attracting increased traffic to the network as a whole. Obviously this implies technical compatibility between HSR and existing rail as a prime requirement.

High-speed rail is more successful at competing with air than the car, and there is evidence for the widely quoted 3-hour rail journey time threshold. Where rail journey times can be brought close to or below 3 hours, HSR can be expected to take a major share of origin-destination aviation markets, although it achieves a significant market share up to around 4 hours. However, the evidence relates to countries with dense cities, where well located city rail terminals are more convenient for most passengers than are airports, and shorter rail journey times may be needed to compete with air where cities are less dense, as in the United States. On the other hand, rail has advantages in terms of comfort and reliability which may yield benefits even when door-to-door journey times are similar to or somewhat longer than air. A key area for further research is the value of business travel time for long distance journeys, and how it varies with mode and circumstances such as waiting at airports.

Of the measured external benefits of HSR investment, reduced congestion is the most significant. Relief of road congestion is, however, unlikely to be a major part of the case for high-speed rail except where chronic congestion is spread throughout the day along much of the route. Relief of airport capacity through transfer of domestic legs from air to rail is potentially more important where capacity is scarce and expansion is difficult, costly, and has a serious environmental impact, as in the case of Heathrow. However, according to the HS2 study, even if HS2 served Heathrow directly, the number of slots released by diversion of domestic traffic from air to rail would be relatively small (HS2 Ltd 2009). Obviously in circumstances such as in California, where air currently has a high market share for short-haul trips, such benefits may be very much greater.

Environmental benefits are unlikely to be a significant part of the case for high-speed rail when all relevant factors are considered, but nor are they a strong argument against it provided that high load factors can be achieved and the infrastructure itself can be accommodated without excessive environmental damage. Regarding global warming, key factors are the extent to which the scheme diverts traffic from air, as opposed to conventional rail, and the source of primary energy used to generate the electricity.

The issue of wider economic benefits remains one of the hardest to tackle. Existing evidence tends to suggest that such benefits will not be large except where HSR has a major role in integrating labour markets, but the evidence is inadequate and this is an important area for further research.

Since most of the benefits of a high-speed rail line vary with the volume of traffic, and most of the costs are fixed, generally the higher the volume of passengers the more favourable the case for high-speed rail. The breakeven volume of passengers to justify a new high-speed line is very variable with circumstances, ranging from 3m to 19.2m in the first year of operation under possible assumptions examined, but typically even under favourable conditions at least 9m passengers per annum will be needed. Whilst it appears that all the French high-speed lines comfortably exceeded this volume, it is clear that some proposals are being developed where traffic is very much less dense. The most important variable in determining the breakeven volume is the construction cost, which varies enormously according to circumstances.

Acknowledgements

This paper draws on an earlier paper written for a conference held by the International Transport Forum in Madrid in October 2009. I wish to acknowledge helpful comments on an earlier draft by Peter Mackie, Stephen Perkins, Emile Quinet, Ginés de Rus and Tom Worsley. Responsibility for the final version is of course solely my own.

References

Abrantes, PAL and Wardman, M, 2011, 'Meta-analysis of UK values of travel time: an update', *Transportation Research A*, pp. 1–17.

Ahlfeldt, G, 2009, *The train has left the station: Do markets value intra-city access to inter-city rail connections?* University of Hamburg, http://mpra.ub.uni-muenchen.de/13900/ Accessed 1 August 2016.

Ahlfeldt, G and Feddersen, A, 2009, 'From periphery to core: economic adjustments to high speed rail', *MPRA Paper*, No. 25106, University Library, Munich.

Atkins, 2002, *High Speed Line Study: HSL Business Case*, London.

Beltran, A, 1993, 'SNCF and the development of high-speed trains', in Whitelegg, J, Flink, T and Hulten, S (eds.), *High Speed Trains: Fast Tracks to the Future*, Leeds: Leading Edge Press, pp. 30–37.

Bonnafous, A, 1987, 'The regional impact of the TGV', *Transportation*, Vol. 14, pp. 127–137.

Brand, D *et al.*, 2001, *Application of benefit-cost analysis to the proposed California high speed rail system*, Transportation Research Record.

Brocker, J *et al.*, 2004, *IASON deliverable 6*.

Bullock, R G, Jin, Y, Ollivier, GP, Zhou, N, 2014, 'High-speed railways in China: a look at traffic', *China transport topics*, No 11, Washington, DC: World Bank Group. http://documents.worldbank.org/curated/en/2014/12/23031378/high-speed-railways-china-look-traffic Accessed 1 August 2016.

Campos, J and Gagnepain P, 2009, 'Measuring the intermodal effects of high speed rail', in G de Rus (ed.), *Economic Analysis of High Speed Rail in Europe*, Fundación BBVA, Madrid.

Cascetta, E, Pagliara, F, Brancaccio, V and Preston, J, 2010, 'Evaluating regeneration impacts of the Channel Tunnel Rail Link', Paper given at the 12th World Conference on Transport Research, July 11–15, Lisbon, Portugal.

CE Delft, 2003, 'To shift or not to shift, that's the question', *The environmental performance of the principal modes of freight and passenger transport in the policymaking context*. Delft.

CE Delft, 2008, *Handbook on Estimation of External Costs in the Transport Sector, Deliverable 1 of the Impact project prepared for the European Commission (DG TREN) in association with INFRAS*, Fraunhofer Gesellschaft – ISI and University of Gdansk, Delft.

Conseil General des Ponts et Chaussees, 2006, *Les Bilans LOTI des LGV Nord Europe et Interconnexion Ile de France* http://www.sncf-reseau.fr/en/node/2284 Accessed 1 August 2016.

COST 318, 1998, *Interaction between High Speed Rail and Air Passenger Transport*, European Commission: Directorate General of Transport.

de Rus, G, 2012, *Economic evaluation of the high speed rail*, undertaken for The Expert Group on Environmental Studies (Ministry of Finance, Sweden).

de Rus, G and Nash, CA, 2009, 'In what circumstances is investment in HSR worthwhile?' in G de Rus (ed.), *Economic Analysis of High Speed Rail in Europe*, Fundación BBVA, Madrid.

de Rus, G and Nombela, G, 2007, 'Is investment in high speed rail socially profitable?' *Journal of Transport Economics and Policy* 41(1), 3–23.

Flyvbjerg, B, Skamris Holm, MK and Buhl, SL, 2003, 'How common and how large are cost overruns in transport infrastructure projects?' *Transport Reviews*, Vol. 23, pp. 71–88.

Gibson, S, Cooper, G and Ball, B, 2002, 'Capacity charges on the UK rail network', *Journal of Transport Economics and Policy*, Vol. 36, No. 2, pp. 341–354.

Giuntini, A, 1993, 'High speed trains in Italy', in Whitelegg, J, Flink, T and Hulten, S (eds.), *High Speed Trains: Fast Tracks to the Future*, Leeds: Leading Edge Press, pp. 55–65.

Gómez-Mendoza, A, 1993, 'History and the AVE', in Whitelegg, J, Flink, T and Hulten, S (eds.), *High Speed Trains: Fast Tracks to the Future*, Leeds: Leading Edge Press, pp. 48–54.

GRACE, 2005, *Generalisation of Research on Accounts and Cost Estimation. European Commission Project under the Transport RTD of the 7th Framework Programme*, Institute for Transport Studies, University of Leeds. Deliverable 7.

Graham, DJ, 2005, *Wider Economic Benefits of Transport Improvements: Link Between Agglomeration and Productivity*, Imperial College, London.

Harman, R, 2006, *High Speed Trains and the Development and Regeneration of Cities*, report for Greengauge 21.

Hensher, DA, 1977, *Value of Business Travel Time*, Pergamon Press, Oxford.

HS2 Ltd, 2009, *High Speed Rail London to the West Midlands and Beyond*, London.

Kluhspies, J, 2010, *Prospects and Limitations of High-speed Ground Transportation Systems: the Maglev Option*, Paper given at the 5th International Symposium on Networks for Mobility, Stuttgart, September 30–October 1.

Kroes, E, 2000, *Air-Rail Substitution in the Netherlands*, Hague Consulting Group.

Laird, JJ, Nellthorp, J and Mackie, PJ, 2005, 'Network effects and total economic impact in transport appraisal', *Transport Policy*, Vol. 12, pp. 537–544.

Lyons, G, Jain, J and Holley, D, 2007, 'The use of travel time by rail passengers in Great Britain', *Transportation Research Part A*, Vol. 41, pp. 107–120.

Marks, P, Fowkes, AS and Nash CA, 1986, 'Valuing long distance business travel time savings for evaluation: a methodological review and application', PTRC Summer Annual Meeting.

Matsuda, M, 1993, 'Shinkansen: The japanese dream', in Whitelegg, J, Flink, T and Hulten, S (eds.), *High Speed Trains: Fast Tracks to the Future*, Leeds: Leading Edge Press, pp. 111–120.

Mohring, H, 1976, *Transportation Economics*, Ballinger Publishing, Cambridge MA.

National Audit Office, 2001, *The Channel Tunnel Rail Link*, London.

Network Rail, 2009a, *Comparing the environmental impact of conventional and high speed rail*, Available from http://www.networkrail.co.uk/newlinesprogramme/ Accessed 1 August 2016.

Network Rail, 2009b, *New lines programme strategic business case*, Available from http://www.networkrail.co.uk/newlinesprogramme/ Accessed 1 August 2016

Office of Rail Regulation (ORR), 2009, *National Rail Trends 2009–10 Yearbook*, London.

Oosterhaven, J and Elhorst, JP, 2003, 'Indirect economic benefits of transport infrastructure investments', in Dullaert *et al.*, *Across the Border: Building on a Quarter Century of Transport Research in the Benelux*, Antwerp, de Boeck.

Pagliara, F *et al.*, 2010, 'High speed rail accessibility impact on property prices: evidence from St Pancras International Station in London', XVI PANAM July 2010.

Polino, M-N, 1993, 'The TGV since 1976', in Whitelegg, J, Flink, T and Hulten, S (eds.), *High Speed Trains: Fast Tracks to the Future*, Leeds: Leading Edge Press, pp. 38–47.

Preston, J and Wall, G, 2008, 'The ex-ante and ex-post economic and social impacts of the introduction of high speed trains in south east England', *Planning, Practice and Research*, Vol. 23, No. 3, pp. 403–422.

SACTRA (Standing Advisory Committee on Trunk Road Appraisal), 1999, *Transport and the Economy*, London.

Steer Davies Gleave, 2004, *High Speed Rail: International Comparisons, Final report*, Commission for Integrated Transport.

Steer Davies Gleave, 2006, *Air and Rail Competition and Complementarity, Final report*, European Commission, DGTREN.

Union Internationales des Chemins de Fer, 2012, *High Speed Rail. Fast Track to Sustainable Mobility*, UIC, Paris.

Vickerman R, 2009, 'Indirect and wider economic impacts of high speed rail', in G de Rus (ed.), *Economic Analysis of High Speed Rail in Europe*, Fundación BBVA, Madrid.

Wardman, M, 2001, 'A review of British evidence on time and service quality', *Transportation Research E*, Vol. 37, No. 2, pp. 107–128.

Wardman, M, 2004, 'Public transport values of time', *Transport Policy*, Vol. 11, pp. 363–377.

Wilken, D, 2000, 'Areas and limits of competition between high speed rail and air', Paper presented at the Think-Up Project Workshop, Dresden.

Part II
California's bold HSR adventure

Transforming transport culture in America?

12 Background on high-speed rail in California

Elizabeth Deakin

Over the last half century, a number of proposals have been floated to build high-speed rail (HSR) in California. Some proposals aimed to connect the metropolitan areas of Northern and Southern California. Others were regional, serving heavily-used corridors in the southern part of the state or travelling eastward to connect Los Angeles with Las Vegas. Many of the proposals were never more than exploratory, while a few received serious attention from policy-makers and investors. Eventually, however, each one was shelved – until the 1990s, when concern about congested transportation infrastructure and a new wave of growth led public officials to take another look.

In the early 1990s the state established a commission to investigate the feasibility of constructing and operating an HSR system that would connect the major cities of Northern and Southern California. In 1996, the commission released its findings, which concluded that such a system would be feasible. That same year, the Legislature established a new state agency, the California High-Speed Rail Authority, and charged it with planning and designing an HSR system for the state. The Authority issued its initial plan in 2002, and the Legislature began investigating how to fund the system's construction. In 2008, California voters passed Proposition 1A, a ballot measure that provided for $9.95 billion in bond sales to support HSR. An additional $3.3 billion in federal funding was subsequently secured, and a recent state law gives the HSR project a portion of the revenues from California's greenhouse gas cap and trade auctions. However, debate continues over the feasibility and desirability of the project.

The project

The California HSR project is a complicated overlay of often contradictory political, economic, environmental and technical plans, many of which are still being worked out, even after 20 years of planning. There are both technical and political reasons for the long planning period. Project development for HSR in California poses numerous challenges. Mountain ranges surround the heavily populated coastal areas, making construction of new infrastructure costly. Earthquakes are a major hazard in the state, requiring specialized designs. Land values are high, particularly in the San Francisco Bay Area and the coastal areas of the Los Angeles mega-region. The massive Central Valley, where such cities as Sacramento, Fresno, and Bakersfield lie, is one of the most productive agricultural regions in the entire US; it's easy to build there, but it also raises issues about adverse effects on a major state and natural resource. In addition, throughout the state are climate zones where high value crops such as wine grapes and citrus thrive, as well as habitat for rare and endangered species. California cities vie for the jobs and economic development that infrastructure projects bring, but state planning law gives residents numerous opportunities to challenge the local impacts on their communities, and they frequently do so. Federal and state environmental laws require thorough review, and state law also calls for mitigation of adverse impacts. Taken together, these factors, which epitomize planning in California, make the planning and design of a massive new infrastructure project like HSR particularly challenging. They have also led to uncertainty about what is actually proposed to be built.

The California HSR project is intended to connect the three coastal metropolitan areas of California – the San Francisco Bay Area, the Los Angeles mega-region, and San Diego – which are among the wealthiest in the US, while also increasing linkages to the state capitol in Sacramento and improving accessibility for California's less affluent Central Valley cities such as Fresno, Bakersfield and Merced. HSR will not reach Sacramento or San Diego until a second phase, however, and as the project is currently conceived there are no plans to directly serve a number of other large Californian cities (see Table 12.1).

HSR is intended to increase intercity passenger capacity within the state, where growth has already put pressure on available airports and highways and another 10 million people are expected by 2050, bringing the state population to 50 million. Californians are highly mobile, but they have also opposed major airport and highway expansions mostly because of concerns about their community and environmental impacts. High-speed rail is seen as having a comparatively benign impact on the natural and built environment.

The decision was made early on to use steel wheel on rail technology (not maglev) and to design for operating speeds of up to 220 mph (350 km/h) in California's HSR project. The first phase of the system would connect Los Angeles and the San Francisco Bay Area, with interregional travel times of 3 hours or less. A second phase would add links to the San Diego and Sacramento metropolitan regions.

While the broad-brush design concept appears to be settled, the HSR plan's specifics have been contentious and the details have changed repeatedly over the years. A major debate arose over the route into the Bay Area and whether the Altamont Pass, nearer to Oakland and San Francisco, or the Pacheco Pass, nearer to San Jose, should be used. (The latter was eventually selected.) On the San Francisco Peninsula, some cities protested that the line should be underground rather than run at the surface. (Their lawsuits have so far been dismissed.) In the Central Valley, farm interests sued over property takings and reductions in access due to the line. (Some cases have been settled; others continue.) Yet elsewhere,

Table 12.1 California cities and regions and HSR proposals

Rank	City	Population	Region	Regional population	HSR phase
1	Los Angeles	3,928,864	LASA	18,679,763	I*
2	San Diego	1,381,069	San Diego MSA	3,263,431	2**
3	San Jose	1,015,785	Bay Area CSA	8,713,914	1
4	San Francisco	852,469	Bay Area CSA	8,713,914	1
5	Fresno	515,986	Fresno-Madera CSA	1,129,859	1
6	Sacramento	485,199	Sacramento CSA	2,544,026	2
7	Long Beach	473,577	LA CSA		NP
8	Oakland	413,775	Bay Area CSA		NP
9	Bakersfield	368,759	Bakersfield MSA	874,589	1
10	Anaheim	346,997	LA CSA		1
11	Santa Ana	334,909	LA CSA		2
12	Riverside	319,504	LA CSA		2
13	Stockton	302,389	Bay Area CSA		2
14	Chula Vista	260,988	San Diego MSA		2
15	Irvine	248,531	LA CSA		1
16	Fremont	228,758	Bay Area CSA		NP
17	San Bernardino	215,213	LA CSA		2
18	Modesto	209,286	Modesto-Merced CSA	806,843	2
19	Oxnard	205,437	LA CSA		NP
20	Fontana ***	204,950	LA CSA		2
33	Palmdale	158,259	LACSA		1
66	Burbank	105,366	LA CSA		1
--	Tulare / Kings County		Visalia-Porterville MSA (Tulare Co.) + Hanford-Corcoran MSA (Kings Co.)	459,863 + 150,965	Y
****	Millbrae (SFO)	22,703	Bay Area CSA		Y

Note on HSR Phase: 1= Phase 1, 2 = Phase 2, NP = not currently planned, Y = Wye proposal
* Additional stations currently under consideration for Norwalk or Fullerton and for Los Angeles International Airport (LAX) (34 million boardings in 2014)
** Other Phase 2 stations may include: East San Gabriel Valley (El Monte, West Covina or Pomona), Murrieta (riverside County), and Escondido (San Diego County)
*** Ontario International Airport vicinity
**** Millbrae is adjacent to the San Francisco International Airport (22 million boardings in 2014)

Note on abbreviations:
Bay Area CSA combines San Francisco-Oakland-Hayward, San Jose-Sunnyvale-Santa Clara, Napa, Santa Rosa, Vallejo-Fairfield, Santa Cruz-Watsonville, and Stockton-Lodi Metropolitan Statistical Areas
LA CSA combines Los Angeles-Long Beach-Anaheim, Riverside-San Bernardino-Ontario, and Oxnard-Thousand Oaks-Ventura Metropolitan Statistical Areas
Sacramento CSA combines Sacramento-Roseville-Arden-Arcade and Yuba City Metropolitan Statistical Area, and Truckee-Grass Valley Micropolitan Statistical Area

Source: US Census. City population data are 2014 estimates. Regional data are 2015 estimates. Airport boarding data from FAA.

cities have welcomed the prospect of the new system, gearing redevelopment plans to the station area in Fresno and building terminals to accommodate it in Anaheim and San Francisco.

Even though broad corridors for the system have largely been agreed upon, selection of particular alignments for each HSR section requires detailed technical studies, and alternatives identified during these studies must be subjected to additional community input and environmental review. The Authority's consultants have been directed to search for alignments that avoid or minimize environmental impacts, minimize community disruption, and at the same time provide for designs that are efficient from construction and operation perspectives. This is a tall order, and a time-consuming one; it has led to uncertainties that have been frustrating for advocates as well as opponents.

The uncertainties over routing, together with local controversies, have meant that the Authority cannot state definitively how many stations would be built and where they would be located. Early on the Authority decided on a policy preference for downtown station locations that could help support urban growth policies designed to reduce greenhouse gas emissions, consistent

Figure 12.1 California HSR Phase 1

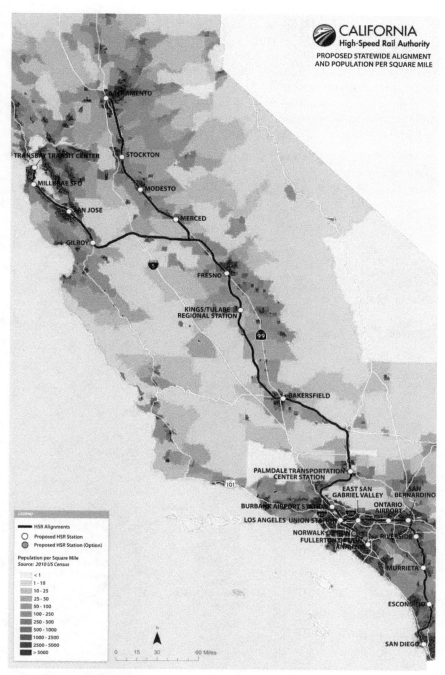

Figure 12.2 California HSR proposed route and population density

with state mandates. However, station locations require not only detailed routing decisions but also negotiations with the cities that would host the station sites. Consequently, maps have continued to show alternative routes and station locations have been tentative until quite recently, when several station agreements have been finalized.

In the current plan, Bay Area stops would be located in San Francisco, Millbrae (San Francisco International Airport), San Jose, and Gilroy. Stops in the Central Valley would include Merced, Fresno, Visalia, and Bakersfield. In the

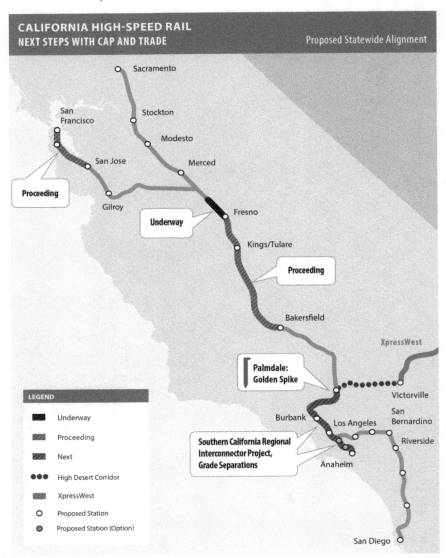

Figure 12.3 California HSR route status

greater Los Angeles region, stops would include Palmdale, San Fernando, and Los Angeles (Union Station). Additional stops at the northern and southern termini and in the Central Valley are also possibilities. At many of the stations, Amtrak and other interregional and regional rail services would provide connections, providing for HSR access via a transfer to or from another system. The current plan calls for upgrades on key links that would allow HSR to extend its reach.

When the HSR services would actually be up and running has been another sore point. The funds in hand are not enough to build the whole system, and those that are currently available come with strings attached. For example, there's a limit on how much can be spent on upgrading existing facilities to nearly-high speeds vs. building new ones that meet the full high speed criteria. The Authority must select an initial segment, buildable with the funds it can count on, that will make sense operationally (see Figure 12.3); meanwhile it is still looking for funds for full build-out. Proposals to build the initial segment in the Central Valley, between Merced and the northern reaches of the San Fernando Valley, led to charges that the new line would be a waste of money because it would fail to serve its big-city markets. A recent proposal would shift the start-up to connect Silicon Valley to the Central Valley (CHSRA 2016), where it potentially could link the jobs-rich technology centre with communities with affordable housing. The shift would delay the start of the project by several years and the larger objective of allowing a speedy trip by rail between the Bay Area and LA would be postponed until 2029.

Costs and funding

The California HSR project's cost and its financing have both been controversial. According to the CHSRA, the project is now projected to cost approximately $64.1 billion in year-of-expenditure dollars (CHSRA 2016). Capital funding to develop the high-speed rail project will come from federal, state, local and private sources, with different funding sources engaging in different development stages of the project. However, the total costs of building the project have been revised several times over the years, and the prospects for full funding remain uncertain.

Changing cost estimates have been a major issue. In its 2009 business plan, CHSRA estimated the cost of building Phase I to full HSR standards at $36.4 billion (CHSRA 2009). In the draft of the 2012 business plan, the price tag for a full HSR system design had climbed to $65.4–$74.5 billion (CHSRA 2012). The increase was attributed to costly design elements needed to traverse difficult terrain, preserve access, and protect the environment, including viaducts, tunnels, embankments, and retaining walls. The increase also reflected higher anticipated prices for construction. Faced with outcry over the price hike, the CHSRA's revised 2012 business plan dropped the full high-speed rail system option and proposed instead a blended system costing $53.4 billion to $62.3 billion. Subsequent plans showed relatively stable costs; the 2014 business plan projected costs at $67.6 billion and the 2016 draft plan's cost estimate was $64.2 billion. The cost figures are not directly comparable because they are presented in current dollars for the year of the estimate, and in some cases it is unclear whether economies have been achieved or costs have simply been put into other agencies' budgets. Nevertheless, the change in numbers illustrates the big jump in costs from the original proposal, as well as the CHSRA's subsequent efforts to hold costs down.

Some observers see the design changes to the lower-speed, blended system as a realistic step. However, the changes provoked lawsuits in which the petitioners claimed that the CHSRA plan had departed from conditions set by voters in passing the Prop 1A bond measure. The litigation wended its way through the courts over several years, and eventually the courts ruled that the CHSRA's actions were within accepted bounds of discretion (Tos v. CHSRA). However, litigation continues, challenging whether the latest plan meets voter stipulations.

The second issue is the lack of definitive funding. Early business plans projected that as much as two-thirds of the HSR system's construction funding would come from the federal government. This assumption has been widely questioned, since federal funding for rail projects has traditionally been modest and the current US Congress has been specifically unwilling to appropriate funds for HSR projects. However, a recent state law has partially filled the funding gap with a portion of the revenues from California's quarterly auctions of greenhouse-gas emissions allowances, and the CHSRA now believes that it has secured sufficient funding to construct the initial segment of the system as proposed in its 2016 draft business plan.

While capital costs for an initial usable segment may have been located, HSR systems also incur costs of operation and short-term maintenance, as well as the longer-term costs of system renewal. The system was promoted as not requiring an operating subsidy, but it is debatable whether this would be workable, especially in the early years. Consultants for the CHSRA have modelled and projected capital and operating costs on an annual basis for a 50-year time horizon, assuming the Phase I line is fully built, and have estimated cash flows (Henley and Kao 2016, Ramey 2016). They conclude that losses will occur only for the first couple of years, turning positive and generating net cash flow thereafter.

Operations and maintenance (O&M) costs are highly project-specific and reflect operating decisions as well as system design choices. While most of the cost assumptions used in the cash flow analysis are within industry norms, they are subject to uncertainties (e.g. useful life of components in actual operation). Sceptics also question the cash flow results because they depend not only on cost models but on ridership and revenue forecasts that some critics of the HSR proposal believe are wildly inflated. Much is as stake since both future public willingness to invest and prospects for attracting private partners depend on the credibility of the cost and ridership estimates.

Ridership forecasts and competing travel modes

Forecasting high-speed rail trips for California city pairs is difficult in part because HSR is a new mode for the state and in part because long-distance travel of any sort is relatively rare, so data are limited. For example, in California's most recent state-wide travel survey, over 42,000 households were asked to report all inter-regional trips they made in an 8-week period; only 68,000 trips were reported, and the majority of these were 100 miles or less. In addition, 5 per cent of the households were responsible for 25 per cent of the reported trips (Caltrans 2013). Given the scarcity of data on actual travel within a typical 'HSR range' of 200–800 km, and none on actual HSR use, planners have used a combination of methods to come up with HSR ridership forecasts, drawing upon state-wide travel survey data but also using data from air travel surveys and stated preference studies, in which participants are asked what choices they would make under various scenarios of the future. In addition, forecasting requires assumptions to be made about travel times and costs, access times, out of pocket costs, and other key variables, not only for HSR but also for the other intercity travel modes (car, air, conventional rail, bus) against which HSR will compete in the future (e.g., in 2030 or 2050). Leavitt *et al.* (1992) and Levinson *et al.* (1997) provided early and substantially differing analyses of these factors; current debates over the prospects for short-haul and low-cost airlines, airport capacity expansion, and fuel efficient and self-driving cars suggest that a wide range of analyses and assumptions are still being made.

Researchers who have examined the accuracy of forecasts for major infrastructure projects have found that overestimates of ridership are common, as are underestimates of costs; such errors have been attributed not only to forecasting difficulties and technical errors but also to 'optimism bias' and outright misrepresentations (Flyvbjerg *et al.* 2002; Flyvbjerg *et al.* 2003; Flyvbjerg 2008). The researchers advocate greater transparency in discussing assumptions and other potential sources of error, and advise the use of independent peer review to curb excesses.

The CHSRA's ridership projections have faced scrutiny by a number of groups over the years. Reviewers criticized previous ridership forecasts both for technical modelling problems and because of the assumptions made. Reviewing early forecasts, researchers at the University of California questioned the way stated preference data were used as well as assumptions and model adjustments made in the forecasting process (Brownstone *et al.* 2010). Analysts for a libertarian think tank, the Reason Foundation, concluded that both the 2008 and the 2012 CHSRA ridership projections could be as much as 200 per cent too high due to unrealistically high costs of auto operation assumed (Vranich and Cox 2013). Responding to such criticisms, the CHSRA established a technical advisory group of highly respected experts to review its forecasting methods, and responding to their advice, the modelling consultants have made major model revisions. In the view of the advisory committee, recent forecasts have been greatly improved (Koppelman 2015), and a range of forecasts is now being produced along with probabilities that each estimate will actually occur. The results, however, may offer so wide a range as to offer little assurance to decision-makers and potential investors. For example, the 2014 forecasts for 2029 ranged from 15 million annual passengers to nearly 55 million, with a median forecast of 28 million (Cambridge Systematics 2014).

Community and environmental impacts

Benefits and costs are not limited to riders and expenditures, and as is the case elsewhere, California is looking at broader impacts in evaluating HSR (de Rus and Nombela 2007). Advocates of CA HSR foresee it offering a low energy, low emissions form of intercity travel that will provide a comfortable, reliably fast ride, relieve pressures for airport expansion and highway building, create linkages that improve the economic performance of major cities and smaller ones, and offer local economic development opportunities and urban revitalization around stations. Critics retort that the energy and other resources required for new construction take years to offset, and that the effects of land takings for new right of way will be negatively felt in the local economies, as will severance impacts. From this perspective, strategies that improve the performance of existing modes without requiring significant new infrastructure expansion are a better approach. Operations improvements, use of pricing strategies to manage demand, and gradual incorporation of new technologies to increase the capacity of time-tested systems are seen as far less of an economic or community and environmental risk than investing in HSR.

Equity concerns are also at issue in California, because long-distance travel improvements are seen as mostly serving the affluent, who disproportionately make such trips, while costs are more widely distributed. Some argue that HSR will help motivate metropolitan areas to invest strategically in local transit connections and station area development, which will spread benefits more widely; others argue that spending the money on those local transportation and development projects directly would make more sense than spending it on HSR in hopes of generating positive secondary urban impacts.

The CHSRA has developed mitigation plans to offset construction and longer-term impacts and has put programmes in place to help local communities take advantage of job opportunities created by the construction of HSR in the state. The agency also is working with local and regional agencies to coordinate its investments with their transportation and urban development plans.

Looking forward

As of March 2016, the CHSRA has 110 miles of railbed under contract for design and construction and has active construction underway on portions of the Phase I route. There is a long way to go before HSR will be operating, and continued risk that challenges to the project and doubts about its performance will stop it in its tracks. Recent polls indicate that a majority of Californians support HSR, but opponents are attempting to mount ballot box challenges to its continued funding. Will the system get built from San Francisco to Los Angeles and offer high speed travel options? Will it eventually extend to Sacramento and San Diego, totalling 800 miles with up to twenty-four stations? While some observers argue that the project is a boondoggle and should be stopped, author James Fallows, an open advocate of HSR in California, asserts that this is one of a long line of bold ventures – from the Louisiana Purchase and the Panama Canal to the Interstate Highway System and new rail systems such as BART – where we have been better at noting imperfections and worrying about problems than we are at envisioning benefits (Fallows 2015). In the chapters that follow, key issues and perspectives from both sides of the debate are examined in greater detail.

References

Brownstone, D, Hansen, M and Madanat, SM, 2010, *Review of 'Bay Area/California High-Speed Rail Ridership and Revenue Forecasting Study'*. No. UCB-ITS-RR-2010-1.

California Department of Transportation, 2013, *2010–2012 California Household Travel Survey Final Report*.

Cambridge Systematics, Inc., 2014, *California High-Speed Rail 2014 Business Plan Ridership and Revenue Forecasting technical memorandum prepared for Parsons Brinckerhoff for the California High-Speed Rail Authority*, April 2014.

CHSRA 2009, Report to the Legislature, http://www.hsr.ca.gov/docs/about/business_plans/BPlan_2009_Legis_FullRpt.pdf Accessed 1 August 2016.

CHSRA 2012, California High-Speed Rail Program Revised 2012 Business Plan: Building California's Future, http://www.hsr.ca.gov/docs/about/business_plans/BPlan_2012_rpt.pdf Accessed 1 August 2016.

CHSRA, 2016, *Connecting and Transforming California: Draft 2016 Business Plan*. Feb. 18, 2016.

de Rus, G and Nombela, G, 2007, 'Is investment in high speed rail socially profitable?', *Journal of Transport Economics and Policy*, vol. 14, no. 1, pp. 3–23.

Fallows, J, 2015, 'California High-Speed Rail: A Minor End, an Important Beginning', *The Atlantic*, Jan. 6, 2015.

Federal Aviation Administration, 2015, *Calendar Year 2014 Passenger Boardings at Commercial Service Airports*, http://www.faa.gov/airports/planning_capacity/passenger_allcargo_stats/passenger/media/cy14-commercial-service-enplanements.pdf Accessed 1 August 2016.

Flyvbjerg, B, 2008, 'Curbing optimism bias and strategic misrepresentation in planning: Reference class forecasting in practice', *European Planning Studies*, vol. 16, no. 1, pp. 3–21.

Flyvbjerg, B, Bruzelius, N and Rothengatter, W, 2003, *Megaprojects and Risk: An Anatomy of Ambition*, Cambridge University Press.

Flyvbjerg, B, Holm, MS and Buhl, S, 2002, 'Underestimating costs in public works projects: Error or lie?' *Journal of the American Planning Association*, vol. 68, no. 3, pp. 279–295.

Henley, M and Kao, L, 2016, Draft 2016 Business Plan 50-Year Lifecycle Capital Cost Model Documentation, WSP/Parsons Brinckerhoff Report prepared for the California High Speed Rail Authority, February 17, 2016.

Koppelman, FS, 2015, *The Ridership Technical Advisory Panel Technical Memo: Review of progress on revenue and ridership forecasting*, December 16, 2015.

Leavitt, D, Vaca, E and Hall, P, 1992, 'High speed trains for California strategic choice. Vol. I: Comparison of technology and choice of route', *Institute of Urban and Regional Development (IURD) working paper*, no. 564, University of California at Berkeley.

Levinson, D, Mathieu, JM, Gillen, D and Kanafani, A, 1997, 'The full cost of high-speed rail: An engineering approach', *Annals of Regional Science*, vol. 31, pp. 189–215.

Ramey, K, 2016, *High, Medium, Low Cash Flows*, *Technical Supporting Document prepared by KPMG for the California High-Speed Rail Authority*, Feb. 2016.

Vranich, J and Cox, W, 2013, *California High Speed Rail: An Updated Due Diligence Report*, Reason Foundation.

13 High-speed rail and smart growth in California

Peter Calthorpe

Introduction and overview

At one time, housing, urban development and transit were co-evolving partners in city building; the urban centre and its streetcar suburbs defined a uniquely American form of metropolis. This form was at once focused on the city and decentralized around transit-rich suburban districts. It offered the best of both worlds, vital urban centres and walkable mixed-use suburbs. During the post-World War II decades, this balance was disrupted by the elimination of the streetcar systems along with the proliferation of freeways, mass-produced tract housing, and suburban shopping centres and office parks.

The 1956 Federal Highway Act, which authorized the Interstate Highway System, helped to establish a new pattern of sprawl development that came to define American communities and lifestyles for generations to come. It steered the American Dream away from small towns, streetcar suburbs, and central cities toward today's auto suburbs. The Interstate system fit the enthusiasm for autos that marked the post-war era and it created jobs, increased mobility, and generated economic growth. It also enabled, shaped and supported new patterns of development that ultimately changed America's identity – it was, in the end, much more than just an infrastructure investment.

Since the demolition of America's streetcars in the 1940s and 1950s, transit, particularly in the suburbs, has been more a safety net than a true alternative to the car. Built with the car in mind, most of our communities lack the density and urban form to support frequent or convenient transit services. Suburban destinations are too dispersed for transit to be an attractive alternative to the auto. Not surprisingly, transit's share of trips across the country today is much lower than it was in the 1960s, only carrying about 6 per cent of the work trips in the US as a whole (APTA 2015, US DOT 2015).

Meanwhile, the highway systems in most urban areas have become congested. Yet most traffic engineers now agree that we cannot build enough new freeways to significantly reduce congestion. Many areas lack the budgets or the available rights-of-way to add significant highway capacity. In addition, citizen groups in many areas have emerged to oppose highway expansion because of its negative community and environmental impacts. Not believing that a significant shift in travel behaviour is possible, some communities have limited growth. But local growth controls have often driven development farther into the regional hinterland, in many cases worsening the traffic and associated problems that the growth restrictions were trying to avoid.

Thus, a challenge of the times is how to manage urban development in a way that is compatible with a well-functioning transportation system.

In this context, it is notable that for work trips to city centres across the country, transit mode share is double the national average at 10 per cent. In metropolitan regions that have thriving city centres – Portland, Seattle, San Diego, San Francisco, New York, Washington DC, and many others – transit ridership has increased. In these places, transit is seen as essential to healthy regional growth and downtown revitalization. New rail systems have not only provided choice for commuters – a way to get around despite congestion on the highways – but have increased land values along their corridors. What's more, many of the most productive urban centres could not function without the extensive transit systems put in place over the past century. In San Francisco, 49 per cent of downtown commuters take transit; in Chicago, it is 61 per cent; and in New York City, 76 per cent. Even in smaller cities, a dense city core coupled with transit connectivity from suburban stations can attract a substantial share of commuters to transit, as evidenced by Portland, where transit carries 27 per cent of the commuters to the CBD, or San Diego and Sacramento, each of which has one in eight people getting to work downtown by transit (Pisarski 2006).

In these successful regions, a new balance is emerging between suburb and city, and between cars and other modes of transportation. By creating compact, mixed-use centres and a range of housing options for a diverse population, walking and cycling become realistic travel options and transit can thrive. Environmental impacts of transportation and urban development are reduced and natural resources are protected. Collectively, these strategies have come to be known as 'smart growth' (Kelbaugh 1989, Calthorpe 1993, Ewing and Hodder 1998). Increasing numbers of cities and towns across the United States are implementing smart growth strategies to update their communities and recalibrate travel options to match today's economics, demographics, and lifestyles.

High-speed rail (HSR) can support this new approach to urban development. It can move people efficiently between urban centres, while supporting and helping to shape urban development patterns that are consistent with a robust economy, modern lifestyles and a healthy environment. Like the Interstate Highway System in its time, high-speed rail can be more than transportation infrastructure – it can be the backbone of a new set of urban and regional development patterns and investments.

This chapter begins by discussing the benefits of the emerging smart growth approach to urban development. It then goes on to explain why smart growth is so relevant to California, presenting the results of a study of growth scenarios for 2050. Next the chapter explains how high-speed rail supports smart growth by stimulating station area development and connecting growth centres through the state. The final section summarizes the chapter.

The benefits of smart growth

Smart growth is the US term for a planning approach that seeks to build communities that provide a range of transportation, employment, and housing options, preserve and enhance natural and cultural resources, and promote a healthy environment. This is accomplished through infill development, urban renewal and redevelopment, and urban expansion at densities and in configurations that support walking, cycling and transit and promote public health (ICMA and US EPA 2015). Similar planning approaches are widely used in other countries and the strategies are frequently referred to as sustainable development, compact development, and urban intensification.

Smart growth fits well with emerging economic and demographic trends. Like many other countries, the United States has systemic forces to reckon with in the next generation: an aging population, a more diverse set of household types, and the likelihood of slow income growth for the middle class. In the 2010 Census, 15 per cent of the population was over 65; this will jump to over 21 per cent by 2040 (US Census 2011). Household structure has changed dramatically; just 20 per cent of US households are traditional families with kids, and single person households are a fast-growing demographic, accounting for nearly a third of all households in 2010. Household incomes reflect these trends as well as larger factors in the economy, such as globalization and the substitution of technology for labour. Income and wage data show that most income growth in the last decade has been concentrated in the top brackets; for the middle class, wages have been stagnating for decades (US Census 2015).

These demographic and economic factors are being reflected in increased demand for moderately priced housing, smaller units, and a growing market segment that prefers to live in or close to city and town centres where access to services is easier. These trends are likely to accelerate as more Baby Boomers (those born following WWII, 1946 to 1964, when there was a marked increase in the US birth rate) retire over the next two decades. Thus there is a need to adjust the housing stock to fit the changing populace, and to find a more frugal form of prosperity.

Smart growth strategies respond to these trends and challenges systematically, tapping into both technology and design solutions. For example, new energy efficiency technologies are making buildings more efficient to operate; more compact development layouts lead to lower land and infrastructure costs and lower housing prices. A different mix of housing types – fewer large single-family lots; more bungalows and town-homes – provides more housing choices for a more diverse population. Some of the housing types have less private space, but can be served by parks and other shared community spaces.

Smart growth also leads to fewer miles driven. Compact development patterns shorten the distances between activities, and with bike and pedestrian-friendly street designs, walking and cycling become a realistic travel option for many. Transit can operate effectively because smart growth creates centres with sufficient activity to support frequent service. Households still have cars but they also have, and use, other travel options for many trips.

Environmental benefits result from smart growth land use and transportation patterns. On the land use side, smart growth's compact forms lead to less land consumed and more farmland, habitat, and open space preserved. A smaller urban footprint results in lower development costs and fewer miles of roads, utilities, and services to build and maintain, and fewer impervious surfaces. This leads to less polluted storm runoff, and more water directed back into aquifers. More compact buildings need less energy to heat and cool, resulting in lower utility bills and lower demand for new power plants; compact buildings and development patterns also require less irrigation water and lower demand for new water supply. Once again, there is less water and air pollution and less carbon in the atmosphere with smart growth.

On the transportation side, smart growth strategies lead to less fuel consumed, less need for foreign oil supplies, less air pollution, and lower carbon emissions. Fewer vehicle miles travelled also means less congestion, lower road construction and maintenance costs, and fewer auto accidents. Health is improved by fewer accidents and cleaner air, and is reinforced by more walking and cycling. And more walking leads to more people on the streets and more vibrant and attractive communities.

In short, the good news is that social, economic, and environmental challenges have a shared solution in smart growth. Smart growth is well suited to an aging population, for whom home upkeep, yard maintenance, and driving is a growing burden, and for working families seeking lower housing, utility, and transportation bills. Smart growth helps create urban environments in which walking, cycling, and transit are competitive travel modes, and reduces vehicle-miles of travel. Both moves reduce the environmental impact of urban development and help improve public health.

The benefits of smart growth have been the subject of much debate and study. The preponderance of evidence now demonstrates that land use/transit integration does increase transit ridership, can revitalize declining neighbourhoods, and can reduce overall auto dependence and carbon emissions. Simply put: 'Research shows residents living near stations are five to six times more likely to commute via transit than are other residents in a region.' (Cervero *et al.* 2004). Other detailed studies show that compact development that is walkable, mixed use, and transit served can reduce overall vehicle miles travelled (VMT) by 25 to 40 per cent (Ewing 2008). The complex interaction of land use and travel behaviour has resulted in many new tools to model outcomes, and while specific results sometimes vary, the outcomes always affirm the positive relationships.

Smart growth and Vision California

California is the most populous state in the US, with over 39 million residents, 95 per cent of whom live in urban areas. The state is home to several of the largest corporations in the world and, were it a country, California's economy would be the world's seventh or eighth largest. Currently, the state is projected to grow to a population of nearly 50 million by 2050 (State of California Department of Finance 2014a).

California is well-known for environmental leadership. A recent example is its commitment to greenhouse gas (GHG) reduction. In 2006, California adopted landmark climate legislation, Assembly Bill (AB) 32, calling for the reduction of greenhouse gas emissions in the state to 1990 levels by 2020. Then-Governor Arnold Schwarzenegger's Executive Order S-3-05 called for an even deeper reduction by 2050, to 80 per cent below 1990 levels, and current Gov. Jerry Brown' s Executive Order B-30-15 underscored California's commitment to action, establishing a California greenhouse gas reduction target of 40 per cent below 1990 levels by 2030. The emissions reduction targets are what scientists have deemed necessary to prevent serious and irreversible harm from global warming.

To achieve these substantial emissions cuts, California is pursuing new and improved technologies and management practices for every sector of the economy: power production, buildings, industry, farming and forestry. While it is likely that the state can meet or exceed its 2020 target, the 2030 and 2050 targets remain a challenge. Consequently, in 2008 the State Legislature passed Senate Bill (SB) 375, which calls for the state's metropolitan areas to reduce GHG through changed land use patterns and improved transportation. Under SB 375, smart growth is an important strategy for reducing VMT.

To better understand how smart growth could work in California, the California Strategic Growth Council and the California High-Speed Rail Authority sponsored an investigation of alternative state-wide land-use/transportation futures for 2050 (Calthorpe Associates 2011). The study, Vision California, created and evaluated two alternative scenarios for handling 40 years of growth, to a total state population of 60 million. One alternative, dubbed 'Trend', assumed a continuation of the current development pattern dominated by low-density suburban growth dependent on freeways for trunk-line transportation. This alternative was compared with a 'Green Urban' alternative that assumed a large share of infill and compact development built around transit, with HSR connecting major sub-centres.

The Green Urban alternative assumed that 35 per cent of growth would be urban infill; 55 per cent would be formed from a more compact, mixed-use, and walkable form of suburban expansion; and only 10 per cent would be standard low-density development. In addition, the Green Urban alternative would push the auto fleet to an average 55 miles per gallon (MPG), its fuel would contain one-third less carbon, and all new buildings would be 80 per cent more efficient than today's norm. This set of assumptions does not represent a green utopia, but it is heading in that direction.

In the Green Urban alternative, large lot single-family detached homes would be a smaller share of the state's housing supply, declining from 40 per cent of the total today to 30 per cent in 2050. The market share of small-lot homes and bungalows would increase slightly, and town-homes would double to 16 per cent. Multifamily flats, condos, and apartments would remain the same share of the market, comprising about a third of the housing in the state. Given current trends, this is a reasonable shift, reflecting market realities while also making the housing stock more diverse and affordable.

The analysis calculated the amount of land required in the two scenarios and drew upon the best available research and empirical evidence on the relationship between development patterns and demand for public services. Rates of land consumption by land development category were based on analyses of urbanized land within existing communities in California, and calibrated with analyses of historical changes in land cover/urbanization per California Farmland Mapping and Monitoring Program (FMMP) data (http://www.conservation.ca.gov/dlrp/fmmp). The analysis showed that the quantity of land needed to accommodate the next 40 years of growth was reduced 75 per cent by the Green Urban alternative, from more than 5,600 square miles in the Trend future to only 1,500 square miles. By comparison, the state's current developed area is 5,300 square miles. This difference would save up to 900 square miles of farmland in the highly productive Central Valley, as well as open space in the coastal regions of the state.

The more compact future in the Green Urban alternative would mean smaller lots to irrigate, saving an average of 3.4 million acre-feet (around 4,000 Gl) of water per year – enough to fill the San Francisco Bay annually or to irrigate 6.5 million acres (2.6 million hectares) of farmland.[1] Less developed land also translates to fewer miles of infrastructure to build and maintain. The cumulative savings to 2050 were estimated to be around $47 billion for the state, or $6,500 for each new household, including one-time capital costs as well as ongoing costs for operations and maintenance. In addition, the Green Urban future would cost less for police and fire services, as coverage areas would be smaller.

In the Green Urban future, auto dependence would drop dramatically – in fact, average vehicle miles travelled throughout the state would be reduced 40 per cent, to 18,000 miles per household, from a Trend projection of 28,600 where outward expansion and longer trips were anticipated. Closer destinations, better transit service, and more walkable neighbourhoods all contribute to this significant shift. Households would still have cars, but somewhat fewer would have second and third cars, and the cars would be more efficient and would be used less.

The implications of this reduction in auto use are far-reaching. In terms of congestion, it is the equivalent of taking 18.6 million cars off the road (Research and Innovative Technology Administration 2006). There would be fewer roads and parking lots built, less land covered with impervious surface, and less runoff water to be cleaned and stored. In fact, the need for new freeways and highways would be reduced by 4,700 lane-miles, a saving of around $400 billion for the state.

Less driving means fewer accidents, in this scenario potentially saving around 3,100 lives and $5 billion in associated hospital costs per year.[2] Less driving means less air pollution and a lower incidence of respiratory diseases (US Environmental Protection Agency 2008). More walking means healthier bodies and less obesity, affecting diabetes rates and all of the associated health costs (Bassett *et al.* 2008).

Significantly, the Green Urban alternative comes very close to achieving the targeted level of carbon reductions. When the savings in vehicle miles travelled are combined with low-carbon/high-MPG cars, emissions from transportation are reduced by close to 12 per cent compared to today's levels, despite the 50 per cent increase in population assumed. New buildings would be far more efficient and compact, would use far less energy, cost less to operate, and emit fewer carbon emissions than their counterparts today; however, since most buildings would predate new standards, the improvement is not enough to achieve the building sector's proportionate share of reductions (which could come from building retrofit programmes, however).

The average household would save money in the Green Urban scenario compared to the Trend alternative. Utility bills, outdoor watering bills, and vehicle operating costs would all be lower. Total savings could amount to several thousand dollars.

The actual implementation of a smart growth alternative would likely differ from the one tested in the Vision California study; for one thing, under SB 375 each metropolitan region can devise its own way forward, and their plans to date show considerable variation. In addition, long term forecasts of population growth rates, energy prices, and technologies available are unavoidably speculative. Nevertheless, the two alternatives illustrate the sorts of choices that would need to be made if California is to meet its GHG reduction goals. The state will need to make use of all of the strategies within reach: the technologies employed, the kinds of homes built, the ways people travel, and the kinds of communities they inhabit. The key will be designing the right mix of strategies, taking a 'whole systems' approach.

The relevance of HSR

California's high-speed rail system, planned to eventually stretch over 500 miles, would connect the major urban areas of the state's north and south and also link to smaller urban centres in the Central Valley. The HSR system would offer a competitive alternative to driving or flying between the connected centres. But significantly, it would also provide impetus for enhanced local transit systems as well as urban revitalization and other market-wise development opportunities. Thus, HSR is a complement to – indeed, a catalyst for – the smart growth plans being developed across the state under SB 375.

HSR is relevant to urban planning because each HSR station offers economic opportunities both inside the station and in the blocks around the station. Cafes, restaurants, shops selling reading materials and traveller conveniences, transportation services, hotels and other lodging, and tourist agencies are some of the enterprises that thrive around downtown rail stations and would be supported by traffic to and from HSR. Existing businesses could increase their sales; new businesses could be established. Major rail stations in other parts of the US and HSR station areas in other countries offer examples that could inform California cities and perhaps inspire them (Nakamura and Ueda 1989, Nuworsoo and Deakin 2009, Bertolini 2008, Bertolini *et al.* 2012). In addition, public improvements around station areas – to transit infrastructure, sidewalks, streetscape, and more – could not only complement the HSR station but also add value to the larger station area (Nuworsoo and Deakin 2009, Loukaitou-Sideris 2013). The prospects for such station area development depend on local governments' willingness to accommodate private initiatives and in some cases to partner with them through complementary public investments.

HSR is relevant to local regional transit planning because convenient access to HSR will be a major determinant of travellers' willingness to use it rather than drive or fly to their destination; good local and regional transit access can be a major factor in HSR's success (Nuworsoo and Deakin 2009). At the same time, by linking HSR to regional transit systems, HSR would contribute riders to those transit systems, adding to their performance statistics. Linkage to HSR could also provide impetus for improving local systems and services so that long distance passengers could reach their destinations seamlessly. HSR station locations with direct transit access have been among the most successful in Europe and Asia.

Transit linkages to HSR could deliver benefits over large areas, especially in the two major markets, Los Angeles and the Bay Area. Those two large regions with their numerous sub-centres would benefit if in addition to taking HSR long distance, transit connections could be made at the origin and destination ends as well. In Southern California alone, HSR's twelve stations would link with about 2,200 miles of local and regional transit with 200 stations. In the Bay Area, the rail connection between Silicon Valley and San Francisco would finally be expanded and improved, and connections would be made to San Francisco Muni, the Bay Area Rapid Transit (BART) rail system, and numerous other local and regional bus and rail services through the Transbay Terminal. These connections open up the possibility that HSR plus transit could be just as fast as air plus car or taxi for many trips between the two metropolitan regions.

HSR would provide a boost to economic development in ways that support smart growth. With HSR stations planned for downtowns rather than bypassing them, HSR will support city centres and provide activity that could stimulate new commercial development downtown. While most HSR trips will be interregional, in Los Angeles and the Bay Area, some of the longer trips between regional sub-centres are likely to also benefit from the fast train service. In the Central Valley, cities and towns would be linked to the coast in ways that offer much-needed economic development opportunities.

In short, HSR can provide important value to the state's emerging growth plans, both in the HSR station areas and through the enhanced regional and interregional linkages provided. Building from walkable neighbourhoods linked by convenient feeder services to regional transit lines, HSR completes the connections by linking all the regional systems throughout the state. Once the transit investments are committed and land use policies are updated, the two can co-evolve over time, with the transit justifying the higher development values and densities and with the increased densities enhancing ridership. HSR plays a key role by inspiring downtown investments and expanding the destinations reachable by transit. A virtuous cycle is triggered.

Conclusions

This chapter has explained how the demographic, economic, and environmental situation in the State of California makes smart growth strategies consistent with market trends as well as with public policies. By coordinating land use and transportation to deliver more compact, walkable, cyclable, transit-friendly communities, it is possible to deliver housing and transportation systems that match the needs of growing market segments, expanding the range of available choices while reducing development's impact on the environment. The chapter summarized findings from Vision California, a study that compared a smart growth development strategy with trends extended, and found that the smart growth strategy provided important benefits in reduced congestion, lower levels of air and water pollution, and reduced greenhouse gas emissions, with attendant cost savings to government and to consumers. High-speed rail contributes to such a growth strategy by creating development opportunities around downtown station areas and by conveniently connecting urban centres and their transit systems throughout the state.

The preponderance of research supports the conclusion that smart growth delivers transportation and housing benefits, though specific results depend on many factors, including zoning, public investments, local market factors, and the like. There is on-the-ground evidence that both cities and suburbs have benefitted from well-designed transportation-land development plans. The East and Westside light rail lines in Portland have attracted over $2.4 billion in investment within walking distance of their stations (TriMet 2006). In addition, Portland's new $73 million streetcar line through the immensely successful Pearl District has resulted in $2.3 billion in private investments (Center for Clean Air Policy 2009). In Arlington, Virginia, the county invested $100 million to pay for enhancing Metrorail's location, unlocking $8.8 billion in private investment (Arrington and Nikolic 2009). Reconnecting America, a non-profit research centre focused on transit, concludes that every dollar of public investment in transit leverages $31 in private investment (Ohland and Poticha 2007).

Urban form has always configured itself around transportation systems and innovations. From foot to horse through rail to car, our cities have scaled themselves as much to transportation technology as to culture. Today we are rediscovering some of the timeless qualities of our historic urban forms and updating them to contemporary situations. The same can be true for our transit systems. High-speed rail has a role to play in transforming the transportation technology that joins together urban centres and links their transit networks. The HSR connection can help support a transition to an urban pattern and lifestyle that is environmentally sustainable, affordable to the middle class, and constructive to the economy.

Notes

1   San Francisco Bay estimate based on Ritter and Kofoid (1918); agricultural data from Economic Research Service (2010).
2   Bureau of Transportation Statistics, 'National Transportation Statistics 2009' (US Department of Transportation 2009), table 2-1. The fatality rate per mile travelled is assumed to hold consistent from 2009 until 2050. Hospital costs data from National Highway Traffic Safety Administration, 'The Economic Impact of Motor Vehicle Crashes 2000,' (US Department of Transportation 2002), 60.

References

American Public Transit Association (APTA), 2015, *Transit Fact Book. Appendix A. Historical Tables*, Washington, DC, http://www.apta.com/resources/statistics/Documents/FactBook/2015-APTA-Fact-Book-Appendix-A.pdf Accessed 1 August 2016.

Arrington, GB and Nikolic, S, 2009, 'Turning the "D" in TOD into Dollars,' *Seattle Daily Journal of Commerce*, May 29, 2009.

Bassett, DR Jr, Pucher, J, Buehler, R, Thompson, DL, Crouter, SE, 2008, 'Walking, Cycling, and Obesity Rates in Europe, North America, and Australia,' *Journal of Physical Activity and Health*, vol. 5, no. 6, pp. 795–814.

Bertolini, L, 2008, 'Station areas as nodes and places in urban networks: An analytical tool and alternative development strategies,' *Railway Development*, Physica-Verlag HD, 2008, pp. 35–57.

Bertolini, L, Curtis, C, Renne, J, 2012, 'Station Area Projects in Europe and Beyond: Towards Transit Oriented Development?', *Built Environment*, vol. 38, no. 1, pp. 31–50.

California Farmland Mapping and Monitoring Program (FMMP). http://www.conservation.ca.gov/dlrp/fmmp Accessed 1 August 2016.

Calthorpe Associates, 2011, *Vision California*, Berkeley, CA. Final report is available at www.calthorpeanalytics.com Accessed 1 August 2016.

Calthorpe, P, 1993, *The Next American Metropolis: Ecology, Community, and the American Dream*, Princeton Architectural Press.

Center for Clean Air Policy, 2009, *Cost-effective GHG Reductions through Smart Growth and Improved Transportation Choices: Executive Summary*, Washington, DC: Center for Clean Air Policy.

Cervero, R, 2004. *Transit-oriented Development in the United States: Experiences, Challenges, and Prospects*, Transportation Research Board.

Ewing, R, 2008, *Growing Cooler*, Washington, DC: Urban Land Institute.

Ewing, RH and Hodder, R, 1998, *Best Development Practices: A Primer for Smart Growth*, Washington, DC, USA: Smart Growth Network.

ICMA and US EPA, 2006, *This is Smart Growth*. https://www.epa.gov/sites/production/files/2014-04/documents/this-is-smart-growth.pdf Accessed 31 October 2016.

Kelbaugh, D, 1989, *The Pedestrian Pocket Book: A New Suburban Design Strategy*, Princeton Architectural Press in association with the University of Washington.

Loukaitou-Sideris, A, 2013, 'New Rail Hubs Along High-Speed Rail Corridor in California: Urban Design Challenges,' *Transportation Research Record: Journal of the Transportation Research Board*, vol. 2350, pp. 1–8.

Nakamura, H and Ueda, T, 1989, 'The Impacts of the Shinkansen on Regional Development,' *The Fifth World Conference on Transport Research*, Yokohama, Vol. III.

Nuworsoo, C and Deakin, E, 2009, 'Transforming High-speed Rail Stations to Major Activity Hubs: Lessons for California,' *Proceedings of the 2009 Transportation Research Board 88th Annual Meeting*, p. 44.

Ohland, G and Poticha, S, eds., 2007, *Street Smart: Streetcars and Cities in the Twenty-first Century*, Oakland, CA: Reconnecting America.

Pisarski, A, 2006, *Commuting in America III: The third national report on commuting patterns and trends (No. 550)*, Transportation Research Board.

Research and Innovative Technology Administration (RITA), 2006, 'Table 5-3: Highway Vehicle-Miles Traveled (VMT),' *State Transportation Statistics 2006*, Bureau of Transportation Statistics.

Ritter, WE, Kofoid, CA, eds., 1918, *University of California Publications in Zoology*, vol. 14, Berkeley: University of California Press.

State of California Department of Finance (CA DOF), 2014a, *Report P-1 (Total Population): State and County Population Projections, 2010–2060*, Sacramento, California.

TriMet, 2006, *At Work in the Field of Dreams: Light Rail and Smart Growth in Portland*, Portland, OR: TriMet.

US Census, 2011, *Changing American Households*, Nov. 4, 2011.

US Census, 2015, *Income and Poverty in the United States*, Sep. 2015.

US Department of Transportation, Bureau of Transportation Statistics, 2015, *National Transportation Statistics Annual Report 2015*.

US Economic Research Service, 2010, *Western Irrigated Agriculture*, US Department of Agriculture, http://www.ers.usda.gov/Data/WesternIrrigation/ Accessed 1 August 2016.

US Environmental Protection Agency (EPA), 2008, *National Air Quality: Status and Trends through 2007*, Research Triangle Park, NC: EPA.

14 Institutional evolution and the politics of planning HSR in California

Blas Luis Pérez Henríquez and Elizabeth Deakin

'Spain can build it. China can build it. France can build it. Germany can build it. England can build it. Japan can build it. But oh, we can't build it. No, we can build more airport runways, more freeways over the next 50 years. That's twice as expensive. So I'm not saying it's cheap; I'm just saying it's cheaper than the alternative, and it's a hell of a lot better.'

Edmund G. 'Jerry' Brown, Governor of California (2012)

Introduction and analysis framework

California's transportation institutions are under legislative mandate to improve their environmental performance while providing the transport infrastructure and services needed to support the state's growing population and its dynamic and expanding economy. In an era of tight budgets and scepticism about government, moving toward greater sustainability is stressing the governmental structures set up to deliver transportation systems, which for over a century have primarily served a car-centric development model. Today that model is increasingly questioned (e.g., Hickman and Banister 2014). However, restructuring transportation institutions and establishing a financing system to deliver a more diversified, well-integrated, inter-modal transport system has proven to be a significant challenge for the state. Adding high-speed rail (HSR) into the mix increases the challenge. While HSR is no longer a new mode by world standards, it is new for California and except for the 'near'-high speed stretches of Acela service in the Northeast Corridor, there is no experience with HSR in the United States on which to draw. Thus HSR is an innovation in the California context.

California, like others before it, is therefore learning-by-doing with HSR, and its ambitions are expansive. If carried out as proposed, the CA HSR would be the largest infrastructure investment in the state and one of the largest in the nation. Moreover, supporters expect that HSR will be a transformational investment that will not only rebalance intercity travel toward more sustainable mode choices, but also trigger smarter urban development. Not surprisingly, such bold claims have led to equally bold criticisms. The project's opponents scoff at its supporters' expectations, arguing that the projected ridership of HSR does not justify its large public investment and doubting that its land use impacts will be positive ones.

By any account, CA HSR project's planning and decision-making has been complex. This is not unusual for a project of its size; in a democratic society any major public investment has to negotiate many interests, represented by an array of stakeholders. Moreover, it is predictable that decision-makers are pressed by those who have interests at stake regarding whether and how HSR should progress. Some would benefit from the status quo, while others would benefit from the proposed plans for HSR and still others from adjustments to the plans. Some are ideologically in favour of rail projects while others are ideologically opposed. Some may simply benefit from participating in the planning and design of the project (or in challenges to it) whether or not it proceeds. The specifics of the HSR project have been in flux, and how to pay for its construction remains uncertain, with only a fraction of the funding needed for the Phase I system identified. The fact that planning has now gone on for decades without finally resolving routing or financing issues adds to the uncertainties about the project. This complex decision field is not an easy one for political leaders and public administrators to navigate. California's environmental review process, which gives aggrieved stakeholders a venue for litigation over questions of procedure as well as substantive environmental issues, further adds to the complexities.

This chapter considers key aspects of the institutional environment and organizational arrangements (North 1990) that have shaped and will continue to influence the planning, management and execution of the high-speed rail project in California. In particular, the chapter considers legal ground rules and political positions that have set the context for HSR implementation. The analysis is grounded in the literature on governance and is based on a critical review of public documents, websites, and media reports, drawing as well as from twenty-five interviews with key stakeholders, conducted by the authors in 2014–2016. Assessing this information under the interdisciplinary lens of policy analysis, and borrowing from the New Institutional Economics, the chapter aims to offer insights on how the California political economy has shaped its HSR project.

Several threads of research on public policy and decision-making inform the analysis set forth in this chapter. Neustadt and May (1986) show that history can inform decisions today, but care must be taken to make sure that the analogies drawn are apt. From the experiences of other countries, we know that planning and implementing HSR has often taken decades, and that financing has been a challenge for many HSR systems. California history has also influenced the HSR project, even though the technology is new to the state. In particular, elements of the legislation establishing the California High Speed Rail Authority (CHSRA) and Proposition 1A, the state bond measure providing partial funding, reflect lessons learned from previous transportation projects and illuminate a desire to avoid making the same mistakes that plagued those projects. Whether the right analogies were drawn remains an important question.

Organizational theorists and institutional economists assert that public administrators need to understand the context in which institutions emerge and function in order to understand the strengths and limitations of different institutional arrangements; they point out that organizational performance is path dependent (history matters) and influenced by leadership and other stakeholders (people matter), as well as by institutional arrangements and ecosystems (Williamson 1975; Ostrom, Cox and Schlager 2014). By reviewing the legislative expectations established for planning the CA HSR system, it is the intent of this chapter to illuminate how early decisions have shaped both organizational behaviour and the results to date. Accordingly, the following section focuses on the legislative history and related processes that have governed and in many ways delimited the development of HSR in California. Section three then turns to the role of the governor in offering leadership for the project and (depending on the preferences of the office holder) in shaping, constraining, or supporting HSR development through the budgetary process. The final section comments on lessons that can be drawn from the analysis.

History matters: understanding the legislative and political constraints on HSR in California

Chapter 12 has provided background information on California and the HSR system and that material will not be repeated here. Instead, this section will take a closer look at the factors that led to the creation of an independent government agency for high-speed rail planning and at the same time established a number of constraints on its actions.

While high-speed rail had been discussed in California since the 1960s, California began the current round of HSR planning in the 1990s, when the Intercity High-Speed Rail Commission was created to determine the feasibility of an HSR system spanning the state. The Commission, staffed by Caltrans with consultant assistance, investigated the financial, engineering and environmental issues that would be posed in building HSR in alternative corridors, but did not attempt to design proposed routes or determine station locations. In 1996, the Commission issued a report that concluded that HSR was feasible in California (IHSRC 1996). Responding to the Commission's report, in that same year the California Legislature created the California High Speed Rail Authority (CHSRA) to carry the work of the Commission forward.

Even though the 1996 report was preliminary, by the time it had been issued the proposal for California HSR had already garnered supporters and detractors, and academics had begun to produce assessments of its pros and cons, including its likely costs, its impacts on alternative intercity modes, and its effects on territorial development, economic performance, and environmental quality. (See, e.g., Hall and Banister 1993; Leavitt et al. 1992a, 1992b; Leavitt et al. 1994; Sands 1993; Levinson et al. 1997; Levinson et al. 1999.) California interest groups were beginning to take positions as well. HSR supporters believed that fast trains would provide an important alternative to increasingly crowded intercity highways and air transport. Detractors argued that HSR was a poor fit for California, where few travellers had experience riding trains of any sort, auto ownership was ubiquitous, and several airlines offered reasonably priced short-haul air service. HSR advocates argued that a well-designed system would attract private investment; doubters countered that several possibilities had already been explored and abandoned by the private sector. HSR advocates spoke of transforming the geography of regions; opponents doubted that such changes would be forthcoming or that they would be acceptable to Californians if they were.

Both sides made assumptions about the ability to offset problems with existing modes. For example, highway advocates argued that it would be cheaper to widen highways or construct new ones than to build a new rail system; HSR supporters countered that highway proposals were increasingly blocked by controversy over their adverse impacts on air quality, neighbourhoods, and the natural environment, and their full costs were extremely high. Air transport advocates believed that better air traffic control and newer aircraft would solve problems of capacity, noise, and emissions; others pointed out that airport expansion projects had been stopped on community and environmental grounds in several Californian cities, that the state's major airports were operating under legal restrictions on operations, that decades of promises for quiet aircraft and higher capacity operating systems were still only promises, and that airports and airlines would benefit from using available capacity for more profitable long-distance flights. New technologists suggested that intelligent transportation systems would make HSR a white elephant, envisioning automated highways and driverless cars. HSR advocates countered that such technologies were unlikely to be widely available before the middle of the twenty-first century, and even then were likely to be complements to HSR rather than competitors.

There was widespread acknowledgement that existing transportation technologies were heavily implicated in social and environmental problems – global warming, petroleum dependence, community disruption, congestion, noise, air pollution. There also was growing impatience with traditional approaches to addressing these problems, which had relied heavily on the possibilities for improvement offered by technological change, but were slow in delivering results. Legislation such as the federal Intermodal Surface Transportation Efficiency Act of 1991, which among other provisions declared the completion of the Interstate Highway System and identified five broad corridors for the study of high-speed rail, had begun to restructure transportation programmes to be more intermodal and to take greater responsibility for avoiding or mitigating the problems transportation systems could create. The California Legislature, dismayed at the inability of the state to manage congestion effectively or deliver new projects on time and on budget, had increasingly devolved planning and financing responsibilities to regional and local agencies. California had also experienced litigation over purported 'bait and switch' moves by county-level transportation agencies that had submitted lists of projects to voters when seeking sales tax support and then attempted to substitute different projects once the funds were in hand; also, there had been public outcry in Southern California over the development of large bureaucracies with highly paid staff but slow transit project delivery. The Legislature reportedly wanted to reduce the chances of such abuses for high-speed rail.

In this context, California's SB 1420, the legislation that created the CHSRA, set forth a number of legislative findings that provided the framework for the CHSRA's activities:

a.   California, over the past decades, has built an extensive network of freeways and airports to meet the state's growing transportation needs.
b.   These facilities are not adequate to meet the mobility needs of the current population.
c.   The population of the state and the travel demands of its citizens are expected to continue to grow at a rapid rate.
d.   The cost of expanding the current network of highways and airports fully to meet current and future transportation needs is prohibitive, and a total expansion strategy would be detrimental to air quality.
e.   Intercity rail service, when coordinated with urban transit and airports, is an efficient, practical, and less polluting transportation mode that can fill the gap between future demand and present capacity.
f.   Advances in rail technology have allowed intercity rail systems in Europe and Japan to attain speeds of up to 200 miles per hour and compete effectively with air travel for trips in the 200 to 500 mile range.
g.   Development of a high-speed rail system is a necessary and viable alternative to automobile and air travel in the state.
h.   In order for the state to have a comprehensive network of high-speed intercity rail systems by the year 2020, it must begin preparation of a high-speed intercity rail plan similar to California's former freeway plan and designate an entity with stable and predictable funding sources to implement the plan.
i.   Utilizing existing human and manufacturing resources to build a large network of high-speed rail systems will generate jobs and economic growth for today's population and produce a transportation network for future generations.
j.   Upon confirmation of the need and costs by detailed studies, the private sector, together with the state, can build and operate new high-speed intercity rail systems utilizing private and public financing.

The legislation went on to specify that the Authority would include a board appointed by the Governor and the Legislature, an executive director appointed by the board, and other staff as needed. It directed the Authority to plan for an intercity high-speed rail service consisting of interlinked conventional and high-speed rail lines and associated feeder buses, coordinated with and connected to commuter rail lines and urban rail transit lines, through the use of common station facilities whenever possible.

The Authority was authorized to evaluate alternative HSR technologies, conduct engineering, environmental, and right of way studies, study and select a proposed route, station locations, and a proposed franchisee, propose financing methods including taxes, bonds, and other indebtedness as needed to pay for the construction of the network, and enter into contracts and accept grants, fees, and allocations from local, state, or federal government agencies, foreign governments, and private sources. The plan, upon completion, was to be submitted to the Legislature and the Governor for approval by statute or to the voters of the state, and if the latter, was to be placed on the ballot unless 'the Secretary of the Business, Transportation and Housing Agency or the Director of Finance notifies the Secretary of State that the financial plan is not consistent with the state's transportation needs or the fiscal condition of the state.' Finally, the law set a sunset date of 2000 for the authority, signalling the Legislature's desire for prompt action.

The legislation reveals the thinking about HSR at the time – that additional intercity capacity was needed and would be better filled by an efficient rail system than by additional highways or airports, that a major new state plan was needed to confirm the need for the system and figure out its financing, that a plan could be put together quickly, building on the work already in hand, and that once that plan was done, the system could be built and operated with the state and private sector working together and utilizing both private and public financing.

It is noteworthy that the Authority was established as an independent entity, not as part of the California Department of Transportation (Caltrans). Caltrans did have a small rail division that worked with local counterparts and Amtrak on the provision of the state's intercity rail services, which ran in Southern California between San Diego, Los Angeles, Santa Barbara and San Luis Obispo, in the Central Valley between Bakersfield, Oakland and Sacramento, and in Northern California between San Jose and Oakland to the Sacramento region. (No passenger rail service was available through the mountains between Bakersfield and the LA region; only a bus bridge was provided.) The Caltrans Rail Division also had experience with capital rail projects, working with Federal Rail Administration grants on track, equipment, and other capital needs, and had overseen the 1996 HSR study. Nevertheless, Caltrans was not directed to carry the study forward and instead was replaced by the CHSRA. According to a former legislative staffer, Caltrans were not selected for the follow-on HSR work because the Legislature wanted quick turnaround, a system plan in a year or two, something they were not convinced Caltrans could deliver. In addition, the former staffer related, legislators expected that an independent commission could bring in international experts to advise the staff about technical and financial aspects of the project, with less red tape than would be involved were an established state agency to take on the job.

SB 1420 was signed into law in late September 1996 and the CHSRA got underway a few months later. Its first business plan was issued in 2000 (CHSRA 2000). That plan estimated that an HSR system connecting San Francisco to Los Angeles via the Central Valley could be built for $25 billion and would generate net revenues for the state. It proposed funding the HSR via a sales tax and recommended that work proceed on the environmental studies, as required by law.

The sales tax proved to be a non-starter, but the environmental studies were authorized and a programme-level environmental EIS/EIR was prepared. The CHSRA, which by then had been given an indefinite life, continued to develop plans for the system, but also faced lawsuits about its environmental reviews (see Chapter 12).

As the project analyses progressed, the estimated costs for the HSR system increased. The increases were due both to rising construction costs generally and to design considerations (avoiding or mitigating impacts, contending with conflicts over right of way, dealing with the challenges of California topography). By 2006 the cost estimate for the system had risen to $45 billion.

Although the Legislature first approved a vote on the plan years earlier, the vote was delayed twice, and it wasn't until November 2008 that a funding plan was actually placed on the ballot: Proposition 1A, entitled the Safe, Reliable High-Speed Passenger Train Bond Act for the 21st Century. The text to be put before the voters was approved as Assembly Bill 3034, which passed the State Assembly by 58 votes to 15 and the State Senate 27-10, with legislators lining up largely along party lines. The November ballot was chosen as the time to ask the voter approval because it was a presidential election year and a big turnout was expected; in California this tends to be favourable for Democrats and expenditure requests. The California Secretary of State provided the proposition's language to voters via mail and on the internet in a voter guide; as is standard practice for propositions, the voter guide included a 'quick reference guide', a one paragraph summary of the proposition, brief statements by proponents for and against it, and a short explanation of what a yes vote or a no vote means, as well as a lengthier impartial analysis of the law and potential costs to taxpayers prepared by the Legislative Analyst, arguments in favour of and rebuttals against the ballot measure prepared by proponents and opponents, and the full official text of the proposed law. For Prop 1A the Legislative Analyst included an overview of the state's previously incurred bond debt and a discussion of how Prop 1A would affect the state's debt level and the costs of paying off the debt over time (CA Secretary of State 2008).

Prop 1A asked the voters to approve the sale of $9.95 billion in general obligation bonds (bonds the state would be obligated to pay back), with $9 billion available for HSR pre-construction and construction activities. Expenditures on preconstruction activities could not exceed 10 per cent of the allotted amount. The remaining $950 million was to go to capital improvements to passenger rail systems that would expand capacity, improve safety, or connect riders to the high-speed train system. The bond funds would be available when appropriated by the Legislature after submission of a detailed funding plan for each corridor or segment of a corridor and review of the funding plan by a separate committee of experts on high-speed rail and finance. In addition, approval by the Director of Finance was to be required before appropriated bond funds could be spent. Among other requirements, the bond funds could not be used for more than 50 per cent of the costs of any particular usable segment and no funds could be used for operations.

The text of Prop 1A also specified many aspects of the system on which the bond money could be spent. It defined HSR as 'a passenger train capable of sustained revenue operating speeds of at least 200 miles per hour where conditions permit those speeds.' It stated that 'As adopted by the authority in May 2007, Phase 1 of the high-speed train project is the corridor of the high-speed train system between San Francisco Transbay Terminal and Los Angeles Union Station and Anaheim.' Prop 1A further established a number of design and performance criteria for the HSR system, stating:

> The high-speed train system ...shall be designed to achieve the following characteristics:
>
> a. Electric trains that are capable of sustained maximum revenue operating speeds of no less than 200 miles per hour.
> b. Maximum nonstop service travel times for each corridor that shall not exceed the following:
>   1 San Francisco-Los Angeles Union Station: two hours, 40 minutes.
>   2 Oakland-Los Angeles Union Station: two hours, 40 minutes.
>   3 San Francisco-San Jose: 30 minutes.
>   4 San Jose-Los Angeles: two hours, 10 minutes.
>   5 San Diego-Los Angeles: one hour, 20 minutes.
>   6 Inland Empire-Los Angeles: 30 minutes.
>   7 Sacramento-Los Angeles: two hours, 20 minutes.
> c. Achievable operating headway (time between successive trains) shall be five minutes or less.

The proposition also specified that trains would be able to bypass or pass through intermediate stations at mainline operating speed, that a maximum of twenty-four stations would be served, and that there would be no station between Gilroy and Merced (an area where farmland conversion to housing projects has been controversial). It required that between specified city pairs there be the ability to travel from station to station without changing trains. It mandated that the HSR alignment follow existing transportation or utility corridors to the extent feasible, avoid disturbing wildlife, and be designed to reduce urban sprawl, with stations located to have good access to transit 'or other modes of transportation.'

Asked why so many specifics were deemed necessary, former legislators, staffers and transportation and environmental group representatives who were active in its drafting and negotiation offered a variety of explanations. First, there was concern among members of the Legislature that the funds be spent on building an HSR system and not on 'endless planning and excessive administrative salaries and other flights of fancy', as one put it. Hence there was a limitation, thought to be a generous one, on the amount that could be spent on preconstruction activities. Second, the specifications of how funds could be spent and the requirement for specific findings about each proposed expenditure were seen as consumer protections, making sure that the funding plans were technically competent and also making sure that the funds could not be raided to cover shortfalls elsewhere in the budget or to support other unrelated projects, transportation or other. Informants commented that bad experiences with administrative excesses and diversions of funds had led to these precautions. There had been voter outrage and in some cases, litigation over this sort of action in the past and Prop 1A provisions were designed to avoid such problems. Third, several provisions were added to address concerns that were raised by community groups and environmentalists in the initial planning phase and during environmental review. These groups feared that the HSR project would support sprawl, harm the natural environment, and require auto access with massive parking structures. With language specifically directing the CHSRA to avoid these problems, several key stakeholders were willing to withdraw their opposition, and it was hoped that similar concerns among the broader public would be assuaged. In addition, funds for other rail projects were included as a gesture to advocates for existing rail and transit systems who felt that they were already providing important services but were severely underfunded. Finally, provisions limiting the bond share to 50 per cent and banning operating subsidies were included both because there was an expectation that federal, regional, local and private funds could be secured to help support the system, and because there was a political strategy to counter opponents' claims that the system would be a money sink with the state taxpayers having to bail out its failure. (The $9 billion figure was based on state support for about a third of the original cost estimate of $25 billion.)

It is not clear what voters actually understood about the proposition and the different takes on it presented in the text, as the Legislative Analyst's analysis, and the comments of the proponents and opponents present substantially different interpretations. The Legislative Analyst's discussion states that, assuming 30 years to pay off both principal ($9.95 billion) and interest ($9.5 billion), costs of the bonds would be about $647 million per year. The Legislative Analyst also reports that once the system was built there would be 'unknown costs, probably in excess of $1 billion a year, to operate and maintain a high-speed train system', adding that the costs would be 'at least partially, and potentially fully, offset by passenger fare revenues, depending on ridership.' The proponents' statement in favour of the bond measure, signed by Chamber of Commerce presidents from San Francisco and Los Angeles among others, argued that investing in HSR will reduce greenhouse gases (GHGs) and dependence on foreign oil, would be cheaper than building new highways and airports to meet population growth, and would require no new taxes. Opponents, represented by the anti-tax Howard Jarvis Taxpayers Association among others, called the project a boondoggle that might never get built and stated that it would necessitate tax increases.

Opposition to the measure also came from some train supporters, who (undeterred by the funds in the measure for existing trains) argued that rather than build a new high-speed rail system, the state would be better off improving the intercity rail systems it already had and linking them more effectively to urban transit. In addition, while many supporters cited community and environmental benefits from HSR, opponents argued that congestion relief, energy savings and pollution reduction would be better obtained by investing in urban transport systems, where most of the trips in the state are made, rather than in intercity services. Route choices were seen as positive and supportive to local interests in some areas but the same route choices were seen as fatal flaws by others, particularly those who were convinced that a route through the Altamont Pass between the Bay Area and the Central Valley would serve more people and that a route through the Tejon Pass from Bakersfield to the LA Basin would provide faster service.

Ultimately, the voters supported the measure and Prop 1A became law. However, the fight over HSR was hardly over. Indeed, Prop. 1A's detailed but sometimes ambiguous specifications, intended to direct CHSRA action, have ended up being grounds for additional challenges to the HSR project. In addition, with rising system costs, the share of the project costs that the bonds would cover had shrunk substantially, making the financial uncertainties even more problematic.

Leadership matters: gubernatorial decision-making and fiscal turmoil for the CA HSR project

While the California State Legislature played a major role in shaping the HSR project, governors in California also have been important players in HSR development. The California governor oversees the agencies charged with implementation of the laws of the state and has a number of important formal powers including proposing and signing the state budget (over which the governor has a line item veto), and appointment of administrative agency heads, state judges, and numerous members of boards and commissions. The governor also can propose legislation and may issue executive orders and administrative orders that set objectives and direct the work of administrative agencies. Formal powers are only part of the story, however, as the governor of California has vast practical, informal powers that can be used to persuade, cajole, and steer legislative action and public opinion. California governors have access to regional, state-wide and national media to communicate with the public and can utilize their networks of connections with legislators, other government officials, and interest groups to mobilize interests in support of the policies they wish to pursue.

The initial planning phase for the California HSR project took place under two governors, Pete Wilson and Gray Davis. Wilson, a San Diego Republican who had served as mayor of that city and as US Senator, was governor of California 1991–1999, the period in which the current round of HSR planning commenced. He signed the legislation establishing the CHSRA. Wilson was succeeded by Gray Davis, a Democrat, who had served in a variety of government posts since serving as Jerry Brown's chief of staff as during Brown's term as governor in the 1970s. Davis took office in 1999 and was governor when the CHSRA's first plan was submitted in 2000.

According to Rod Diridon, whom Davis had appointed chairperson of the CHSRA, Davis was 'a strong supporter of HSR' [and under his administration] 'we were proceeding rapidly with the project.' The 2000 plan identified general corridors connecting San Francisco, Sacramento, Merced, Bakersfield, Los Angeles, Riverside, and San Diego; based on this work, with Davis' encouragement, the Legislature authorized that planning continue and extended the sunset date for the CHSRA until December 31, 2003 (AB 1703, 2000). Two years later, SB 796 repealed the expiration date, making the Authority permanent. In addition, during Davis' tenure the Legislature first authorized a vote on state debt bonds totalling $9.95 billion for HSR, though that vote was postponed.

Political and financial turmoil over the HSR project was already brewing, however. The state budget had been negatively impacted by the dot.com bubble bursting in 2001, which significantly reduced tax revenues for the state. Additional complications lingered from an electricity market crisis which had resulted in brownouts and severe price fluctuations. Voter anger over the resulting problems eventually made Davis lose his job – he was recalled from office shortly after the beginning of his second term in 2003. He was replaced by Arnold Schwarzenegger, a Republican, who won a special election following Davis' recall and went on to win in a subsequent election, serving as governor 2003–2011.

By most accounts, Schwarzenegger did not start his political career with very much interest in environmental matters or in HSR. However, early in his administration, Schwarzenegger became aware of efforts of an alliance of business associations, regional non-governmental organizations, environmentalists and academic institutions in Silicon Valley to minimize the cost of energy bills through efficiency gains and technological innovation, while also accounting for reduced GHG emissions as an important co-benefit of the reduced energy consumption practices (Pérez Henríquez 2009). Schwarzenegger and his advisors saw this as an opportunity to link environmental sustainability with economic growth and began promoting investment in clean technologies as a way to generate green jobs and transition to a clean and prosperous economy.

In 2006, the California Legislature launched an ambitious state plan to decarbonize the state's economy and contribute to the international effort to address global warming. AB 32, the California Global Warming Solutions Act of 2006, requires California to reduce its GHG emissions to 1990 levels by 2020 – a reduction of approximately 15 per cent of the emissions expected under a 'business as usual' scenario. To further support the state's climate action goals, the Legislature in 2008 enacted SB 375, The Sustainable Communities and Climate Protection Act, which aims to reduce GHG emissions through coordinated transportation and land use planning and the development of more sustainable communities. Schwarzenegger signed both bills (AB 32 2006; SB 375 2008) and went a step further, issuing an executive order directing state agencies to reduce GHG emissions to 80 per cent below 1990 levels by 2050 (CA EOS305).

While HSR had been touted at least since the mid-1990s as a way to reduce energy use and emissions, it did not figure prominently in the short term actions that California was taking to reduce GHG emissions. In fact, HSR barely survived during the Schwarzenegger era, both because of delays in putting the HSR financing measure before the voters and because of restrictions to the CHSRA's budget during California's budget crisis years.

The bond issue was important because bond sales were intended to provide the state contribution to HSR construction costs. Under Article XVI of the California Constitution, the California State Legislature can't borrow more than $300,000 unless the Legislature agrees to enter into the debt '...by a two-thirds vote of all the members elected to each house of the Legislature and until, at a general election or at a direct primary, it shall have been submitted to the people and shall have received a majority of all the votes cast for and against it at such election.' Thus, to use debt financing for HSR, the proposed debt had to be submitted to a popular vote. Timing of such votes typically depends on economic conditions and on other bond items on the ballot. For HSR, the vote was deferred repeatedly.

The Legislature had initially authorized the bond measure to be placed on the ballot in November 2004. However, to avoid conflict with another transportation initiative, the vote was postponed (SB 1169). The bond measure was then scheduled for the November 2006 ballot; but that spring, Governor Schwarzenegger proposed to indefinitely postpone the vote and instead to provide $1.3 million to the CHSRA, enough to pay pending obligations and staff salaries but not enough to continue environmental work. As the Legislative Analyst's Office (LAO) saw it, this would essentially have terminated the project. The LAO recommended, instead, that the budget bill make funding for the Authority contingent on moving forward with the bond measure (LAO 2006). Budget negotiations led to AB 713, which further pushed back the bond measure to the November 2008 ballot.

The Schwarzenegger recommendations for indefinite postponement came as a result of discussions with Michael Genest, whom Schwarzenegger had appointed in December 2005 as head of the California Department of Finance. Genest had asked the governor to make a decision about the future of HSR in California and had recommended the elimination of the CHSRA from the budget in order to generate savings of $14.3 million for the period 2006–2007. According to Genest, Schwarzenegger, who was born in Austria and was familiar with the heavily-used and highly reliable railway systems in that part of Europe, responded that there was 'hope' in many communities of the state about the high-speed rail system. His response to the suggestion by his director of finance to 'kill the project' was that 'you never kill hope,' and in a close call, the CHSRA remained a small line item in the governor's budget proposal. Whether this made him a supporter of HSR or simply unwilling to take the heat for its demise is unclear. Some argue that he kept the plan alive at a time when budget problems could easily have led to it being eliminated. Others argue that his approach amounted to starving the project rather than killing it: as the LAO put it, funding only the staff amounted to terminating the project without saying so directly. It may well be that Schwarzenegger was primarily focused on the money aspects; he also vetoed bills that would have expanded the CHSRA's duties, but he did so while expressing his support for the project. For example, he stated, 'I strongly support efforts to provide a reliable high-speed rail system throughout California…' as he vetoed a bill asking for further studies on HSR's labour force effects. He vetoed another bill that wanted to impose Californian content quotas in the HSR supply chain, stating that he did so because it 'could result in unnecessary additional costs' and also citing the potential for 'delays in the constructing of high-speed rail in California….'

Subsequent budget proposals from the governor again proposed only enough funds for CHSRA to pay staff salaries and cover costs already committed, and each time the LAO noted that such a budget would be akin to terminating the project. In each case, the Legislature provided additional funds and work continued.

Thus, a series of gubernatorial decisions during the Schwarzenegger years kept the CHSRA and the project alive but did not allow for expeditious action. Negotiations with the Legislature generally led to somewhat better budget outlook for the CHSRA, allowing the CHSRA to continue its work on key environmental and technical studies but not to move forward with great speed. At this point it was becoming clear that HSR would not be operating by 2020 as originally envisioned.

On November 2008, with the electoral cycle that put President Barack Obama in the White House, The Safe, Reliable High-Speed Passenger Train Bond Act for the 21st Century was finally put on the ballot as Proposition 1A. Voters approved the measure with 52.6 per cent in favour, out of 12,399,370 voting. With this vote, the state was authorized to sell $9 billion in general obligation bonds for HSR – enough at the time to cover perhaps 20 per cent of the estimated costs of the project.

The passage of the bond measure came as the economy worsened, right after the housing bubble had burst and the state was caught up in the global recession triggered by the collapse of the subprime mortgage markets. President Barack Obama, who had campaigned on infrastructure investment to jumpstart growth, promoted federal funding for infrastructure as a way to aid economic recovery, and Congress passed the American Recovery and Reinvestment Act (ARRA 2009) to help deliver specific projects. In 2009 the Obama Administration offered $8 billion of federal funding to intercity passenger rail projects throughout the United States as part of this recovery effort. However, during the same political cycle several states (Florida, Texas, Ohio and Wisconsin) which had been planning to develop HSR developments elected Republican governors, who cancelled or rejected federal support for these projects. Governor Schwarzenegger took a different approach, welcoming the federal funds; according to former federal staffers he lobbied strongly for the funds for California and furthermore pushed for the funds to be designated for HSR. California ultimately secured about $3.5 billion in federal funding for the CA HSR, with $2.6 billion from ARRA. The ARRA funds, however, came with strings attached, requiring that they be spent relatively quickly (the current deadline is 2017) and in the areas with the most severe economic need – sensible requirements for economic recovery funds but not necessarily the best way to assure a successful HSR project.

Throughout this period the California project continued to face difficulties, ranging from litigation over the adequacy of its environmental reviews and its compliance with Prop 1A (see Chapter 12) to criticisms by the LAO, which found the CHSRA business plans wanting. In the review of the 2009–10 budget proposal, for example, the LAO severely criticized the CHSRA's financing plans for lacking specificity. Even stronger criticisms were levelled by LAO after the Federal Rail Administration, which became a major player once federal funds were secured, recommended that the first project should be run between two small Central Valley cities – a proposal that immediately engendered derision as the 'train to nowhere'. During this period considerable pressure was put on the CHSRA to make use of independent peer reviewers regarding costs, ridership forecasts, and other aspects of project planning and design.

Edmund G. 'Jerry' Brown, the current governor, took office in January 2011 and was re-elected to a final term ending in January 2019. Unlike the Schwarzenegger Administration, which was ambivalent about HSR, the Brown Administration has been supportive of it. (Indeed, Brown, who had been governor in the 1970s when in his 30s, supported HSR then.) Brown has increased the CHSRA budget and has pushed forward with construction. To be sure, the situation Brown has faced has made it somewhat easier to support HSR than it was for his predecessor: the Californian economy has rebounded, the project has overcome a number of legal challenges, and environmental clearances are further along. In addition, Brown has enjoyed substantial public support, and polls show that he also has broad support for his economic and environmental agenda.

Yet problems remain. A 2011 LAO report suggested that the staff was too small to handle the transition from planning to construction, that reliance on consultants was too heavy, that the independent Board was not necessarily responsive to budgetary concerns, and that the cost and ridership projections were out-dated and likely underestimated costs. The report recommended that the Authority, which had heretofore been an independent agency, be moved to Caltrans, where it could more easily draw on the expertise of right of way agents and project engineers (LAO 2011). This move (which also helped avoid layoffs at Caltrans) was done as part of a larger Brown administration reorganization of the state's transportation agencies in 2012. The 2012 draft business plan (CHSRA 2012) showed year of expenditure costs for Phase I of the HSR system at nearly $100 billion ($65–75 billion in 2010 dollars), raising outcry about excessive costs and forcing the CHSRA to go back to the drawing boards to find a less costly strategy. The current 2016 plan (CHSRA 2016) proposes a Phase I budget of $64.2 billion, but sceptics question whether the costs will be that low. The LAO has continued to raise concerns about the project's financial feasibility, in particular, emphasizing the lack of specifics about how to pay for all of Phase I. Litigation continues over environmental issues and Prop 1A compliance. With the CHSRA focused on keeping costs down and pushing forward to get its project under construction as deadlines loom, some cities report feeling ignored when they ask to discuss mitigation.

Private sector funding for the project, contemplated in the original legislation, has yet to materialize. Statements of interest from potential operators make it clear that in its current state the risks would have to be shared; and continued litigation, a still-uncertain alignment, and restrictions on the use of available funds all add to the risks perceived. Investors want a degree of predictability that the unstable plans for the project have not yet delivered. Also, paraphrasing the comments of one potential operator, the involvement of organizations with HSR operating experience is coming very late in the process after many commitments have been made that could be hard to alter.

Political support for the project continues, especially in the Governor's office. As he launched his second term, Brown has doubled down on the state's bet on green growth, as well as on climate policy ambition and scope of action. In Executive Order B-30-15, the governor directed that 'State agencies shall take climate change into account in their planning and investment decisions, and employ full life-cycle cost accounting to evaluate and compare infrastructure investments and alternatives.' While opponents have already challenged aspects of this executive order, and some have argued that it will pose a new challenge for the CHSRA due to the heavy carbon burden that HSR construction entails, others point out that the Agency is already accounting for and offsetting a large share of the GHG burden through design decisions, requirements for the use of green materials, best technology construction vehicles and practices, and mitigation strategies.

The Brown Administration and the Legislature reiterated support for HSR by allocating, through the California Air Resources Board (CARB), a portion of funds from cap-and-trade auctions to HSR. This move has provided hundreds of millions of dollars in the past 2 years to the CHSRA – $250 million in FY 14–15, $650M in FY 15–16 (CARB 2016). The use of cap-and-trade proceeds for the HSR project has been criticized by some environmentalists as not likely to achieve the quick reductions in carbon that other expenditures of the funds could produce, and by some social justice advocates as not as helpful to disadvantaged communities as, say, urban transportation projects or home insulation and window retrofits.

CARB in its 2016 report to the Legislature on cap-and-trade proceeds and expenditures notes that it does not have year-by-year estimates for the HSR project, and so cannot comment on its near-term benefits. CARB goes on to say the following about this use of funds:

> The High Speed Rail Project is expected to reduce GHG emissions by 44 million MTCO2e over its operating life... [and] is expected to greatly benefit disadvantaged communities by creating thousands of direct construction-related jobs in Central Valley communities, which have some of the highest unemployment rates in the country. Over time, the project will lead to permanent operations, maintenance, and manufacturing jobs. As of November 2015, the project has employed over 200 craft labor workers in the Central Valley and contracted with 100 small businesses located within disadvantaged communities. The project has created a pipeline for workers from disadvantaged communities to apprentice in the construction trades.

In addition, connecting the Silicon Valley to the Central Valley offers the potential to transform the Central Valley's disadvantaged communities by opening up new job markets for people living in the Central Valley, creating linkages between higher education institutions in the Central Valley and high-tech industries in the Silicon Valley, and incentivizing high-tech companies to locate certain functions in the Central Valley where commercial real estate is less expensive.

In other words, the use of cap-and-trade funds is being justified in large part not on HSR's near-term emissions reductions but on its anticipated economic benefits.

The CHSRA recently issued its 2016 business plan with a new proposal to build its first section connecting the Silicon Valley to the Central Valley. Noting that this proposal would expend most of the available funds, the LAO comments that the plan still does not say how the remainder of Phase I would be financed, and recommends that the Legislature decide whether that section meets their approval as a usable segment in the event that further construction is not possible (LAO 2016).

At this point, the CHSRA states that it intends to finish its environmental reviews for all of Phase I in the next 2 years and to proceed with major construction on a usable Silicon Valley to Central Valley line. If it succeeds in doing so, it is possible that the first true HSR line in the United States will be built (if not fully operational) during Jerry Brown's governorship. It remains to be seen, however, whether this will prove feasible, given the continued opposition to the project and the opportunities for litigation presented by environmental reviews and the ambiguities of Prop 1A.

Supporters argue that once the environmental documents are completed and the first section of the HSR system is operating, investors will come forward – ranging from real estate developers who want a piece of the action around the stations to international rail companies who see a profit potential. The supporters believe that carbon trading funds will remain available (i.e., that the Legislature will agree to continue the programme past its current 2020 deadline) and that additional federal funds will eventually flow again for the project. Opponents say that they will keep fighting the project, hoping that the next governor will be less enthusiastic about it, that legislative support will wane as it becomes clear that the plan cannot be financed, and that eventually the entire venture will be halted.

Discussion

Public policy is about trade-offs, and any investment made can be viewed as diverting resources from priorities other stakeholders may see as more urgent. Budgeting is by its nature a highly political process, often generating the debate over investments and funding sources that is normal in democracies. The debates over policies, investments and budgets can be trenchant when there is disagreement about whether the government should even have a role in the provision of a product or service, or what that role should be. This is clearly the case with California's HSR.

The legislation for California's HSR project made it clear that there was an expectation of private sector involvement in the financing of HSR after an initial plan for the HSR system was prepared and approved. It also opened the door to federal, regional, and local funding and funding by foreign governments. So far, however, non-state funding has been limited, with support coming from the federal government and some local funding being provided for stations. International interest has been expressed, but has not led to commitments of funds and is unlikely to do so until some of the risks of the project are removed. The stipulation that operating subsidies cannot be provided raises the stakes for potential investors, but continuing litigation and debates over priorities are even more troubling.

Thinking on organizational design for the project has clearly changed over time. Initially the CHSRA was established as an independent agency intended to do its assigned work and close down. As a result it was set up with a small staff with much of the planning work done by private contractors. The heavy use of contractors, initially seen as a way to avoid a creating a huge bureaucracy, became a liability when budgets were cut, threatening to leave the CHSRA staffed with project managers but no projects to manage. Use of state employees with needed skills in planning, engineering and right of way acquisition came to be seen as a good move.

While leadership for HSR in California has come from the Legislature as well as from the governor of the state, the governor's role as initiator of the budget has had a definite impact on the CHSRA's operations. Gubernatorial support appears to have kept the project afloat during difficult times (though some would say barely afloat) and has moved it forward substantially more recently. Currently the thinking among supporters is to get enough built to demonstrate viability, then seek additional funds to finish the project. Nevertheless, governors serve for limited terms, and opponents hope that they can keep the fight going until a governor who does not endorse the project takes office. In the meantime they hope to nibble away at support from others by underscoring the project's still unresolved financial problems. If the next governor continues support for the project, HSR's future would clearly be brighter.

References

American Recovery and Reinvestment Act of 2009 (ARRA), Public Law 111–5.
California Air Resources Board, California, 2016, *Climate Investments Using Cap-and-Trade Auction Proceeds, Annual Report to the Legislature*, http://arb.ca.gov/cc/capandtrade/auctionproceeds/cci_annual_report_2016_final.pdf Accessed 1 August 2016.
California Assembly Bill (AB) 32, 2006, *The California Global Warming Solutions Act of 2006*.
California AB 1703, 2000, *An Act to Amend Sections 185020 and 185032 of the Public Utilities Code, Relating to Transportation*, January 3.
California Executive Order B-30-15 (Brown), 2015, April, http://www.climatechange.ca.gov/state/executive_orders.html Accessed 1 August 2016.
California High Speed Rail Authority, 2000, *2000 Business Plan*, http://www.hsr.ca.gov/About/Business_Plans/2000_Business_Plan.html Accessed 31 October 2016.
California High Speed Rail Authority, 2012, *Draft Business Plan*, http://www.hsr.ca.gov/docs/about/business_plans/BPlan_2012Draft_web.pdf Accessed 1 August 2016.

California High Speed Rail Authority, 2016, *Draft Business Plan*, http://www.hsr.ca.gov/about/business_plans/draft_2016_Business_Plan.html Accessed 1 August 2016.

California Intercity High Speed Rail Commission, 1996, *High-Speed Rail Summary Report and Action Plan: Final Report*, Sacramento, CA.

California Legislative Analyst's Office (LAO), 2011, *High-Speed Rail Is at a Critical Juncture.*

California Legislative Analyst's Office (LAO), Various Years, *Budget Analysis. High Speed Rail.*

California Secretary of State, 2008, *Proposition 1A Official Voter Information Guide*, http://vig.cdn.sos.ca.gov/2008/general/analysis/pdf/prop1a-analysis.pdf Accessed 31 October 2016.

California Senate Bill (SB) 375, 2008, *Sustainable Communities Act.*

California SB 796, 2003, *High-Speed Rail Authority*, September 19.

California SB 1169, 2004, *Safe, Reliable High-Speed Passenger Train Bond Act for the 21st Century*, June 24.

California SB 1420 (Kopp), 1996, *Transportation: High-Speed Rail Act.*

Hall, P and Banister, D, 1993, 'The Second Railway Age,' *Built Environment*, vol. 19, no. 3, p. 157.

Hickman, R and Banister, D, 2014, *Transport, Climate Change and the City*, Routledge Advances in Climate Change Research. Abingdon, UK: Routledge.

Leavitt, D, Vaca, E and Hall, P, 1992a, 'High Speed Trains for California Strategic Choice: Volume I: Comparison of Technology and Choice of Route,' *University of California, Berkeley, Institute of Urban and Regional Development (IURD) working paper*, no. 564.

Leavitt, D, Hall, P and Vaca, E, 1992b, 'CalSpeed: High-Speed Trains For California. Volume II: Detailed Segment Descriptions, Cost Estimates, and Travel Times Calculation,' *University of California Transportation Center (UCTC) Working Paper*, no. 105.

Leavitt, D, Cheng, P, Vaca, E and Hall, P, 1994, 'Potential for Improved Intercity Passenger Rail Service in California: Study of Corridors,' *University of California, Berkeley, Institute of Urban and Regional Development working paper*, no. 612.

Levinson, D, Mathieu, JM, Gillen, D, and Kanafani, A, 1997, 'The Full Cost of High-Speed Rail: An Engineering Approach,' *The Annals of Regional Science*, vol. 31, pp. 189–215.

Levinson, D, Kanafani, A and Gillen, D, 1999, 'Air, High Speed Rail, or Highway: A Cost Comparison in the California Corridor,' *Transportation Quarterly*, vol. 53, pp. 123–132.

Neustadt, RE and May, ER, 1986, *Thinking in Time: The Uses of History for Decision-Makers*, The Free Press.

North, D, 1990, *Institutions, Institutional Change and Economic Performance (Political Economy of Institutions and Decisions)*. Cambridge, UK: Cambridge University Press.

Ostrom, E, Cox, M, and Schlager, E, 2014, 'An Assessment of the Institutional Analysis and Development Frameworks and Introduction of the Social-Ecological Systems Framework,' in Sabatier, PA and Weible, CM (eds) *The Theories of the Policy Process*, 3rd Edition, Westview Press.

Pérez Henríquez, BL, 2009, 'Sustainable Silicon Valley: A Model Regional Partnership,' in Vollmer, D, (ed.) *Enhancing the Effectiveness of Sustainability Partnerships*. Washington, DC: National Academies Press.

Sands, B, 1993, 'The Development Effects of High-Speed Rail Stations and Implications for California,' *Built Environment (1978–)*, pp. 257–284.

Williamson, OE, 1975, *Markets and Hierarchies*, New York, pp. 26–30.

15 High-speed rail and economic development

Business agglomerations and policy implications

Jin Murakami and Robert Cervero

Introduction

High-speed rail (HSR) investments in the United States have been justified in part as an economic stimulus, helping to increase firm productivity, resulting in new jobs and businesses as well as higher wages and income. Subscribing to this view, in 2009 the Obama Administration pledged US$8 billion to thirteen HSR projects across thirty-one states under the American Recovery and Reinvestment Act (ARRA) as part of the response to the deep recession of 2008. The federal HSR stimulus money was subsequently rejected by the newly elected governors of Wisconsin, Ohio and Florida, fearing that the proposed HSR projects would be too costly to taxpayers and that the project risks would outweigh the economic benefits. As a result, federal funds to construct HSR lines have been redirected to key corridors in other states where the economic benefits of intercity railway investments are thought to be high and projects are ready for implementation (Figure 15.1).

It is widely accepted that the primary benefits of HSR investments are the direct ones that accrue to users, mainly in the form of travel-time savings. To the degree that they occur, economic development benefits are mostly second-order and indirect in nature. In addition, both theory and international experiences raise the question of whether the economic benefits conferred by HSR investments are truly generative, representing net increases in economic productivity and real increases in income and wealth, or largely redistributive, simply transferring taxpayer monies and economic activities from one physical location to another.

In recent years, some researchers have questioned the net downstream benefits of HSR investments (Levinson 2010; Levinson et al. 1999; Levinson et al. 1997; Givoni 2006). Doubts largely turn on the question of whether gains are truly generative, or are pecuniary and redistributive in nature. However, the relocation of businesses, such as from a highway corridor to an HSR station area, need not always have a zero-sum outcome. To the degree that rail stations support higher development densities, benefits might accrue from the agglomeration economies of highly-skilled, knowledge-based workers being in close physical proximity to each other. Not all businesses, however, benefit from physical clustering; and some, like manufacturing plants and distribution centres, likely value low-density development with good highway access far more than proximity to an HSR stop.

Examining the potential economic development impacts of HSR is important from a public-policy perspective because the ability of these investments to recover their full lifecycle costs through direct user fees, especially in automobile-oriented societies like the United States, has been questioned by many. Economic justification of these multi-billion dollar investments could therefore hinge crucially on their abilities to generate external benefits, such as stimulating new generative economic activities.

Most of our knowledge about the impacts of HSR systems is drawn from two sources: inferences from studies on the impacts of metropolitan rail systems on land use and development activities; and comparative insights gained from experiences with HSR in other countries, notably Japan and France. The transferability of metro-rail experiences to HSR is subject to question, because intra-metropolitan rail systems' economic impacts take place within a totally different context. Metro rail investments influence firm locations and economic activities within metropolitan labour-sheds and trade-sheds. Economic activities that might benefit from improved rail access within an urbanized region tend to occur on a regular basis – e.g., daily access to labour and workplaces, regular and routine access to consumer outlets serving households in a region, etc. Thus the accessibility benefits conferred by new metro rail systems can be expected to influence the location of firms seeking improved access to labour and customers as well as households seeking better access to workplaces and shops. HSR systems, on the other hand, serve mainly inter-city, inter-regional, and transnational

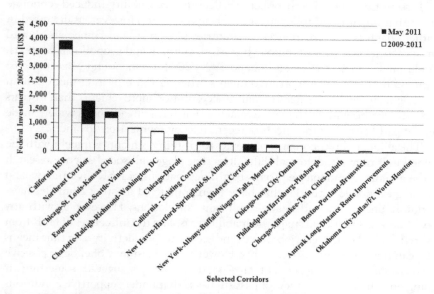

Figure 15.1 High-Speed Intercity Passenger Rail Program: Federal investment highlights, 2009–2011

travel markets, on a more sporadic basis. As with air travel, the vast majority of households and workers within a region make long-distance trips on a less-than-routine, irregular basis. A family might take an HSR train or catch a flight to go to major leisure destinations or visit relatives, but for most the infrequency and irregularity of such travel does not prompt locational or lifestyle adjustments.

With the increased globalization of economic production, some firms and businesses do carry out inter-city, transnational, and international business transactions on a fairly regular basis. These tend to be highly specialized business-service firms with highly-skilled, knowledge-based labour whose clients are spread throughout a state, country, or region of the globe. To the degree that HSR enhances physical access of financial analysts, engineering consultants, legal advisors, and other specialists to their spatially dispersed business clients, then areas surrounding HSR stations can be expected to attract new knowledge- and service-based firms and investments drawn by those accessibility advantages. And to the degree that the higher densities supported by HSR stops (vis-à-vis highway corridors) yield agglomeration benefits – in the form of productivity gains, knowledge spill-overs, and innovations allowed by increased face-to-face interactions, subcontracting, and external transactions – the demand to be in these choice locations will intensify. With a finite, limited supply of land near HSR stops, rents and property values will rise as companies bid up the price of doing business in these preferred locales. Thus a different economic dynamic is likely to be unleashed by the opening of an inter-city HSR compared with an intra-city metro rail station, represented by a different composition of firms and businesses drawn to station locations.

Lessons from abroad perhaps better reflect the accessibility-induced economic shifts that might occur following an HSR investment. However, as discussed in earlier chapters, the experiences in countries like Japan and France are shaped in substantial part by their unique historical, cultural, and geopolitical contexts. Additionally, some analysts (Giuliano 1995, 2004; Graham and Marvin 1996) contend that future transport investments, whether intra- or inter-metropolitan in design, are likely to generate smaller accessibility improvements than in years past, in part because of the improvements that have already been widely made and in part because of the effects of recent telecommunication advances.

The ability to link economic outcomes to HSR investments is fraught with the same kinds of methodological difficulties that plague all social science research – the absence of randomized trials. Past investigations of HSR investments and ensuing economic activities that have been conducted in other countries have certainly uncovered statistically significant correlations. However as with any post-hoc, cross-sectional study, the inability to isolate the influences of HSR from everything else that affects job growth and economic productivity over time means one can never demonstrate causality. However, the existence of enough positive correlations across independent cross-sectional studies suggests something is going on. The consensus view of past studies is that under supportive conditions HSR can be a contributor to real economic growth, but is never sufficient in and of itself (Givoni 2006; Levinson 2010).

This chapter probes the economic development impacts of HSR by focusing on the kinds of companies that have been drawn to HSR stations, based on experiences in the country with the longest history of HSR services: Japan. Using location quotients and other metrics, we study the kinds of firms and businesses that have been most attracted to Japan's Shinkansen HSR station environs and how patterns vary across station groupings. We then investigate the degree to which districts around proposed HSR stations in California and stations slated for 'Core Express' services in the North Corridor have been attracting similar types of economic activities as in Japan. Based on Japan's experiences, we also speculate about the settings that are most likely to reap economic development benefits along the two most populous US corridors scheduled for HSR services, California and the Northeast Corridor. The chapter concludes by discussing the public-policy implications of the research findings.

Literature review

HSR investments have transformed the economic geographies of city-regions in Asia and Europe to varying degrees. Countries like China, Korea, Taiwan, and Spain have invested heavily in HSR in recent years, partly to meet rising demands for inter-city travel but also in hopes of stimulating economic growth. This is despite the fact that empirical evidence on HSR's impacts on economic growth, drawn mainly from Japan, France, and Germany, has been mixed and inconclusive.

The most studied HSR system is the world's oldest, the Shinkansen in Japan, where the Tokaido Line connecting the mega-cities of Tokyo and Osaka opened in 1964. Sands (1993) reviewed the development effects of the Shinkansen's Tokaido line in the early 1990s. He found that the cities and regions served by the Shinkansen line experienced higher employment and population growth rates than areas not served by HSR. Particularly high rates of growth were recorded for information exchange industries (business services, banking services, real estate) as well as higher education in areas surrounding Shinkansen stations. Buoyant population and commercial growth was also recorded along secondary intra-metropolitan transit corridors that connected to Shinkansen stations. Focusing on longer-term impacts, Banister and Berechman (2000) concluded that the Shinkansen (and other railway systems) influenced Japan's employment growth patterns at the regional and local levels and increased station-area land values as a function of travel times to Tokyo station and other large cities. The degree to which the Shinkansen network was the dominant agent behind recorded growth could not be confirmed by either Sands (1993) or Banister and Berechman (2000), at least not in a pure causal sense.

Cervero and Bernick (1996) examined the likely redistributive effects of Shinkansen on urban activities. Their analysis showed that some 30 years after Tokaido services began, the economic roles of intermediate cities, like Nagoya and Kyoto, within the nation's urban hierarchy had weakened. With a hub-and-spoke design that delivered the greatest incremental increases in accessibility to

Tokyo and Osaka, the Shinkansen delivered the lion's share of economic benefits to these two cities. It is, of course, not the physical infrastructure itself that induces economic change, but rather the quality of services, most notably speed when it comes to HSR. Takagi (2005) reported that in more recent times the Tokaido Line's high-speed services have become slower because of the increased number of intermediate stops, inferring that Shinkansen's economic benefits have likely also slowed down. In Chapter 3 of this volume, the authors note that Nagoya has held its own better than most other intermediate cities because of the importance of Toyota to the city's economy, and that when the competition was between Osaka and Tokyo, the latter had the advantage.

Across Europe, experiences to date suggest that, as in the case of Japan, the economic development benefits of HSR systems have accrued mainly to large cities at the expense of smaller and intermediate ones. Gutiérrez, González, and Gómez (1996) predicted that Europe's planned HSR network would increase territorial polarization between major cities and their hinterlands, with major urban centres like London and Paris becoming the chief beneficiaries of this new spatial order. Vickerman (1997) similarly predicted that long-term economic development in peripheral small cities would be suppressed if global and regional firms that locate in large cities are able to capture the bulk of HSR's accessibility benefits. To a large degree, experiences have borne out these predictions. In London, for example, new HSR links have been credited with attracting global finance and business service jobs to districts near central terminal stations, such as King's Cross-St Pancras, which through multiplier effects has spurred the regeneration of once-distressed urban districts (GLA 2008; Bertolini and Spit 1998). Freeman (2007) documents that London's HSR-served hubs have claimed a relatively large share of the city's 'creative businesses', ones that thrive on face-to-face communications for the exchange of knowledge and ideas.

In France, the TGV has also been viewed as a catalyst for Paris-based global and regional firms to expand their potential markets in Europe. Cervero and Bernick (1996) argued that the first generation of TGV services benefited secondary cities, such as Lyon and Lille, every bit as much as Paris. However, Garmendia, Ureña, Ribalaygua, Leal, and Coronado (2008) examined the development impacts of HSR lines on small and large intermediate cities in France and Spain and found the impacts of HSR services on residential growth to be quite modest. There was some evidence that small cities attracted immigrant households in the wake of HSR investments. With regard to intermediate cities, Ureña, Meneraut, and Garmendia (2009) concluded that Spain and France's HSR systems helped them attract mid-level business and technical consultancy firms, urban tourism, and interregional conferences; see Chapter 6 for more discussion. HSR was credited with strengthening the central-place hierarchy of intermediate cities in relation to smaller ones.

The spatial and economic-growth ramifications of new HSR investments in today's fast-changing informational age are yet to be told. Some see 'edge city' station locations as a competitive boon (Garreau 1991; Hall 2009), especially where HSR services link edge cities directly to major international airports

(Kasarda 1999, 2001). Kasarda (2009, 2010) contends that the connection of airport cities with high-speed rail services will stretch clusters of aviation-linked businesses and associated residential development some 30 kilometres outward from major international airports. Edge cities connected to airport hubs via HSR can reap competitive advantages in the global marketplace by dramatically expanding labour-, trade-, and knowledge-sheds. Experiences in Lyon, France, could be a harbinger of things to come. The integration of an HSR station with an airport terminal on the eastern edge of Lyon spawned the construction of nearby hotel, conference, and retail facilities. In recent years, the Satolas airport TGV station has become a focal point of Lyon's marketing and economic development strategy. Lyon's success lends credence to Thompson's (1995) arguments that HSR-airport interchanges combined with state-of-the-art telecommunication facilities are poised to reap an economic windfall by facilitating commercial trade and exchange worldwide without the diseconomies of congestion.

Methods and data

This study investigates the locational characteristics of job markets around both already developed and newly proposed stations on the Japanese Tokaido Shinkansen, Northeast Corridor, and proposed California HSR systems. The analysis focuses on market trends around planned stations with an eye toward exploring whether public policies might be able to harness and leverage these trends to induce greater economic benefits. Trends in the Northeast Corridor and California are compared to job market experiences in Japan. Such comparisons, we believe, shed light on the kinds of long-term economic development impacts that might occur along the US corridors scheduled for HSR and importantly, the kinds of public policy interventions that might meaningfully influence outcomes. Our analysis does not predict likely economic development impacts but rather applies interpretative methods to investigate station-area employment patterns that might unfold and the roles that public policies might play in leveraging positive outcomes.

This analysis assumes that the economic development impacts of HSR investments are largely confined to areas within 5 km around stations. In studies of urban transit systems, 'station catchment area' is often defined as a much smaller radius, e.g. 500 to 1,000 metres from the station. However, because of the potentially much larger accessibility benefits conferred, the station catchments of HSR systems arguably stretch considerably farther (Catz and Christian 2010). In addition, the locations of many of the proposed HSR stations in California are not finalized and may shift by more than 500 metres. For these reasons, this analysis looks at job market profiles within 5 km of the station locations studied for the three corridors studied (Figures 15.2, 15.3, and 15.4).

Table 15.1 presents key data on the three corridors under study. The Tokaido corridor between Tokyo and Osaka is fairly comparable to the Northeast Corridor, connecting Boston, New York, Philadelphia, and Washington, DC, in

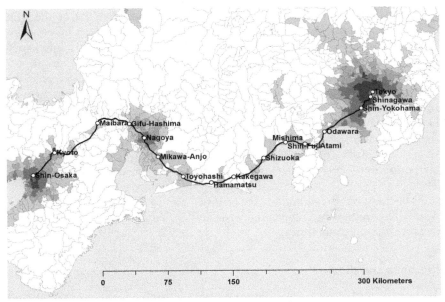

Figure 15.2 Seventeen Shinkansen stations on the Tokaido Line

Table 15.1 Comparative Statistics: Tokaido Shinkansen, Northeast Corridor and California HSR

	Tokaido Shinkansen	Northeast Corridor	California HSR
Opening year	1964 (46 years)	2000 (Acela Express)	2029?
Service distance km (end points)	552.6 (Tokyo and Shin-Osaka)	584.7 (Boston and Washington DC)	695.2 (San Francisco and Los Angeles)/ Anaheim with eventual extensions to Sacramento (N) and San Diego (S)
# of stations	17	30	Up to 25
Max. speed kph	270	241	354
Travel time	2 hrs. 20 mins (2010)	6 hrs. 40 mins (2010)	2 hrs. 40 mins (San Jose–LA Estimate)
Passengers per day	378,000 (FY2009)	n.a. (FY2015)	96,000 (Phase I Estimate for 2030)
Ave. # of jobs in 5 km	259,769 (2006)	178,645 (2008)	110,817 (2008)
Ave. # of inhabitants residing in 5 km	397,645 (2005)	219,925 (2007)	174,868 (2007)

Sources: Central Japan Railway Company (2011); Government of Japan (2010a, 2010b); Amtrak (2011, 2015); California High-Speed Rail Authority (2010, 2014); U.S. Census Bureau (2011); ESRI (2010).

terms of role: both are the economic spines of large mega-regions. The California HSR, in contrast, will connect the state's large metropolitan areas by running through the largely agricultural Central Valley with stops at intermediate sized cities there. The Tokaido line averages very high urban densities compared to the other two. The average number of jobs and population within 5 km of the Tokaido Shinkansen's business stations are around twice as large (dense) as the averages within 5 km of existing or planned stations on the Northeast Corridor and California HSR.

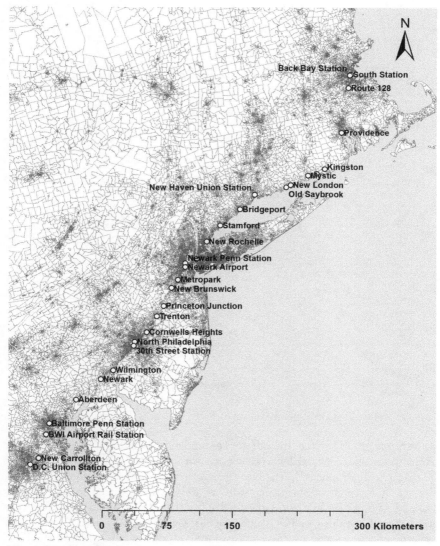

Figure 15.3 Amtrak stations on the Northeast Corridor

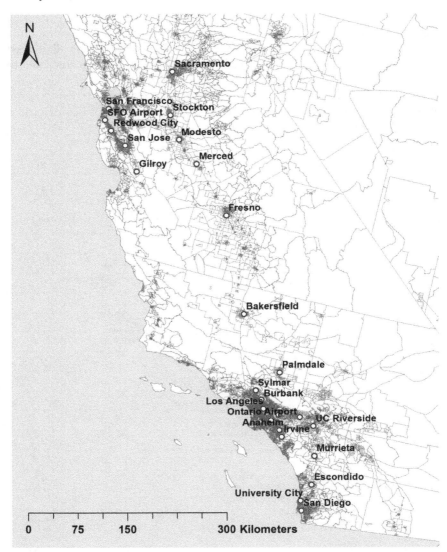

Figure 15.4 Proposed HSR stations in California

In terms of rail service, the differences are large. Along the Tokaido corridor Shinkansen offers several levels of service with differing numbers of stops, but all maintain high speeds. In the Northeast Corridor, Amtrak operates the Acela Express at fourteen of the thirty stops as well as lower-speed intercity trains (Northeast Regional) on the same tracks; however, track limitations and other restrictions limit the speed at which any of the trains can operate. (The federal government, states and Amtrak are currently joining forces to improve the HSR service by replacing aging bridges, expanding constrained stations, and upgrading track and power systems.) In California, only conventional trains connect the major cities, often with delays due to required transfers.

Our analysis classifies types of economic activities around the developed and proposed HSR stations[1] with respect to their market sizes, growth trends, job-population balances, and business specializations. To build a typology for each of the three corridors, cluster analysis is applied. The technique of agglomerative hierarchical clustering systematically combines cases into a reasonable set of clusters on the basis of their similarities (i.e., squared Euclidean distances) across input variables (Aldenderfer and Blashfield 1984). The job market profile for each station catchment area is quantified by four measures: (1) total job number; (2) recent change in total job number; (3) job-population gap index; and (4) job location quotient. The gap index and location quotients used for cluster analysis were computed as follows:

$$\text{Gap index} = \frac{\begin{array}{c}(\# \text{ of jobs within 5km of a station } - \\ \# \text{ of population within 5km of a station})\end{array}}{\begin{array}{c}(\# \text{ of jobs within 5 km of a station } + \\ \# \text{ of population within 5 km of a station})\end{array}}$$

Where the station catchment has more jobs than population, the Gap Index becomes closer to +1; where the station catchment has more population than jobs, the Gap Index becomes closer to -1.

$$\text{Location quotient (the sector i)} = \frac{\dfrac{(\# \text{ of jobs in the sector i within 5 km of a station})}{(\# \text{ of all jobs within 5 km of a station})}}{\dfrac{(\# \text{ of jobs in the sector i in the region})}{(\# \text{ of all jobs in the region})}}$$

where the Sector i is seven business categories (Heavy Industry [20], Manufacturing [30], Logistics [40], Knowledge Business [50], Social Service [60], Leisure Service [70] and Other Service [80]); and the Region comprises Tokyo, Kanagawa, Shizuoka, Aichi, Gifu, Shiga, Kyoto, Osaka and Hyogo (Tokaido Shinkansen), Massachusetts, Rhode Island, Connecticut, New York, New Jersey, Pennsylvania, Delaware, Maryland and the District of Columbia (Northeast Corridor), or California (California HSR).

Precise locations of the seventeen stations on the Tokaido Shinkansen were obtained from the geographic information system (GIS) shapefile provided by the Japanese National and Regional Planning Bureau (Government of Japan [GOJ] 2011). Also, GIS point shapefiles for the thirty Amtrak stations on the Northeast Corridor were extracted from the National Transportation Atlas Database (US Bureau of Transportation Statistics 2011). For the proposed HSR station sites in California, station locations were identified based on the public outreach materials and preliminary alternatives analyses that were posted on the CHSRA's official website as of Fall 2010 (CHSRA 2010, Monkkonen 2008). GIS point shapefiles for these stations were produced using online satellite imagery techniques.

Japan's job market data in 2001 and 2006 were extracted from the Establishment and Enterprise Census of Japan (GOJ 2010a). Population data in 2005 came from the Population Census of Japan (GOJ 2010b). These census data were then spatially related to the seventeen station catchment areas along the Tokaido Shinkansen. US job market data in 2002 and 2008 were collected from the ZIP Business Patterns (US Census Bureau 2011). US population data (at the census block group levels) for 2007 were obtained from Esri. Both the ZIP code and block-group level datasets in the US were geographically reassigned to the 5 km catchments of the thirty existing Amtrak stations on the Northeast Corridor and seventeen proposed HSR stations in California.

Table 15.2 Correspondence table: seven common business categories across Japan and the United States

Japan: major industrial categories 2006	United States: NAICS (2-digit codes) 2008	Common: business categories [code]
Steel Utility Construction	Mining, quarrying, oil and gas extraction (21) Utilities (22) Construction (23)	Heavy Industry [20]
Manufacturing	Manufacturing (31)	Manufacturing [30]
Wholesale and retail Transportation	Wholesale trade (42) Retail trade (44) Transportation and warehousing (48)	Logistics [40]
Information Finance and insurance Real estate Multiple service	Information (51) Finance and insurance (52) Real estate and rental and leasing (53) Professional, scientific and technical services (54) Management of companies and enterprises (55) Administrative and support services (56)	Knowledge Business [50]
Educational Medical	Educational services (61) Health care and social assistance (62)	Social Service [60]
Restaurant and hotel	Arts, entertainment and recreation (71) Accommodation and food services (72)	Leisure Service [70]
Other service	Other services (81)	Other Service [80]

To calculate location quotients that were comparable across the three settings, a correspondence table was created between fourteen Japanese major business categories and the eighteen North American Industry Classification System (NAICS) codes (Table 15.2). The job market data from Japan and the United States were aggregated into seven core business categories: Heavy Industry [20]; Manufacturing [30]; Logistics [40]; Knowledge Business [50]; Social Service [60]; Leisure Service [70]; and Other Service [80].

It is important to note that this analysis method is based on current economic development patterns, not prospective ones. The analysis does not account for changes in activity that may result from growth and change in the regions, or from exogenous planning interventions. It does, however, provide insights into the economic base in each station area. Since it is generally easier to build upon an existing base than to transform an area's economic base into something new, by reviewing the current clusters we get an indication of how readily economic development might occur, or how difficult it might be.

Results of cluster analysis

Tokaido Shinkansen

Our cluster analysis quantitatively classified the seventeen Shinkansen stations into eight job market types: (1) Global Business Centre; (2) Waterfront Information Centre; (3) Regional Business Centre; (4) Large Leisure City; (5) Large Business City; (6) Medium Intermediate City; (7) Small Manufacturing City; and (8) Small Leisure City. These titles reflect the size, specialization and balance attributes of station-area job markets. Table 15.3 summarizes the characteristics of the eight groupings by presenting statistical averages for the variables used to form clusters.

Table 15.3 reveals that agglomeration patterns along the Tokaido Shinkansen were highly varied. With more express trains, Tokyo and Shinagawa stations have attracted world-class finance and information business activities. Secondary business and leisure service clusters have formed around Shin-Osaka, Nagoya, and Kyoto stations. Despite a slowdown in growth, the Shin-Yokohama station area remains a large and important business cluster on the western edge of Tokyo. Other intermediate cities served by HSR, however, have generally experienced job losses. From the mapping of location quotients in Table 15.3, we note that medium-size intermediate cities exhibit employment characteristics that most closely resemble those of their corresponding regions. The smallest clusters along the Shinkansen corridor – Kakegawa, Gifu-Hashima, Maibara, and Atami – feature small manufacturing and leisure service activities. In recent years, they have witnessed slight job gains.

Table 15.3 Tokaido Shinkansen: business agglomeration types and statistics for key clustering variables

Type	# of jobs, 2006	Change in # of jobs, 2001–06	Job-population gap index [+1~–1]*, 2006/05	Location quotients [common business code]**, 2006	Stations***
Global Business Centre	3,121,398	40,879	0.497		Tokyo
Waterfront Information Centre	1,710,524	139,542	0.334		Shinagawa
Regional Business Centre	892,298	172,152	0.078		Shin-Osaka Nagoya
Large Leisure City	476,752	121,561	–0.14		Kyoto

				Shin-Yokohama
Large Business City	438,888	−20,787	−0.234	
Medium Intermediate City	158,086	−6,910	−0.214	Toyohashi Hamamatsu Shizuoka Shin-Fuji Mishima Odawara
Small Manufacturing City	59,848	6,285	−0.299	Mikawa-Anjo Maibara Gifu Hashima Kakegawa
Small Leisure City	23,794	2,650	−0.216	Atami

Notes:
*Formula: (Jobs−Population)/(Jobs+Population); Closer to +1, the catchment area has more jobs than population; Closer to −1, it contains more population than jobs.
**Heavy Industry [20], Manufacturing [30], Logistics [40], Knowledge Business [50], Social Service [50], Leisure Service [70], and Other Service [80].
*****Bold stations** offer express train services, the 'Nozomi'.

Table 15.4 Northeast Corridor: business agglomeration types and statistics for key clustering variables

Type	# of jobs, 2008	Change in # of jobs, 2002–08	Job-population gap index [+1~-1]*, 2008/07	Location quotients [common business code]**, 2008	Stations***
Global Business Centre	1,982,781	91,293	0.18		New York City
Regional Service Centre	378,595	49,215	0.062		Washington, DC
Large Business City	216,560	–2,753	–0.167		South Station, Back Bay, New Haven, Stamford, Princeton, Philadelphia, 30th Street, Wilmington, Baltimore
Medium Airport Centre	64,528	11,700	0.217		BWI Airport

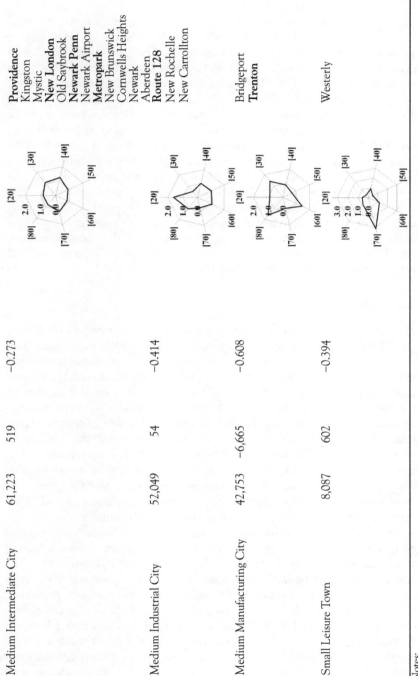

Medium Intermediate City	61,223	519	−0.273	Providence Kingston Mystic **New London** Old Saybrook **Newark Penn** Newark Airport **Metropark** New Brunswick Cornwells Heights Newark
Medium Industrial City	52,049	54	−0.414	Aberdeen **Route 128** New Rochelle New Carrollton
Medium Manufacturing City	42,753	−6,665	−0.608	Bridgeport **Trenton**
Small Leisure Town	8,087	602	−0.394	Westerly

Notes:
*Formula: (Jobs−Population)/(Jobs+Population); Closer to +1, the catchment area has more jobs than population; Closer to −1, it contains more population than jobs.
**Heavy Industry [20], Manufacturing [30], Logistics [40], Knowledge Business [50], Social Service [60], Leisure Service [70], and Other Service [80].
*****Bold stations** offer high-speed intercity train services, the 'Acela Express'.

Northeast Corridor

The thirty Amtrak stations were also grouped into eight categories, similar to those of the Tokaido Shinkansen. Table 15.4 shows that stations along the Northeast Corridor are characterized by contrasting business activities. Served by the Acela Express, stations in New York City and Washington, DC, are home to knowledge- and service-based businesses that cater to both global and regional markets. Jobs in both areas have been on the upswing. In contrast, economic activities in the region's secondary business and medium-size manufacturing cities have slowed around the Amtrak stations. Baltimore-Washington International Airport (BWI) today supports an active and growing business cluster, taking on some of the characteristics of an emerging aerotropolis, while economic activities around the Newark Airport have been more modest and only weakly tied to HSR. As was found along Japan's Tokaido line, medium-size intermediate cities along the Northeast Corridor have employment compositions that most closely match those of their surrounding regions, suggesting that current rail stations themselves have had no particular drawing power that appeals to particular kinds of firms. This could change, of course, with the introduction of upgraded and faster train services at existing Amtrak stations.

California HSR

Business activities around twenty-five possible station locations in California were similarly clustered into eight categories. Table 15.5 summarizes key attributes of eight job market types. The California typology has some of the same business agglomeration patterns found on the Tokaido Shinkansen and Northeast Corridor, but is not identical. Because of the considerably smaller number of types of jobs within 5 km of the planned downtown San Francisco station relative to that found in New York City and Tokyo, and also because of compositional differences, we assigned the title of 'regional' instead of 'global' business centre to this planned station. Within 5 km of San Francisco's Transbay Terminal are numerous knowledge-based businesses, in fields like finance, law, insurance, and engineering, but the area's overall employment base is not as globally connected as that of New York or Tokyo. Nevertheless, many knowledge-based and high-tech firms within San Francisco's planned station catchment serve worldwide clients and markets. Stations planned for Los Angeles and Sacramento, on the other hand, are surrounded by service-based jobs whose customer base is mostly at the regional and state levels. San Jose, Anaheim, Irvine and University City (San Diego) have planned stations in areas characterized by secondary business clusters and edge cities that are experiencing modest rates of growth. Burbank's planned station stands out for its nearby large media cluster. Ontario International Airport (38 miles east of Los Angeles) forms a sizable manufacturing-logistics cluster, while activities near San Francisco International Airport and San Diego are heavily oriented toward tourism services. California's intermediate stations, located in the Central Valley, have few firms that specialize in knowledge- and service-based activities. Local-serving retail, light manufacturing, and agri-businesses – activities that generally benefit the least from spatial clustering and enhanced accessibility to state-wide markets – characterize many of the Central Valley's station areas.

Implications

If the trends and experiences in Japan are repeated in the United States, planned HSR investments in the United States are likely to be associated with territorially uneven and highly localized economic development impacts. This is because there are many station areas in the US cases where there is little currently in place for which HSR will be a significant contributor.

In the Northeast Corridor and California, if the Japanese example applies, HSR is likely to produce agglomeration benefits that accrue mostly to globally connected business centres, and secondarily to specialized areas such as international airports and leisure-service hubs. Such shifts would occur mostly at the expense of many small, intermediate cities. This will be all the more magnified as regions and states continue to shift toward knowledge- and service-intensive businesses.

Regional business centres

If the US follows the same path as did Japan, the economic development impacts of HSR will likely concentrate in globally connected business centres and in regional service centres (e.g., New York, San Francisco, Washington, DC, and Los Angeles), mimicking Japan's experiences with HSR stations in Tokyo, Osaka and Nagoya. This will especially be the case when both public agencies and private entities aggressively embark on large-scale urban regeneration projects that appeal to high value-added businesses (Murakami 2010; Curtis et al. 2009). Around the newly opened Shinagawa Shinkansen station in Central Tokyo, for example, the national government, the privatized Central Japan Railway Company (JR Central), and private real estate developers joined forces to co-develop prestigious office towers and shopping malls (Figure 15.5). The project features high-quality public green plazas and attractive pedestrian-ways as a lure to firms and workers that place a premium on liveability and are drawn to urban amenities when deciding where to open a business or take on a new job.

Japan's commercial redevelopment efforts aim not only to increase business passengers on the Tokaido Shinkansen but also to promote land value capture around the terminal stations. Figure 15.6 shows that Tokyo, Shinagawa and Nagoya have experienced rising commercial land prices within 5 km of the Shinkansen stations, fuelled by large-scale redevelopment projects created through public-private partnerships. In contrast, other HSR station settings have seen commercial property values fall. Compared to many private intracity railway corporations that built suburban railways outside of Tokyo and Osaka, the former Japanese National Railways was passive in promoting and leveraging

Table 15.5 California HSR: business agglomeration types and statistics for key clustering variables

Type	# of jobs, 2008	Change in # of jobs, 2002–08	Job-population gap index [+1~−1]*, 2008	Job location quotients [common business code]**, 2008	Stations
Regional Business Centre	458,621	29,306	0.114		San Francisco
Regional Service Centre	207,182	3,504	−0.202		Los Angeles Sacramento
Large Business City	175,787	4,834	−0.073		San Jose Anaheim Irvine University City
Large Airport Centre	155,603	28,954	0.119		Ontario Airport

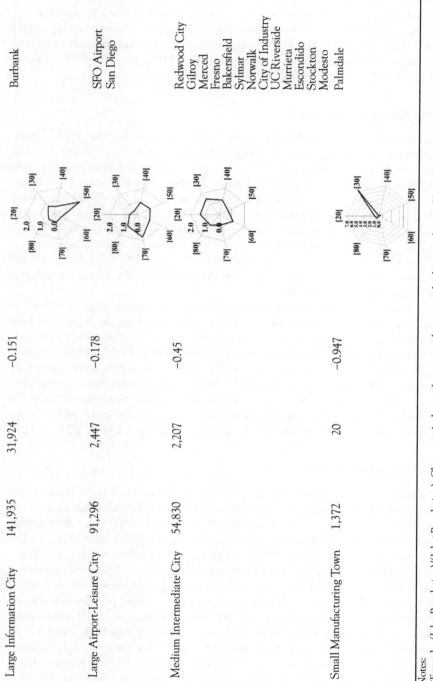

Burbank

SFO Airport
San Diego

Redwood City
Gilroy
Merced
Fresno
Bakersfield
Sylmar
Norwalk
City of Industry
UC Riverside
Murrieta
Escondido
Stockton
Modesto

Palmdale

Large Information City	141,935	31,924	−0.151
Large Airport-Leisure City	91,296	2,447	−0.178
Medium Intermediate City	54,830	2,207	−0.45
Small Manufacturing Town	1,372	20	−0.947

Notes:
*Formula: ((Jobs−Population)/(Jobs+Population); Closer to +1, the catchment area has more jobs than population; Closer to −1, it contains more population than jobs.
**Heavy Industry [20], Manufacturing [30], Logistics [40], Knowledge Business [50], Social Service [70], and Other Service [80].

land development around Shinkansen stations. However, in response to recent market pressures to re-urbanized city centres, the privatized JR Central has sought to maximize real-estate revenue streams, largely from commercial property redevelopment around the Nagoya Shinkansen station. Its proceeds from land development have shot up markedly, from JPY24.3 billion in FY1999 to JPY66.7 billion in FY2009 (JR Central 2011).

Edge cities and aerotropolis

Recalling that Hall (2009) and Kasarda (2010, 2009) predict that HSR systems will attract knowledge-intensive businesses, convention hotel services, and/or time-sensitive industries, the California system offers several promising sites where the groundwork for such development has been laid. For example, we would expect to see development around such sites as Burbank on the north-eastern edge of Hollywood and University City on the northern edge of San Diego. HSR investments also hold promise for attracting globally linked businesses near and around international airports (e.g., BWI Airport on the southern edge of Baltimore and north-eastern edge of metro Washington, DC, SFO Airport on the southern edge of San Francisco, Ontario Airport and Irvine on the eastern and southern edges of Los Angeles).

Some observers question whether automobile-dependent edge cities will be able to sustain dense agglomerations and suburban transit nodes because of high external costs (e.g., traffic congestion, air pollution, and airport noise) that could cancel out accessibility benefits (Lang 2003; Tomkins et al. 1997). In lieu of massive roadway and parking infrastructure, HSR could provide a new layer of intercity mobility, relieving suburban gridlock, improving environmental conditions, and sustaining polycentric transit-served urban forms in the United States (as experienced around the Shin-Yokohama Shinkansen station in suburban Tokyo) (Cervero 2005, 2003; Leinback 2004; Cervero and Bernick 1996).

Leisure service cities

Our research also suggests that an HSR system might be able to enhance the economic advantages of tourist-oriented clusters in relatively large cities (e.g., Kyoto on the western side of Japan, Anaheim and San Diego in Southern California) rather than small towns (e.g., Atami at the southwestern end of Greater Tokyo or Westerly on the southwestern shoreline of Rhode Island). Japan's ancient capital city, Kyoto, has seen appreciable gains in the number of regional businesses, local services, and educational institutions within 5 km of the terminal station. It has also become one of Japan's most popular cultural and leisure destinations. Taking advantage of Kyoto's historical resources and national location, the privatized JR Central aggressively marketed new high-speed 'tourist services' that connected Greater Tokyo and Kyoto (13.4 per cent of JR Central's revenues were from hotel and leisure service businesses in FY2006 [Central Japan Railway Company 2007]). Anaheim (home of Disneyland) and San Diego in

Figure 15.5 Transit-joint redevelopments around the newly opened Shinagawa Shinkansen station, 2003

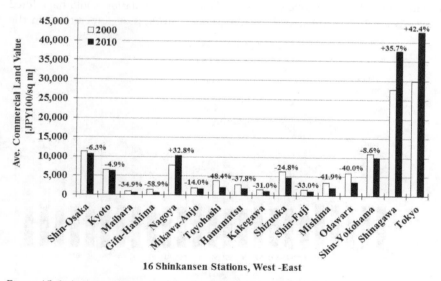

Figure 15.6 Average commercial land values within 5 km of the sixteen Shinkansen stations, 2000 and 2010

Southern California have a number of entertainment, recreational, cultural, hotel, and food-service businesses within 5 km of the proposed HSR stations. The cities could likewise be promoted as easy to reach leisure destinations for tourist markets in Northern California.

Other intermediate cities

Japanese experiences reveal that very small and intermediate cities failed to reap economic development benefits from HSR largely because of their manufacturing- and service-industry economic bases. This is also how employment growth is trending in small and intermediate cities along the Northeast Corridor and around several of the planned California HSR stations. However, the Japanese experience also reflects operating decisions. In the case of Japan, the spatial redistributions of economic activities between major and minor cities have been strongly associated with the Tokaido Shinkansen's intercity service patterns over the last two decades. Figure 15.7 illustrates that the privatized JR Central set up the 'Nozomi' services that skip through eleven of the seventeen Tokaido Shinkansen stations. The Nozomi services have increasingly replaced the 'Hikari' services that, since 1992, were designed to stop at five of the eleven intermediate stations (Odawara, Shizuoka, Hamamatsu, Gifu-Hashima, and Maibara). Apparently, these five intermediate stops have become less attractive destinations for business passengers and less profitable for the privatized JR Central. New intercity service patterns have been matched by falling commercial land values in the minor intermediate cities (presented in Figure 15.6).

Public policies might have intervened to alter market trends. For example, expanded local feeder services as well as land use deregulation could have lured new private investment and thus strengthened business agglomerations in the

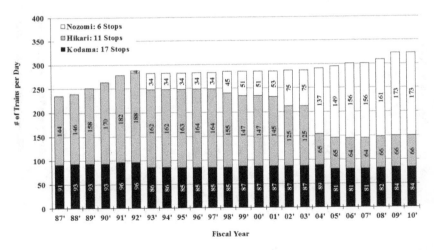

Figure 15.7 Changes in the Tokaido Shinkansen's intercity service patterns, 1987–2010

station catchment areas. Nevertheless, the comparative advantage of the small intermediate cities in areas like agriculture and traditional manufacturing are the kinds of economic activities that find little value in being near a high-speed passenger rail station in a clustered configuration.

Without both clear regional strategies and proactive local efforts, proposed HSR projects in the United States could end up saddling local governments of medium-sized cities with high ancillary costs like expanding local bus services and upgrading sewer-water facilities without an expanded tax base from high value-added industries. Regional policies should aim to redress such potential inequities.

Strategies for leveraging economic development potential

We believe that, on the whole, the economic development impacts of HSR investments in major city-regions of the United States are likely to be more redistributive than generative, unless there are major interventions to change direction. Past experiences from Japan and market trends around areas planned for HSR services in the US suggest this to be the case. However, net overall benefits can accrue from spatial redistribution, in the form of strengthening the global competitiveness (and the associated spill-over benefits) of large urban centres. HSR's business relocation effects within one region need not be a simple 'zero-sum' game. The knowledge-intensive businesses, time-sensitive industries, and tourist-oriented services shifting from elsewhere to higher density, more accessible, and high amenity nodes, like New York City, Washington, DC, San Francisco and Los Angeles, could generate net increases in wealth and economic development that benefit metro-regions at large (Cervero and Aschauer 1998; Weisbrod and Weisbrod 1997).

Some observers maintain that the direct user benefits of new HSR and local transit systems alone will unlikely be large enough to cover the full lifecycle costs of HSR investments in a traditionally automobile-oriented society like the US. External accessibility and agglomeration benefits, if leveraged by proactive public policies that reward efficiencies and appeal to high value-added businesses, could help tilt the benefit-cost equation in HSR's favour. The net economic impacts of HSR investments will likely be negative unless public policies appropriately guide market shifts to station catchment areas that, based on Japan's experiences, offer comparative business advantages.

Four policy responses are recommended for leveraging the economic development impacts of HSR:

1   Polycentric development as a global competition strategy. HSR investments in the United States are in a position to strengthen major city-regions' polycentric form and in so doing increase global competitiveness. This could occur by efficiently linking central business districts, edge cities, international airports, and tourist destinations. Such integration could offer more advantageous business locations and localize greater development benefits in the station catchments. Economic linkages might also be

improved over an even larger mega-regional level (e.g., between city pairs within states), dramatically expanding the market-sheds and labour-sheds of firms seeking a competitive edge – e.g., enhanced co-matching between businesses seeking specialized labour inputs and workers seeking the most promising and gratifying employment opportunities. If synergetic and spill-over effects conferred to globally-connected establishments by HSR are to be fruitfully leveraged, strategic planning needs to occur on a larger geographic scale to reflect the mega-territorial reach of an inter-city HSR investment. This speaks to the need for more proactive state, sub-state, and inter-state land-use planning and growth management. Institutionally, there needs to be a close geographic correspondence between the trans-metropolitan coverage of expanded economic interactions and the territorial space in which land-use planning and growth management takes place. In general, current regional planning structures in the US, like councils of government (COGs) and metropolitan planning organizations (MPOs), are too geographically constrained to carry out the scale of planning needed to successfully tie HSR investments to mega-scale economic development.

2   Pro-business state assistance as a regional development strategy. HSR investments in the US will likely need 'pro-business' policy interventions to guide HSR-induced economic activities at the sub-state level. Permissive zoning, targeted public infrastructure investments, expanded and improved feeder bus services that tie into HSR stations, flexible funding programmes, and expedited environmental reviews could help leverage private investment and facilitate the location of co-dependent business activities that are naturally drawn to HSR stations. Public-private co-ventures should be aggressively pursued in this regard. Both sides bring to the table the kinds of complementary resources (e.g., eminent domain powers of government and the entrepreneurial instincts of private investors) needed to share near-term risks and downstream benefits inherent with mega-projects like HSR.

3   Land value capture as an infrastructure financing strategy. HSR authorities should aggressively pursue joint development opportunities, recouping costs by capturing a portion of the accessibility and agglomeration benefits that would be capitalized into commercial land values near major intercity terminals. Properly designated value capture applications for HSR projects could balance global corporate profits and local public interests, discourage excessive levels of rent-seeking investments, and maximize long-term revenue streams by encouraging high-density, mixed-use, and amenity property packages around HSR terminals. Useful lessons on recapturing accessibility and agglomeration premiums created by investments in fast train services can be drawn from experiences in Hong Kong under its Rail+Property programme (Cervero and Murakami 2009).

4   Transit-oriented development as a community improvement strategy. With the help of federal and state funding programmes, local governments in small and intermediate cities can play pivotal roles in assembling land parcels, promoting affordable housing, providing feeder bus services,

and rationalizing parking policies (so as not to detract from high-quality pedestrian environments) around HSR stations. Local business entities also need to proactively seize upon community development opportunities created by HSR projects. Under the right market conditions, the provision of high-quality pedestrian infrastructure and urban designs could create a liveability premium in the vicinity of HSR stations of large urban centres. This in turn could help business centres attract and retain highly-skilled, knowledge-based workers. HSR investments, backed by public-private co-ventures that leverage high-quality transit-oriented development, could be a boon to economic growth and expansion in select urban markets for years to come. Successful transit-oriented developments (TODs) around HSR stations, however, are likely to be considerably different than that of metropolitan rail systems, thus the same design templates should not be employed. Whereas housing is often a prominent feature of urban-rail TODs in the US, due to HSR's logistical designs, busy intermodal connections, and the potentially higher nearby land prices that are bid up by time-sensitive firms, office and retail uses are apt to be more common in HSR TODs. To the degree TODs are embraced as strategies for charting more sustainable urban futures, as stressed in California's landmark Senate Bill 375 (carbon emission legislation), new forms of TODs conducive to HSR services should be pursued.

Note

1 In our analysis, we exclude the proposed California Hanford/Visalia/Tulare stop because the multiple station options publicized by CHSRA contain too few nearby business establishments for job market analysis.

References

Aldenderfer, M. S., and Blashfield, R. K. 1984, *Cluster analysis: Quantitative applications in the social sciences* (No. 07-044), Beverly Hills: Sage Publications.

Amtrak 2011, 'Amtrak National Factsheet: FY2010' Retrieved June 15, 2011, from http://www.amtrak.com/servlet/ContentServer?c=Page&pagename=am%2FLayout&c id=1246041980246 *Accessed 1 August 2016.*

Banister, D., and Berechman, J. 2000, *Transport investment and economic development*, London and New York: Routledge.

Bertolini, L., and Spit, T. 1998, *Cities on rails: The redevelopment of railway station areas*, London: E & FN Spon.

California High-Speed Rail Authority 2010, 'Proposed route map'. Retrieved October 20, 2010, from http://www.hsr.ca.gov/Programs/Statewide_Rail_Modernization/Project_Sections/index.html

Catz, S. L., and Christian, A. 2010, 'Thinking ahead: High-speed rail in Southern California' (ITS Working Paper), University of California, Irvine, CA.

Central Japan Railway Company 2007, *Databook 2006*, Nagoya, Japan: JR Central.

Central Japan Railway Company 2011, 'Fact Sheet 2010'.

Cervero, R. 2003, 'Growing smart by linking transportation and land use: Perspectives from California', *Built Environment*, vol. 29, no. 1, pp. 66–78.

Cervero, R. 2005, 'Progress in coping with complex urban transport problems in the United States', in G. Jönson and E. Tengström (Eds.), *Urban transport development: A complex issue* (pp. 118–143), Berlin: Springer.

Cervero, R., and Aschauer, A. D. 1998, *Economic impact analysis of transit investments: Guidebook for practitioners* (Transit Cooperative Research Program Report 35), Washington, DC: Transportation Research Board.

Cervero, R., and Bernick, M. 1996, 'High-speed rail and development of California's Central Valley: Comparative lessons and public policy considerations', (IURD Working Paper 675), University of California, Berkeley, CA.

Cervero, R., and Murakami, J. 2009, 'Rail and property development in Hong Kong: Experiences and extensions', *Urban Studies*, vol. 46, no. 10, pp. 2019–2043.

Curtis, C., Renne, J. L., and Bertolini, L. (Eds.) 2009, *Transit oriented development: Making it happen*, Farnham: Ashgate.

Esri. 2010, 'Esri updated demographics'. Retrieved April 1, 2010, from http://www.esri.com/data/esri_data/demographic.html

Freeman, A. 2007, 'London's creative sector: 2007', Update (Working Paper 22). London, England: GLA Economics.

Garmendia, M., de Ureña, J. M., Ribalaygua, C., Leal, J., and Coronado, J. M. 2008, 'Urban residential development in isolated small cities that are partially integrated in metropolitan areas by high-speed train', *European Urban and Regional Studies*, vol. 15, no. 3, pp. 249–264.

Garreau, J. 1991, *Edge city: Line on the new frontier*, New York: Anchor Books.

Giuliano, G. 1995, 'The weakening transportation-land use connection', *Access*, vol. 6, pp. 3–9.

Giuliano, G. 2004. 'Land use impacts of transportation investments: Highway and transit', in S. Hanson and G. Giuliano (Eds.), *The geography of urban transportation* (3rd ed., pp. 237–273), New York: The Guilford Press.

Givoni, M. 2006, 'Development and impact of the modern high-speed train: A review', *Transport Reviews*, vol. 26, no. 5, pp. 593–611.

Government of Japan 2010a, *Establishment and Enterprise Census 2006*. Retrieved September 7, 2010, from http://www.stat.go.jp/english/data/jigyou/index.htm *Accessed 1 August 2016*.

Government of Japan 2010b, Population Census 2005. Retrieved September 7, 2010, from http://www.e-stat.go.jp/SG1/estat/eStatTopPortal.do *Accessed 1 August 2016*.

Government of Japan 2011, *Geographic Information Systems download service*.

Graham, S., and Marvin, S. 1996, *Telecommunications and the city: Electronic spaces, urban places*, London, England: Routledge.

Greater London Authority (GLA) 2008, *London's central business district: Its global importance*, London, England: GLA Economics.

Gutiérrez, J., González, R., and Gómez G. 1996, 'The European high-speed train network', *Journal of Transport Geography*, vol. 4, pp. 227–238.

Hall, P. 2009, 'Magic and seamless webs: Opportunities and constraints for high-speed trains in Europe', *Built Environment*, vol. 35, no. 1, pp. 59–69.

Kasarda, J. D. 1999, 'Time-based competition and industrial location in the fast century', *Real Estate Issues*, pp. 24–29.

Kasarda, J. D. 2001, 'From airport city to aerotropolis', *Airport World*, vol. 6, no. 4, pp. 42–44.

Kasarda, J. D. 2009, 'Airport cities', *Urban Land*, pp. 56–60.

Kasarda, J. D. (Ed.) 2010, *Global airport cities*, Twickenham: Insight Media.

Lang, R. E. 2003, *Edgeless cities: Exploring the elusive metropolis*, Washington, DC: Brookings Institution Press.

Leinback, T. R. 2004, 'City interactions: The dynamics of passenger and freight flows', in S. Hanson and G. Giuliano (Eds.), *The geography of urban transportation*, 3rd ed., pp. 30–58, New York: The Guilford Press.

Levinson, D. 2010, 'Economic development impacts of high-speed rail' (Working Paper for the Department of Civil Engineering), University of Minnesota, Minneapolis, MN.

Levinson, D., Kanafani, A., and Gillen, D. 1999, 'Air, high speed rail, or highway: A cost comparison in the California corridor', *Transportation Quarterly*, vol. 53, pp. 123–132.

Levinson, D., Mathieu, J. M., Gillen, D., and Kanafani, A. 1997, 'The full cost of high-speed rail: An engineering approach', *The Annals of Regional Science*, vol. 31, pp. 189–215.

Monkkonen, P. 2008, 'Using online satellite imagery as a research tool mapping changing patterns of urbanization in Mexico', *Journal of Planning Education and Research*, vol. 28, pp. 225–236.

Murakami, J. 2010, The transit-oriented global centers for competitiveness and livability: state strategies and market responses in Asia (Dissertation Research Paper for the University of California Transportation Center, UCTC-DISS-2010-02), University of California, Berkeley, CA.

Sands, B. 1993, 'The development effects of high-speed rail stations and implications for California', *Built Environment*, vol. 19, no. 3/4, pp. 257–284.

Takagi, R. 2005, 'High-speed railways: The last 10 years', *Japan Railway and Transport Review*, vol. 40, pp. 4–7.

Thompson, I. B. 1995, 'High-speed transport hubs and Eurocity status: The case of Lyon', *Journal of Transport Geography*, vol. 3, no. 1, pp. 29–37.

Tomkins, J., Topham, N., Twomey, J., and Ward, R. 1997, 'Noise versus access: The impact of an airport in an urban property market', *Urban Studies*, vol. 35, no. 2, pp. 243–258.

Ureña, J. M., Meneraut, P., and Garmendia, M. 2009, 'The high-speed rail challenge for big intermediate cities: A national, regional and local perspective', *Cities*, vol. 26, pp. 266–279.

US Bureau of Transportation Statistics 2011, National Transportation Atlas Database 2011.

US Census Bureau 2011, ZIP Code Business Patterns (ZBP): Download comma-separated value (csv) files.

US Federal Railroad Administration 2011, High-Speed Intercity Passenger Rail Program.

Vickerman, R. 1997, 'High-speed train in Europe: Experience and issues for future development', *The Annals of Regional Science*, vol. 31, pp. 21–38.

Weisbrod, G., and Weisbrod, B. 1997, Assessing the economic impact of transportation projects: How to choose the appropriate technique for your project (Transportation Research Circular 477), Washington, DC: Transportation Research Board.

16 Environmental impact of high-speed rail in California

Elizabeth Deakin

Overview

California's proposed high-speed rail (HSR) system is advocated as a sustainable way to increase the state's intercity transportation capacity, offering a fast, reliable, and convenient travel option that is also environmentally sound. Like any major infrastructure project, however, the system is expected to have significant effects on the natural and built environment. This chapter discusses the environmental impacts that the California HSR system could produce and the strategies that are being proposed to improve its environmental performance.

To set the context for the discussion, the chapter begins with a brief overview of the California High Speed Rail Authority's proposed system. The chapter then reviews the complex environmental review process that is underway and some of the issues it raises. Since the final design and the detailed project-level environmental assessments are not yet complete, a number of gaps remain in the environmental analyses available at this time. However, the programmatic review completed for the overall system concept identifies the range of impacts that are likely and has also been provided for public engagement, flagging the impacts that have raised the greatest concern. Additional environmental documents for segments in the Central Valley provide additional data and insights.

The chapter reviews several of the key environmental issues raised about HSR: its air quality and greenhouse gas impacts; its effects on agriculture and on communities; and its ability to support local plans and aspirations for development. The chapter also addresses environmental uncertainties. Many of these uncertainties result from questions about the demand forecasts for the project, which in turn stem in part from questions about growth patterns as well as system costs and the operations plans that would be feasible. The future performance of competing modes and future urban development and transport also affect HSR environmental performance and are sources of additional environmental uncertainty, since technological advances, policy changes, and planning interventions could all alter HSR environmental impacts.

The chapter draws data from the scholarly and professional literature and from project documents and websites produced by project proponents, supporters and critics. In addition, it is informed by interviews with twenty key informants

(CHSRA officials, environmental advocates, neighbourhood activists, and subject area experts) as well as by urban design studies for selected station areas.

The chapter focuses heavily on the Central Valley because that is where most of the Phase I HSR alignment and several of its initial stations will be located. Impacts also will occur in the major urban areas served by the trains. Chapter 19 discusses some of the issues that have arisen with regard to the proposal to extend HSR up the San Francisco Peninsula.

The CHSRA proposal

The California High Speed Rail Authority (CHSRA) has developed a proposal for a system of high-speed trains spanning the state (see http://www.hsr.ca.gov for details). The proposed system would use electric propulsion and steel-wheel-on-steel-rail technology. The majority of the system would operate on dedicated (exclusive) dual track, but shared track operations would be used in sections with extensive constraints. The proposed station locations are multi-modal hubs and most are in city centres. Intermediate stations would provide off-line platforms to allow express services to pass through.

The system is being developed in phases and within phases, in usable segments. The first phase would provide service between San Francisco and Los Angeles with an extension to Anaheim, running on about 500 miles of tracks. A second phase would extend services north to Sacramento and south to San Diego, bringing the total length of the system up to about 800 miles of rail lines. A 'blended' system design would allow for 'one-seat' services (no transfer required) over existing tracks (to be upgraded) at the urban ends of the lines. Fares and operational details are still to be determined, but preliminary assumptions used in forecasting ridership and revenue call for fares of $86 or less (one way), with two to four trains per hour during the peak period, depending on the station pair, and fewer off-peak (Cambridge Systematics 2014).

Timing, inflation rates, construction prices, and design-build contracting have altered cost figures for the system substantially over time. CHSRA's 2016 estimate for the cost of the Phase I system is $64.2 billion in year-of-expenditure dollars. This is substantially higher than the $40 billion estimate provided in 2008, but less than the $67.6 billion estimate made in 2014, and it includes $2.1 billion in new investments in tracks and grade crossing removals for a 'blended service' extension to Anaheim.

To date, only a portion of the needed funding has been identified. State Proposition 1A – dubbed the Safe, Reliable High-Speed Passenger Train Bond Act for the 21st Century – authorized the issuance of $9.95 billion in general obligation bonds for HSR; it was approved by the California voters by a margin of 52.6 per cent to 48.4 per cent in November 2008. The federal government provided an additional $3.48 billion for CA HSR, with $2.344 billion made available through the American Recovery and Reinvestment Act (ARRA) and $715 million in additional federal funds announced in October 2010. Prop 1A allowed for up to $1.125 billion for administration and preconstruction costs, and bond funds also have been committed to match the federal funds ($2.6 billion), to fund so-called 'bookend' projects in Northern and Southern California ($1.1 billion), and to support regional connectivity projects laid out in the proposition ($950 million). These commitments leave $4.166 billion for construction of the new system. In 2014, the California Legislature substantially increased funding by approving two one-time appropriations as well as continuous appropriation of a portion of the state's cap and trade funds for the project; these funds currently are adding $500–600 million a year for HSR, and can be used for either planning and construction costs or loan repayments. However, additional funds would be needed to complete the promised San Francisco to Los Angeles/Anaheim Phase I system, and would be sought from federal, state, and private sources.

In addition to the stipulations on what can be funded imposed by Prop 1A, federal funds must be spent in accordance with federal conditions and approvals. The Federal Railroad Administration had directed that the federal funding awarded to the project had to be spent on a single section of the project in the Central Valley (Szabo 2010). In response to this mandate, the CHSRA initially approved a 65-mile segment running between two small Central Valley cities, Madera and Corcoran, with one station in downtown Fresno and the other east of Hanford, with funds set aside to connect the tracks to existing rail lines if necessary. With additional funds from the cap and trade auctions beginning to flow, the CHSRA recently proposed a new alternative, to build a first segment from the Silicon Valley (San Jose) to the Central Valley just north of Bakersfield, at a cost of about $18.8 billion and with an opening date of 2027. Public comment is currently being solicited on this proposal, and legislative hearings are being held. Additional changes to the plans may occur in response to the comments received. Nevertheless, construction is underway. Initial construction includes relocation of a highway to make room for HSR tracks, reconstruction of a bridge to allow for HSR clearance, and trenching for a below-grade section.

Environmental review process and objectives

In the US, as in a number of other countries, government agencies proposing or approving projects that will have a significant impact on the environment must comply with legal and regulatory provisions that require impact assessments. In general, the project sponsor's purpose and objectives for proposing a project must be identified, as must a reasonable range of alternatives to the preferred course of action, including a 'no project' alternative. Full disclosure must be made of the anticipated environmental effects of the proposed action and alternatives. Environmental assessments of this sort can help decision-makers weigh anticipated project benefits against environmental as well as economic costs, and may help them to identify design revisions or mitigation strategies to reduce the likelihood or consequences of adverse effects.

Assessments carried out in the EU and elsewhere have evaluated key environmental attributes of high-speed rail both for existing systems and for proposed investments. A broad suite of impacts of concern have been noted, ranging from irreversible commitments of land and other resources, to population exposures to emissions and noise during construction and operations, to local and regional issues such as impacts on traffic congestion. In recent years energy consumption and the global issue of climate change have become prominent considerations. Some of the studies aim at comprehensiveness while other studies limit their focus to a few key impacts such as energy use or emissions. (See, for example: de Rus 2009, rev. 2012; Kosinski, Schipper and Deakin 2010; Kishimoto *et al.* 2012.) The approaches used frequently assess the impacts for a specified 'target' year or set of years, and present 'average' or 'most likely case' effects for the policy or project being evaluated. There is a growing body of research that seeks to improve the environmental assessment of HSR and other transport modes by broadening the scope of the analysis to include life cycle assessments (LCAs – see, for example, Chapter 17). However, such analyses are not currently required under US law; and indeed many observers of the environmental review process, while supportive of the added information LCAs can produce, also point out that such additional analyses add complexity and uncertainty to an already complex and uncertain process. (See, for example: Plevin *et al.* 2013.)

The California HSR programme must undergo review under both state and federal environmental law, with the CHSRA the lead agency for the California Environmental Quality Act (CEQA), and the Federal Rail Administration of the US Dept. of Transportation the lead for compliance with the National Environmental Policy Act (NEPA[1]). NEPA requires preparation of a statement of the environmental effects that rise to significance; CEQA goes a step farther by also calling for mitigation of adverse effects when feasible. The documents produced for major projects with significant effects are called Environmental Impact Statements (EISs – federal) and Environmental Impact Reports (EIRs – state). For the HSR project joint EIR/EIS documents are being prepared.[2]

Because of the size and complexity of the project and the many urban and natural environments it will affect, a decision was made to proceed with a tiered environmental review. The first tier, called the Program EIR/EIS, was scoped to cover the overall state-wide proposal and was designed to support decisions on whether to proceed, to help select a preferred corridor and station locations, and to choose options for phasing in the system. The environmental analysis in the Program EIR/EIS relied primarily on existing data and was carried out at a planning level, describing the alternatives in fairly general terms and looking at potential impacts within broadly defined impact zones. The HSR proposal was compared to two alternatives: a 'no project' alternative and a 'modal' alternative that included a mix of highway and air transport capacity improvements such as additional highway lanes, additional passenger terminal gates, additional runways, and associated improvements. (Buses and conventional rail carry small amounts of traffic currently and were not included in the modal alternative.)

For the EIR/EIS, the baseline year for the analysis was 2020 (because at the time it was thought that the project could be delivered by then – construction was expected to start by 2012). Existing (2003) conditions were first compared to 2020 'no project' conditions, to account for anticipated population growth, socio-economic change, technological change, new patterns of development, and other factors. The direct, indirect, and cumulative effects, positive and negative, of the alternatives were then assessed, and the impacts of the three alternatives – the 2020 'no project' alternative, the proposed HSR alternative, and the 'modal' alternative – were compared. Finally, the alignment and station options within segments of the HSR alternative were compared.

Models of travel demand for high-speed rail are an important element of the environmental assessment because impacts are heavily dependent on ridership projections. Furthermore, many assumptions critical to environmental assessment are based on modelling done by other agencies. These include population and employment projections, forecasts of future development patterns, composition of the vehicle fleet and its emissions, and capital and operating costs and user fees for the various competing modes, among other factors. Such forecasts and assumptions about the future are necessarily uncertain, and if they change, so too can the environmental impacts.

Challenges to the models and assumptions fed the debate over the environmental assessments. In addition, the use of a tiered environmental document, in which detailed analyses are deferred to later steps, appears to have caused a certain amount of uncertainty among reviewers about the level of detail to be expected and anxiety among affected interests over the potential effects on their homes, jobs, and lifestyles.

The Program EIR/EIS was completed in 2008, but litigation was filed contesting the adequacy of the analysis (Town of Atherton vs. CHSRA, 2008).[3] The back story on the litigation was that the southerly Pacheco Pass had been identified by the CHSRA as the preferred route from the Bay Area through the mountains to the Central Valley. However, the route had potentially severe impacts on pristine wetlands, parkland, and habitat; along portions of the right of way, the private railroad that owned the track was resistant to sharing it with the high-speed train; and the Pacheco Pass route also meant that the route from San Jose north to San Francisco would be up the Peninsula, where the litigants wanted the new train only if it could be placed in a tunnel. A number of the plaintiffs were in favour of a more northerly route through the Altamont Pass to the Central Valley, arguing it would serve trips from the Bay Area to Sacramento more effectively and would be closer to much of the region's population; however, the CHSRA rejected the route because it expected difficulties obtaining right of way and because crossing the Bay to San Francisco would require extremely costly bridging.

The trial court found for the plaintiffs on several counts, and while appeals were filed, the CHSRA made revisions to its analyses and the environmental documentation. After additional rounds of litigation the revised EIR/EIS was eventually certified, but the process added 2 years of delay to the project timetable.

The second tier of environmental review documents examines impacts of project sections in greater detail. These documents typically include data based on fieldwork done for the project and base impacts and impact zones on preliminary design and engineering. Currently, nine project sections plus a wye connector[4] have been identified for separate analysis. Two Section EIR/EISs have a final decision, Merced to Fresno (2012) and Fresno to Bakersfield (2014), although additional work on station location is being performed in Bakersfield at the city's request. The CHSRA has identified completion of the remaining EIR/EISs as a high priority item since construction cannot proceed until the relevant environmental reviews are final and certified.

Among the impacts of the HSR project identified as potentially significant, both in the Program EIR/EIS and in Section EIR/EISs, are the following:

- Air quality
- Greenhouse gas emissions
- Water quality
- Noise
- Vibrations
- Visual impacts
- Impact on flora and fauna – especially endangered and threatened species
- Impacts on habitat
- Waterways, wetlands, and nature preserves or biologically sensitive habitat areas affected
- Parklands lost, trails crossed
- Effects on use and enjoyment of the natural environment – parks, wildlife, views
- Encroachment into areas of highly erodible or otherwise sensitive soils
- Disruption to rail and road transport during construction
- Permanent impacts on rail operations due to, e.g., loss or relocation of sidings
- Permanent traffic circulation changes – increased circuity; delay due to ROW protection
- Traffic and parking impacts around stations
- Disruption, relocation of utilities
- Waste disposal impacts (construction and long-term)
- Takings of homes and businesses – full and partial
- Loss of access to urban and rural parcels
- Severance of parcels and resulting economic impacts
- Takings/disturbance of prime and unique farmland/farmland of state or local importance
- Impacts on water channels and irrigation systems
- Impacts on historic and cultural resources
- Archaeological impacts.

Comments from the public indicated particular concerns about effects on neighbourhoods – noise, visual impact, takings, severance, traffic, and circulation changes – as well as potentially harmful impacts on agricultural activities and on parks, endangered species (eleven of which could be affected), and habitat. The importance of these issues was underscored by their being underlying factors in much of the litigation the CHSRA has faced. In addition, questions were raised about the project's impacts on air quality – already a severe problem in much of California and particularly in the Central Valley – during the extended construction phase. Subsequently the CHSRA has taken a number of steps to avoid or mitigate these impacts.

Impact assessment and mitigation strategies

The CHSRA initially listed three major objectives for the project: maximize ridership and revenue potential, maximize intermodal connectivity and accessibility, and control operations and maintenance costs. Each of these strategies has potential for avoiding or minimizing environmental impact. By maximizing HSR ridership, much of which will be attracted from trips that would otherwise be made by plane or car, emissions from those alternative modes can be reduced both from operations changes (assuming that airlines adjust offerings accordingly) and from reduced need for highway and airport capacity expansions. Maximizing ridership also makes efficient use of the resources that are committed in building and operating HSR. Maximizing connectivity and accessibility should increase the range of trips for which HSR is feasible (by allowing convenient transfers to other systems and services) and also should allow environmentally favourable modes to be used to reach the HSR station.

The CHSRA added several additional objectives as the plans for the project developed. They included assuring cost-effective constructability, minimizing impacts on sensitive environmental and natural resources adjacent to the project corridor, minimizing community disruptions, assuring consistency with regional and local plans, and supporting transit-oriented development within a half mile of the stations. These objectives often involve trade-offs between environmental performance and costs.

The CHSRA has preferred routes that use existing rail right of way (most of which are privately owned), or alternatively, properties directly adjacent to rail right of way (ROW) in a highway corridor, all strategies that minimize disturbance of additional areas. For some segments, cost and constructability considerations have led to route choices that minimize distances and reduce the need for viaducts and tunnels, although these considerations were sometimes traded off to serve additional markets. In addition, viaducts and tunnels have been included in preliminary designs when their use would avoid takings or disruption of sensitive areas or communities, but their exceptionally high costs may make it financially impossible to utilize these design features when other options are available.

Citizen concerns have played an important role in influencing ROW and design choices, in some cases to the point of eliminating certain corridors from further consideration. In particular, concerns about potential impacts on coastal bluffs, beaches, views, historic areas, parklands, and sensitive communities along the coast between South Orange County and San Diego led to a decision to eliminate right of way options along the coast from South Orange County to San Diego.

Air quality impacts, energy and greenhouse gas emissions, farmland preservation, community impact, and HSR's impacts on local and regional plans have been major issues in the environmental assessments. Each is discussed briefly below.

Air quality

The federal Clean Air Act requires the Environmental Protection Agency (EPA) to establish National Ambient Air Quality Standards (NAAQS) to protect public health and welfare, including heath of 'sensitive' populations such as asthmatics, children, and the elderly, and to protect against damage to plants and animals, buildings, and the natural environment, including visibility. Standards have been set for six 'criteria' air pollutants: ozone (an indicator of photochemical oxidants formed in the presence of sunlight from precursor emissions of volatile organic compounds and oxides of nitrogen), carbon monoxide, nitrogen dioxide, sulfur dioxide, lead, and particulate matter (PM2.5 and PM10) (US EPA 2016). These standards are reviewed every 5 years and have been revised from time to time based on the most recent available data on health and welfare effects. The State of California has its own air quality standards which differ somewhat from the federal ones (California EPA 2015).

Much of California remains in the nonattainment category for ozone and PM2.5 emissions standards under both federal and state law. In the regions to be served by HSR, the Bay Area and San Diego were classified by the US EPA (2016) as 'marginal' for ozone, the Sacramento region is classified as 'severe', and the San Joaquin region (the southern portion of the Central Valley) and the Los Angeles/South Coast region are classified as 'extreme' in terms of their violations of the air standards. Such areas must maintain plans showing how they will reduce emissions to acceptable levels, and penalties can be applied for failure to implement the plan or show reasonable progress toward attainment of the standards.

Passenger transportation sources are a relatively small share of the overall air pollution burden. The California Air Resources Board (CARB) state-wide emissions inventory data for 2012 show that cars and light duty trucks emitted about 14 per cent of the reactive organic compounds; aircraft accounted for about 1.7 per cent, with the rest coming from industrial processes, surface coatings, consumer products, agricultural operations, and trucks, ships, and other motor vehicles. Regional differences can be significant but in general passenger travel remains small compared to other sources. For the San Joaquin Valley, for example, CARB's 2015 inventory of emissions shows that passenger vehicles and light duty trucks account for 16.3 tons a day of volatile organic compounds emitted into the air, and aircraft account for 4.5 tons a day, out of a total of 1,815.5 tons a day (CARB 2015). As additional regulations on vehicle emissions take effect and as the vehicle fleet becomes less dependent on gasoline and diesel fuels, emissions are expected to decline further. Whether and when this will be sufficient to attain the national air quality standards is uncertain, however. CARB has developed a scenario plan for standards attainment by 2030–31 that would require a 45 per cent state-wide decline in emissions of organic compounds and particulates by 2030–31. Achieving such a reduction would require substantially increased use of low emission and zero-emission passenger vehicles (ZEV) powered by electricity and hydrogen (with 50 per cent renewable energy generation), with liquid fuels for combustion engine vehicles heavily sourced from renewable feedstock (CARB 2015). These targets are ambitious, but they also are consistent with greenhouse gas emissions reduction targets set by the state.

In the meantime, serious levels of pollution persist. As a result, construction emissions for major infrastructure such as HSR are an issue. With current air pollution levels posing serious health risks (including acting as a trigger for asthma attacks, affecting as many as one out of seven children in the air basin), air pollution officials in San Joaquin County have argued that rail construction should not add to the emissions burden. They have argued that if the best available technologies for construction equipment result in a net increase in emissions, mitigation should extend to funding other sources of pollution reduction. Concerns also extend to emissions from the quarrying of gravel and production of concrete for the project.

In response to these concerns, the CHSRA has developed a programme of actions designed to avoid, minimize, and offset emissions during construction and afterward. They include mandating the use of low emissions construction equipment and construction practices, as well as providing funds for offsetting remaining emissions by, e.g., replacing irrigation pumps, buying new school buses, replacement or retrofitting of old truck engines, and other similar projects. The intent is to zero out construction emissions of particulate matter and volatile organic compounds. The subsequent operation of HSR will not produce tailpipe emissions, and the net emissions in and out of the region would depend on electricity sources.

Energy and GHG emissions

California has committed by statute (AB32 2006) to reduce greenhouse gas (GHG) emissions to 1990 levels by 2020, with a further reduction target of 80 per cent below these levels by 2050 specified through Executive Order (EO S-3-05 2005). A recent Executive Order (EO B-30-15 2015) established a 2030 target of a 40 per cent GHG reduction below 1990 levels. To accomplish these reductions, the state is pursuing a range of strategies targeting practically every source of emissions within the state. These strategies include increasing the amount of electricity derived from renewable sources to 50 per cent; doubling the efficiency savings achieved at existing buildings; seeking up to a 50 per cent reduction in petroleum use; developing new policies to reduce emissions of short lived but powerful climate pollutants; and managing agriculture, forests, and natural preserves so that they can store carbon. Transportation accounts for 37 per cent of the GHG inventory, with cars, SUVs, and light duty trucks responsible for about three-quarters of that, so the state is also encouraging the use of personal vehicles with low GHG emissions and has started the development of a freight strategy to encourage GHG emissions reductions from that portion of the vehicle fleet. In addition, state law requires regional planning to consider transportation and land use strategies to reduce GHG (SB375 2008), and this has resulted in plans promoting cycling and walking, increased transit use, and higher density and more compact development including infill.

Consistent with these mandates, among the policies that the CHSRA is pursuing are the following (CHSRA 2016):

- Minimize energy use and GHG emissions through design and in construction.
- Make life cycle performance of components, systems, and materials a priority.
- Minimize carbon intensity (embodied carbon) of major materials while maintaining durability and quality.
- Maximize station access for pedestrians, cyclists, and transit riders.
- Adaptively reuse existing structures and facilities whenever feasible.
- Divert 75 per cent or more of construction wastes from landfill.
- Recycle all steel and concrete.
- Use 100 per cent renewable energy for operation.

The environmental assessments for the HSR project assert that by committing to zero net greenhouse gas emissions during construction and 100 per cent renewable energy during operations, the main GHG emissions remaining would be due to the system's life cycle aspects, some of which might also be reduced by green materials and practices as suppliers increasingly reduce and offset their own carbon content.

A number of additional mitigation measures are currently under discussion or planned. For example, coordination of station area plans with local and regional transit services is intended to reduce access-related emissions and traffic impacts. Tree planting in the Central Valley will be used as a carbon emissions mitigation measure, as will the replacement of fossil fuel-burning irrigation pumps with electric pumps, and the replacement of or retrofit of vehicles with more efficient engines, strategies that have the potential to also aid in the retention of agriculture.

Impacts on agriculture

The preferred route through the Central Valley of California connects the coastal areas of the state with inland urban areas, but it also raises issues about potentially adverse impacts on farming and ranching. While it is home to over 6.5 million people, the Central Valley, 40–60 miles wide and 450 miles long, is also one of the most productive agricultural areas in the world. It produces more than half of the fruits and vegetables grown in the US, including practically every sub-tropical crop, and is the leading US producer of almonds, walnuts, pistachios, artichokes, pomegranates, dates, kiwis, and figs. It also is a major producer of grapes, livestock, and dairy products (USDA 2015). While Sacramento at the north is the state capitol and has a diversified economy, most of the rest of the cities and towns in the valley base their economies on agriculture. In the southern, San Joaquin, portion of the Central Valley, direct, indirect, and induced effects of agricultural production and processing accounted for 37.8 per cent of regional employment, almost 30 per cent of regional labour income, and 34.2 per cent of regional total value added (UCAIC 2009).

Although agriculture is a major economic force, Central Valley residents are among the state's poorest. Low incomes reflect the lack of economic diversity in the area, low wages and skill levels for most agricultural jobs, and low education levels among the area's population (PPIC 2006). Population growth in the Central Valley has been driven by both natural increase and migration, mostly from other parts of California. Lacking the pull of good jobs, the Central Valley's major attraction has been its affordable housing prices. With urban growth has come a gradual loss of agricultural land.

High-speed rail requires acquisition of agricultural land for right of way and in some cases for stations and other facilities. Both federal and state laws are triggered by this impact. The federal Farmland Protection Policy Act (FPPA) requires federal agencies (in this case, the Federal Rail Administration) to examine potential direct and indirect effects on farmland of a proposed action and its alternatives before approving any activity that would convert farmland to non-agricultural use. Farmland subject to FPPA requirements includes forestland, pastureland, as well as cropland. In California, loss of farmland is a potentially significant impact under CEQA, and state policy is to avoid takings of farmland that are under agricultural protection. At present, substantial acreage is protected under the California Land Conservation Act, commonly known as the Williamson Act, under which property owners may voluntarily enrol agricultural and open space lands in 10-year contracts with local government, restricting use to agriculture, open space, and compatible uses in return for tax breaks. Alternatively the landowner or a group of landowners can request the creation of a Farmland Security Zone (FSZ), an agricultural preserve that offers greater property tax reductions but also has a minimum initial term of 20 years. In the Central Valley, much of the agricultural land – 60–80 per cent in several counties – is under Williamson Act contracts or FSZs.

Losses of agricultural land are not limited to the Central Valley; according to a report by the Department of Conservation's Division of Land Resource Protection (DLRP 2015), 43 per cent of recent losses were in Southern California, with San Diego, Riverside, and San Bernardino Counties accounting for much of the change. However, 30 per cent of the agricultural land conversion occurred in the southern (San Joaquin) portion of the Central Valley. Most losses are to development at the periphery of existing cities, and to a lesser degree to rural housing including large lot or ranchette development and to water projects. Farmland is also idled from time to time if crop prices plunge or inputs (such as water) are too scarce, or if development leaves agricultural land marooned amidst urban development (a situation that can make agricultural noise, smells, and chemical use problematic or require costly alternative management practices).

Increased efficiencies in agricultural production have partially made up for the losses but the effects are uneven.

In this context, agricultural land takings and severance of parcels, potentially resulting in remnants that would not be practicable to farm, were analyzed in detail for each of the HSR alignments and alternatives. During the environmental reviews, agricultural interests in the Central Valley raised additional concerns about potential problems arising from the train's construction and operation, including impacts on irrigation systems, the effects of train noise and vibration on animals, and effects of train-generated winds on bees. Technical advisory panels were formed to respond to these issues and a series of white papers was issued as public information documents and as background for the environmental analyses. The analysis then looked at takings of farm and grazing lands for the various line and station alternatives, as well as impacts that would rise to a level that would result in the removal of farmland from agricultural use. (Lesser impacts, such as reduced productivity due to construction or operation of HSR, were referred to the economic impact section of the analysis.)

While preservation of agriculture is an important objective, most cities also approve urban development to accommodate population growth, and they seek to improve their economic outcomes by attracting new economic development. In the environmental assessment, the CHSRA asserted that the 'no project' alternative would result in extensive farmland conversion to house the expanding population, while in comparison, the HSR alternatives would convert farmland for construction of the project but would also support local plans for focusing future growth on land that is already urbanized or is planned for urban uses. The 'modal' alternative was also assessed to require more agricultural land than HSR.

The strategies proposed by the CHSRA to reduce impacts on agriculture include avoiding farmland when selecting the HSR alignment, as well as situating the alignment adjacent to existing railroad rights-of-way or highways, or along property lines, strategies that would avoid bisecting properties or creating oddly shaped parcels that would be difficult to farm. Overpasses or viaduct would be used to minimize impacts on waterways; and overpasses and underpasses designed to allow farm equipment to cross the alignment, with additional farm roads if necessary, were identified as ways to reduce adverse impacts due to added circuity. Since farmland is also a major source of habitat, passageways would be designed to avoid, minimize, and/or mitigate any potential impacts to wildlife movement.

Community impacts

Community impacts include the direct effects of acquisition and relocation of homes, businesses, and public and private community facilities and institutions (government offices, schools, police and fire stations, senior centres, churches, parks and recreation facilities, theaters/cinemas, etc.), as well as the indirect effects of changes in access to them. These impacts can cumulatively generate changes in neighbourhood quality, safety and security, changes in employment opportunities and in tax revenues, as well as changes in social interaction and community cohesion. Disproportionate impacts may fall on low income or minority communities or on people with special needs due to disabilities.

For the HSR environmental assessments, an inventory was conducted of all facilities within a quarter mile of proposed alignments and a half mile of stations and other facility sites. In addition, public outreach was used to identify issues of particular concern. Residents and business owners flagged property takings, noise, congestion, and devaluation of property along the tracks as potential negatives. In the Central Valley, they also identified employment opportunities, increased business activity, improved accessibility, and jobs and sales during construction as possible benefits. This was in marked contrast to the reactions of residents along the San Francisco Peninsula, many of whom noted the potential problems but were uninterested in the possible economic development boost.

Central Valley communities were hard hit by the recession of 2008 and the bursting of the housing bubble that helped to precipitate it. Unemployment increased sharply, and over the next several years property tax revenues fell because of foreclosures, and sales tax revenues also declined. Recovery has been gradual, with the extended drought affecting employment in agriculture and related industries. This context explains the communities' higher interest in HSR's potential for supporting economic development than has been found in the more affluent and job-rich Bay Area.

The use of electric power and advanced-design track interfaces for HSR would reduce noise compared to existing diesel passenger trains. Design practices that would be employed to avoid adverse community impact include use of existing transportation corridors, grade separation from roadways, and use of tunnels or trenches to reduce noise and visual impact.

In the Central Valley, both housing and commercial property takings would be necessary to locate track, stations, and related facilities. The environmental assessment assumed that the housing impact would be minor because there are available vacancies in the sub-region (if not in the immediate neighbourhood) and relocation assistance would be provided. For commercial facilities it was assumed that relocation likewise would be feasible with normal assistance. For community facilities, the assessment recommended replacement occur before the existing facilities are removed.

For the cities with downtown HSR stations, it was assumed that the station areas would attract new businesses and additional development, resulting in primarily beneficial social impacts including increased employment opportunities and tax revenues. These employment and tax increases would be felt as a benefit throughout the city/county and beyond, including communities that would not have an HSR station. However, the environmental assessments acknowledged that in communities without HSR stations or maintenance facilities, community impacts would tend to be negligible or adverse rather than beneficial. This is due to the effects of possible property takings along some of the alignments as well as visual changes, noise, and changes in local access and circulation, all of which could reduce property values and quality of life. Communities with stations or maintenance facilities would see some of these impacts offset by new development (commercial and residential). In Central Valley cities such as Merced and Fresno, infill development and redevelopment opportunities were also assumed to relieve some of the pressures to develop agricultural lands, partially offsetting losses of farmland to track construction.

Somewhat more controversially, it has been proposed that the HSR alternative would improve accessibility to labour and customer markets, particularly for high wage employment sectors, thereby potentially improving the state's overall economy, and that this effect would be stronger for HSR than for the modal alternative. See Chapter 15 for further discussion of this issue.

Support for state, regional, and local planning goals

California's 2006 climate legislation, Assembly Bill (AB) 32, was complemented in 2008 with legislation promoting the reduction of vehicle miles travelled (VMT) and vehicle use. SB 375 calls for reducing emissions through changed land use patterns and improved transportation alternatives.

Under SB 375, in collaboration with the state's metropolitan planning organizations (MPOs), CARB set regional targets for the reduction of greenhouse gas emissions. The MPOs were then required to develop a 'sustainable communities strategy' (SCS) to demonstrate how the region could meet the greenhouse gas emission targets, or, should the sustainable communities strategy fall short of meeting the targets, prepare an 'alternative planning strategy' (APS) that, if implemented, would meet the targets. These 'strategies' are expected to take into account expected growth in the region as well as the particular needs of various economic groups, and include the general location of various land uses, their densities and intensities, the transportation networks and services to be provided, and the transport demand management strategies to be implemented. However, SB 375 specifically leaves the final say over land use with local cities and counties. Neither the SCS nor an APS supersedes a city's or county's general plan or requires it to be changed to be consistent with the regional plan. Consistency is only required in determining eligibility for CEQA streamlining incentives and for transport funding incentives: SB 375 mandated that decisions relating to the allocation of transportation funding be consistent with the Sustainable Communities Strategy, and also strengthened requirements for public involvement and provided CEQA incentives for development projects that are consistent with an approved SCS. How powerful these stipulations prove to be remains to be assessed.

Additional changes in legislation and regulations have appeared as implementation of SB 375 has moved forward. Of particular note is SB 743, which (among other things) directed the Governor's Office of Planning and Research to develop new CEQA guidelines to balance congestion management and its emphasis on level of service with state-wide goals promoting infill development, cycling and walking, and reduction of greenhouse gas emissions. For areas within a half mile of a major transit stop, new CEQA standards apply.

The CHSRA has identified transit-oriented development (TOD) around its stations as one of its objectives, and also as a mitigation strategy. Even though the catchment area for HSR stations will surely be much larger, having TOD in the immediate vicinity around stations could support ridership, especially for those with downtown destinations. From a downtown station, many destinations would be within walking distance and many more might be accessed via rail and bus, and shuttles and taxis serving the station. At the same time, downtown stations have the potential to mitigate certain unwanted impacts, for example by reducing the traffic that auto access and egress to stations would produce. In addition, cities could capture benefits from HSR by promoting land uses that HSR riders would benefit from, such as restaurants and hotels. Offices, shopping and housing also have developed around HSR stations in other countries (see, for example, Chapters 3 and 15).

Figures 16.1 and 16.2 are taken from a study by Deakin *et al.* (2010) investigating infill development around the proposed HSR station in Fresno. (A similar study for two other potential station areas was done as well; see Deakin *et al.* 2009.) Figure 16.1 presents an analysis of infill potential, showing that there is a vast amount of un- and under-developed land that could be developed. Figure 16.2 is an example of the sort of infill development that might be implemented.

How realistic are such concepts? Fresno's recent update of its general plan calls for this sort of infill, but the designs reflect possibilities for development that have not been checked against market realities. With a high unemployment rate, a flattened real estate market, and heavy current reliance on the automobile for nearly all travel, Fresno may not be a particularly good prospect for new infill development at the current time, but HSR multimodal stations could change the prospects and become hubs for such development.

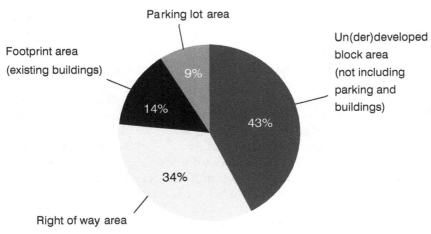

Figure 16.1 Infill development potential – Fresno

San Joaquin Light and Power
Corporation Building   Infill Development   Alexander Pantages Theater

Figure 16.2 Infill examples

Weighing the costs and benefits

Although the environmental impacts of any major construction project are likely to be both positive and negative, the CHSRA's description of the HSR project on its website emphasizes the positive:

> California high-speed rail will connect the mega-regions of the state, contribute to economic development and a cleaner environment, create jobs and preserve agricultural and protected lands. By 2029, the system will run from San Francisco to the Los Angeles basin in under 3 hours with trains capable of over 200 miles per hour. The system will eventually extend to Sacramento and San Diego, totalling 800 miles with up to twenty-four stations. In addition, the Authority is overseeing the implementation of a state-wide rail modernization plan that will invest billions of dollars in local and regional rail lines to meet the state's twenty-first century transportation needs.
>
> The California High Speed Rail Authority is committed to building a high-speed rail system that minimizes impacts to the natural and built environment, encourages compact land development around transit stations, and helps California manage pressing issues with climate change, traffic and airport congestion and energy dependency. Not only will the high-speed rail system alleviate pressure on California's current transportation system, it will provide immediate and long-term environmental and community benefits to residents for decades to come.

(CHSRA 2016)

While the website provides links to draft and final environmental documents, amounting to hundreds of pages, for the determined reader, no overview of environmental impacts is provided – as of spring 2016, the links on the CHSRA website on environmental planning simply stated, 'Coming Soon.' Links to environmental mitigation only discuss reports on farmland takings and potential takings that were agreed as part of settlements with agricultural interests. Additional links provide brief information on sustainability policy, greenhouse gas reduction estimates, and civil rights impacts, but without considerable effort it would be difficult to arrive at an informed view of the issues and impacts.

As the previous section has illustrated, some of the likely impacts of HSR – its land takings, its impact on surrounding communities – depend on the final choices in alignment and design, while other impacts, such as air quality and greenhouse gas emissions, depend on utilization of the system and the extent to which it attracts riders from other modes, especially air and automobile. The benefits and costs depend not only on how and where HSR is built but when it is delivered and how it operates, since it will be competing with modes that themselves are changing in response to economic and environmental challenges and opportunities.

Some of the construction projects being carried out as part of the HSR project should generate few regrets. For example, improvements in public safety due to grade separation of existing as well as planned rail can be costly but will also produce safety benefits regardless of HSR status. Electrification of the Caltrain connection between San Jose and San Francisco will reduce exposure to air pollutants and noise while also cutting operations-generated GHGs. Other project elements, however, are more speculative and more controversial. Several analysts have been highly critical of economic benefits claims; for example, Enthoven *et al.* (2010) question the magnitude and basis of employment forecasts. A large number of analysts (Gillen and Levinson 1996; Levinson 1996; Levinson *et al.* 1996; van Wee *et al.* 2003; Kemp 2004; Morris 2009, among others) show that when the costs of construction are included, benefits per HSR passenger are considerably lower than when operations alone are considered – a point made decades earlier by Lave (1977). Cox and Vranich (2008), among others, note that technological improvements in other modes will narrow the gap between HSR and air or auto. Still other analysts, while less critical of HSR in general, note that the environmental benefits are likely to be modest and net benefits will depend largely on travel considerations (Kosinski *et al.* 2010).

More generally, many analysts have characterized the California HSR project as a 'megaproject' – one whose complexity, time frame, large size, and huge cost lead to risks of optimism bias (overconfidence, unduly favourable interpretations of evidence) and strategic misrepresentation (intentional lying) (Pickrell 1992; Flyvbjerg *et al.* 2003; Altshuler and Luberoff 2003). The increases in costs over time have been one source of concern, but an even bigger source of concern appears to be the major changes in the ridership forecasts. Forecasts prepared by Charles River Associates in 2007 estimated that the 'investment grade' ridership would be about 37.9 million riders a year in 2020 (the then-estimated build-out year); their sensitivity analysis suggested a high ridership of up to 69.1 million riders annually. Forecasts prepared 7 years later by Cambridge Systematics for 2030 projected a much higher 65.5 million riders in the 'base case' and up to 96.5 million riders for the high estimate. 2014 ridership forecasts, also by Cambridge Systematics, present a more modest midrange estimate for Phase 1 of 29.1 million riders in 2029 and 34.7 million by 2040, but with a range as large as 14.8 to 54.4 million for 2029 and 17.0 to 64.8 million for 2040. In discussions with policymakers and interest group leaders, the frequently changing forecasts repeatedly came up as undermining confidence in the project, even among those who recognized that as plans develop and context evolves, changes in forecasts are likely.

The accuracy of costs and forecasts are an environmental issue because some environmental impacts are a function of costs and ridership. Environmental impacts that are a direct function of ridership include emissions savings due to diverted trips, impacts from the traffic levels that will be experienced in station areas, and the potential for business growth related to passenger services. If ridership falls short, the impacts due to operations and ridership, both positive and negative, could be significantly different from those projected. On the other hand, environmental costs will result from building the system, whether or not there is good ridership: the environmental impacts due to right of way and facility location do not change – takings, severance, circuity, impacts on parks, farmland, visual impact. Also, costs that are a function of the number of trains operating will accrue regardless of how many seats are filled – noise, vibrations, and a significant portion of energy consumption and emissions.

The CHSRA has made numerous decisions in its choice of right of way, station location, and design preferences that tend to avoid or mitigate environmental problems. For the most part these choices add to the monetary costs of the project in order to avoid, minimize, or compensate for environmental costs. For example, downtown terminals can be difficult to site and build, and the payoffs may not accrue to the system because California metropolitan areas are not dominated by the central district; most are multinucleated, and even when local governments are committed to strengthening their downtowns through infill and densification it may take many years for markets to respond. If they do so, there is the risk of gentrification with infill and densification that could displace current residents and businesses to outlying areas. Whether the net social benefits exceed the costs is not entirely clear.

There is also the question: *Costs and benefits compared to what?* The CHSRA has compared its proposed project to a no project future scenario and to a scenario in which plausible changes are made to the air and auto-highway modes. However, it is easy to imagine a wide variety of futures for the next 15–25 years:

• HSR construction compared to new construction of equivalent capacity for air and highway travel, e.g., widened roadways, more flights, more runways, assumed to be needed to handle growth.

- Effects of additional use of air and auto modes with little or no capacity expansion or technological change (and resulting congestion, emissions, etc.).
- Use of technologically advanced air and auto modes in the future, e.g., advanced highway operations, highly efficient motor vehicle technologies, automated vehicles, quiet and fuel efficient aircraft, more effective air traffic control – all resulting in competing modes carrying more traffic in the future with little or no physical expansion (but perhaps heavy expansion in IT and vehicle technology).
- Continuation of current subsidies and services, e.g., subsidies to minor airports, subsidies to transit services that feed HSR stations.
- Cuts in subsidies, up to eventual elimination of support for airports, air traffic control, and Amtrak services.

Each of these options or a combination of them could be used to forecast how HSR would fare, with widely differing results likely. Figuring out 'most likely' trajectories is not a simple matter, because existing plans only help a little – for the most part there is not enough detail., and assumptions and time horizons differ. Scenarios thus may be the best way to proceed, but they do not settle controversies, as the emergence of competing scenarios and forecasts has revealed (see Chapter 2).

Scenarios also may be a way to address additional questions with environmental consequences – to size up how important the questions are. Some questions that might fall into this category are:

- How use of rail ROW would affect ability to move more freight by rail (only sketchily analyzed to date in publicly available studies).
- Longer term effects of global warming – e.g., flooding, storms affecting CA airports (could change cost functions and performance of airports).
- Induced travel – how many new trips would be made that are not made now? (Could be negative from an environmental perspective, though from a mobility perspective it could be a positive outcome.)
- Effect of comfort, ability to use time more effectively during travel; effect on mode choice. (SP surveys address this in part, but how well do they predict especially for Californians with limited train experience?)
- How AB 32 and SB 375 plans will change local investments in higher densities, transit; how they will affect investments in highways and airports.

Addressing such questions could provide useful insights not only for HSR but for other modes as well.

Summing up: risks, but potential as well

To sum up, high-speed rail in California will affect the environment in a variety of ways. Both positive and negative impacts on the natural and built environment are likely. Some of the impacts, such as severance of properties, visual impact of structures, and changes in street connections and rail spur availability, will be determined by the choice of right of way and elevation, independent of actual ridership. Other impacts, such noise from trains, will depend on service frequency and speeds. Still other impacts, such as air pollution reduction and GHG emissions avoidance, will depend on a combination of design, equipment, and operations, choices, how many passengers are attracted to HSR, and what share of total passengers would otherwise have travelled by car or air. For the latter set of impact calculations, the future performance of cars, highways, aircraft and airports will also determine the comparative performance, and hence the net environmental benefits, of HSR.

Concerns about ridership forecasts mean that there are also concerns about the ability of California's HSR project to achieve the levels of energy savings, emissions reductions, and GHG avoidance it has claimed. Ridership estimates have improved in recent years in response to peer reviews, but there is no way to fully reduce uncertainties.

HSR's environmental impact also depends on how fast the technology of competing modes improves. HSR performance will look far better if cars in 2030 get 30 mpg than if they achieve 45 or 50 mpg. Likewise, if aircraft become far more fuel efficient (and airlines can afford to use such aircraft in the California markets), HSR's projected advantage over air travel would be diminished.

Many impacts of HSR will depend on the specific alignment and elevation design decisions being developed now. Mitigation of these impacts will likely add costs to the project. An analysis of HSR's changing impacts over time (including a life cycle analysis) is worth doing, but the comparison to other modes likewise should include realistic life cycle comparisons.

Urban impacts will depend not only on HSR plans but also on state and local actions that shape the context in which HSR will operate. If the next 10–12 million people and their jobs are located mostly in low density developments at the fringe of metropolitan areas, it seems likely that driving will continue to be the best option for many trips in the HSR range. If a substantial portion of population and economic growth is accommodated around transit lines through urban infill and densification, HSR may be easily accessible to a higher share of the population and employment centres and therefore more attractive. California's new initiatives to reduce greenhouse gases through regional and local planning under SB 375 could spur the latter response.

Notes

1 Federal regulators have asserted that their authority preempts CEQA challenges to projects they have approved, but this remains far from settled. See Tos v. CHSRA, CA Ct. App., 2014.
2 With decades of practice and litigation over NEPA and CEQA, an intricate practice of environmental review has developed. Here I aim to provide a broad outline which communicates the essence of the EIR/EIS process (and the litigation that followed, in this case), but in so doing I leave out many details and run the risk of oversimplification.

3 Litigation also was filed challenging the CHSRA's compliance with Prop 1A (Tos v. CHSRA, 2011).
4 A wye is a y-shaped or triangular connection between rail lines with switches at the three junctures, allowing trains to travel in multiple directions.

References

Altshuler, AA and Luberoff, D, 2003, *Mega-projects: The changing politics of urban public investment*, Brookings Institution Press.

California Air Resources Board (CARB), 2015, *Mobile Source Strategy Discussion Draft*, Oct. 2015, at http://www.arb.ca.gov/planning/sip/2016sip/2016mobsrc_dd.pdf Accessed 1 August 2016.

California Department of Conservation Division of Land Resource Protection (DLRP), 2015, *California Farmland Conversion Report 2015*, http://www.conservation.ca.gov/dlrp/fmmp/Documents/fmmp/pubs/2010-2012/FCR/FCR 2015_complete.pdf Accessed 1 August 2016.

California Executive Order (EO) S-3-05, 2005, https://gov.ca.gov/news.php?id=1861 Accessed 1 August 2016.

California Executive Order (EO) B-30-15, 2015, https://gov.ca.gov/news.php?id=18938 Accessed 1 August 2016.

California High Speed Rail Authority (CHSRA), 2016.

California Senate Bill (SB) 743, 2013, *Environmental quality: Transit oriented infill projects, judicial review streamlining for environmental leadership development projects, and entertainment and sports center in the City of Sacramento*, September 27.

California Statutes of 2006. AB 32, *The Global Warming Solutions Act*.

California Statutes of 2008. SB 375, *Sustainable Communities Act*.

Cambridge Systematics, Inc., 2014, *California High-Speed Rail 2014 Business Plan Ridership and Revenue Forecasting*, technical memorandum prepared for Parsons Brinckerhoff for the California High-Speed Rail Authority.

Cox, W and Vranich, J, 2008, 'California's High Speed Rail Proposal: A Due Diligence Report,' *Policy Study No. 370*, Reason Foundation, http://reason.org/files/1b544eba6f1 d5f9e8012a8c36676ea7e.pdf Accessed 1 August 2016.

Deakin, E, Shirgaokar, M, Duduta, N, *et al.* 2009, *Transit Oriented Development for High Speed Rail (HSR) in the Central Valley, California: Design Concepts for Stockton and Merced, Report to the California High Speed Rail Authority*, California High Speed Rail Authority.

Deakin, E, *et al.* 2010, *Transit Oriented Development for High Speed Rail (HSR) in the Central Valley, California: Design Concepts for Fresno, Report to the California High Speed Rail Authority*, California High Speed Rail Authority.

de Rus, G, (ed.) 2009, rev. 2012, *Economic analysis of high speed rail in Europe*, Madrid: Fundación BBVA.

Enthoven, AC, Gridley, WC and Warren, WH, 2010, *The Financial Risks of California's Proposed High-Speed Rail*, http://www.cc-hsr.org/assets/pdf/CHSR-Financial_Risks-101210-D.pdf Accessed 15 November 2016.

Flyvbjerg, B, Bruzelius, N and Rothengatter, W, 2003, *Megaprojects and risk: An anatomy of Ambition*, Cambridge University Press.

Gillen, D and Levinson, D, 1999, 'The full cost of air travel in the California corridor,' *Transportation Research Record: Journal of the Transportation Research Board*, vol. 1662, pp.1–9.

Kemp, R, 2004, *Environmental impact of high-speed rail*, Institution of Mechanical Engineers, High Speed Rail Developments.

Kishimoto, PN, Paltsev, S and Karplus, VJ, 2012, *The Future Energy and GHG Emissions Impact of Alternative Personal Transportation Pathways in China*, Joint Program on the Science and Policy of Global Change.

Kosinski, A, Schipper, L and Deakin, E, 2010, 'Analysis of high-speed rail's potential to reduce CO_2 emissions from transportation in the United States,' *Working Chapter, Global Metropolitan Studies Program*, University of California, Berkeley, November 2010.

Lave, C, 1977, 'The Negative Energy Impact of Modern Rail,' *Transit Systems Science*, vol. 195, pp. 595–596.

Levinson, D, 1996, 'The Full Cost of Intercity Transportation,' *Access Magazine*, vol. 9, pp. 21–25.

Levinson, D, Mathieu, J-M, Kanafani, A and Gillen, D, 1996, *The full cost of intercity transportation: A comparison of air, highway, and high speed rail*. Research report UCB-ITS-RR-96-3.

Morris, EA, 2009, 'High-Speed Rail and CO_2,' *Freakonomics, New York Times*, July 24, 2009, at http://freakonomics.blogs.nytimes.com/2009/07/24/high-speed-rail-and-co2/ Accessed 1 August 2016.

Pickrell, D, 1992, 'A Desire Named Streetcar: Fantasy and Fact in Rail Transit,' *Planning: Journal of the American Planning Association*, vol. 58, no. 2, pp. 158–76.

Plevin, RJ, Delucchi, MA and Creutzig, F, 2013, 'Using Attributional Life Cycle Assessment to Estimate Climate-Change Mitigation Benefits Misleads Policy Makers,' *Journal of Industrial Ecology*, vol. 18, no. 1, pp. 73–83.

Szabo, J, Federal Railroad Administrator, to Roelof van Ark, CEO, California High Speed Rail Authority, 2010, *letter of November 3, 2010 regarding expenditures of federal funds received in 2010*.

Town of Atherton *et al.* v. California High Speed Rail Authority, 2009, California Superior Court of the County of Sacramento, Case No 34-2008- 80000022. Filed Nov. 26, 2009.

University of California Agricultural Issues Center, 2009, *The Measure of California Agriculture*, University of California, Davis. At http://aic.ucdavis.edu/publications/moca/moca09/moca09.pdf Accessed 1 August 2016.

US Environmental Protection Agency, 2016, *The Green Book Nonattainment Areas for Criteria Pollutants As of October 01, 2015*.

van Wee, B, van den Brink, R and Nijland, H, 2003, 'Environmental impacts of high-speed rail links in cost–benefit analyses: A case study of the Dutch Zuider Zee line,' *Transport Research Part D*, vol. 8, no.4, pp. 299–314.

17 Uncertainties in the life cycle assessment of high-speed rail's energy and environmental impacts

Mikhail Chester, Megan Smirti Ryerson, and Arpad Horvath

Introduction

A variety of methods for environmental assessment are in use today. The focus of each assessment and the methods chosen for the analysis are driven by the knowledge goals of those conducting the study. These goals can range from identifying and creating an inventory of likely impacts to developing an understanding of their consequences over time, and can extend to identifying ways to avoid, minimize, or mitigate, or compensate for adverse effects.

In the last several decades there has been increasing interest in framing environmental assessments from a life cycle perspective. Life cycle assessment (LCA) is a framework for assessing the cradle-to-grave effects of products, processes, services, activities, or the complex systems in which they reside. LCA accounting provides a more rigorous understanding of the environmental impacts of the entire system, including how upfront design and construction decisions lead to long-term effects. Environmental LCA can thus aid in the planning, design, construction, and operation of systems to minimize energy consumption, emissions that cause climate change and harm to human health, and a host of other environmental and resource depletion impacts.

While there are a number of variations in LCA methods, two approaches in common use today are dubbed 'attributional' LCA and 'consequential' LCA. Attributional LCA tracks energy and material flows through a product's production process, during use, and in decommissioning, disposal or recycling. Attributional LCA has frequently been used to evaluate how the environmental footprint of a product could be reduced. As it is typically implemented, an attributional LCA accounts for the full range of environmental impacts using average data (e.g., average fuel economy and emissions of the vehicle fleet in the years being studied) and presents the results in the same terms. In contrast, a consequential LCA estimates how flows to and from the environment would be affected by various policies or actions under consideration, and focuses on the elements of the system that are affected by the choice under consideration, omitting factors that are not changed. By taking a broad systems view of the environmental impacts of a proposed action, the consequential LCA approach can help avoid pushing a problem from one system to another, which can happen if a narrow perspective is taken. Dynamic changes due to competition with other modes and their consequences also can be considered. However, the broad scope of consequential LCA and its forward perspective raises a number of issues about data and methods.

This chapter examines the issues raised in conducting a life cycle analysis for intercity travel modes, specifically high-speed rail and air transport. The chapter first presents a brief overview of life cycle assessment (LCA), highlighting some of the challenges the method poses. The chapter then discusses the interrelated uncertainties that surround key factors that influence mode choice for intercity travel and the choices operators make to attract customers, fend off competition, and manage costs and impacts. We focus on energy and emissions among the many environmental impacts that intercity travel modes may impose, because these are impacts of great policy concern worldwide, whereas many other impacts, such as noise, loss of habitat, property takings, and changes in the pattern of development stem from more localized and context-specific decisions. The chapter goes on to presents an analytic model that helps to conceptualize responses to changing costs for both travellers and operators. We focus on air transport as the chief mode of competition for HSR as an intercity travel mode. The chapter then presents a life cycle analysis of HSR for California and discusses its implications. The final section presents conclusions.

Background on life cycle assessment

The development of an LCA proceeds in four steps: i) goal and scope definition, ii) inventory analysis, iii) impact assessment, and iv) interpretation (International Organization for Standardization 2006). In goal and scope definition, the practitioner must identify the environmental analysis questions they'd like the LCA to answer. The practitioner then identifies the analytical system boundary to perform the assessment. The system boundary will depend on the environmental questions being asked.

Both attributional and consequential assessments have been conducted for transportation projects and policy investigations. Attributional analyses typically present information on technological performance (e.g., emissions per vehicle-km, seat-km or per passenger-km) and are commonly carried out using average data (e.g., average MPG for the on-road vehicle fleet). Often the performance of a proposed intervention is compared to a baseline, usually current conditions or trends-extended.

Whether an attributional LCA is appropriate or a consequential LCA is needed depends on what questions are being asked. However, it is unlikely that an attributional LCA can by itself indicate the environmental consequences, since environmental consequences depend not just on attributes but market penetration rates, patterns of use, etc. Attributional LCAs are useful if the question is how to improve technological performance, but if the question is what impact a proposed project will have on, say, regional emissions, then additional information is needed. For example, suppose that a manufacturer introduced a new electric vehicle that could operate in automated mode. It would be useful to know that automated electric cars (EVs) typically produce only a fraction of the emissions per passenger mile that a conventional gasoline powered car does. However, to predict the impacts on regional emissions resulting from replacing a portion of the vehicles in a region with automated EVs, one would also want to know how many such vehicles would be in use. If the concern is limited to regional emissions, an analysis of out-of-region vehicle manufacture might be omitted, but power requirements and how that power is generated might be relevant, along with any specialized infrastructure needs for the vehicles (e.g., specialized lanes or control centres, charging stations, specialized disposal facilities). It would also be necessary to estimate how many person-kilometres the vehicles would serve, whether the automated EV would be used instead of a gasoline or diesel-powered vehicle or is used for trips that used to be made by transit or bicycle, and whether the new technology would make trips possible that would not otherwise be made. Furthermore, producers of conventional vehicles might change their designs and performance (fuel economy, emissions, safety features) to be more competitive with EVs; transit operators might adjust their own vehicle fleet, hours and frequencies of operation, and other operational details to compete more effectively. Alternatively, however, the conventional vehicle producer or transit operator might make changes to reduce production in light of lost market shares. In other words, to understand the regional environmental effects of the introduction of automated EVs would require knowledge not only of the vehicle's energy and emissions characteristics but also of the support infrastructure they would need, the market share they would capture and the effects on the competition and their environmental impacts. Consequential LCAs attempt to take these broader systems effects into account by including them in the analysis.

The consequences of the approach chosen and the assumptions made can be substantial. For example, Chester and Horvath (2010) report findings from alternative scenarios for light rail transit (LRT). If only emissions per mile are reported, LRT is far more efficient than a typical car. If, however, LRT must be built before it can be offered, the impacts of construction double the total emissions attributable to LRT. If the system is assumed to operate 90 per cent full, it remains more environmentally friendly than an automobile, but if it is only 10 per cent full its performance is no better than the average car.

LCA results are affected by the analyst's choices regarding system boundaries, data sources, model specifications, and level of aggregation. As an example of system boundary effects, Chester and Horvath (2010) report that including airport equipment, such as baggage tractors, can result in vastly different findings about air transport emissions; in the case they studied, they found that airport equipment generates three to nine times more carbon monoxide emissions than actually flying the aircraft. Likewise, results will likely differ if travel datasets and models aggregate all trip purposes for origin-destination (OD) pairs than if they report trips individually, distinguish business travel from personal travel in model specification and parameter estimation, and account for travel party size. A different result will be produced if it is assumed that 'green energy' will be used than if the assumption is that regional energy markets will simply shift sales of less-green energy elsewhere.

Because of the uncertainties associated with these analytical choices, some scholars argue that consequential LCA should be used for examining alternative scenarios to understand the range of potential environmental outcomes than for predicting a single most-likely outcome (Delucchi 2011, Sathre *et al.* 2012). In addition, it is important to explicitly acknowledge the choices made in setting up the analysis.

Uncertainties associated with operating decisions and passenger forecasts for intercity travel

In performing environmental assessment of the intercity transportation system that accounts for mode shift effects and can therefore reflect on the consequences of the investment, models are needed that capture how operations and passengers will respond to the system change. However, capturing the actions of operators and passengers in a modelling framework is a challenging proposition, due to high levels of uncertainty in the inputs as well as the limits of current understanding of the behaviour of individuals and organizations. Uncertainties include labour costs, fuel and energy prices, vehicle technologies deployed, fares, and travel times, which interact with each other and with passenger demographics, travel needs and preferences to affect mode choice. In the case of California high-speed rail (HSR), the analysis is further complicated by the fact that this would be a new mode with which few Californian travellers have any experience.

While intercity transportation is offered by conventional rail, bus, auto, and air, we will focus only on the aviation system in comparison to HSR. Omission of bus and conventional rail modes will have minor effects on our assessment since their current roles in intercity transport in California are small. While auto plays a large role in intercity transportation, a 2008 study provides an argument for omitting it as well. The Office of the Inspector General (OIG) investigated two scenarios of improvement to the rail service travel times in the Northeast Corridor (US Federal Railroad Administration 2008). The first scenario was 3-hour travel time between Boston and New York and 2.5-hour travel time between New York and Washington; the second scenario cut travel times by 0.5 hours on both segments. The study found that the loss in air ridership would be 10.6 per cent under scenario one and 20.3 per cent under scenario two, while the loss in auto ridership would be 0.3 and 0.6 per cent. In other words, HSR would significantly affect air transport but have a negligible effect on intercity auto use in the Northeast Corridor. In part, this reflects the auto's far higher share of total trips in the corridor (auto is between 80 and 90 per cent of the intercity trips) and in part it reflects the service similarities between air and HSR, versus the significant differences between HSR and auto. The report's authors concluded that those who choose auto in this corridor do so for a reason, for example the airport/HSR station access or egress times may be long, or they may be travelling to multiple destinations. Such passengers would be very unlikely to switch modes. We believe that similar conditions would be in play in California, so we focus on uncertainties related to the HSR and aviation systems as the key competitor for HSR.

We explore the uncertainty surrounding several key inputs used by these two modes of transportation: fuel and labour costs, technology choices, fares, and travel times. We use data that are largely drawn from before the economic downturn which began at the end of 2007. Data for several years thereafter showed declines in travel, and then recovery began. By about 2012 intercity travel in the US had largely returned to its previous levels and patterns are not substantially different from those reflected in the earlier data we use here.

Operating costs for HSR and air: overview

Operating costs for HSR have varied considerably from country to country where HSR systems have been deployed. Table 17.1 presents the reported operating and direct maintenance costs for HSR systems in Europe (de Rus 2009). The costs are in 2006 dollars; EU costs have changed relatively little 2006–2016.

In comparison, CHSRA estimates that its Phase I system will cost roughly a billion dollars per year in operations and maintenance (O&M) costs and will carry roughly 25 million riders a year by 2029 (Cambridge Systematics 2016). Costs, revenues, and ridership are acknowledged to be uncertain and have been subjected to a risk analysis with ranges for forecasts and probabilities attached. Only a portion of the estimated ridership is forecast to be travelling the full length of the Phase I system between the Los Angeles metropolitan region and the San Francisco Bay Area; many HSR trips are expected to begin or end in the Central Valley. Ridership estimates include over 4 million trips that begin or end

Table 17.1 Operating cost for European high-speed rail systems

Country	Type of train	Seats	Operating cost per seat-mile ($)
France	TGV Reseau	377	0.182
	TGV Duplex	510	0.150
	Thalys	377	0.288
Germany	ICE-1	627	0.241
	ICE-2	368	0.336
	ICE-3	415	0.202
	ICE 3 Polyc.	404	0.238
	ICE-T	357	0.244
Italy	ETR 500	590	0.323
	ETR 480	480	0.318
Spain	AVE	329	0.310

Source: de Rus *et al.* 2009

beyond the regions directly served by the system, as well as half a million short trips (under 50 miles) in the Bay Area and Los Angeles.

The forecasts suggest average O&M costs on the order of $40 per forecast rider. Specific trip length estimates were not available to us for this analysis. However, if California HSR trips are projected to average 200 km, the cost per km would be well within the range of those in the EU. If trips are longer, the estimated cost per km would be low compared to the EU experience.

As for air transport, the US costs differ substantially between low cost carriers and 'legacy' carriers, with costs per assigned seat mile ranging from 11 cents for the low cost carriers to about 14 cents for the legacy carriers (MIT 2015). Costs also differ by vehicle type.

Labour costs and fuel prices

Uncertainties regarding operator costs lead to uncertainties about the vehicle technologies, fares, and ultimately operational profile the operators will choose. This is true for both airlines and HSR operators. For HSR in California, labour costs are necessarily speculative and must be based on the range of rail operator costs experienced in the US. Fuel costs will depend on electricity sources and prices, which are likely to change over time.

For airlines, fuel and labour are the largest components of operating cost (Ryerson and Hansen 2010). From 2000–2009, about 50 per cent of airline operating expenses comprised fuel and labour. However, as shown in Figure 17.1, labour costs were relatively stable through most of this period, while fuel prices were volatile; the relative shares of fuel and labour saw a large shift as fuel prices rose (Air Transport Association 2010). Aviation fuel price increased more than threefold from 2004 to 2008 and then quickly fell back to pre-2004 levels. Uncertainty regarding the direction and slope of the fuel price curve going forward makes future airline operations costs highly uncertain.

Environmental considerations also add to the uncertainty over the future price of fuel. State, federal, and international initiatives are looking to regulate the amount of CO_2 released into the atmosphere, and such a constraint on CO_2 emissions is a resource constraint imposed on production processes. It is well known that such constraints can be represented through shadow prices on the associated resources and that fuel price increases will most likely follow (Plaut 1998). As a result, CO_2 emissions policy also adds to the uncertainty related to the future fuel price.

Turning again to the California HSR, an explanation of cost differences between the CHSRA estimates and the EU experience could be the significantly lower expected cost of energy. Comparing industrial energy prices by end-use sector from the United States and Europe, we find that in some instances the energy prices in Europe are double those experienced in the United States (European Commission 2010, US Energy Information Administration 2010).

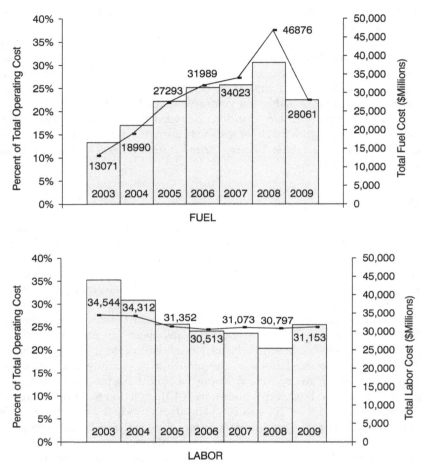

Figure 17.1 Fuel and labour as percentage of airline operating costs, 2003–2009

Vehicle technologies

New transportation vehicles currently in research, development, and deployment stages offer extensive options for the transformation of intercity transportation. They also intensify uncertainty, because an operator has numerous choices for vehicles; as each vehicle offers a different mix of operating cost and service quality, an operator can choose one or a mix of vehicles that meet its needs.

In the aviation system, vehicles are segmented by their propulsion systems: aircraft with turboprop engines and aircraft with jet engines. For the short haul markets (under 1,000 miles) that would be in competition with HSR service, turboprops, regional jets, or narrow body jets can be used. Turboprops are noted for their low fuel consumption; regional jets, with 30–90 seats, are noted for their passenger service quality; and narrow body jets, with 105–150 seats, balance

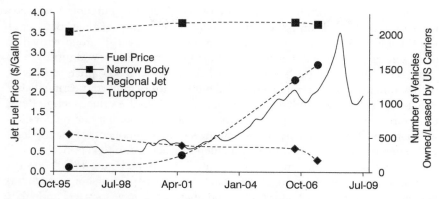

Figure 17.2 Aircraft trends for short haul travel and US jet fuel price paid by airlines (dollars per gallon)

operating costs and passenger service quality (Ryerson and Hansen 2010). The choice of aircraft presents opportunities to deploy vehicles to offer customized service as well as to meet environmental and operating cost objectives.

Figure 17.2 shows the change in United States airline ownership and leasing levels (summed to represent vehicle presence in the market) of these three different aircraft types, gathered from US Department of Transportation data, overlaid on the jet fuel purchase price from 1996–2009. Recent years have witnessed a shift away from turboprops toward regional jets, while the narrow body aircraft share has remained stable. While regional jets are less fuel efficient on a per-seat basis, they continued to be owned or leased in greater numbers even as fuel prices increased. One possible explanation is that despite high operating costs, the regional jet enables high frequencies and a high level of service that is valued by passengers. Turboprops offer a lower level of passenger service in the form of comfort, speed, and perceived safety. Another possible explanation is that airlines expected the fuel price surge to be temporary. In any case, these trends make it clear that costs alone do not always determine vehicle choice; passenger preferences can be a key driver for airline decision making (Wei and Hansen 2005).

Fares

Transport fares may be set based on costs, but they also may reflect a variety of other factors, including demand patterns, load balancing needs, level of competition, and desire for market share (Borenstein and Netz 1999). Today an airline may vary its fares based on demand at a particular time of day, day of the week, or season, as well as how far in advance the ticket is purchased, whether it is refundable, seat size and legroom, baggage allowances, and refreshments and amenities provided. Some HSR services are also differentiating fares in this way.

Fares are an important determinant of mode choice, but how passengers react to fares depends on passenger trip purpose and value of time. Berry *et al.* (1996) noted two distinct types of air passengers: a 'tourist' group with high price sensitivity, low willingness to pay for frequency, and low disutility from connecting flights; and a 'business traveller' group with low price sensitivity, high willingness to pay for frequency, and high disutility from connecting flights. Adler *et al.* (2005) found that heterogeneity extends to the value given to flying time, schedule, and on-time performance. Crozet reports similar findings for HSR in Chapter 4. Thus both trip purpose and the various components of the trip itself will generate different time values and different reactions to ticket prices.

Air fares have become more differentiated over time. Figure 17.3 shows the cumulative per cent of passengers who paid a given fare per mile for all segments between 350 and 500 miles for the second quarter of two years: 1993 and 2008. Data are shown in 2008 dollars and are taken from the Bureau of Transportation Statistics' Airline Origin and Destination Survey (DB1B), a 10 per cent sample of airline tickets purchased domestically. The distribution of passenger fares has a steeper slope in 1993, representing a more limited distribution of fares compared with 2008. In 1993, 50 per cent of passengers pay less than $350–$500, a fare much lower than the 50 per cent of passengers paying less than $420–$600 in 2008. While there is a longer tail to the distribution in 1993, such that a small percentage of passengers paid fares not seen in 2008, the bulk of passengers paid a limited range of fares compared with 2008. Cascetta, in Chapter 5, reports that competition on the Italian HSR lines has resulted in increased differentiation by fare and amenities, suggesting that competitive strategy applies to HSR as well.

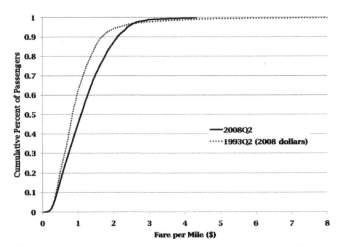

Figure 17.3 Distribution of total system passenger one-way fares per mile

Travel times

Travel times are well known to be an important determinant of mode choice. The travel times offered by intercity rail and air modes depend on the technology chosen and the operating decisions made. Operating decisions of import for HSR are the number of stops made between city pairs, the duration of stops (dwell time), and whether transfers are required. Speed can also be adjusted in operations and will affect costs as well as travel time. Air travel times likewise reflect technologies and operating choices.

Currently there is some thinking that HSR is likely to have less time in terminal (checking in, going through security, and waiting) than for air travel, though others question this, pointing out that rail and air are both subject to security challenges. HSR access time could be equal to, better than, or worse than that for airports, depending on the number of stations built in the major metropolitan areas and noting that there are multiple airports offering flights between the Los Angeles metro area and the Bay Area.

Evidence that there are travel time bands in which different modes are competitive appears in US data as well as in data from other countries. As shown in Figure 17.4, a study on travel time and market share in EU city pairs that have HSR service showed that for travel times under 3–4 hours, the market share for HSR is consistently higher than 50 per cent (Steer Davies Gleave 2006). This highlights the strong potential for intermodal competition in short-to medium-haul intercity transportation corridors. (See also the chapters in this volume on experiences in France, Spain, and Japan.) For the US, Coogan *et al.* (2009) report on the intercity mode shares for the two mega-coastal corridors: the California Corridor and the Northeast Corridor. California, a region with considerable short-haul air service but limited intercity rail service, has an intercity mode share dominated by auto for short distance and auto and air for medium-haul distances. Figure 17.5 shows the breakdown between city pairs, with distances in miles by driving. Figure 17.6 displays the rail and air mode shares on the Northeast Corridor (auto share excluded). In both corridors, longer distances equal higher mode share for air. However, the intercity rail travel times are very competitive with air transportation in the Northeast Corridor, and rail captures a much larger mode share than in California.

While HSR and air are likely to be competitors, there also is potential for them to serve as complementary modes. For example, HSR could bring passengers to a hub airport for air travel; this could either expand the catchment area of the airport or divert passengers from small local feeder flights. In addition, HSR could replace air services in markets that the airlines cannot serve profitably. Both strategies have been employed in Germany, as Rothengatter discusses in Chapter 7. However, a study by Charles River Associates (2000) found that for California, HSR as an airport access mode would account for less than 1 per cent of ridership and revenue potential and there has been little further investigation of complementary options in California since then.

Summing up

How, then, will passengers shift between air and HSR if the two are present in the same market? Factors that create uncertainty are cost estimates, especially fuel costs since these are likely to be volatile; the technologies chosen by the various modal operators, which are likely to reflect operating costs and customer preferences; pricing strategies for fares, which also are likely to reflect not only costs but other market factors; and travel times, a function of operations design that typically reflects technology choices, patterns of demand, and costs. The evidence from analogous situations suggests that competition between HSR and air is likely to be strongest for trips under 500 miles.

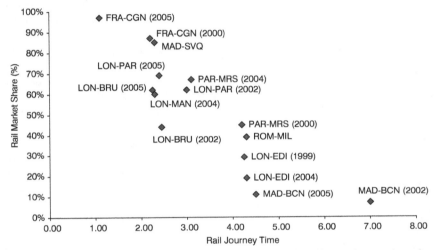

Figure 17.4 Rail market share (compared with air) against rail travel time for select European intercity transportation corridors

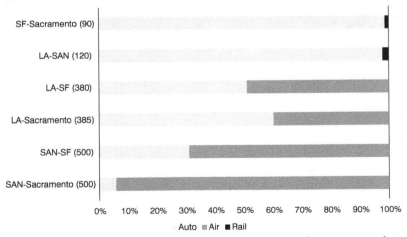

Figure 17.5 Mode share and distance for certain California Corridor city pair markets

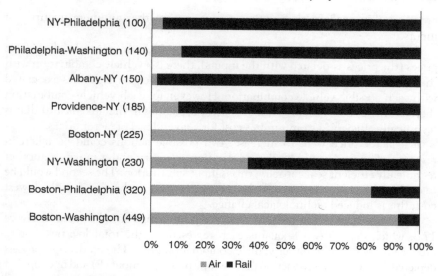

Figure 17.6 Mode share and distance for certain Northeast Corridor city pair markets

An analytic model of intercity transportation choices

Models created to forecast intercity transportation choices are often highly complex and become more so when uncertainties are taken into account, as the modelling efforts for the California HSR project illustrate (Cambridge Systematics 2014). Here we present an analytic (conceptual) model that is intended to clarify the way the various uncertainties introduced in the previous section affect intercity transportation choices. The model can be used to explore passenger and operational profiles without the need to identify one single value of each input, and is intended to support the exploration of possible responses to changes in the costs of inputs – which could be changed environmental costs, such as higher fuel prices due to greenhouse gas reduction policies, or costs associated with traveller value of time.

In the context of intercity transportation, we have noted that a variety of vehicle technologies can be used to provide intercity passenger travel. Both the suppliers and the users provide inputs to produce travel: suppliers provide fuel, labour, equipment, facilities, and other capital while users must provide their travel time including access, wait, transfer, and possible delay time as well as time in route (at different values of time) and must also be willing to pay fares. We can view the mode of transport, which we will represent here in simplified form as the vehicle technology, as the means of transforming inputs into outputs. This production process for intercity passenger travel can be represented by a total logistics cost function. Some possible production processes, represented by vehicle technologies, inputs and output, are shown in Figure 17.7. We will assume that these represent technically efficient production processes, i.e., processes that produce the maximum output from the minimum quantity of inputs.

For each vehicle type or combination in Figure 17.7, at a given level of factor prices (the prices associated with the inputs), there is a vehicle combination with the lowest total logistics cost. There are many possible seat capacities associated with each possible vehicle combination. However, for each vehicle combination there is only one seat capacity (or set of seat capacities in the mixed case) that is technically efficient, i.e., minimizes cost for a given level of factor prices.

If a factor price were to increase, two possible actions could be taken in response. The first would be the substitution of inputs and a move to another technically efficient seat capacity; this is input substitution. The second would be to change the production process that converts inputs to the output at the lowest cost; this is induced technological change.

Input substitution and induced technological change are illustrated in Figure 17.8, which depicts two isoquants each representing the total logistics cost to produce output O with either vehicle combination i or j. The production process depicted is a two input production process: one passenger input (P) and one supplier input (S). At a baseline factor price p^0_S for all inputs, point X1 represents the optimal point of production for vehicle combination i; point X2 represents the optimal point of production for vehicle combination j. Let C(X1) and C(X2) represent the total logistics cost at the point of optimal production for vehicle combination i and j respectively. At a baseline (supplier) factor price of p^0_S, C(X2) < C(X1), point X2 is on a lower budget line than point X1; therefore vehicle combination j has a lower cost to produce the same output as vehicle combination i.

If there is an increase in the factor price of fuel (a supplier input) represented by p'_S, a new budget line and point of tangency exists for each vehicle combination. The shift from the optimal costs at p^0_S to the optimal costs at p'_S – C(X2) to C(X4) and C(X1) to C(X3) – represents input substitution. Furthermore, at p'_S, C(X3) < C(X4), such that optimal point of production for vehicle combination

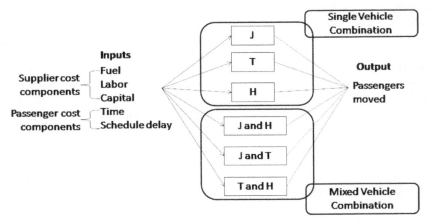

Figure 17.7 Inputs and output of single and mixed vehicle production processes

i is on a lower budget line than vehicle combination *j*. This change in vehicle combination with the lowest total logistics cost represents induced technological change.

The analytical framework shows how, from a total cost perspective considering user costs as well as supplier costs, input substitutions and technological changes could result from changes in factor prices and the preferred modal mix could change.

Ryerson (2010) developed analytic total logistics cost models for an intercity transportation corridor serving multiple passenger groups. The models are sensitive to fuel price and incorporate multiple classes of vehicles serving passengers with differentiated values of time. She combined the analytic models with empirical models of the cost relationships between fuel price and operating cost for intercity transportation vehicles to gain insights into the impact of fuel price on optimal service mixes in representative corridors. Optimal service mix is conceived as choosing the vehicles and service frequencies that provide the minimum total logistics cost (vehicle operator cost and passenger cost) for the intercity transportation corridor. Applying this approach, Ryerson found that a mix of vehicle technologies can help manage fuel price increases and that an increase in fuel price causes vehicles to become more differentiated with respect to the value of time of the passengers, i.e., by sorting passengers to different types of vehicles according to their values of time. She further found that the minimum cost vehicle combination is highly sensitive to fuel price in a small transition zone within which the cost ordering of vehicle combinations changes significantly. As the transition area is in the range of fuel prices forecast between

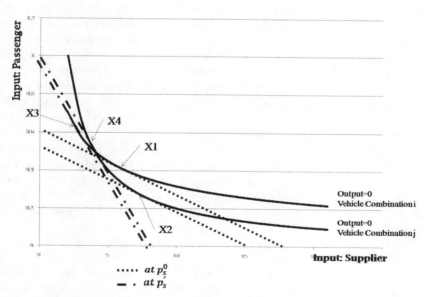

Figure 17.8 Illustration of input substitution and induced technological change

the years 2010–2035, the results indicate fuel price changes between 2010 and 2035 may dramatically alter the most cost-effective ways to provide intercity passenger transport. In her analysis, high-speed rail is part of a mixed vehicle service that can reduce total logistics cost, suggesting that an integrated air and rail strategy could be an effective tool to manage intercity transport costs and fuel consumption (as well as greenhouse gas emissions).

A life cycle assessment of CA HSR

Environmental LCAs of air and HSR systems have assessed vehicle, infrastructure, and energy production processes, including manufacturing and maintenance, in addition to energy used for propulsion. In the case of new long-distance transportation infrastructure, traditional materials such as steel, concrete, and asphalt have large environmental footprints from aggregate mining, furnace emissions, and in the case of concrete, direct process CO_2 emissions in the production of cement (United States Environmental Protection Agency 2010). Construction equipment and processes can cause significant local and regional impacts. As countries around the world look to deploy new aviation and HSR services, the assessment should account for the use of new materials and improved manufacturing and maintenance processes. This may include the changing effects of greening electricity mixes, as well as new types of equipment and improved construction management practices that can significantly reduce environmental effects.

Energy use, either as jet fuel for aircraft or electricity for HSR, relies on supply chain activities that also consume energy and produce environmental impacts. LCAs of air and HSR systems account for energy production systems by assessing primary fuel (i.e., crude oil, coal, natural gas, uranium, etc.) extraction, processing, transport, and distribution. Each process in the supply chain consumes energy and produces environmental impacts including air emissions, noise, land use, hazardous waste generation, and wastewater production. Emerging efficiency gains in engine design and air traffic control, the potential of using biofuels, and the generation of electricity from larger shares of renewables may significantly alter the energy supply chain for air and rail transport, and environmental assessments must account for these changes.

Estimated life cycle greenhouse gas emissions and respiratory impact potential of future auto, aircraft, and HSR travel in the California Corridor are shown in Figure 17.9. This is an attributional life cycle approach in that it shows what the greenhouse gas and respiratory impacts are in 2030 to 2050, allocated to the vehicle, infrastructure, and energy production components per passenger mile travelled.

The life cycle results show that there are significant greenhouse gas emissions and respiratory impact potential from vehicle, infrastructure, and energy production processes (Chester and Horvath 2012). These are the result of many processes including vehicle manufacturing energy use, gasoline extraction and refining, and concrete use for HSR infrastructure. Some of these pollutants are

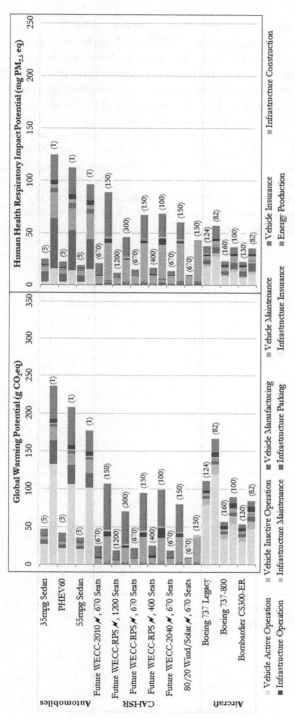

Figure 17.9 Life cycle GHG emissions and respiratory impact potential (per passenger mile travelled) 2030 to 2050

released locally and some remotely, and the emissions may occur over many decades. Overlaying a decision-maker boundary could provide additional insights as to which parties have the ability to reduce these impacts, both directly and in the supply chain (e.g., a vertically-integrated plane or train manufacturer).

The results show that for HSR, the infrastructure construction emissions are as large as propulsion, suggesting that mitigation strategies should assess the benefits and costs of reductions in initial construction as well as operation. The contrasting of life cycle per passenger mile effects by long-run high and low occupancy highlights the *potential* of each mode, that is, how 'clean' or 'dirty' they can be. The sensitivity of these normalized per passenger mile travelled results is shown in Figure 7.10.

As long-distance transportation decision-makers develop plans to deploy new HSR systems, comparisons like the one in Figure 17.10 will be valuable for identifying the breakeven ridership that will be needed for rail to have a

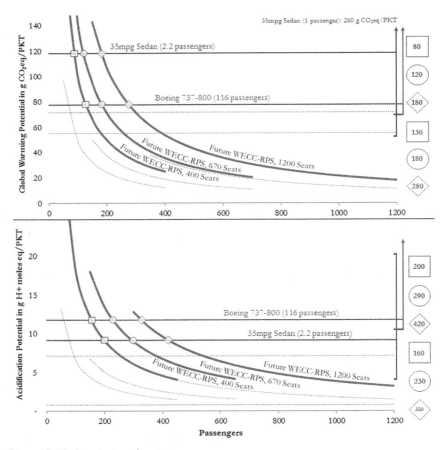

Figure 17.10 Sensitivity of emissions to occupancy

lower long-run footprint than air travel. With the assumptions and data shown in Figure 17.10, with at least 280 passengers (roughly 40 per cent occupancy), California HSR will in the long run have a lower greenhouse gas footprint than future automobile and air travel, and with at least 330 passengers (roughly 50 per cent occupancy) it will have lower acidification potential. These sorts of breakeven ridership estimates can serve as a goal for planners and operators.

HSR environmental assessments that are intended to inform policy and decisions should use consequential LCA to assess how strategies that lead to changes in long-distance travel help meet environmental goals. For example, a region with a greenhouse gas reduction goal may want to understand how the implementation of an HSR system will reduce the transportation system's emissions footprint. Attributional LCA does not provide a direct assessment of outcome; it produces long-run average estimates of modal performance. The consequential approach instead assesses how the implementation of HSR infrastructure produces upfront emissions that later lead to reductions by attracting ridership away from more emissions-intense automobiles and aircraft. This is shown in Figure 17.11 for greenhouse gas emissions and acidification potential of the CA HSR (using CHSRA 2011 forecasts).

The cumulative curve (light grey line in the bar chart portion of impact) for the consequential approach shows that HSR will begin providing greenhouse gas and acidification impact reductions in the third decade after construction begins. Construction effects (black bar to right of axis in first two decades) create an initial puff of emissions that will require automobile (medium grey solid and medium grey dotted bars to left of axis starting in decade 2) and air (light grey solid and light grey dotted bars to left of axis starting in decade 2) travel reductions to offset.

Note that Figure 17.11 does not make any assumptions about the no project alternative. A separate analysis would have to be conducted to evaluate the consequences of relying on air and highway transport with no high-speed rail. If doing so can be accommodated by operational and vehicle technology changes, e.g., advanced air traffic control systems, improved operations at airports, improved aircraft technologies for the air system, improved vehicles and fuels, increased automation for highway operations, the results would likely be significantly different than if it is necessary to add runways, widen highways, or build new airports and highways to accommodate growth.

Conclusions

The energy and environmental assessment of HSR travel requires a systematic approach that can assess future behaviour and mode choices, emerging technologies, emerging fuel mixes, and life cycle processes. LCA is a valuable framework for assessing HSR effects as it provides a methodology for capturing geospatial variations across large and complex systems. However, practitioners should decide what types of questions they would like to inform with LCA to determine whether attributional or consequential system boundary framing

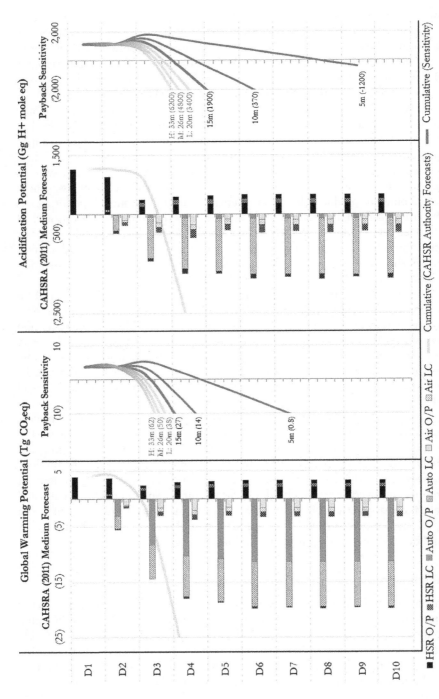

Figure 17.11 Consequential LCA of California HSR: greenhouse gas and the potential for acidification impacts

is appropriate. Any analysis is only as good as the data it incorporates, and as California and other regions around the world assess the feasibility of deploying HSR, it is imperative that high-quality information about key parameters be developed so that assessments can be robust and the results can be positioned for informing policy and decision making. At the same time, forecasting the future is necessarily uncertain, and it is advisable to test multiple scenarios to explore the range of possible outcomes. While well designed studies and scenario testing can help reduce risks, analysts should nevertheless acknowledge the empirical, methodological, and scientific limitations that long-term forecasts entail.

References

Adler, T, Falzarano, C and Spitz, G, 2005, 'Modeling service trade-offs in air itinerary choices', *Transportation Research Record: Journal of the Transportation Research Board*, no. 1915, pp. 20–26.

Air Transport Association, 2010, *Quarterly Cost Index: US Passenger Airlines*.

Berry, S, Carnall, M and Spiller, P, 1996, 'Airline hubs: Costs, markups and the implications of customer heterogeneity', *National Bureau of Economic Research Working Paper*, No. 5561, Washington, DC.

Borenstein, S and Netz, J, 1999, 'Why do all the flights leave at 8 am?: Competition and departure-time differentiation in airline markets', *International Journal of Industrial Organization*, vol. 17, pp. 611–640.

Cambridge Systematics, Inc., 2014, *California High-Speed Rail 2014 Business Plan Ridership and Revenue Forecasting*, technical memorandum prepared for Parsons Brinckerhoff for the California High-Speed Rail Authority.

Cambridge Systematics, Inc., 2016, *2016 California High-Speed Rail Business Plan Ridership and Revenue Risk Analysis*, Technical Report, Prepared for CHSRA.

Charles River Associates, 2000, *Independent Ridership and Passenger Revenue Projections for High Speed Rail Alternatives in California*, Boston, MA: Charles River Associates.

Chester, M and Horvath, A, 2010, 'Life-cycle environmental assessment of California high speed rail,' *University of California Access magazine*, vol. 37, at http://www.uctc. net/access/37/access37_assessing_hsr.pdf Accessed 1 August 2016.

Chester, M and Horvath, A, 2012, 'High-speed rail with emerging automobiles and aircraft can reduce environmental impacts in California's future', *Environmental Research Letters*, vol. 7, no. 034012.

Coogan, M, Hansen, M, Kiernan, L, Last, J, March, R, Ryerson, MS and Yatzeck, R, 2009, *Approaches to Addressing Aviation Capacity in Coastal Mega-regions*, Washington, DC: Airport Cooperative Research Program Project 3–10.

Delucchi, MA, 2011, 'Beyond lifecycle analysis: Developing a better tool for simulating policy impacts,' in JM Ogden and L Anderson (eds.), *Sustainable Transportation Energy Pathways*, Institute of Transportation Studies, University of California Davis.

de Rus, G, (ed.) 2009, rev. 2012, *Economic Analysis of High Speed Rail in Europe*, Madrid: Fundación BBVA.

European Commission, 2010, *EU Energy and Transport in Figures*, *Statistical Pocketbook 2010*, At: http://ec.europa.eu/transport/facts-fundings/statistics/doc/2010/pocketbook2010_ contractor.pdf Accessed 31 October 2016.

Farrell, AE and Sperling, D, 2007, *A Low-Carbon Fuel Standard for California, Parts 1 & 2*. University of California.

Finnveden, G, Hauschild, MZ, Ekvall, T, Guinée, J, Heijungs, R, Hellweg, S, Koehler, A, Pennington, D and Suh, S, 2009, 'Recent developments in life cycle assessment,' *Journal of Environmental Management*, vol. 91, no. 1, pp.1–21.

Hawkins, TR, Singh, B, Majeau-Bettez, G and Strømman, AH, 2013, 'Comparative environmental life cycle assessment of conventional and electric vehicles,' *Journal of Industrial Ecology*, vol. 17, no. 1, pp. 53–64.

International Organization for Standardization, 2006, *14044: Environmental Management – Life Cycle Assessment – Requirements and Guidelines*, Geneva, Switzerland: International Organization for Standardization.

MIT Global Airline Industry Project, 2015, At: http://web.mit.edu/airlinedata/www/Expenses&Related.html Accessed 1 August 2016.

Plaut, PO, 1998, 'The comparison and ranking of policies for abating mobile-source emissions', *Transportation Research Part D: Transport and Environment*, vol. 3, pp. 193–205.

Plevin, RJ, Delucchi, MA and Creutzig. F, 2013, 'Using attributional life cycle assessment to estimate climate-change mitigation benefits misleads policy makers,' *Journal of Industrial Ecology*, vol. 18, no. 1, pp.73–83.

Ryerson, MS, 2010, *Optimal Intercity Transportation Services With Heterogeneous Demand and Variable Fuel Price*, University of California Transportation Center.

Ryerson, MS and Hansen, M, 2010, 'The potential of turboprops for reducing aviation fuel consumption', *Transportation Research Part D: Transport and Environment*, vol. 15, pp. 305–314.

Ryerson, MS and Hansen, M, 2011, 'Capturing the impact of fuel price on jet aircraft operating costs with Leontief technology and econometric models,' *Transportation Research Part C: Emerging Technologies*, vol. 33, pp. 282–296.

Sathre, R, Chester, M, Cain, J and Masanet, E, 2012, 'A framework for environmental assessment of CO_2 capture and storage systems,' *Energy*, vol. 37, no. 1, pp. 540–548.

Steer Davies Gleave 2006, 'Air and rail competition and complementarity final report', in *Transportation*, European Union.

Stratton, RW, 2010, *Life cycle assessment of greenhouse gas emissions and non-CO_2 combustion effects from alternative jet fuels*. Diss. Massachusetts Institute of Technology.

US Energy Information Administration, 2010, *Independent Statistics and Analysis: Forecasts & Analysis. Average Retail Price of Electricity to Ultimate Customers: Total by End-Use Sector*.

US Environmental Protection Agency, 2010, *Available and Emerging Technologies for Reducing Greenhouse Gas Emissions from the Portland Cement Industry*, Washington, DC, USA: United States Environmental Protection Agency.

US Federal Railroad Administration, 2008, *Analysis of the Benefits of High-Speed Rail on the Northeast Corridor*, Washington, DC: US Department of Transportation.

Wei, W and Hansen, M, 2005, 'Impact of aircraft size and seat availability on airlines' demand and market share in duopoly markets', *Transportation Research Part E: Logistics and Transportation Review*, vol. 41, pp. 315–327.

18 Equity analysis of California high-speed rail

Cornelius Nuworsoo

Introduction

The California high-speed rail (HSR) project, which began construction in 2014, plans to link the state's four largest metropolitan areas (Sacramento and San Francisco to the north; Los Angeles and San Diego to the south) with the first true high-speed train system in the United States. According to studies by the California High Speed Rail Authority (CHSRA), the high-speed rail network is projected to carry between 22.6 and 32.6 million passengers per year by 2030. Who will be the main beneficiaries of this new transport system? Are there particular groups that will benefit little? This chapter presents an overview of the debates about equity that have surrounded the project and an analysis of the relative social equity of California's high-speed rail system for different segments of the population. Equity is defined here as 'fairness in the distribution of goods and services among the people in an economy' (Friedman 2002).

The debates over the equity of the HSR project are first discussed. These include debates over what income and demographic groups are expected to benefit most from the system as well as debates over differential impacts on the wellbeing of communities and regions. The chapter then focuses on the issue of who is most likely to receive direct user benefits from HSR through an analysis of long-distance travel reported in the 2012 California Household Travel Survey (CHTS). This analysis reveals the current demographic profile and travel patterns of long-distance travellers in the state and the relative geographic accessibility of long-distance travellers to proposed high-speed rail station areas. If travel profiles and patterns in the future are similar to those currently reported, the implications for HSR can be derived.

Debates over the equity of high-speed rail

Supporters of high-speed rail in California contend that it will increase travel choices, reduce the energy and environmental impact of long-distance travel within the state, and reduce pressures for airport expansion and highway widening. They also assert that HSR will be an economic boon to the cities it serves by supporting development around station areas. Detractors of the HSR project challenge all of these assertions. They retort that CA HSR lacks a realistic funding plan, that its ridership and revenue models are flawed, and charge that as a result of these problems, the system will soak up public funds and deliver only minor economic and environmental benefits (APTA 2012). They contend that California currently lacks the density to make HSR viable and are dubious that HSR stations will attract enough new development to make a difference. They question whether property along major rail lines will be attractive to developers outside of a few urban locations and point to evidence that areas supporting fast travel rarely have many origins and destinations close together (Grengs *et al.* 2010). They worry that the facility will create problems of its own including noise, access traffic, visual intrusion, and barrier effects. They worry that if existing rail rights of way are used, as has been proposed for parts of the CA HSR alignment, conflicts with critical freight operations could result (Schweiterman and Scheidt 2007). They argue that Californians lack a rail habit and point out that the state has well established highway and short-haul air transport systems that would offer tough competition for a new HSR entrant.

A major criticism of CA HSR is that it will serve a relatively small segment of the population at considerable public expense, requiring public subsidies that will divert resources from other worthy projects. The critics argue that this poses a serious equity problem because HSR will mainly serve urban elites that travel long distances frequently, rather than average citizens who only occasionally take long-distance trips. As Randle O'Toole of the Cato Institute stated in a 2009 editorial, '...the train's only advantage is for people who are going from downtown to downtown. Who works downtown? Bankers, lawyers, government officials, and other high-income people who hardly need subsidized transportation. Not only will you pay $1,000 for someone else to ride the train; that someone probably earns more than you' (O'Toole 2009). Others make similar claims about economic elitism, but add arguments about race: 'Since the fares will be about the same as regional jet, probably the same people who use regional jet, that is to say, a largely Anglo, middle and upper income customer base [will use HSR]. Low income people and many people of color likely won't be able to afford the fares' (Brenman 2011).

Critics of the CA HSR project also raise equity concerns about HSR's impacts on particular communities and regions. They argue that many local communities through which the system passes will be burdened by the project without receiving significant benefits. In addition, some are concerned that disparities among regions will be magnified by HSR service. They worry that richer cities will benefit from HSR to expand their labour and housing markets, drawing attention and resources away from less prosperous cities, which would end up in a comparatively worse situation (Monzón *et al.* 2013).

Opposition to the local impacts of California HSR has come mainly from two areas of the state: the Central Valley and the San Francisco Peninsula. In each case, local residents argue that they will bear the brunt of negative effects of the project while others will reap the benefits (Williams 2013). In the Central Valley, locals have brought lawsuits and otherwise argued that building HSR threatens farmland, both directly, through takings, and indirectly, by creating a barrier that severs agricultural parcels and requires circuitous travel. Locals are also upset about the land acquisition process, arguing that they have been in 'financial limbo for years as the authority weighs different paths for the train, leaving farmers wary of planting crops or investing in new equipment in case their land ends up being gobbled up' (Tavlian 2011). Propelled by concerns about adverse local impacts, in 2011 local farmers and ranchers joined by Kings County filed a multi-part lawsuit against the project, arguing that the emerging designs for the project did not match project design and performance descriptions in voter-approved Proposition 1A, which authorized bond sales for HSR (Tos v. California High-Speed Rail Authority, 2011, 2014). While several of the plaintiffs' complaints were dismissed by the trial court and several favourable trial court rulings were later overturned on appeal, a remaining challenge is still being litigated as of 2016.

Opposition to HSR in the San Francisco Peninsula has also centred on the proposed route's local impacts. On the Peninsula, the proposed alignment uses an existing rail corridor, and local residents have long complained about the current rail service's noise, barrier effects, traffic and safety impacts, and visual impacts. When HSR was proposed to run along the same right of way, first as a replacement for the current diesel train service and more recently as a 'blended' system with electrification of the current 'Baby Bullet' rail service between San Francisco and San Jose, a number of residents protested. Some lobbied for undergrounding the rail services – an extremely costly proposal for the 30–40 mile stretch in question, and one that the affluent local communities did not want to fund themselves. Several of the towns filed lawsuits challenging the adequacy of the environmental impact reports prepared for the project. (See in particular Town of Atherton v. California High-Speed Rail Authority, 228 Cal. App.4th 314, 175 Cal. Rptr. 3d 145, 2014.) Most of the elements of these lawsuits were dismissed, although two lawsuits did require the CHSRA to spend about a year each time revising its environmental documents slightly (Rosenberg 2013). Residents continue to express dismay over the potential negative impacts on their communities, worrying that the effects of the project could reduce property values along the corridor.

Regional equity issues also have surfaced. High-speed rail is promoted as an economic development tool in California and elsewhere in the world (Nuworsoo and Deakin 2009), and proponents of the California project have asserted that HSR can help economically depressed areas access markets in the more prosperous metropolitan areas, while providing valuable construction and redevelopment jobs in all areas along the route (Ehlers *et al.* 2011). However, others argue that regional economic effects are uncertain and that 'these effects depend predominantly on the manner in which the urban actors react to the new opportunities offered by improved accessibility' (Monzón *et al.* 2013). Opponents insist that the increased market access that HSR provides is likely to help firms in the larger metropolitan areas to outcompete firms in the newly connected smaller cities, in which case HSR could potentially increase disparities among regional economies (Martin 1997).

One reason that there is so much contention about the role that HSR might play and the equity of its impacts, is that there is no direct experience in the US on which to base investigations. With no HSR systems in operation, studies of travel behaviour must either draw inferences from the experiences of other countries with HSR, extrapolate from experiences with other long-distance modes (air, auo, rail, bus), or rely on econometric models and 'stated preference' studies that attempt to describe the new mode to prospective users to gauge their reactions. In addition, there is relative scarcity of long-distance travel data compared to everyday travel data; most large-scale travel surveys record person trips on a given day, but the average person is not likely to make a long-distance trip on the survey day. Indeed, Americans averaged only 0.067 long-distance trips per day in 2001 and Californians averaged only 0.093 trips per day in 2008 (Bierce et al. 2012).

It is nonetheless possible to glean useful inferences from the available data on long-distance travel. Sources include long-distance trip records reported in national surveys sponsored by the federal government, as well as those from surveys conducted by state and metropolitan agencies and airport authorities. Such surveys cannot inform every inquiry about HSR equity – e.g., they cannot tell us whether HSR lines will create troublesome noise problems or attract new development – but they can offer insights about who makes long-distance trips and who does not, and where and for what purposes such trips are being made. As such, the data offer insights into how HSR might perform if travellers continued trip-making patterns much as they are today – or how much current behaviours might have to change to break the mould and significantly change travel outcomes. Accordingly, in the remainder of this chapter, data from two surveys, the National Household Transportation Survey and the California Household Travel Survey, have been analyzed to extract information about long-distance trips and draw inferences about the equity of HSR.

Evidence from long-distance travel studies: nationwide data

The National Household Travel Survey (NHTS) is periodically produced by the Bureau of Transportation Statistics (BTS) of the US Department of Transportation (US DOT). The most recent survey was conducted in 2009 and the one prior to that was conducted in 2001. Data are collected on the trips taken by household members on the survey day and include information on the mode of transportation used, the trip purpose, trip length, and day and time of travel. The 2009 NHTS sample size was 150,147 households, including a national sample of 25,000 households and add-on samples from twenty states and metropolitan areas that together added 125,147 households. Results presented here are from the 2001 and/or 2009 surveys as re-weighted to represent the population as a whole.

In the US, long-distance travel is typically defined as a trip that is 50 miles or more from home, totalling 100 miles or more round-trip. According to the Federal Highway Administration (US DOT 2006), Americans make about 2.6 billion long-distance trips on average per year. Given a population size of more than 300 million, it is clear that long-distance trips constitute only a small fraction of daily travel. While Americans typically make three or four person trips per day (Bierce *et al.* 2012), long-distance trips typically occur a little less than once a month (US DOT 2006).

The nationwide data show that long-distance trips are not evenly distributed across the US population: 61 per cent of Americans make no long-distance trips at all in a given year, while 5 per cent of the population makes 25 per cent of the long-distance trips (US DOT 2006). Differences in long-distance trip rates reflect geographical/spatial structure and differences in modal availability as well as socioeconomic differences.

Long-distance travel also varies substantially with location in the United States. Those living in the more intensely settled coastal regions of the Atlantic and Pacific Rim make fewer long-distance trips per capita than those in the middle regions of the nation, with trip rates ranging from 8.4 long-distance trips per year in the Mid-Atlantic region to 11.2 long-distance trips a year in the West North Central region. This most likely reflects the concentration of population and activities in the large urban areas on the two coasts, which allow for more activities to be accomplished locally than is possible in smaller and more dispersed areas. On the other hand, those living in the largest metropolitan areas (of 3 million or more population) are twice as likely to make a trip of 1,000 miles or more than those living in small towns or rural areas (US DOT 2006). This is likely a reflection of income and lifestyle as well as the nature of work in the larger metro areas.

National survey data show substantial differences in long-distance trip-making among different income groups, and point to the interaction of income and place. For example, higher income people in rural areas make the most long-distance trips per household, while low-income people in inner cities take the fewest long-distance trips (US DOT 2006).

Mode choice for long-distance trips varies with context as well as with demographics. Americans make approximately 90 per cent of commute trips by private auto (US DOT 2009); and a similar share, approximately 90 per cent of long-distance trips, are also by private auto (US DOT 2006). Air travel accounts for 7 per cent of all long-distance trips made by US households, with the remaining 3 per cent by bus, train, and all other modes.

One reason for the high auto share is that most long-distance trips are relatively short. Forty-five per cent of all long-distance trips in the US are made within the same state (US DOT 2006), and the average long-distance trip by private vehicle is 220 miles one-way. Bus and train trips are substantially longer, averaging 400 miles. Air trips average 1,500 miles (USDOT 2006).

Auto share drops quickly as trip lengths exceed a few hundred miles. For trips under 300 miles the auto share is 97 per cent, but auto share is only 22 per cent of trips over 2,000 miles (US DOT 2006; Sharp *et al.* 2001).

Low-income households depend more on private vehicles for long-distance trips than do higher income households. Households with incomes greater than $50,000 use the automobile for 87 per cent of long-distance trips, while households with incomes less than $50,000 use the automobile for 92 to 93 per cent of long-distance trips (Sharp *et al.* 2001). This gap widens as income increases. For households with an income greater than $100,000 per year, the share of long-distance trips by air increases sharply, principally for trips of 400 miles or more. Fewer than half of trips that are 1,000 miles or more are made by car among the high income groups. However, for low-income households earning less than $25,000 per year, the share of trips by auto remains above 50 per cent until trip length reaches 2,000 miles or more (US DOT 2006).

There also is an association between level of education and the number of long-distance trips taken. Adults with a high school education or less make only 34 per cent of all long-distance trips even though they represent 49 per cent of the adult population over 18. Adults with a bachelor's degree or higher make 37 per cent of all long-distance trips even though they represent only 24 per cent of the general population (Sharp *et al.* 2001).

From these national data, we can see that most Americans make long-distance trips relatively infrequently and a small share of the population accounts for a disproportionate share of long trips. Higher income people make more trips than average, as do the better educated, residents of major metropolitan areas, and affluent rural residents. Currently the majority of long-distance trips are a few hundred miles or less and are made mostly by auto, with air transport capturing an increasing share of trips as trip distance exceeds 300 miles. This has important implications for HSR, suggesting that in the US market the competition would be mostly with the auto, with air-rail competition important principally for trips in the 300–600 mile range.

Findings from the California Household Travel Survey

While national data provide useful insights, data from California can capture local socioeconomic conditions and thus better inform an assessment of the California case. In this section an analysis based on California long-distance travel surveys is presented.

California conducts a state-wide survey of travel, the California Household Travel Survey (CHTS), approximately every 10 years in order to support travel analysis and forecasting in the state. The most recent surveys were conducted in 2001 and 2012. In the 2012 survey, a total of 42,431 California households provided their travel information (California Department of Transportation 2013).

The CHTS contains a small proportion of data records on long-distance trips. Out of the 175,861 trips recorded by the 2001 CHTS, a mere 4,287 trips (or 2.4 per cent) were determined to be long-distance trips. In addition, the majority (57 per cent) of the long-distance trips that were captured in the 2001 CHTS were less than 100 miles in length. The 2012 CHTS made a deliberate attempt to gain a deeper perspective on long-distance travel by asking for separate logs on long-distance trips. Survey respondents were asked to record (in a long-distance log) the long-distance, inter-regional household trips that occurred in the 8 weeks preceding the survey. The data records were compiled into six different but related databases including information on characteristics of *households* and *persons* within households, *activities* conducted and *places* visited by persons, *vehicles* owned by households, and *long-distance trips* to places visited. As a result of this effort, data were collected for 68,193 inter-regional trips (vs. 460,524 shorter, in-region trips).

While some results presented here are from the 2001 survey, the primary dataset used in this analysis is the 2012 CHTS, which was released in June 2013 by the California Department of Transportation (Caltrans). The 2012 CHTS contains geocoded trip data at the latitude and longitude level, allowing comparison of trip patterns to proposed California High-Speed Rail (CA HSR) station locations. For state-wide level analyses, the California Department of Transportation reports that the 2012 CHTS has a margin of error ranging between 0.02 and 0.20 (except for trip rates of zero vehicle households at 0.34) for 90 per cent and 95 per cent confidence intervals (Caltrans 2013).

Analysis of the CHTS data for this investigation involved a series of tasks: linking demographic information in the persons and households data files with trip records in the long-distance trips and places data files; extraction and data checking of long-distance trip records; geocoding proposed HSR station locations; calculation of distances between trip origins and destinations and the nearest HSR stations; and determination and comparison of average access distances by demographic characteristics of long-distance travellers. Trip distances between origins and destinations were calculated using the great circle distance, i.e., the shortest distance 'as the crow flies.' Actual route distances would be longer, but great circle distances offer a reasonable first approximation of distance and are sufficient for assessing relative access distances rather than actual route length.

Since at the time of the analysis, station locations were considered tentative, all proposed station locations, including siting alternatives, were geocoded and considered in the analysis. 'As the crow flies' distances were used to calculate the nearest proposed rail station to each trip origin and destination in the travel data files.

Equity analysis involved the assessment of long-distance travel behaviour by various population groups as well as an analysis of the relative accessibility of travellers of various demographic characteristics including ethnicity, age, income, and trip purpose.

Profile of long-distance travellers in California

The 2001 CHTS showed that the distribution of long-distance trips was strongly skewed towards the shorter of the long-distance trips (Figure 18.1). Nearly 60 per cent of all long-distance (interregional) trips were less than 100 miles, while 25 per cent were between 100 miles and 200 miles. The number of trips dropped

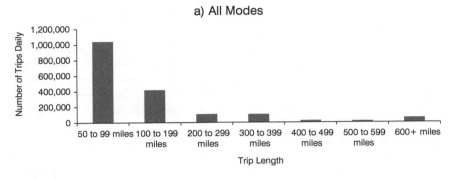

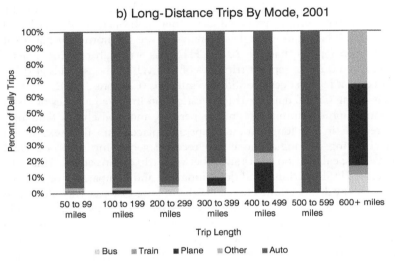

Figure 18.1 Distribution of long-distance trip lengths per day in California, 2001

off precipitously for distances longer than 200 miles. This trend persisted in the 2012 CHTS data.

There were notable differences in the numbers of long-distance trips in different parts of California, with the most long-distance trips made by residents in the largest metropolitan areas of the San Francisco Bay and Southern California (Bierce *et al.* 2012).

In 2012, approximately 97 per cent of all long-distance trips by California residents were destined for locations within the United States, and approximately 79 per cent of all long-distance trips were destined for locations within California – of which a total of 16 per cent ended up in the top five cities of San Francisco, Los Angeles, Sacramento, San Diego, and San Jose. The preponderance of in-state long-distance trips vis-à-vis the minor percentage to the top five cities, which are major air service markets, suggests a large market for long-distance travel across California outside major air service markets. Similar to the findings for the US as a whole, California residents

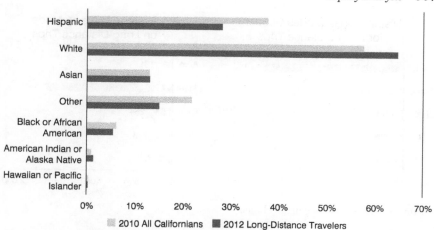

Figure 18.2 Comparative distributions by race and ethnicity

made 84 per cent of all long-distance trips by auto, with an average trip length of 131 miles; the next highest share went to air travel with nearly 13 per cent of long-distance trips and an average trip length of 1,614 miles. On average, approximately three people travelled together on long-distance trips of which those by the auto/van/truck passenger travel mode averaged three people and those by plane averaged two people (Caltrans 2013).

Long-distance travel by race and ethnicity

Figure 18.2 compares the distribution of long-distance travellers in California in the 2012 CHTS by race and ethnicity versus the distribution in the population as a whole in the 2010 US Census. Whites are over-represented among long-distance travellers in California, making almost two-thirds of all long-distance trips although they constitute less than three out of every five Californians. People of Hispanic origin were under-represented in long-distance travel. Other racial groups are more proportionally represented when compared to their shares of the California population. Another noticeable disparity relates to the 'other' race category, which includes multi-racial residents who appear to be substantially underrepresented in long-distance trips.

HSR is inherently a long-distance travel mode. If one assumes that the racial distribution of HSR riders will be similar to the (current) racial distribution of long-distance travellers in California, then whites will be overrepresented among the riders and other groups will be under-represented. In other words, a trends-extended analysis suggests that California's investment in HSR is likely to serve whites disproportionately.

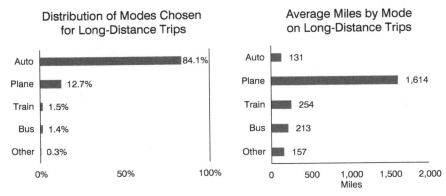

Figure 18.3 Long-distance mode choice

Distribution by mode choice

Figure 18.3 provides insight into the modes chosen for long-distance travel in California. It shows that the automobile is the primary mode used for long-distance travel, accounting for more than four out every five long-distance trips by California residents. Air travel captures nearly 13 per cent of the longer interregional trips, dwarfing the frequencies with which intercity trains and buses are chosen. Consistent with the predominance of whites in long-distance travel in general, the 2001 CHTS revealed that whites were over-represented in all long-distance modes in absolute numbers. Thus if the choice patterns persist, high-speed rail will likely be used more by the majority group than minority groups.

Mode choice by trip distance

The overwhelming majority (84 per cent) of long-distance trips in California are made by private automobile and the auto dominates mode choices for trips up to about 600 miles. Over 600 miles, air travel is the predominant mode choice. Air travel also is a key service provider in the critical 300–600 mile range; where HSR would be offering competing service in California, the car is the dominant mode choice.

At uncongested freeway speeds, trips of 300–600 miles take 4+ to 10 hours of driving. By HSR such trips could be shortened by many hours. Air trips in the same distance range take 2–3 hours depending on the aircraft and airspeeds used, and accounting for extra time spent in the air terminals. Assuming HSR access time is not much different from time to the airport, but security and wait time in HSR terminals is considerably less, HSR trips could be as fast as many air trips. These findings suggest that HSR might draw mostly from trips currently made with the auto, but could also attract trips from air travel. Of course, fares or other out of pocket costs would be important as would travel party size (because four

Table 18.1 Distribution of long-distance trips by mode and distance

	Under 300 miles	300 to 599 miles	600 or more miles	Modal Total
Car	85.2%	6.8%	0.0%	91.9%
Bus	0.7%	0.3%	0.4%	1.4%
Train	0.4%	0.0%	0.2%	0.6%
Plane	0.4%	0.5%	1.7%	2.7%
Other	1.8%	0.6%	1.1%	3.5%
Distance Total	88.5%	8.2%	3.3%	100.0%

Source: author's analysis of 2001 CHTS

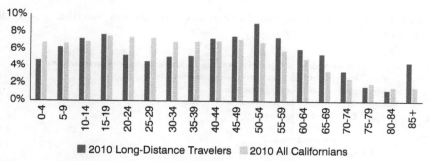

■ 2010 Long-Distance Travelers ▨ 2010 All Californians

Figure 18.4 Comparative age distribution of long-distance travellers v. general population

or five travellers could ride together in one automobile, but would pay separate fares by HSR or air).

Distribution by age

Figure 18.4 shows comparative age distribution of long-distance travellers vs. the general population of California. Long-distance travellers in California tend to be middle-aged adults between the ages of 40 and 70 as well as teenagers. They constitute 50 per cent of the population, but make 58 per cent of the long-distance trips in California. The senior population also makes proportionately high long-distance trips. These findings suggest that HSR will most likely be used mostly by middle-aged adults, with teenagers and seniors as additional market segments.

Distribution by income

Figure 18.5 compares the income distribution of long-distance travellers in California and the population as a whole. There are disproportionately more long-distance travellers in the upper-income groups (above $75,000 annual household income) than the share of those in these income brackets within the population

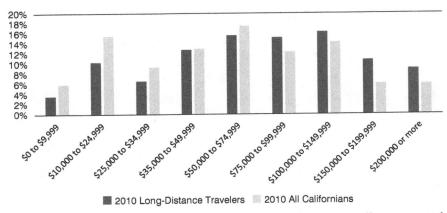

Figure 18.5 Comparative income distribution of long-distance travellers v. general population

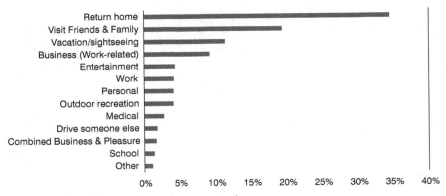

Figure 18.6 Distribution of long-distance trips by purpose

as a whole. There are proportionately fewer long-distance travellers in the lower income groups (under $35,000 per year) than in California as a whole.

Details in the 2001 CHTS revealed that those who earn less than $25,000 per year used the automobile for 89 per cent of their long-distance trips, but also rode the bus proportionately more than those in the upper income groups. The share of long-distance travel by plane tended to increase with income while the auto dominated across all income groups. If HSR draws mainly from auto trips then it could serve all income groups across the board, but likely would be used less often by those in the lower income brackets.

Distribution by trip purpose

Figure 18.6 shows the distribution of long-distance trips by primary trip purposes. Virtually all trips must return home at some point; ignoring those trips the most common purposes for long-distance travel among California residents are visiting friends and family and vacation, i.e., social and recreational trips, followed by those that are work-related. One question these data pose for HSR concerns travel party size; social and recreational trips are often made with family members or friends and this can affect the economics of travel by car vs. other modes. This also may explain why so many of the trips are by car.

Spatial distribution of long-distance trip origins and destinations

Figure 18.7 is a map of the distribution of long-distance trip origins and destinations in California, as reported in the 2012 CHTS. The map shows that places where travellers undertake activities are concentrated in the major metropolitan areas of San Francisco and Sacramento in the north and Los Angeles and San Diego in the south. Other noticeable concentrations follow the proposed corridor of the HSR across communities in the Central Valley.

Proposed station locations track the heaviest concentrations of long-distance trip origins and destinations. However, Figure 18.8 shows wide variability in the distribution of long-distance trip destinations from the nearest proposed

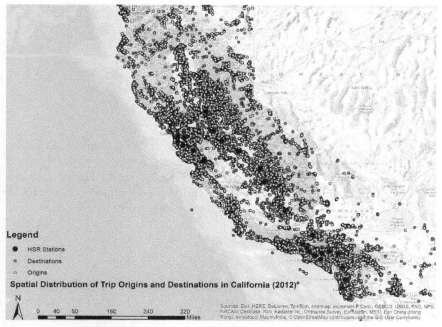

Figure 18.7 Spatial distribution of long-distance trip origins and destinations in California

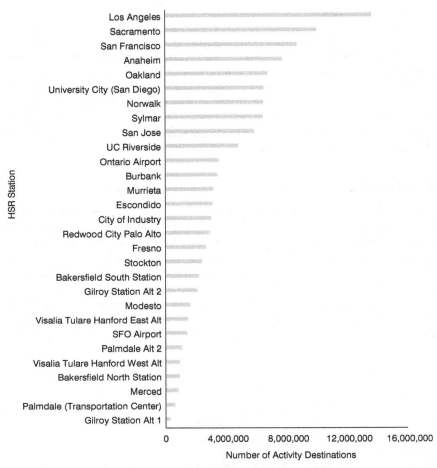

Figure 18.8 Nearest long-distance trip destinations by nearest HSR station

stations. Consistent with the spatial distribution of trip origins and destinations, station locations in the largest metropolitan areas in the state depict the highest proximity to trip destinations The proposed HSR station in Los Angeles, for instance, would be the nearest station for nearly 14 million places of activity for California residents, whereas stations in smaller cities would serve only a small number of activities.

Distance to nearest HSR station by race of long-distance traveller

Figure 18.9 shows the distribution of access distances to nearest HSR stations by race and ethnicity of the long-distance traveller, for both trip origins and trip destinations as reported in the CHTS. If the 2012 pattern of long-distance trips were being made on HSR, whites would be the group worst off in terms of

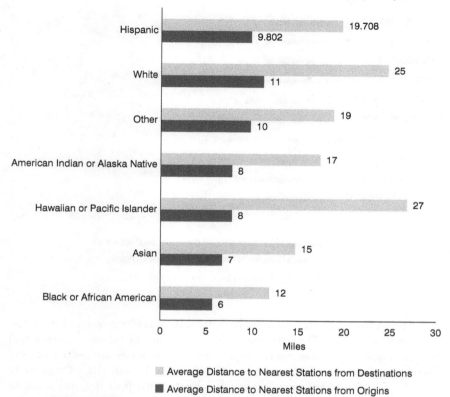

Figure 18.9 Comparative access distances by race and ethnicity

distance to stations. Minority groups would be better off in this regard than the white population of long-distance trip-makers because their long-distance trip origins and destinations are located closer to the proposed HSR stations.

Distance to nearest stations by income

Figure 18.10 shows the distribution of access distances to nearest HSR stations by income group for both trip origins and destinations as reported in the CHTS. It is noteworthy that lower-middle and middle income household members have somewhat longer than average access distances than either their richer or poorer counterparts. This finding is consistent with assertions that HSR would benefit the wealthy more than those who are less well-off, but the fact that lower income groups are also closer to stations is worth considering. This may create new opportunities for them to travel but it also may expose them to higher levels of station-related negative impacts.

Figures 18.10 and 18.11 together confirm that the majority (67 per cent) of those who make long-distance trips in California are whites. The figures also

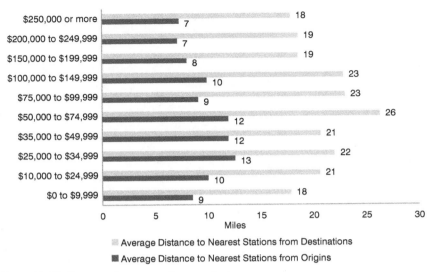

Figure 18.10 Comparative access distances by income group

reveal that whites make up the overwhelming majority of long-distance travellers in all income groups. Thus differences in accessibility by income category will most adversely impact those in the middle income categories irrespective of race. The finding supports the assertion that HSR would benefit the affluent more than those in the middle class and to a lesser extent the poor in terms of access irrespective of ethnic composition.

Distance to nearest stations by age of long-distance traveller

Figure 18.12 shows the distribution of access distances to nearest HSR stations by age group. There is little discernible pattern in terms of access by age as distances only vary slightly from the average for the population as a whole. The chart suggests that seniors above age 65 would have slightly longer access distances than the average for the population of long-distance travellers except for those above age 80. However, age effects are minimal.

Distance to nearest stations by trip purpose

Figure 18.13 shows the distribution of access distances to nearest HSR stations by trip purpose. It is clear that access distances would be shortest for trips related to work and school, while distances to HSR stations would be longer for long-distance trips for vacations and outdoor recreation. This finding is consistent with the assertion that HSR might be used disproportionately by those making business trips. Travellers on business trips are likely to travel shorter access distances than others.

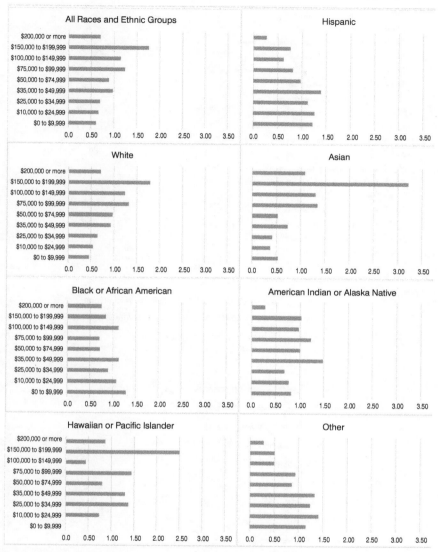

Figure 18.11 Ratios of sample population to state population by income and race/ethnicity

Distance to nearest stations overall

The compactness of cities shapes the average travel distances between trip origins and destinations (activity locations) and proposed HSR station locations. The placement of the HSR station also affects average distances. Figure 18.14 shows how average distances to stations compare. Although the Sacramento station is within an urbanized area, its location at the northern

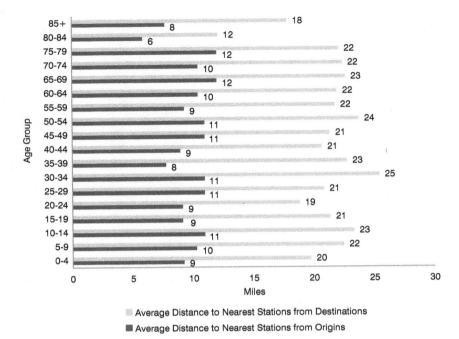

Figure 18.12 Comparative access distances by age group

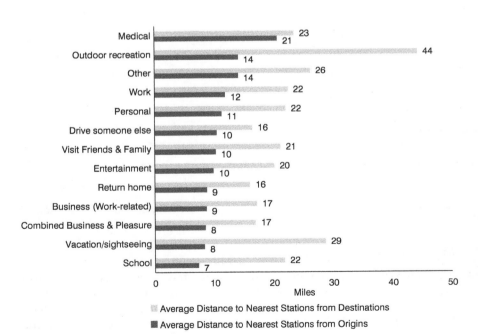

Figure 18.13 Comparative access distances by trip purpose

terminus of the proposed HSR system means it would be likely to serve not only the desired origins and destination in the Sacramento area but also origins and destinations further north, resulting in one of the largest average access distances. In general, stations in the larger and more compact urban areas like Los Angeles, San Diego, and San Francisco would experience lower access distances than stations in smaller and lower density Central Valley communities such as Bakersfield and Visalia, which would likely experience considerably higher than average access distances. The access distances will also affect mode choice to the stations, with longer distance access trips most likely to be made by car, especially outside the major metro areas.

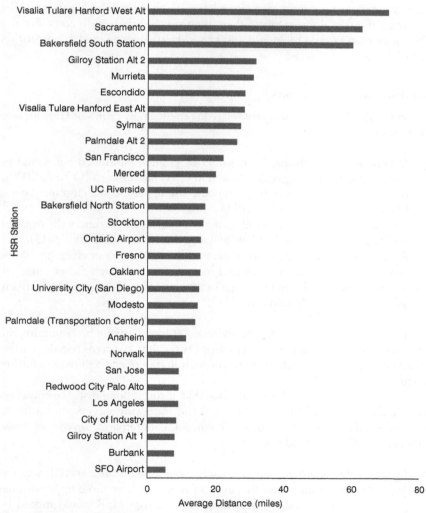

Figure 18.14 Overall access distances to proposed HSR stations

Overall, the analysis of the CHTS data indicates that if trip patterns remain similar to current ones and travel behaviour also remains similar, the CA HSR project would principally serve white, relatively affluent travellers, including many business travellers, who are currently making long-distance trips by auto. This is not, however, a unique feature of HSR but rather is the reality of long-distance travel. Interestingly, proposed station locations serve high and low income long-distance travellers better than the middle income groups, most likely because of settlement patterns and station locations that are predominantly in or near city centres. The majority of trips in the long-distance range are currently made by auto and so competition with the auto would be a major consideration; while travel time differences between auto and HSR are relatively clear, at this early stage of the project, costs are more speculative. In addition, whether the traveller is making the trip alone or with others (hence could share auto costs, but not HSR or air costs) would be an important consideration when modal competition with the auto is considered.

Summary and conclusions

To summarize, key points of equity-related contention by critics of HSR include the following:

- Income equity: high-speed rail would be publicly subsidized but would be more beneficial to economic elites than to average citizens (O'Toole 2009).
- Racial disparity: a largely Anglo, middle and upper income customer base is likely to use HSR (Brenman 2011).
- Localized adverse impacts: local residents would bear the brunt of the negative effects of the project while others will reap the benefits (Williams 2013).
- Regional disparities: the motivation to achieve mobility or efficiency above other considerations can also lead to situations in which richer cities are likely to gain while disadvantaged cities would end up in comparatively worse situations (Monzón et al. 2013).

The first two of the issues can be addressed at least partially by examining the evidence on long-distance travel. The latter two equity concerns remain matters of debate empirically as well as in the research literature and will require further monitoring.

The analysis presented here indicates that if future long-distance travellers are like those observed in recent national and state-wide surveys, and if future travellers make similar trips to their current counterparts, several of these criticisms are likely to hold true:

- Income – There are disproportionately more long-distance travellers in the upper-income groups than the share of households in those upper income groups, thus as a mode serving long-distance trips HSR would indeed be likely to benefit the wealthier groups more than those who are less well-off.

- Race/ethnicity – With the exception of Asians, minority groups are disproportionately represented in the lower income brackets in California. Whites have higher incomes and make a disproportionate share of long-distance trips, accounting for almost seven out of every ten long-distance trips although they constitute a little more than five of every ten Californians. The analysis reveals, however, that HSR stations are located closer to minority long-distance trip-makers on average than majority trip-makers. Thus, the anticipated benefit to whites could be tempered by more distant locations from HSR than other groups.
- Local impact – Origins and destinations of long-distance trips are concentrated in the major metropolitan areas of San Francisco and Sacramento to the north and Los Angeles and San Diego to the south. The large urban HSR stations are thus likely to attract more HSR trips than the smaller suburban and small city stations. However, outlying stations may generate considerable travel for access to HSR. This has implications for the localized burdens (from traffic, for example) that various communities might bear.

The study findings indicate that if past travel patterns continue, HSR riders are likely to be disproportionately white and affluent and are most likely to be making work-related trips by HSR. This is consistent with overall findings about long-distance travel in the distance range HSR would serve. On the question of station area impacts, the analysis does not address highly localized issues such as noise propagation, barrier effects, or visual impact, but does suggest that station locations are closer to the rich and the poor than to the middle income and that peripheral stations are likely to draw traffic from longer distances (and hence would generate more traffic) than those located in major city centres. With regard to regional impact, the analysis suggests that long-distance travel is more prevalent in the major city centres, which would support a finding that such centres will benefit the most.

These findings do not dismiss all potential for the efficacy of HSR to society. A previous study summarizes the rationale for implementing a high-speed rail system in California. It identified reasons that relate to the growth of the state's population vis-à-vis congestion on the highways and at the airports within the state, as well as competitiveness in energy consumption and air pollution (Nuworsoo and Deakin 2009).

There are arguments for reducing air pollution and energy consumption if large proportions of long-distance trips were to switch from the private automobile, which dominates such travel, to any of the large capacity, shared modes like buses, trains, and planes. For instance, the Bureau of Transportation Statistics (BTS) shows that the energy intensity (that is, energy consumption per passenger mile) is two to four times as high for the private automobile as it is for the large capacity surface modes like rail and intercity bus (BTS 2006). Similarly, a more detailed study of the total energy use, which includes such components as construction, operating, and maintenance of vehicles and infrastructure as well as fuel production, shows similar ratios for energy intensity and greenhouse gas emissions (Chester and Horvath 2009). High-speed rail is one of these high capacity modes and is likely to help reduce both energy consumption and greenhouse gas emissions.

There are also arguments about the cost competitiveness of HSR relative to other alternatives. A mid 1990s study of the proposed California high-speed rail system analyzed its cost competitiveness relative to highway and air transportation (Levinson *et al.* 1996), and found it to be the least costly in terms of social costs alone, but not in terms of total costs. The study concluded that California HSR would be most effective if treated as an alternative to highway use and a complement to air transportation. A subsequent study (Brand *et al.* 2001) assessed that the benefits of the California high-speed rail system would outweigh its costs by a factor of two. The study considered both user and non-user benefits in the calculations.

Such benefits should continue to be tracked as the HSR project is refined, since air pollution reduction and reduced demand for expansion of other modes could be of value in evaluating equity concerns (since low income and minority communities often bear the brunt of externalities from highway modes, for example). In addition, detailed analyses of impacts around stations and rail lines may reveal cost-effective ways to reduce or compensate for localized adverse impacts.

The question remains: what can be done to address potential equity issues that may arise in terms of accessibility and use of HSR? Here it is worth noting the main reasons the issues relate to: (a) the individual choice to engage or not engage in long-distance travel, which differs by racial/ethnic group but is not necessarily a function of a person's ethnic group; (b) income distribution, which historically favours majority groups over minority groups; and (c) trip purpose, which favours occupational travel which in turn reflects on income. In urban public transportation, society has attempted to address equity in offering lower fares for the youth and seniors. Similar types of treatments can help promote equity in the use of high-speed rail. Broader social policies that reduce income disparities and employment disparities may do even more to narrow the gap over the longer run.

References

American Public Transportation Association, 2012, *An Inventory of the Criticisms of High-speed Rail. With Suggested Responses and Counter-points*. Retrieved from: http://www.apta.com/resources/reportsandpublications/Documents/HSR-Defense.pdf Accessed 1 August 2016.

Bierce, E, Kurth, D and West, R, 2012, *Long-distance Travel – An Update from a 2011 Web-Based Travel Survey for the California High-Speed Rail Authority*. Transportation Research Board. Retrieved from: http://trid.trb.org/view/1243063 Accessed 1 August 2016.

Brand, D, Kiefer, MR, Parody, TE and Mehndiratta, SR, 2001, 'Application of Benefit-Cost Analysis to the Proposed California High-Speed Rail System,' *Transportation*

Research Record: Journal of the Transportation Research Board, No.1742, TRB, National Research Council, Washington, DC.

Brenman, M, 2011, *High-speed Rail and Social Equity*, Legal services of Northern California, Race Equity Project.

Bureau of Transportation Statistics, 2006, *National Transportation Statistics*, Table K-6.

California Department of Transportation, 2002, *2001 California Household Travel Survey* [Data file, code book, and user's manual].

California Department of Transportation, 2013, *2010–2012 California Household Travel Survey*.

Chester, MV and Horvath, A, 2009, 'Environmental assessment of passenger transportation should include infrastructure and supply chains,' *Environmental Research Letters*, vol. 4, no. 2, 024008 http://iopscience.iop.org/1748-9326/4/2/024008/pdf/1748-9326_4_2_024008.pdf Accessed 1 August 2016.

Ehlers, E, Goldberg, J, Metcalf, G, Reilly, M, Sedway, P and Teitz, M, 2011, *Beyond the Tracks: The Potential of High-speed Rail to Reshape California's Growth*, San Francisco Planning and Urban Research (SPUR).

Friedman, LS, 2002, *The Microeconomics of Public Policy Analysis*, Princeton University Press, Princeton, NJ.

Grengs, J, Levine, J and Shen, Q, 2010, 'Intermetropolitan Comparison of Transportation Accessibility: Sorting Out Mobility and Proximity in San Francisco and Washington DC,' *Journal of Planning Education and Research*, vol. 29, no. 4, 427–443.

Levinson, D, Gillen, D, Kanafani, A and Mathieu JM, 1996, *The Full Cost of Intercity Transportation – A Comparison of High Speed Rail, Air and Highway Transportation in California*, University of California at Berkeley.

Martin, F, 1997, 'Justifying a high-speed rail project: Social value vs. regional growth,' *The Annals of Regional Science*, vol. 31, no. 2, 155–174.

Monzón, A, Ortega, E and López, E, 2013, 'Efficiency and spatial equity impacts of high-speed rail extensions in urban areas,' *Cities*, vol. 30, pp. 18–30.

Nuworsoo, C and Deakin, E, 2009, 'Transforming High-speed Rail Stations to Major Activity Hubs: Lessons for California,' Paper presented, *88th Annual Meeting of the Transportation Research Board*, January, 2009. http://digitalcommons.calpoly.edu/cgi/viewcontent.cgi?article=1045&context=crp_fac Accessed 1 August 2016.

O'Toole, R, 2009, *High-Speed Spending*, The Cato Institute, Retrieved from: http://www.cato.org/publications/commentary/high-speed-spending Accessed 1 August 2016.

Rosenberg, M, 2013, 'California high-speed rail finally wins Peninsula lawsuit,' *San Jose Mercury News*, Retrieved from: http://www.mercurynews.com/ci_22688893/california-high-speed-rail-finally-wins-peninsula-lawsuit Accessed 1 August 2016.

Schwieterman, JP and Scheidt, JL, 2007, 'High-speed rail in the United States: Proposed routes and rights-of-way', *Journal of Transportation Law, Logistics and Policy*, vol. 74, no. 4, 435–444.

Sharp, J, Bose, J, Giesbrecht, L, Memmott, J, Khan, M and Roberto, E, 2001, *A Picture of Long Distance Travel Behavior of Americans Through Analysis of the 2001 National Household Travel Survey*, Washington DC: Bureau of Transportation Statistics.

Tavlian, A, 2011, 'Kings County sues high-speed rail authority,' *Fresno Bee*, Retrieved from: http://www.fresnobee.com/2011/11/14/2614819/kings-co-sues-high-speed-rail.html Accessed 1 August 2016.

US Census Bureau, 2010, 'Demographic profile, California,' Retrieved Oct. 27, 2013 http://www.census.gov/2010census/news/press-kits/demographic-profiles.html

US Department of Transportation, Federal Highway Administration, 2006, *NPTS Brief*, Retrieved from: http://nhts.ornl.gov/briefs/Long%20Distance%20Travel.pdf Accessed 1 August 2016.

US Department of Transportation, Federal Highway Administration, 2009, *Summary of Travel Trends, 2009 Household Travel Survey*, Retrieved from: http://nhts.ornl.gov/2009/pub/stt.pdf Accessed 1 August 2016.

Williams, J, 2013, *California High-Speed Rail Project Angers Locals*, Retrieved from: http://www.realclearpolitics.com/articles/2013/10/21/california_high_speed_rail_project_angers_locals_120397.html Accessed 1 August 2016.

19 NIMBY reactions to HSR

Conflicts over the proposed right of way

Michael O'Hare and Ander Audikana

Introduction

'Mode of failure analysis' is an underappreciated exercise in project and programme planning, directed at anticipating the most likely ways implementation can go wrong. The spirit is properly to modify the programme design so as to minimize the likelihood of the greatest risks, and to be prepared with repair and response mechanisms to keep it viable after one comes to pass, though in practice it often degenerates into project proponents arguing that this or that proposed risk is exaggerated and not worth attending to. High-speed rail (HSR) has many opportunities to fail before the first passenger takes a trip. This chapter attends to a characteristic risk of any system dependent on an exclusive right-of-way (ROW) constrained to connect an origin and a destination in an unbroken line: so-called NIMBY (Not In My Back Yard) opposition from stakeholders near or on any proposed route. The NIMBY phenomenon, reified by the acronym, is already salient in the California HSR policy debate (Dungan 2010) and is part of a constellation of phenomena which include LULU (Locally Unwanted Land Use), BANANA (Build Absolutely Nothing Anywhere Near Anything), NOPE (Not On Planet Earth), and (the authors' personal favourite), NIMTO (Not In My Term of Office).

Whether HSR is good for California is a debate outside the scope of this discussion, which proceeds as though that question is settled in the affirmative. The present questions are, can local opposition to ROW and station location hinder or halt the programme? If so, why should this be, and what can be done about it?

We begin with a parable:

> On a cold northern night, a small-town resident driving by a frozen pond opens the window of his car to throw out an apple core, and just at that moment, hears a cry for help. Stopping the car and getting out, he realizes a child has fallen through the ice. Without thinking, he wades into armpit-deep water and saves the child.
>
> Later, a familiar scene; flashing red lights, police radios going on and off, people milling about, and the driver sitting shivering on a log wrapped in a

blanket. A TV reporter thrusts a microphone before him. 'You saved that little girl! How do you feel now?'

'I'll tell you how I feel; I'm furious. My clothes are ruined, I'm freezing cold, I could have drowned, and I'm late for dinner. It's completely unfair that I was the one this happened to; we have a fire department for this kind of thing! I'm going to sue everyone; the kid's parents, the town, and the owner of the pond.'

Everyone we've told this story to finds it ridiculous, unimaginable, absurd. The hero would say something completely different, like 'I'm just so glad I was able to help; her poor parents!' Abstracting the example, one would think that *the opportunity to incur a significant but manageable risk or cost in the service of one's community* would always seem like a piece of good fortune to be seized, but local opposition to generally beneficial land uses – as exemplified in NIMBY – confounds this expectation.

This chapter addresses the problem of NIMBY reactions to proposals for selecting the right-of-way for California's HSR. The chapter begins with a discussion of the NIMBY phenomenon and the problems it poses: the potential to stop good projects or transform them into projects that are less desirable. It discusses the roots of the NIMBY reaction in real facility impacts, but notes that the nature of the discourse over localized impacts often ranges far beyond an impact assessment. The limited ability in a democratic society of information, compensation, or authority to overcome such opposition is also discussed. The chapter concludes that political leadership is perhaps the only way to overcome the NIMBY problem.

Facility siting analytics

A NIMBY is either a local opponent of a facility (in which case the term has a pejorative intent, implying selfishness or cupidity [Hermansson 2007]) or a land use opposed locally. The term appears to have originated in 1980 in a newspaper article (Livezey 1980), though a similar phrase for the same phenomenon is in the title of a 1977 journal article (O'Hare 1977). Here we will use it in the second sense, more generally to describe the political conflict associated with something people generally want, but few want near them.

Good investments left on the table

The key elements of a NIMBY dispute are:

- a location-specific proposed land use,
- that prospective neighbours see as noisome (dangerous, noisy, ugly, and/or reputationally damaging, etc.), and
- that creates net benefits for a large population including many stakeholders far from its site.

Note that an ill-conceived facility – something with negative total net benefits – opposed by neighbours is just a bad idea, not a NIMBY. The core of the NIMBY problem is the likelihood of not building something *that's good for society as a whole, counting the local costs it imposes*, because it is politically impossible in any particular location.

NIMBY opposition derives from real perceived costs and fairness judgements

Local opposition to NIMBYs derives from a combination of perceived costs, among which are often real costs, and a combination of process-related perceptions including mistrust of government or business, and a sense of unfair treatment (Hunter and Leyden 1995; Gibson 2005). Most of the early research on NIMBYs concerned things like hazardous waste processing and disposal sites and liquefied natural gas (LNG) terminals that posed real risks (however large or small in fact) of toxic or other injury to neighbours; a famously enduring NIMBY episode is the search for a disposal site for nuclear waste in the United States (Bewick 2010; O'Hare 2011). However, local opposition also obstructs construction of things like airports (on grounds of noise, traffic, land taking and community disruption), landfills (Feinerman, Finkelshtain *et al.* 2004), and social service facilities like homeless shelters (Gibson 2005), projects whose physical or health risks to neighbours are small and neighbours are mainly concerned about economic or symbolic costs.

The strategic disposition of a NIMBY dispute begins with an expectation of local costs conditional on operation (or construction) of the new facility. Neighbours face a decision, when a project is proposed, whether to incur costs to oppose it, using a variety of well-known tactics. The project developer has a variety of response options, and a successful enterprise depends on correctly reading the neighbours' decision structure. Figure 19.1 illustrates the generic choice facing possible NIMBY project opponents as a decision tree. One branch, labelled 'Oppose' has costs of time, attention, stress, and money, and leads to two outcomes, 'Build' and 'No-build' with probabilities attached, the successful implementation of the project and its failure or abandonment respectively. In turn, 'Build' leads to a variety of results, with associated probabilities. The other action choice, 'Accept', may have immediate costs (for example, social pressure if other neighbours have chosen the other branch) and similarly leads to two possible project outcomes with possible consequences. A NIMBY conflict arises when enough neighbours see the 'Oppose' branch as preferred.

Project advocates can change this decision tree in two generic ways. First, they can change participants' probabilities of different outcomes, by sharing information and evidence from expert analysis or by reference to comparable projects elsewhere. Second, they can decisively attach additional consequences that change the net value of being at the end of different branches. Both approaches impose costs on the project, costs that may not be recoverable if the project does not proceed (or is so transformed by mitigation efforts that it no longer is net beneficial).

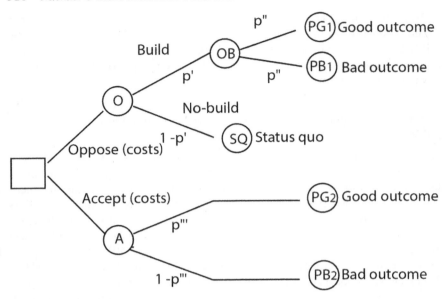

Figure 19.1 Decision of a project neighbour

Collective action and strategy

The distribution of costs and benefits in a facility siting conflict is central to the probable outcome, and to effective strategies for countering NIMBY opposition. In particular, a project disfavoured by neighbours almost always imposes large *per capita* costs on them (or they think it will), while the positive net benefits balance depends on small *per capita* benefits delivered to a very large population, many of whom don't necessarily know they are in it. In the case of a new rail line proposed to pass through a town but not stop in it, the beneficiaries include the entire population of the region served by the line insofar as it benefits the economy, the population of the earth insofar as rail travel inhibits climate change, and the people who will ride the train when it is operational.

Mancur Olson provided the key theoretical explanation of why a small group with high individual stakes in a decision will have a great strategic advantage over a large, diffuse group even when the latter has more to gain or lose in total (Olson 1971). A small group of neighbours is able to identify and coerce slackers in an opposition effort, feels responsible to each other and to its community, and can condition private benefits on participation, while the population of a large polity faces powerful free-rider incentives to remain tacit and has to act through a complicated, slow-moving, bureaucratic and legislative machinery.

Olson's model is the basis for the analysis of the NIMBY problem in a previous analysis by the lead author and colleagues (O'Hare, Bacow *et al.* 1983), which shapes the analysis presented here and, less directly, much of the other research in the field. Briefly, we argued that neither the legal right to proceed with a project (permits, etc.) nor a demonstration persuasive to a neutral third party or objective observer that local costs are actually small, is likely to make the 'Accept' branch of a local opponent's choice preferable to 'Oppose'. We also argued that local opposition will, by Olson's model, make use of a range of well-known means of opposition that seem efficacious to this small group, including litigation and extra-legal means (of which the classic meme is 'standing in front of the bulldozers with baby carriages'). The large, diffuse group of project beneficiaries often cannot deliver the political force necessary to overcome determined local resistance.

As expected, HSR has given birth to a variety of civic organizations dedicated to opposing or at least watching the project closely, including maintaining information channels for citizens outside CHSRA's official actions. These organizations are a changing set, but have included several organizations in the San Francisco Bay Area as well as groups in the Central Valley and Southern California. In addition, organizations with broader missions, such as the California Farm Bureau Federation and the Train Riders Association of California, also have taken positions challenging aspects of the project.

Local governments have taken formal actions challenging alignment decisions or the EIR process, as well. The City of Palo Alto unanimously endorsed the HSR plan in late 2008, but the city council found itself the target of its own citizens the next spring when 'more than 50 people marched on City Hall ahead of the council meeting, carrying signs with slogans such as "Too close to my school," "Do it right," and "Revote on Prop 1A"' (the state-wide proposition that authorized bond funding for HSR). Voicing an increasingly popular sentiment, they chanted, 'High-speed rail underground, we don't want to hear a sound.' As a result, the council demanded of CHSRA that the line be underground through Palo Alto and that alternative alignments through the East Bay, or even ending the line in San Jose, be revisited (Oremus 2009). Palo Alto eventually joined a lawsuit against the peninsula route with Atherton, Menlo Park, and some environmental NGOs that took 5 years to resolve (in favour of CHSRA) (Rosenberg 2013). Central Valley challenges to the project have included Madera County and Kings County as well as individual plaintiffs and the California Farm Bureau Federation.

Rail location local costs and benefits

A limited-access transportation link like a freeway or rail line poses a distinctive set of spatially distributed costs and benefits. Near access points, residents may suffer increased local traffic but will enjoy improved access to other stations or intersections and, usually, higher property values owing to commercial and residential development opportunities like transit villages (Dittmar and Ohland 2004). They may also experience destruction of social capital embodied in the traditional habits and relationships of their community as it grows, and a particular group, whose property is used for the project itself, will face displacement from homes and businesses bought or condemned for the project. An access point offers a mixture of benefits and costs, but is probably regarded positively by prospective neighbours (though it appears that intra-city proximity to such nodes does not always significantly affect property values [Ahlfeldt 2009]).

Between access points, along the right of way, are costs with few benefits. Landowners face expropriation or purchase of land and possibly homes and businesses (many for a highway, fewer for rail); and on a wider strip on each side of the alignment, people can expect noise and visual intrusion. At-grade links obstruct local travel across the ROW, while underground placement is less disruptive after, and sometimes during, construction but much more expensive. Elevated tracks or lanes blight the streets beneath them, as anyone who remembers the San Francisco Embarcadero under its freeway, New York's Third Avenue before 1955, or Boston under the Central Artery, can confirm. In rural areas, the number of people affected by a mile of new track is usually small, but the disruption nevertheless may undermine agricultural activities by increasing access costs trans-line, leaving some parcels 'stranded', or reducing the uses for certain parcels because of noise or other impacts. In suburban and developed areas many residents can expect significant disruption of their lives (see Chapter 16).

A high-speed train passing 80 feet away (about the depth of a suburban lot) at 180 mph is a 100 dB experience (Schulte-Werning, Thompson *et al.* 2008), and because it is a line rather than a point source, the intensity decreases only linearly with distance normal to the track, or to about 94 dB a football field distant. Many residents reasonably foresee nearby location of a rail line as reason to move entirely, selling their principal asset for a significant loss, and sound walls of the type that increasingly line freeways are themselves distasteful if only on grounds of visual aesthetic impact.

All these effects have been recognized and detailed in the hundreds of comments received by CHSRA on their Bay Area to Central Valley EIR. In a random sample of thirty-five individual comments (nineteen women, thirteen men and three couples), most of the comments consider the impacts of the proposed routing, questioning the evaluation and conclusions provided by the EIR (Administration 2010). Many asked for a new alignment or proposed to tunnel the new line; a few comments questioned the entire project.

Complicating the siting problem for a rail alignment are the constraints of maximum radius curves, grades, and the requirement that the chain of 'sites' be adjacent. This makes holdouts especially important and assures that while political debate can discriminate among a few alignments several miles apart, once one is chosen, eminent domain taking will almost assuredly be required, so the experience of coercion (actual or latent) is added to the costs affected stakeholders anticipate.

Realigning local incentives

Some governments hold practical power to impose costs for a national or regional purpose (or, of course, for private enrichment of oligarchs and rulers). Thousands of miles of HSR have been put in place not only in China but also in western European countries that no one would judge to be autocracies. Even there, however, the siting problem is not merely technical: selecting the route for the Lyon-Marseille TGV took more than 4 years punctuated by a blockade of the main Paris-Marseille rail line and widespread public demonstrations, and led to an extensive reform of French public participation and deliberation procedures (de Carlo 2006). The insight that determined local opposition cannot be overcome – at least in a democracy – by government coercion at the disposal of a transportation agency or a developer, by legal procedures, or by technical browbeating, leads directly to a search for ways to reduce the motivation of neighbours to oppose projects of this kind.

Compensation

The first classic non-coercive approach to the NIMBY problem is a mechanism to attach compensation of some sort for the costs the project imposes on neighbours so they will not want to oppose the project. A variety of schemes to determine, and to pay, money compensation have been put forward, including structured negotiations with a designated community body (O'Hare, Bacow *et al.* 1983), and an auction of the facility to the site willing to accept the smallest compensation payment (Kunreuther and Kleindorfer 1986).

Compensation schemes are theoretically sound and especially attractive on conventional economic grounds, because a net-beneficial project, by definition, can come up with payments that offset its costs and still show net benefits; the approach is in essence one of converting a policy that meets a Kaldor-Hicks test into a Pareto-superior change. They also have the advantage that, again in theory, projects that look net beneficial but really aren't will be revealed as such, because the local costs are made manifest in the negotiation or auction process. And they are empirically supported by the thousands of cases in which facilities of various kinds, including not only the ideal smokeless, noiseless hi-tech operation whose childless PhD employees commute on bicycles, but also prisons, are accepted because they promise employment and economic growth (even if the promise is not always fulfilled) (King, Mauer *et al.* 2004).

One type of compensation that has particular promise in this context is conditional guarantees like property value insurance. A homeowner displaced by noise can at least be assured that he won't suffer a financial loss when a nearby train alignment makes his home much less valuable. For one reason or another, financial compensation, beyond legally required payment for property taken by eminent domain, has not been featured (beyond vague promises to compensate actual damages) as part of CHSRA's public posture, though a form of in-kind compensation (purchasing agricultural easements to protect the farming culture of the region) was included in the settlement of the second major lawsuit, brought by Central Valley cities and organizations (Sheehan 2013a).

In American law, it has been difficult to establish a compensable taking without actual physical intrusion in highway cases, though takings for noise are well established in the aviation field. Furthermore, compensation, if not established in a negotiated purchase price between CHSRA and a landowner, is at least in theory limited to the market value of the property taken, so owners of land in the noise-afflicted zone described above, but not crossed by the right-of-way, may reasonably fear uncompensated costs.

Process legitimacy

Pure money compensation has a disappointing track record at least in the context of facilities threatening health or injury risk. Here we need to view citizens and stakeholders as optimizing something more complicated than wealth, or even wealth plus some money equivalent of expected health. The most important non-economic factors in triggering and maintaining public opposition to local facilities are approximately the following:

- Aversion to coercion
- Mistrust of government
- Mistrust of private enterprise
- Mistrust of science
- Desire not to be taken advantage of
- Concern for family, especially children
- Local social capital (community, and belonging to it)
- Concern that the siting choice process was unfair
- Suspicion that a siting decision does not rest on sound scientific judgement
- Concern that the whole project is ill-advised on net-benefits grounds
- Fear that costs will be irreversible if rosy predictions are not fulfilled
- Fear of damage to locality and personal reputation.

These factors are all attested in the variety of 'compensation revisionist' research that has appeared over the last 2 decades (Frey and Oberholzer-Gee 1996; Frey, Oberholzer-Gee *et al.* 1996; Gibson 2005; Hermansson 2007), a body of work usefully reviewed and summarized in Schively (2007). These authors, and others, argue or demonstrate that success in the face of NIMBY opposition cannot be achieved by any single administrative device, especially cash payments. Notice that to the degree that opponents think a proposal resulted from an illegitimate political process (or defective science and engineering analysis), accepting money compensation marks the recipient as taking a 'bribe' to compromise on principle. The condemnatory use of the word *bribe* for compensation is political rhetoric and incorrect on the facts; a bribe is a secret payment to change a party's incentives from what they appear to be. This doesn't stop fervent project opponents from saying that the government is 'bribing us to put our lives at stake'.

Fortunately, HSR ROW alignment does not generally raise the issues of toxic injury that characterize siting waste disposal. However, it certainly raises concerns about neighbourhood reputation, as attested in numerous comments on the HSR EIRs; being near to at-grade or elevated tracks is not viewed by most homeowners as prime real estate.

What makes a siting process appear legitimate in the eyes of locally affected parties is not fully understood. It certainly has to do with transparency and access for all to make their views known, but especially in the context of environmental harms it also involves distributional issues recently studied under the umbrella of *environmental justice* (Pastor, Sadd and Hipp 2001). One of the most certain advantages of being richer rather than poorer is having more choice about where one lives, and since neighbourhoods began, the rich have moved to quiet places, where the air and water are cleaner and the views better. The US highway programmes of the 1960s and 1970s were roundly condemned for selecting rights-of-way where land was cheap and displaced residents powerless. Some NIMBY scholarship has recognized the great advantages high-income suburbanites have in deflecting undesired land uses (Brion 1988), advantages that include access to powerful political actors and the ability to hire lawyers and consultants. This kind of advantage is not unique to wealthy suburbs, however: a notable HSR opponent currently serving in the US Congress, along with members of his family, owns large tracts of land directly on and near one of the proposed routes in Kings County in the Central Valley (Sheehan 2013b).

The differential effects of unwanted land uses on rich and poor communities cuts two ways in locating the HSR. On the one hand, alignment through or near poor communities will raise questions of discrimination with echoes of the 'Negro removal' criticism of freeways and urban renewal. On the other hand, and not to put too fine a point on it, the route from San Francisco to Los Angeles goes through Atherton and Palo Alto, comfortably situated communities whose litigation of the peninsula route has already delayed the project by as much as 5 years (Dungan 2010; Rosenberg 2013).

NIMBY discourse

The claims put forward by the peninsula litigants and stakeholders in Mountain View (Samuels 2010) are worth noting as examples of the direction public debate is likely to take, and its tendency to spread to larger issues even when the motivation is local; if a NIMBY can be shown to be a NOPE, prospects of assembling a coalition to stop it are improved.[1] The Mountain View neighbours are seeking underground construction at the HSR Authority's or federal expense (local cost mitigation), assert their unwillingness to pay for the cost difference locally, and seek to double the comment and response period on the draft EIR, though they express support for HSR generally. The Atherton, Palo Alto, and Menlo Park litigants challenge the environmental impact analysis, doubt the ridership and financial viability of the project generally (seeking to demonstrate negative overall net benefits), and propose a completely different route along the East Bay shore. Consider some extracts from comments on the Bay Area-Valley EIR (CHAFR Administration 2010) illustrative of the variety of citizen positions from educated, economically advantaged correspondents:

'As a long-time Atherton resident (30 years), I can speak with authority regarding the impact of the proposed routing.'

letter I022

'I can assure you that I am a genuine "expert" with respect to the impacts of the project you propose.'

letter I192

'I am the co-founder and former CEO of Biolog. Inc., a biotechnology company in Hayward, CA, and I have a high level of expertise in creating, understanding and evaluating business plans.'

letter I199

'I have been advised that it is necessary for me to establish my competence to be considered "expert" in my ability to relate to such a complex issue and document. I have a law degree, am a Chartered Accountant (CPA equivalent) and MBA with distinction from Harvard.'

letter I229

'It is now long after this EIR was "circulated" the first time, and while awareness is up significantly thanks to efforts of groups like mine, public knowledge remains surprisingly ignorant; a true indicator of how poor a job the HSRA has done in reaching out to the communities it will impact.'

letter I241

'If there is more than I can do or say to get this alternative truly considered, please let me know. Beyond providing emails such as these and attending meetings, I feel that my voice is not heard.'

letter I281

'We have 86 houses in Eichler Tract 795 (...). Depending on the alternative chosen, High Speed Rail will have a devastating effect on this area of historic Eichler homes.'

letter I172

'My house is about 600 feet from the current train track. Your report did not measure how my property value would be seriously affected.'

letter I251

'My house is adjacent to the track in Palo Alto close to Peers Park and I'm concerned about how California High Speed Rail (CAHSR) will change things here in my backyard.'

letter I182

'The commonly referred to "Berlin Wall" will literally split our quite little town in half, will be an incredible eye-sore, will depreciate the value of our homes by hundreds of thousands of dollars per home, and will greatly diminish the quality of living. This is not NIMBYism...'

letter I032

In comparison, comments on the Merced-Fresno EIR (CHSR Authority 2012) (many handwritten) included relatively less attention to the decision process (legitimacy) and economic feasibility of the project as a whole, and more attention to (i) the effect of HSR on the agricultural industry, especially loss of agricultural land, more focused on a way of life than convenience or comfort, and (ii) environmental justice concerns:

'I am disabled veteran on dialysis legally blind, and had a heart attack a year ago. We have nowhere to go if you take our house (...) What are you going to do to help? Are you going to kick me out of my house and in to the street?'

(submission 801)

'I don't want it because I am not going to have a place to live.'

(submission 394)

'Farming is a way of life for my family. My grandfather came over from Italy and began farming in 1922. I have lived my whole life in the Le Grand area. We are currently farming with three generations (...) The HSR project threatens to take away this way of life.'

(submission 742)

'First of all I would like it known that I am very much against HST. I am against it because of the fact that I live in an area that won't have the benefit of having a stop. I live in Madera, CA by the way. I realize that this would be a nice way to have faster and quite possibly safer travel thorough the State, but if the closest stop to me is Fresno to the South either San Francisco or Los Angeles when I can just drive to either of those places myself.'

(submission 108)

'Approximately one half of the population of Fresno, Madera and Merced Counties is Hispanic, but HSRA held only one outreach meeting that was specifically designed to inform the Hispanic population about HSR and this leg of the project.'

(submission 952)

The breadth of considerations for which standing in a debate like this may be claimed is almost unlimited. Noteworthy on this score was the demand that the French SNCF, a likely bidder on any US HSR project, be disqualified from the Tampa-Orlando project on grounds of the participation of the French railways in transporting Jews to concentration camps during World War II. This attack led the SNCF to send its president to the US to apologize to Florida elected officials (Anon. 2010), and in California legislation was proposed that would have required HSR contractors to disclose activities during WWII (vetoed by the governor).

It is to be expected that project opponents will use whatever arguments fall to hand and can be presented with a straight face, at least insofar as they are determined that the best outcome is no project in their location. This strategic discourse, that necessarily combines reasonable considerations with assertions and claims that do not bear on the real issues, greatly complicates the task of the agency proposing the project.

Conclusions: leadership is critical

Previous studies have identified attention to leadership as a critical missing piece in understanding the NIMBY problem (O'Hare and Sanderson 1993). When the dust clears, many locally undesired land uses remain undesired, even with the sound engineering and planning analysis and attempts to mitigate harm and compensate for damages that are generally necessary but not sufficient conditions for acceptability. Neighbours of these facilities, assuming they are broadly socially desirable, are being asked to accept costs on behalf of a larger social good, quite in the fashion of the local hero with whose imaginary story we began this discussion. Without appropriate political leadership that both recognizes and credits good behaviour and calls out the easy retreat to 'my fair share…and not a penny more' morality into which project neighbours can easily fall, the complexity of NIMBY conflicts, both in terms of participants and issues, favours paralysis and failure.

Note

1   The Atherton *et al.* lawsuit has accreted the following co-plaintiffs: Planning and Conservation League, the Transportation Solutions Defense and Education Fund, the California Rail Foundation, Community Coalition on High-Speed Rail, Mid-Peninsula Residents for Civic Sanity, Dungan, J. (2010). 'Peninsula cities sue to derail high-speed rail project'. *Mercury News*, San José.

References

CHAFR Administration, 2010, *Bay Area to Central Valley High-Speed Train (HST) Revised Final Program Environmental Impact Report (EIR)*, Vol. 2 *Response to Comments*, Sacramento, CA, California HSR Authority 2.

Ahlfeldt, G M, 2009, *The Train has Left the Station: Do Markets Value Intra-City Access to Inter-City Rail Connections*, Available at SSRN 1355969.

Anonymous, 2010, 'Sous pression américaine, la SNCF fait son mea culpa sur la déportation des juifs', *Le Monde*, Paris.

Bewick, J A, 2010, 'Life after Yucca: Reviving hope for spent-fuel storage,' *Public Utilities Fortnightly*, vol. 148, no. 11, pp. 52–59.

Brion, D J, 1988, 'An essay on LULU, NIMBY, and the problem of distributive justice', *Boston College Environmental Affairs Law Review* vol. 15, 3(2).

CHSR Authority, 2012, *EIR/EIS Merced to Fresno*, C. H. A. F. R. Administration, Sacramento.

de Carlo, L D, 2006, 'The French high-speed Méditerranée train decision process: A large-scale public decision case study', *Conflict Resolution Quarterly*, vol. 24, no. 1, pp. 3–30.

Dittmar, H and Ohland, G, Eds., 2004, *The New Transit Town*, Washington, DC, Island press.

Dungan, J, 2010, 'Peninsula cities sue to derail high-speed rail project', *Mercury News*, San José.

Feinerman, E, Finkelshtain, I, *et al.*, 2004, 'On a political solution to the NIMBY conflict', *The American Economic Review*, vol. 94, no. 1, pp. 369–381.

Frey, B S and Oberholzer-Gee, F, 1996, 'Fair siting procedures: An empirical analysis of their importance and characteristics', *Journal of Policy Analysis and Management*, vol. 15, no. 3, pp. 353–376.

Frey, B S, Oberholzer-Gee, F, *et al.*, 1996, 'The old lady visits your backyard: A tale of morals and markets', *The Journal of Political Economy*, vol. 104, no. 6, pp. 1297–1313.

Gibson, T A, 2005, 'NIMBY and the civic good', *City & Community*, vol. 4, no. 4, pp. 381–401.

Hermansson, H, 2007, 'The ethics of NIMBY conflicts', *Ethical Theory and Moral Practice*, vol. 10, no. 1, pp. 23–34.

Hunter, S and Leyden, K M, 1995, 'Beyond NIMBY', *Policy Studies Journal*, vol. 23, no. 4, pp. 601–619.

King, R S, Mauer, M, *et al.*, 2004, 'An analysis of the economics of prison siting in rural communities', *Criminology & Public Policy*, vol. 3, no. 3, pp. 453–480.

Kunreuther, H and Kleindorfer, P R, 1986, 'A sealed-bid auction mechanism for siting noxious facilities', *The American Economic Review*, vol. 76, no. 2, pp. 295–299.

Livezey, E T, 1980, 'Hazardous waste', *Christian Science Monitor*, Boston.

O'Hare, M, 1977, 'Not on my block, you don't – facilities siting and the strategic importance of compensation', *Public Policy*, vol. 25, no. 4.

O'Hare, M, 2011, *Nuclear Waste Facility Siting and Local Opposition*, Washington, DC, Blue Ribbon Commission on America's Nuclear Future.

O'Hare, M and Sanderson, D, 1993, 'Facility siting and compensation: Lessons from the Massachusetts experience', *Journal of Policy Analysis and Management*, vol. 12, no. 2, pp. 364–376.

O'Hare, M H, Bacow, L, *et al.*, 1983, *Facility Siting and Public Opposition*, New York, Van Nostrand Reinhold.

Olson, M, 1971, *The Logic of Collective Action*, Cambridge, MA, Harvard University Press.

Oremus, W, 2009, 'Palo Alto residents march for high-speed rail tunnel', *Mercury News*, San José.

Pastor, M J, Sadd, J, *et al.*, 2001, 'Which came first? Toxic facilities, minority move-in, and environmental justice', *Journal of Urban Affairs*, vol. 23, no. 1, pp. 1–21.

Rosenberg, M, 2013, 'California high-speed rail finally wins Peninsula lawsuit after five years', *Mercury News*, San José.

Samuels, D, 2010, 'Mountain View lays out rail requests in letters', *Daily news*, Palo Alto.

Schively, C, 2007, 'Understanding the NIMBY and LULU phenomena: Reassessing our knowledge base and informing future research', *Journal of Planning Literature*, vol. 21, no. 3, pp. 255–266.

Schulte-Werning, B, Thompson, D, *et al.*, 2008, 'Noise sources for high speed trains: A review of results in the TGV case', *Noise and Vibration Mitigation for Rail Transportation Systems*, vol. 99, pp. 71–77.

Sheehan, T, 2013a, 'Farmers, state settle last lawsuit over Merced-Fresno high-speed rail line', *Bee*, Fresno.

Sheehan, T, 2013b, 'Rep. David Valadao owns land on high-speed rail routes', *Bee*, Fresno.

20 High-speed rail stations as transportation nodes and places

Lessons for California

Anastasia Loukaitou-Sideris and Deike Peters

Introduction

High-speed rail (HSR) has often transformative effects on cities and regions, potentially increasing both mobility and accessibility in an unprecedented way. HSR systems may also have important physical impacts, altering the built environment of station-neighbourhoods and affecting municipal economies. However, not all cities have witnessed positive effects from HSR, and benefits from HSR systems have been unevenly distributed among cities (Vickerman 2007, Martínez and Givoni 2012). A number of studies have examined the impacts of HSR projects on station cities (Loukaitou-Sideris *et al.* 2013, Murakami and Cervero 2010, Nuworsoo and Deakin 2009). They have observed differential impacts depending on the type of city (first- or second-tier) (Garmendia *et al.* 2012a), its distance from other major cities on the network (Garmendia *et al.* 2012b), the condition of the local economy and land market, and station location (central or peripheral) within a city (Ureña *et al.* 2012). Additionally, most scholars agree on the importance of two factors: connectivity of the HSR station with other transportation modes, and anticipatory planning, i.e., planning for the station area (van den Berg and Pol 1997, Bazin *et al.* 2006, Meer *et al.* 2012).

Connectivity and anticipatory planning appear critical for California as it embarks on an ambitious programme to install a high-speed rail network that would connect its northern and southern parts. Indeed, three top lessons for California emerged from an earlier Delphi survey of high-speed rail experts: 'provide good connections with intra-urban transportation systems,' 'plan stations as intermodal nodes,' and 'develop good urban design station-area plans' (Loukaitou-Sideris *et al.* 2012: 44).

In an early article, Bertolini and Spit (1998: 31) emphasized that 'a railway station's essential feature appears to be its function as an intermodal interchange, rather than merely a place where trains arrive and depart.... The railway system has to offer full connectivity in both the hard sense – the infrastructure – and the soft sense – the services... In the process the railway station turns into "a place to be", not just a "place to pass through".' This observation underscores the importance of a station as both a transportation *node* and a vibrant *place*.

In this chapter, we will examine how to best enhance operational connectivity and intermodal integration of California's HSR stations, and how to achieve a seamless spatial integration of the HSR stations and their surroundings. In doing so we will extract lessons from the HSR systems of Germany and Spain, two countries with well-developed HSR networks that make use of a 'blended' system (where HSR shares tracks with conventional rail) for at least some track segments and whose HSR stations score very highly in terms of connectivity and node and place qualities. The purpose of the analysis is to understand the requirements for high levels of connectivity and spatial integration of HSR stations and offer some guidelines for Californian HSR stations. The chapter draws data from 1) a review of the literature on the connectivity, intermodality, and spatial integration of transit systems; 2) a survey of twenty-six HSR experts from six European countries; and 3) an in-depth look of the German and Spanish HSR systems and some of their stations.

Certainly, cities in California are considerably different from cities in Europe. The urban form of European cities is typically more compact, dense, walkable, and bicycle-friendly than their Californian counterparts. Additionally, European cities have higher levels of intermodality than Californian cities, which are primarily built around the automobile. To these differences one should add that Californian residents are more 'married to their cars' than Europeans. They have higher rates of automobile ownership and more automobile miles travelled per capita. Despite these differences, we will show that the European experience with HSR can provide lessons for California.

Spatial and operational connectivity of stations

HSR station connectivity denotes the spatial integration of the station with its surrounding urban fabric, but also the level of accessibility of the station from different points of origin. Good urban design is the means to achieve the first type of connectivity, which we will call *spatial connectivity*. Frequent HSR services and operational integration between the HSR system and other transportation modes (including walking and cycling) are critical in achieving the second type of connectivity, which we will call *operational connectivity*. The latter is also related to intermodality, as a high level of intermodality denotes a passenger's ability to use more than one transportation mode for a single trip in a convenient and 'seamless' way. A high level of connectivity increases the mobility benefits for transit travellers (GAO 2013). Conversely, poor transit connectivity creates barriers to passenger mobility and may affect transit ridership (Metropolitan Transportation Commission 2005).

Good operational and spatial connectivity enhance the node qualities of a station, while good spatial connectivity also contributes to its place quality (Bertolini 2008). Both types of connectivity are crucial to attracting passengers because they make travel convenient. This appears to be significant for the competitiveness of HSR systems (Loukaitou-Sideris *et al.* 2012). Indeed, one of HSR's biggest advantages over air travel is that it can offer passengers a one-seat ride into the centre of major cities, eliminating time-consuming transfers such as those that predominate at airports. However, this competitive advantage is highly dependent on the level of spatial and operational intermodal connectivity, as well as the transit authorities' ability to deliver convenient and fast service into urban cores in a cost-efficient manner. The integration of high-speed trains with existing intercity and commuter/regional rail systems offers the advantages of higher connectivity as well as potentially lower capital costs and decreased adverse impacts on urban form and the environment. However, an integrated intermodal approach requires careful pre-planning to achieve a high degree of coordination in operations and passenger services. It also requires station infrastructure that accommodates smooth transitions between the different modes (Nash 2003). This can extend to information and ticketing processes as well as to the design and layout of the station and the surrounding area.

Sando *et al.* (2009) stress the role of the built environment in encouraging or discouraging transit use. They argue that a station-area design that connects to all modes of transportation, including walking and cycling, will have the highest rates of ridership. Dill and Schlossberg (2013) looked at the combined effects of transit service and station area design elements on transit ridership at the transit stop/station level. They found that while transit service plays the most important role in predicting transit ridership, characteristics of the built environment, such as the nearby presence of bicycle paths, matter as well. When good transit services and a good physical infrastructure co-exist, connectivity improves and ridership is the highest.

Spatial connectivity

While the importance of smooth linkages between an intermodal transportation facility and the surrounding neighbourhood and city is recognized, only a minuscule part of the HSR literature discusses physical and urban design interventions that can improve spatial connectivity. Loukaitou-Sideris (2013) identifies four spatial zones that must be considered for ensuring good connectivity and access to high-speed rail stations: 1) the station itself; 2) the station-district, generally defined as about a half-mile radius around the station; 3) the municipality at large; and 4) the broader region. Good urban design can enhance the station's spatial connectivity in the first two zones; while good multimodal services can improve the connectivity of the station with the municipality and region at large.

Developing or improving connectivity at HSR stations should consider the station layout, including station signage, ease of locating and entering the station from different directions, wayfinding inside the station for ticketing, access to platforms, connection between different platforms, and access to other services (information systems, food services, restrooms). The flow of pedestrian movement from parking lots and adjacent bus or rail stops to station entrances, ticketing areas, train platforms and other station facilities should be clearly marked and comfortable (avoiding long walks or steps up and down whenever possible, and providing mobility assistance such as elevators and moving sidewalks when distances and elevation changes are unavoidable). Connections between different station platforms likewise should be direct, short, and legible for passengers.

Operational factors important to integrating different transportation systems also can be manifest at the station. This includes line integration or easy transfers (e.g., cross platform or up one escalator, clearly signed as such) and coordinated scheduling, fares, and information systems.

At the station-neighbourhood or district level, a major urban design challenge for spatial connectivity is the bridging of 'the barrier effect,' the gap between the station and its neighbourhood that is created by the bulky railway infrastructure and major parking facilities. The appropriate urban design intervention will vary depending on the guideway type (elevated, surface, or tunnel), and whether the HSR tracks are dedicated or shared – the railway right-of-way is wider and more challenging to bridge when the HSR operates on its own dedicated track in the same corridor as conventional rail (Loukaitou-Sideris 2013). Other issues will include the mix and intensity of development to be permitted around the station. A large literature on transit-oriented development has emerged in the last 3 decades (see, e.g., Cervero 2004) and offers guidance that is likely to be applicable to HSR stations, especially for urban locations.

For the municipality at large, a major planning issue will be establishing good access routes for all the modes that serve the station, which these days can include not only pedestrian and bike connections and bus and rail links but also carsharing and ridesharing modes as well as taxis and rental cars. The municipality will also want to consider how development around the HSR station or stations competes with or complements development in other parts of the city. Regional agencies will often be responsible for the major rail and bus services and in some cases may have certain land use planning responsibilities as well (as is the case of California with its recent legislation on greenhouse gas reduction).

Operational connectivity

Operational connectivity can be enhanced by high levels of intermodality – the availability of different transportation modes converging at the HSR station – and the seamless integration and time-coordination of these modes, so that waiting time for passengers is minimized.

A number of studies have examined ways of enhancing operational connectivity by improving transferring services, supporting facilities, and information systems in multimodal transportation networks for both high- and low-speed modes. For example, HSR can be coordinated with air travel as well as with local transit. Givoni and Banister (2006) have examined intermodal cooperation and integration between air and rail transit at Heathrow Airport in London. They defined integration as 'aircraft and high-speed railway services provided as one complete journey with a fast and seamless transfer between the modes.' They suggest that achieving integration requires that 1) the railway station is designed to offer fast and seamless travel between modes by minimizing the distance of transfers; 2) the station has direct links to a large number of destinations with services at a relatively high frequency (often by making the airport rail station a through station on a main line); and 3) the rail and air travel times are comparable for the same origin-destination pairs (achieved by taking the passenger directly to the destination city's centre). The researchers find that such integration would be mutually beneficial for both transit and airline operators, while also preserving the airport's and HSR station's competitive position, increasing services to other regions, and curbing its environmental impact. However, the private sector must play a significant role in promoting airline/railway integration. Additionally, policy makers should consider the two modes as part of one transport network, rather than separate entities competing in an open market.

Developing the HSR station in close proximity to retail and tourist attractions requires its integration with low-speed modes – walking and cycling. Thus, Pan *et al.* (2010) examine the challenges and opportunities for improving the bicycle-rail connectivity based on surveys of railway passengers in Shanghai. Based on their findings, they recommend the provision of additional bicycle parking spaces and a bicycle rental system for improving the bicycle-rail connection and utilizing the bicycle more fully as an efficient supplement mode for rail transportation in China.

In regards to the efficient time-coordination of different modes with the HSR, the Swiss example of 'clockface scheduling' is referred to as 'the most streamlined delivery of public transport and Europe's best practice for bus, tram, and railway interchange' (Green and Hall 2009: 46). All Swiss trains are programmed to arrive at the interchange stations of all major cities at exactly the same time, at 00 and 30 minutes past the hour. Inter-city trains arrive every 30 minutes, regional trains and buses connecting to the station arrive every 15 minutes, while local trams and buses arrive every 7.5 minutes.

Clever (2007) examines the concept of Integrated Time Transfer (ITT) as utilized in Europe as a way to improve public transportation services. Under ITT, trains, buses, boats, and other means of local and long-distance public transportation not only operate on a fixed-interval schedule, but also connect with each other in ways that minimize transfer times. The advantages of ITT include reduction of transfer times, more frequent services, better spatial coverage, and more profit for operators, while possible disadvantages include longer headways and the unrealistic assumption of the uniform usage of the system throughout the day.

Lastly, an additional factor that can contribute to the increased operational connectivity of HSR involves the provision of seamless information and ticketing for its travellers. Noting that building infrastructure to support connectivity can be expensive and time-intensive, some scholars have argued that more or better-placed signage, real-time information about the schedules of different connecting modes, information kiosks, and ticketing practices that enable passengers to purchase combined transport services can also improve connectivity and attract ridership (GAO 2103, Sauter-Servaes and Nash 2009). In recent years, particular interest has also arisen regarding the development of effective internet-based platforms such as the multimodal route advisory system (MRAS) developed by Chiu *et al.* (2005) that enables travellers to link with multiple modes of public transportation services as well as taxis and shuttles in identifying the shortest, fastest or cheapest multimodal connections. These kinds of services are expected to become standard in coming years and let users take full and optimized advantage of the range of existing connections between modes.

Overall, the existing research demonstrates that transit connectivity and intermodality can provide a wide range of mobility benefits for travellers, and thus increase ridership. While many argue that improving the built environment is crucial to improving connectivity, others have shown that operational connectivity is also very important. Lastly, HSR planners need to consider the integration of the HSR with low- and high-speed travel modes for intra- and inter-city travel.

Expert survey

To complement the findings of the literature and identify the factors that should be considered for good integration of the Californian HSR network and the high connectivity of its stations, we conducted a survey of thirty high-speed rail experts from Europe, twenty-six of whom provided detailed responses. There was an overall consensus among the experts of the critical importance of high connectivity and network integration. As they reasoned:

> 'Finding the right system depends on the opportunities of each territory. But simple rules for success exist: You must consider the new HSR lines as part of a multimodal system. You must ensure interdependencies among the rail lines. A good transportation system is a system that ensures high connectivity.'

> 'The HSR is an important long-distance mode of transport and its integration with the rest of the transport network is probably one of the most, if not the most, important element in its planning.'

Additionally, it was stressed that 'maximum connectivity is reached if users experience the HSR service as much as possible as one door-to-door system.' But how can this be achieved? The experts talked about a combination of spatial and operational measures and ways to enhance the nodal and place qualities of HSR stations.

Station location

An important topic that emerged from the survey entailed the location of HSR stations and the trade-offs of having stations in central versus peripheral city locations. In Spain and France, new HSR stations were often built peripherally, at a distance from city centres in small and intermediate cities, while they are very centrally located in large cities. In contrast, Germany integrated almost all its HSR connections into pre-existing stations in central urban areas. There are trade-offs involved. As one of the experts explained:

'There are two scenarios: The first is that of stations in the city center. It is easier to integrate different services and modes of transportation there. Be careful though because it requires a lot of work to adapt to different modes in the area of the station. Capital works are cumbersome and complex. The second scenario is of stations located on the outskirts of cities. Here it is essential to organize the transportation of passengers to the city center from where the station is located.'

Historic stations usually have the advantage of already serving as the focal point for intercity bus connections and as a major hub of the urban transportation system. However, auto access may be difficult. An expert noted:

'Integrating an HSR station in a densely built district certainly hinders access by car, because of the congestion of the urban street system, but allows access by walking or cycling. Thus, the choice to serve a central station encourages intermodality and sustainable mobility.'

On the other hand, if an HSR station is located at a peripheral location and away from the conventional railway services, it may be possible to connect it to different parts of the metropolitan area via a network of express buses. This is the case in Valence, France – a new station built exclusively for the HSR – that is served daily by seventy-four bus connections. Alternatively, rail extensions may be needed; in Reims and Besançon, a specific rail link was built to connect the new HSR station to the conventional rail network. Additionally, in Reims, the new HSR station is integrated into the urban transport network through the building of a new tramway service.

Despite these examples, the assessment of a French expert is that:

'The experience in France shows that where TGV stations have been created at a distance from conventional (central) station, the TGV station is not well served from the centre and fails to attract services. It also impacts the central station, which becomes less attractive. Therefore, one has to be very careful when building dedicated HSR stations.'

Station design and connections

Many experts emphasized the importance of station planning, design, and programming for enhancing the place qualities of HSR stations for both travellers and non-travellers:

'Plan functions and activities which express mix, flexibility and versatility of the spaces to ensure the presence of different populations and different practices not only related to the trip or for temporal use.'

'It is important to bring new services into the stations to make them attractive. Such services may include retail, restaurant, and even cultural activities.'

Experts referred to the 'need for continuity between the station and its neighbourhood; easy recognition of the access path to the city and other interconnected transport networks' and emphasised that it is important to 'design the space of the station as an urban open avenue/space, permeable and equipped with functions and activities that integrate this space to the surrounding urban fabric.' It was argued that 'the best integration results from an intelligent placement of the public transit network and from avoiding an over-abundance of parking at multimodal stations.'

Others referred to the importance of allowing visual connections, physical proximity and short walking distances from the HSR platform to other transport modes, including conventional rail. There was a lack of consensus, however, as to the desirability of shared or separate station platforms between HSR and conventional trains. Some believed that separate train platforms at stations are preferable:

'It seems important to try and separate the slow and fast trains as much as possible in the stations to allow easy transfer between the services. If the services share a platform, the change between them will necessitate waiting at the platform for one service to depart and the next to arrive.'

On the other hand, some experts believed that sharing station platforms as much as possible is preferable because it maximizes interconnectivity. Most, however, qualified their response on the basis of particular contexts. Thus, the number of trains that arrive or depart from a station should influence the number of required platforms. As explained: 'In Dutch stations there are only a small number of high-speed trains, and separate platforms seem a waste of space, but this is different in Brussels Midi where there are many more high-speed trains' (Trip interview). Some also argued that the type of station (intermediate or terminal) plays a role: 'Separate platforms are essential at intermediate stations where high-speed trains pass through at high velocities. At endpoints they are helpful and convenient, but not essential to ensure efficient service.' Other experts mentioned that the decision about separate or shared platforms should depend on whether trains have similar or different dwell times (amount of time that a train stops at the station).

Lastly, experts referred to the importance of information systems and good way-finding signage for achieving good connectivity. One mentioned: 'Signage is important and especially [information] indicating from what platform the next train will depart'. Much of that information is already available through real-time smart phone apps.

Coordination of different travel modes and services

A third major theme that emerged related to the coordination and seamless connection between the HSR and other travel modes and the goal of complementarity rather than competition among the different modes. Additionally, the need was noted for 'the HSR to stop at airports and have the endpoint within a city transport-hub (intersection of several metro lines), as well as ensure integration into local tram and/or bus networks and park-and-ride facilities.' Operational aspects such as short transfer times were deemed very important for good intermodality.

Several experts stressed the importance of smooth coordination of HSR and conventional rail schedules and services. As one put it: 'Often [HSR] leads to the abandonment of secondary connections on the conventional network. The ideal, however, is to have stops on high-speed trains which are coordinated with local and regional trains.' According to the experts, integration and coordination should extend to the ticketing of different transportation modes, as already happens in Germany: 'Have one ticket for the entire journey even when it involves a plane, a train and a coach.'

Lastly, institutional coordination was mentioned among the managers of HSR and other transportation services. There was suggestion of 'a terminal manager with coordination responsibilities over all kind of operators, spaces and services' and even for 'an overall transport authority for multimodal functions.'

In the end, as most experts noted, the promotion of connectivity at HSR stations requires multiple levels of integration: 'You always should consider the triple integration: spatial, operational, and institutional.'

Review of German and Spanish HSR stations

To better understand how the aforementioned issues are handled in German and Spanish HSR stations and extract lessons for California, we examined six stations in Germany and six in Spain (Table 20.1). These stations were recommended by the HSR experts who participated in our survey as exemplary models for connectivity and intermodality. Data for the case studies was gathered from a variety of sources including government documents and websites, travel guides, and station itineraries for each case study station. In Germany, we visited the case study stations, interviewed representatives of German Railways (Deutsche Bahn – DB), and reviewed publicly available information on new high-speed corridors and station construction projects. In Spain, we interviewed representatives of the high-speed transit operator Renfe, as well as the managers of each of the case study stations. The Spanish station owner ADIF provided us with relevant data such as station plans, annual number of high-speed services, available parking spaces at each station, etc. In what follows, we synthesize our findings by country, since we do not have space to discuss each station separately.

Table 20.1 Stations studied

Germany:	Spain:
Berlin Hauptbahnhof	Madrid Puerta de Atocha
Berlin Südkreuz	Barcelona Sants
Hannover Hauptbahnhof	Zaragoza-Delicias
Kassel-Wilhelmshöhe Fernbahnhof	Málaga María Zambrano
Leipzig Hauptbahnhof	Córdoba Central
Erfurt Hauptbahnhof	Lleida Pirineus

Germany

Germany's rail operations are highly blended, and the optimization of connectivity and intermodality lies at the very heart of its transit system. High-speed operations were originally designed to blend seamlessly into pre-existing rail operations, and high-speed corridors are not exclusive to high-speed passenger rail operations under the ICE label. The overall slower top speeds of the system are usually outweighed by the good overall connectivity of the integrated system, still allowing for impressive door-to-door connections. Depending on location, route and time of day, ICE lines operate at half-hour, hour or two-hour intervals. With the exception of the special case of Limburg-South, there are no exclusive ICE stations or even concourses in Germany. With the exception of the newly built ICE station at Frankfurt Airport, major stations across the country are all located in city centres.

Relying mostly on upgrading existing routes to higher speeds, Germany has built comparatively few new HSR corridors and thus also relatively few completely new HSR stations. Instead, German Railways remodelled and adapted many historic stations and locations to better accommodate its HSR services since the early 1990s. All German cities of over a million inhabitants, namely Berlin, Hamburg, Cologne and Munich, have more than one HSR station, and Germany's largest metro area, the Rhein-Ruhr, features more than fifteen stations with ICE services, all in a region of 10 million people (a size that is comparable to Los Angeles County, and just over half the size of the greater LA metro area).

In the cases where new HSR lines were constructed, German Railways (DB) promoted the re-purposing of secondary rail stations into new, well-linked high-speed rail nodes (Berlin Südkreuz and Kassel-Wilhelmshöhe). Historic inner-city rail stations, meanwhile, underwent vast transformations into multimodal hubs with amplified commercial and retail functions (Berlin Hauptbahnhof, Hannover, Leipzig, Erfurt). The related planning processes have integrated national, regional and local redevelopment efforts at multiple levels.

The German approach of privileging modal connectivity at the station level over achieving top speeds at the corridor level has clearly resulted in a system that is optimally suited to the country's poly-centric settlement pattern. HSR enthusiasts enamoured with DB's integrated rail system often forget that Germany is also the land of speed-limitless Autobahnen, Audi, BMW, Mercedes-Benz and

Porsche, and a country where large portions of the population hardly ever use trains. This has forced DB to re-invent itself as a one-stop mobility provider that not only offers integrated and price-competitive ticketing for rail travel but also interlinks this with various car- and bike-sharing offers, and at times even issues flight numbers and Lufthansa boarding passes for its fastest metro connections.

The following factors are key reasons why and how Germany achieves high inter-modality at its HSR stations:

- With the exception of Limburg, Germany's 150+ ICE stations are *never* exclusive to HSR but are always also served by regional and/or local rail. DB consistently practises the joint/adjacent use of station tracks for both ICE/IC/EC trains and local RB/RE/SBahn trains.
- Stations are located so that they provide quick access to other travel modes and good pedestrian connections to surrounding neighbourhoods. Good intermodal access can be provided either in the city's central core or at a secondary centre, but rarely outside the urban core.
- There is high emphasis on good connectivity with local metro and tram systems. In the case of Berlin Hauptbahnhof, this meant the expensive new construction of the new U55 metro stub. In the case of Kassel-Wilhelmshöhe, regional train tracks directly extend and connect into the local light rail system. Several stations achieve short pedestrian connections by layering tracks atop each other (Berlin Hauptbahnhof, Berlin Südkreuz, Erfurt).
- Most cities provide direct and convenient connections to nearby airports, ideally via rail, but at minimum via frequent and regular bus services.
- Whenever possible, DB cooperates rather than competes with major airlines. As a key case in point, DB and Lufthansa created the DB/LH joint AIRail service for select high-speed routes from Frankfurt Airport to several other German cities.
- DB has long practised integrated ticketing services, easy online, early booking discounts, etc. Its DB Navigator app lets smartphone users check time tables, and receive real time information on arrivals, as well as book and rebook tickets.
- DB Station&Service has long standardized its easy-to-read signs for in-station way-finding. Good way-finding often extends into surrounding neighbourhoods.
- All major stations have good availability of bicycle parking and bike-sharing programmes next to or inside the station.
- All major stations offer car rental services and provide day use and longer-term parking near the station. Due to the availability of strong transit networks, German cities do not typically promote park- or kiss-and-ride at inner city stations the way US cities do, with the unique exception of Berlin Südkreuz station, which has strong car-orientation.
- DB remodelling of stations has sought to promote smooth passenger flows within the stations, ideally via barrier-free access and/or high-capacity elevators and escalators. As stations also include shopping malls, there is a conflict

of interest between quickly moving passengers through the stations versus encouraging potential retail customers to linger near shops and attractions.

- All major stations offer a variety of additional passenger services, including those commonly found in airports (first class and business lounges, boarding areas, information kiosks, travel agencies, free Wi-Fi).

Spain

Spain has a combination of systems, from pure HSR systems (the AVE that rolls along new HSR infrastructure at 185–205 mph), to blended HSR services called ALVIA and ALTARIA that in certain segments roll along new HSR infrastructure and at other segments along the conventional infrastructure at 175 mph, to short distance commuting HSR services called AVANT, that only roll on new HSR infrastructure but with slower trains (150 mph). In Spain, the HSR started as a separate system using mostly dedicated tracks (with the exception of short areas at stations), but technology has developed that now allows HSR trains to share conventional train infrastructure by changing gauge at certain locations, slowing down but not having to stop. This system allows Spanish HSR trains to typically travel at higher speeds than the German ICE trains. One serious drawback is the limited number of changeover location that makes the network less flexible.

In the Spanish cases, intermodality is achieved through:

- A good station location that has easy access to other travel modes and good pedestrian connections to the vicinity. Such a location is either at the city's central core or at a secondary centre, not far from the core and linked to the core via a frequent and direct bus line.
- The location of a central bus terminal inside the station, or directly adjacent to it.
- For cities that have a metro system, the location of a metro stop inside the station.
- Close proximity of HSR platforms to the platforms of other railway services to regional destinations.
- Direct connection to the city airport through a 'fly-away' bus, metro line or both.
- Availability of bicycle parking, and bike-sharing programmes in the station.
- Integration of ticketing services
- Availability of park-and-ride and kiss-and-ride lots. However, the high level of station intermodality decreases the need for large amounts of parking.
- Good information panels within the station and standardized, easy-to-read signs for way-finding.
- Smooth passenger flows within the stations and proximity of different station platforms.
- Availability of a variety of passenger services inside the station, more often seen in airports (such as first class lounges, boarding areas, information kiosks, travel agencies, car rental facilities, etc.)

Additionally, all six Spanish case study stations serve not only as transportation nodes for travel but also as social destinations and vibrant places in the city, incorporating retail stores, cafes, restaurants, and sometimes hotels, museums and gardens. In some of these stations, good station architecture aims to reclaim or create a new architectural landmark in the city – either through the preservation and expansion of significant historic buildings (such as in Madrid Atocha and Lleida Pirineus) or the building of a new structure (such as in Zaragoza-Delicias). Indeed, these six case studies exemplify how a railway station can become both a route for seamless travel and also a place for a variety of other urban activities.

Conclusion: lessons for California

The literature review, survey of experts, and German and Spanish case studies help us draw lessons and recommendations for the Californian HSR stations.

Spatial connectivity

The studied European examples do a good job in their consideration of four spatial zones: the station, the station-neighbourhood, the municipality at large, and the broader region. These four zones should also be considered in the planning and design of the Californian stations.

At the *station scale*, attention should be given to both the aesthetics and the functionality of the station building. In some of the case study stations, existing historic buildings were renovated and expanded – as was the case with Madrid's Puerta de Atocha Station, Lleida Pirineus Station, or Leipzig Hauptbahnhof – or as in the case of Erfurt, partly retained. In other cases, completely new buildings have been built, and many feature significant new architecture. This attention to station aesthetics signifies a desire to create a landmark building in the city, one that serves as both a transportation node and a social place.

Station architecture is not only about aesthetics but also functionality. Thus, the spatial relationship and proximity of train platforms and the pedestrian flow between them should be carefully considered. A variety of passenger services should be easily available at the Californian HSR stations. The Spanish and German cases feature an array of such services, such as business class lounges, multiple information kiosks and ticket booths, cafes, and free Wi-Fi. Some Spanish and German HSR stations feature fully fledged malls within the station structure. The possibility of marrying retail with station activities should be considered for some Californian HSR stations.

For complex buildings such as railway terminals, where passengers have to catch different connections, move from one platform to the other, or access other spaces (ticketing, eateries, restrooms) inside and outside the station, clear, easy-to-read, and frequent signage becomes extremely important. Thus, HSR stations and their immediate vicinity should have clear and standardized way-finding signage, as was the case in the examples studied. Lastly, stations should not only provide park-and-ride and kiss-and-ride lots where needed, but also include adequate bicycle parking.

At the *station-neighbourhood scale*, emphasis should be given on minimizing the barrier created by the tracks and station infrastructure, and integrating the station to the surrounding urban fabric and street network. The case study examples have employed different design strategies, depending on the particular context, including consolidating, covering, trenching or bridging over the rail tracks. Regardless of the physical intervention, easy and safe pedestrian, bicycle, and vehicular linkages between the station and its neighbourhood should be provided. Additionally, the placement of station entrances and the relationship between the station and its surrounding streets and parking structures should be important considerations in station planning.

Operational connectivity

An important operational aspect is the level of connectivity and intermodality of the HSR service with other travel modes. This entails both the location of other transportation modes in close proximity and easy access from the HSR platform as well as the coordinated scheduling of different modes for easy links and short transfer times.

At the *municipality level*, emphasis should be placed on station connectivity via public transit and/or via metro with different areas in the city that represent important destination points (airports, downtown and other sub-centres, theme parks, commercial centres, etc.). The case study stations scored highly in regards to their connections with public transit. In almost all cases, an airport bus connects the station to the local airport. All studied cases have rental car facilities, and many included car-share and bike-share facilities. Because of this good connectivity with transit and the availability of alternative transportation modes, the amount of parking space in the studied stations is considerably lower than the projected parking needs for HSR stations in Southern California.

It is important to consider the major destination points in the city (downtown and other sub-centres, theme parks, commercial centres, airports, etc.), connect them with direct transit lines to the HSR station, and consider ways to boost the utilization of alternative means of transportation to and from the HSR station.

The new high-speed infrastructure compresses time and space, making some of these cities much more accessible. Thus, at the *regional level*, the possible complementarity of the station with the neighbouring stations along the HSR line should be considered in determining the desirable land uses around the station. This is likely more important for second-tier cities that may attract more visitors and tourists if they are only 60–90 minutes away from the first-tier cities. Thus, in Spain, after the advent of the HSR, it became much easier for tourists arriving in Madrid to visit places like Toledo, Córdoba or Seville.

Additional ways to improve the operational connectivity of HSR services with other modes include integrated ticketing options and transfer of luggage services from one mode to the other. Ticketing for HSR services in Germany is fully integrated with all other rail ticketing, with certain tickets even including local fares from and to a passenger's origin and final destination. German transit operator DB has also managed to coordinate its ticketing and services with the services of Lufthansa Airlines. Ticketing and travel service integration and possible discounts for passengers who plan to use more than one transportation mode can make the HSR services more appealing and increase the market for HSR; they should be considered by the Californian HSR.

Last, operational connectivity requires coordination and collaboration among multiple parties (the transit operators of conventional and HSR services) during the planning and operation process. Additionally, collaboration and coordination of municipal, state and federal entities for the provision of unified design and safety standards, signs and maintenance criteria would also help.

In conclusion, high levels of HSR station connectivity result in seamless travel and mobility benefits for travellers. The German and Spanish case studies are exemplary in their achieved levels of intra-city and inter-city connectivity, and they have found ways to integrate local and regional railway services, buses and even airline services in ways that complement one another. This entails both an operational aspect involving coordinated scheduling of different modes for easy links and short transfer times, as well as a spatial aspect (easy physical access from one mode to the other, visual connections between platforms). Additionally, while the HSR stations in Germany and Spain often incorporate services similar to those found in an airport (e.g., first-class lounges, boarding areas, luggage services, etc.), the most successful European stations are not designed as airports (inward-oriented and cut-off from the rest of the city). Instead, they are designed as both functional transportation nodes and outward-oriented, social hubs with high levels of connectivity and good integration with the surrounding city fabric. The Californian HSR stations should aspire for nothing less.

References

Bazin, S, Beckerich, C, Delaplace, M and Masson, S, 2006, 'La LGV Est-Européenne en Champagne-Ardenne: Quels effets sur la cohésion territoriale champ ardennaise?', *Revue d'Economie Regionale et Urbaine*, no. 2, pp. 245–261.

Bertolini, L, 2008, 'Station Areas as Nodes and Places in Urban Networks: An Analytical Tool and Alternative Development Strategies', in Bruinsma, F, Pels, E, Priemus, H, Rietveld, P and van Wee, B, Eds., *Railway Development*, 35–57.

Bertolini, L and Spit, T, 1998, *Cities on Rails: The Redevelopment of Railway Station Areas*, New York: E & FN Spon.

Cervero, R, 2004, *Transit Oriented Development in the United States: Experiences, Challenges, and Prospects*, Vol. 102, Transportation Research Board.

Chiu, DKW, Dickson Computer Systems, Lee, OKF, Leung, H-F, Au, EWK and Wong, MCW, 2005, 'A Multi-Modal Agent Based Mobile Route Advisory System for Public Transport Network', *Proceedings of the 38th Hawaii International Conference on System Sciences*.

Clever, R, 2007, 'Integrated Timed Transfer: A European Perspective', *Transportation Research Record: Journal of the Transportation Research Board*, no. 1571, pp. 107–115.

Dill, J and Schlossberg, M, 2013, 'Predicting Transit Ridership at the Stop Level: The Role of Service and Urban Form', *Transportation Research Board conference*, January 2013.

Garmendia, M, Ribalaygua, C and Ureña, JM, 2012a, 'High-Speed Rail: Implication for Cities', *Cities*, vol. 29, pp. 526–531.

Garmendia, M, Romero, V, Ureña, JM, Coronado, JM and Vickerman, R, 2012b, 'High-Speed Rail Opportunities around Metropolitan Regions: Madrid and London', *Journal of Infrastructure Systems*, vol. 18, no. 4, pp. 305–313.

Givoni, M and Banister, D, 2006, 'Airline and Railway Integration', *Transport Policy*, vol. 13, no. 5, pp. 386–397.

Government Accounting Office August, 2013, *Intermodal Transportation: A Variety of Factors Influence Airport-Intercity Passenger Rail Connectivity*, Washington DC.

Green, C and Hall, P, 2009, *Better Rail Stations: An Independent Review Presented to Lord Adonis, Secretary of State for Transport*, p. 46. http://collections.europarchive.org/tna/20100409091328/http:/www.dft.gov.uk/pgr/rail/passenger/stations/betterrailstations/pdf/report.pdf Accessed 1 August 2016.

Loukaitou-Sideris, A, 2013, 'New Rail Hubs along High-Speed Rail Corridor in California: Urban Design Challenges', *Transportation Research Record*, no. 2350, pp. 1–8.

Loukaitou-Sideris, A, Cuff, D, Higgins, T and Linovski, O, 2012, 'Impact of High Speed Rail Stations on Local Development, A Delphi Survey', *Built Environment*, vol. 38, no. 1, pp. 51–70.

Loukaitou-Sideris, A, Higgins, H, Piven, M and Wei, W, 2013, 'Tracks of Change or Mixed Signals? A Review of the Anglo-Saxon Literature on the Economic and Spatial Impacts of High-Speed Rail', *Transport Reviews*, vol. 33, no. 6, pp. 617–633.

Martínez, H and Givoni, M, 2012, 'The Accessibility Impact of a New High-Speed Rail Line in the UK – A Preliminary Analysis of Winners and Losers', *Journal of Transport Geography*, 25, pp. 105–114.

Meer, A, Ribalaygua, C and Martín, E, 2012, 'High-Speed Rail and Regional Accessibility', in Ureña, JM, Ed., *Territorial Implications of High-Speed Rail: A Spanish Perspective*, pp. 197–216, Aldershot: Ashgate.

Metropolitan Transportation Commission January, 2005, *Transit Connectivity Report*, Oakland, CA. http://mtc.ca.gov/sites/default/files/Transit_Connectivity_Report.pdf Accessed 1 August 2016.

Murakami, J and Cervero, R, 2010, 'California High-Speed Rail and Economic Development: Station-Area Market Profiles and Public Policy Responses,' *High Speed Rail Symposium, University of California, Berkeley Faculty Club*.

Nash, A, 2003, *Best Practices in Shared-Use High-Speed Rail Systems*, San Jose: Mineta Transportation Institute, MTI Report 02-02.

Nuworsoo, CK and Deakin, E, 2009, 'Transforming High-Speed Rail Stations to Major Activity Hubs: Lessons for California', In *Transportation Research Board 88th Annual Meeting*, No. 09-2757.

Pan, H, Shen, Q and Xue, S, 2010, 'Intermodal Transfer Between Bicycles and Rail Transit in Shanghai, China', *Transportation Research Record: Journal of the Transportation Research Board*, no. 2144, pp.181–188.

Sando, T, Mbatta, G and Moses, R, 2009, 'A Proposed Procedure for Developing Transit Station Design Criteria with a Focus on Intermodal Connectivity', Washington, DC: Institute of Transportation Engineers, 2009 Annual Meeting.

Sauter-Servaes, T and Nash, A, 2009, 'Increasing Rail Demand by Improving Multimodal Information and Ticketing', *Transportation Research Record: Journal of the Transportation Research Board*, no. 2117, pp. 7–13.

Ureña, JM, Coronado, JM, Garmendia, M and Romero, V, 2012, 'Territorial Implications at National and Regional Scales of High-Speed Rail', in Ureña, JM, Ed., *Territorial Implications of High Speed Rail: A Spanish Perspective*, London: Ashgate, pp. 204–243.

van den Berg, L and Pol, P, 1997, *The European High-Speed Train and Urban Development: Experiences in Fourteen European Regions*, Brookfield, VT: Ashgate Publishing Company.

Vickerman, R, 2007, 'International Connections by High-Speed Rail: Metropolitan and Inter-Regional Impacts', Paper presented at the World Conference on Transport Research, University of California, Berkeley, June 2007.

21 Conclusions

High-speed rail and sustainability

Elizabeth Deakin and Blas Luis Pérez Henríquez

Learning from international experience

This book has presented analyses of high-speed rail's performance based on the experiences of countries in Asia and Europe where HSR has been built, along with discussions of forecasting and evaluation approaches used in these cases. It also has presented a variety of assessments of California's ongoing efforts to develop a high-speed rail system linking the northern and southern regions of the state. In this concluding chapter we discuss the lessons that can be drawn from the international examples and the California case, focusing in particular on high-speed rail's potential to increase sustainability.

Sustainability as it is used here refers not simply to the ability to endure but more broadly to three specific criteria – the ability to sustain a healthy environment, social wellbeing, and a strong economy. This formulation of sustainability has normative dimensions (requiring agreement on what we mean by health and wellbeing, for example, and what kind of an economy we would prefer) and it also has implicit time dimensions inasmuch as both natural and man-made systems change over time and succession takes place (Costanza and Patten 1995, Holdren *et al.* 1995, Brown *et al.* 1987). In the context of urban and regional systems, sustainability can be thought of as a process of discovery, invention, and change, requiring policy makers to set goals and develop strategies to meet them for the particular context, while recognizing that there are real limits on resources and on human capacities, and that the choices made will affect current and future generations (WCED 1987, Alberti and Susskind 1996). There is no reason to require that every urban or regional project or programme gives equal attention to each of the three objectives or measures them in the same way, although mitigating the risks and dangers of human interference on the planet's climate system, which have potentially catastrophic consequences and a relatively short time frame for action, justifiably demand considerable priority. A transportation system should at the very least account for its economic, social, and environmental effects over its expected lifetime, and to contribute to sustainability it should preferably aim to co-produce benefits in all three domains. Such an accounting requires a more comprehensive analysis of impacts (including consideration of indirect and cumulative impacts) than has typically been done (Litman and Burwell 2006).

Context matters, and as previous chapters have suggested, caution must be exercised in learning from international cases. Many of the countries in which HSR has been implemented have urban and regional structures that fit well with the technology – cities are several hundred kilometres apart, urban densities are high, the central city captures a high share of trips, and urban transit is readily available for local connections. Under these conditions, HSR can provide door-to-door travel times and costs that compete well with air or auto, and that has been the experience in most European and Asian HSR applications to date. However, the cases also indicate that when HSR is extended into thinner markets, for example by serving smaller cities, its economic performance does not match that attained in the first/best market initiatives. However, important social benefits may be gained by connecting communities through HSR, such as territorial integration and better access to high quality jobs and services.

The cases presented in this volume make it clear that there is no generalizable 'best' design: Germany's system intermixes high-speed and conventional links while other countries have emphasized separate HSR systems that connect to the conventional rail system. Both types have been successful. Success depends on matching system designs to the realities of topography, competing modes, and city size and spacing. The cases also show that station location decisions can affect performance: locating stations at the urban periphery can save money for the system providers but raise costs for travellers due to the diminished accessibility of the system.

Some of the systems in Europe and Asia are relatively new whereas others have been operating for decades. For the most part the older HSR systems were introduced when socioeconomic conditions were propitious and competing services had not yet solidified market shares. For example, early HSR systems were built in France and Japan when government agencies controlled intercity travel offerings. Intercity roads were less developed, auto ownership was less prevalent, and short haul air transport was sparse and expensive. In addition, incomes were lower.

In Japan, France, Germany, and Italy, HSR underwent decades of planning and experimentation before decisions were made to deploy the first HSR lines. Decades more were needed to develop their systems as they exist today. In France, the R&D for fast trains for passenger services was a risk the state took on; the state also built up institutional capacity for the deployment and operation of modern rail systems (Mazzucato 2015). In Japan, the government likewise committed significant state resources to develop the technology and deploy the HSR system. In both countries, deployment was based on a government commitment to finance construction and manage operations to cover costs. However, the government was also available to cover costs in times of crisis.

China has a vastly different government and economic model than that of other HSR leaders, but it has followed a similar HSR development trajectory. China introduced HSR at a time when intercity travel was beginning to grow, auto ownership was just beginning to boom, and rail was still a major means of long distance travel. For the Chinese, building HSR through state-owned enterprises was a way to steer intercity travel choices. It also was a jobs creation and economic development policy and a way to develop credibility in the international engineering and construction markets. China's first HSR line began operations in 2007 as part of the plan to provide modern transport infrastructure. Since then, the central government in Beijing has demonstrated a strong political and financial commitment to HSR and has developed the most extensive HSR network in the world. By the beginning of 2016 more than 12,000 miles of HSR lines were in operation in China, more than the rest of the world combined. Despite some major accidents and technical hiccups, China continues to expand its HSR network. By 2020, almost 20,000 miles of HSR tracks will provide fast connections to all major cities. The PRC government's commitment to HSR translates to abundant financing for the project. As Japan did when the HSR technology was first introduced to the world in 1964 at the start of the Tokyo Olympic Games, China now showcases technological prowess and its engineering capacity in infrastructure development and construction as an important export product. China now aims to compete directly with France, Germany, and Japan as a top tier global player in the international HSR industry.

The international examples indicate that in many cases, the institutional framework when HSR systems were first introduced permitted a far higher degree of government intervention in intercity transport decisions than would be possible today. Today, in much of the world, neoliberal economic policies have loosened government controls over intercity transport and promoted private sector engagement, and some of the steps taken in early years to help assure the success of HSR – such as limiting flights between HSR-served city pairs – would be highly controversial and contested today, if allowed at all. More recent projects in the EU have been shaped by policies favouring market competition both across modes (e.g., air vs. rail) and for HSR operations themselves (as illustrated by the Italian case). The idea of evaluating projects based on value for money is widely held, but how to measure value is debated, especially when social and environmental benefits and costs are at issue. Moreover, new considerations on co-benefits emerge in the context of climate change. For instance, diversification of transport modes can constitute a way to mitigate climate risk. This is relevant, for instance, in the context of the San Francisco Bay Area, where its two main airports are vulnerable to flooding due to rising sea levels. Whether market-based solutions are always best has been controversial, as the British case illustrates, and social welfare policies rather than profitability have influenced some investments (as in Spain). The Taiwan case is a cautionary tale about over-exuberant reliance on market approaches and private sector involvement without adequate performance oversight.

Factors affecting HSR performance

The international cases and papers presented in this book indicate that six interrelated factors are critical to the performance of HSR:

- urban and regional structure
- system design
- costs, prices, and benefits
- traveller ability and willingness to pay
- a clear governmental role
- public support
- institutional capacity.

Urban and regional structure, including the distances between cities and the degree to which they are concentrated in centres, affects the viability of HSR since it competes best for distances in the 200–800 km range. Under that distance, automobiles are usually more cost-effective, and above that distance air transport dominates. The numbers are not hard-and-fast, however; for example, in the contested Tokyo region, and to some extent in European cities such as London, shorter trips can be attracted to HSR.

System design includes such factors as line haul operating speed, the number of stops and dwell times during stops, whether some trains can run nonstop between major stations and bypass interim stations or traverse them at speed, route location and station-to-station distances, station locations and connections to other modes, and service hours of operation and frequency. These factors affect door-to-door travel times; and the match between travellers' desired travel times and those available, since time is valuable, are key factors in mode choice. System design also includes factors that affect the system's social and environmental acceptability, including such impacts as land takings, severance, noise, visual intrusion, and their impacts on economic activities and community quality of life.

Costs include the cost to build the system, including mitigation costs, the costs to maintain, operate, and renew or retire the system, and any unmitigated social and environmental costs that the system may impose. *Prices* may be set to cover capital and operating costs and compensate for unmitigated costs, or may by policy recover only some of the costs. However, society pays for costs if users do not. *Benefits* can accrue to users in the form of consumer surplus (the difference between the total value consumers receive and the amount they pay for it) or to society (social benefits equal all the private benefits plus any external benefits of production/consumption).

Traveller willingness to pay is the level at or below which a traveller will accept a price for the trip, taking into account the product or service being provided. For HSR, the evidence indicates that in addition to the fares themselves, access and egress travel times, time required to move through the terminal, the probability of delays, and considerations such as the ability to move around during the trip, work or relax in comfort, and obtain meals and refreshments are factors affecting willingness to pay.

A clear governmental role in HSR has been a key ingredient for every HSR system reviewed here. For the most part, this has meant well-specified and predictable funding support; all of the cases of operating HSR systems presented in this book were sponsored by the central government and some were implemented primarily with public funds, though many lines later recouped costs. Governments have also covered operating costs both as a start-up measure and for lines justified in substantial part on territorial integration and economic integration grounds. While governmental willingness to advance construction funds and to cover operating shortfalls has been controversial (see the European and Taiwanese cases), what seems to be most important is a clear and consistent statement about the government policy. Clear statements that government will not step in (as was the case for the Channel Tunnel services offered between the UK and France) can be valuable by reducing uncertainty about terms and conditions.

Public support matters because its absence can weaken government support or even lose it entirely. In democratic societies, protests, litigation, and other challenges are likely to result if the public does not believe their voices have been heard and taken into account. Modern media make it easy for both supporters and opponents to reach wide audiences with websites and blogs expressing their views on projects such as HSR creating multiple channels for publicizing positions and influencing public opinion. In a 24/7 news cycle and with new media communications, thinking long-term in real time is complex; former New York Mayor Michael Bloomberg stated that 'social media is going to make it even more difficult to make long-term investments' in infrastructure, and Townsend reminds us that when citizens use social networks to discuss governmental plans, these conversations can become 'daily referenda' on elected officials' actions (2014, p. 304).

Institutional capacity matters because well integrated, well connected, and well informed organizations can mobilize readily to act to capture opportunities, while those that are fragmented and lack the connections to sources of power and knowledge may not be able to move their agenda forward (Healy 1998). For a complex project like HSR, lead agencies, or alliances of agencies, need to have both the technical know-how to deliver the system and the political know-how to get it through the decision process, as well as to procure pertinent expert services and/or privatize its operations.

While the specifics have differed in each of the cases considered here, the evidence presented indicates that all of these factors must be positive and aligned for HSR to succeed.

How sustainable is HSR?

If we measure sustainability in terms of covering costs and providing social and environmental benefits compared to other travel options, by most accounts HSR systems to date meet basic sustainability criteria. Most studies indicate that HSR systems have produced net social benefits, though some extensions are contested on these grounds and most systems have taken a number of years to pay off. Most use less energy and produce less pollution and greenhouse gas (GHG) emissions than other modes of intercity transport, and have a smaller environmental footprint than an equivalent addition of highway or air transport capacity.

However, HSR is hardly a panacea for environmental effects. Its energy efficiency and GHG emissions status depend on the electric power it sources, as well as on the number of seats it fills (since the intent is to move people, not vehicles or seats). Construction impacts are substantial, and while it is increasingly possible to obtain 'green' steel and concrete, i.e. products whose environmental impacts have been minimized, internalized in their costs or mitigated, net costs are still likely to remain. In addition, routing and operations of a high-speed rail system create environmental and social impacts that can be substantial; while they also can be mitigated doing so tends to increase construction costs. For example it is almost always many times more costly to tunnel for HSR than to build a line at grade.

Turning to impacts on the broader economy, HSR may restructure territorial relationships and this restructuring may improve overall economic performance, though some places may gain more than others. Faster connections between urban centres can support greater economic activity and productivity, though again, the effects are likely to be uneven. Gains in one location may be accompanied by losses in others, and the economic changes are likely to differ based on the economic bases of the affected cities. In addition to these long-term impacts on the general economy, HSR can create both short-term construction jobs and longer-term permanent employment at and around terminals (with an array of commercial and hospitality services) as well as operations and maintenance services, for instance. Overall, the shifts and gains are likely have net positive effects, including multiplier effects, on the economy.

Experience in Europe and Japan has shown that HSR stations can serve as a focal point and impetus for valued urban development and revitalization. Some of these changes might have occurred anyway but in less environmentally felicitous locations. The coming of HSR can motivate – and may well necessitate – investments in local and regional transport infrastructure to support the HSR system and coordinate it with local and regional systems.

The California case

California has envisioned a state-wide high-speed rail system that delivers not only fast, safe and efficient transportation services but also economic and environmental benefits and positive spill-overs for smart growth. Most agree that there is already substantial market potential for HSR, especially between the San Francisco Bay Area and Los Angeles, and that forecasted growth will increase demand for intercity travel. However, construction costs are high, and route choices are contentious. As planning has unfolded it has become clear that reality is in danger of falling short of the state's ambitious vision.

The reasons for this are varied. Any project of this size and magnitude entails risk and uncertainty (Flyvbjerg et al. 2003). In the case of California HSR, costs, ridership, and willingness to pay for HSR have been issues. The construction of a new rail line in California under any plausible routing or management scenario would be an expensive undertaking, and while the state's population makes enough intercity trips and is sufficiently affluent to make HSR a possibility, air travel and auto travel are well-established alternatives and few Californians have any experience with rail, so that forecasts of mode choice are particularly uncertain. Forecasts have been highly contested, as have claims about environmental performance and economic benefits.

In our assessment, modelling improvements have been substantial and forecasts are now in line with best practices for a long-term project of this nature. Likewise, our assessment is that environmental gains, while modest, are mostly positive, as are economic impacts. However, other major uncertainties remain, the most pressing one being the ambiguous support that the HSR system has had from state and federal government, and the lack of a clear financial way forward for the system. This, in turn, is the result of under-development of needed financial and organizational capacity. In addition, wavering political support may be an issue going forward.

California is proceeding with HSR claiming that state government support is only needed to create a plan and get the system started, and that once it is in place, public-private partnerships of various sorts will be able to carry it forward. While this may eventually prove to be the case, it is a risky assumption. The failure to date to identify a long-term funding source for HSR construction and the uncertainties about whether anyone else will come forward as a major partner has put the state HSR plan on shaky grounds. Some suggest a less charitable assumption, that the intent is to spend so much money that turning back becomes impossible regardless of the costs to government.

Federal funding has been important, but somewhat unpredictable given current Congressional antipathies to passenger rail projects and competition from other states for the limited rail funds available. Regional and local agencies have been willing to coordinate investments with HSR plans and to share costs for multimodal stations, but not to pay for the HSR lines. State bond funds are useful down-payment for the system but are tied up in litigation made possible by the extensive but ambiguous conditions the Legislature imposed on the project. State allocations of greenhouse gas cap and trade funds are potentially a major source of state support, but only if the funds are available after 2020 (when the law authorizing them currently expires). Additional funds would still be needed, however.

California certainly has good reasons to make a major investment in passenger rail modernization. Its growth will necessitate investment in additional transport services. HSR would diversify intercity options beyond air and road travel and would offer attractive features including far faster, safer, and more convenient travel times than intercity travel by auto, equal or better access and egress times than by air, and less propensity for delay than either of the competing modes. Caltrans points to the link between transport and growth in describing its investment rationale to modernize and expand its inter-modal transport network, and also notes the policy mandate to reduce greenhouse gas emissions in its actions. Electrification is the technological roadmap but clean energy sourcing and production will be key to achieve a clean HSR operation in California. Whether these motivations are enough to transform urban and transport infrastructure sustainability remains to be seen.

Wavering public support is an issue because of the particularities of the California political system. California's citizens are no strangers to controversial megaprojects; examples range from the state water project to the California Freeway and Expressway System to the Bay Area Rapid Transit (BART) system. Each one of these projects was controversial, labelled a 'pipedream' or 'boondoggle' or 'planning disaster.' Each was advocated by some and fought bitterly by others. The projects were adjusted and adapted to economic conditions and political demands and implemented over decades. Over time, plans changed, reflecting emerging awareness of ecological risk and social consequences. Some elements were dropped and new elements were added as projects progressed. Today, however, these large-scale initiatives are widely recognized as important contributors to California's wellbeing, though flaws with each of them are acknowledged.

The California HSR is certainly a megaproject of substantial size and complexity. It presents significant risks as well as huge potential benefits in return for a promise to link the San Francisco Bay Area and Los Angeles Metropolitan Area, two of the most productive, dynamic and innovative urban mega-regions in the world. Such a linkage may have much in common with the highly symbolic, as well as economically significant, closeness that the undersea tunnel connecting London and Paris now provides. A difference between HSR and the other HSR systems developed around the world, however, is the lack of clarity about the government position for California HSR. This in turn makes the project vulnerable to political and economic cycles as well as to the divergent ideological perspectives that can emerge over election cycles.

California's political and governance system is open and highly inclusive, epitomized by the many mandates and opportunities for citizens to take action at the ballot box. Some observers view this as creating 'perils of extreme democracy', preventing the state from getting things done (*The Economist* 2011). The process is certainly complex, but allowing citizens a direct say in key decisions can also motivate political will to action. The vote in favour of providing partial funding for HSR provided direction for the Legislature and Governor in this regard, though the severe recession made forward motion difficult. Delays, high cost estimates, and lack of clarity about plans after many more years of planning may now be eroding voter support. As a poll conducted by the Public Policy Institute of California found, 8 years after state voters passed the $10 billion bond to build high-speed rail with 53 per cent support, 52 per cent of adults and 44 per cent of likely voters continue to favour building it. When those who are opposed are asked how they would feel if it cost less, overall support increased to 66 per cent among adults and 59 per cent among likely voters (Baldasarre *et al.* 2016).

HSR compared to what?

Even if California's HSR system meets tests of sustainability and its proponents figure out a way forward financially, assuaging public concerns about costs, there remains the question of whether it is the right investment for the state. Intercity travel is a small portion of overall travel in California, and some question the wisdom of public investments in a mode that will likely serve a small share of trips made mostly by business travellers and the affluent. Others question the need for new intercity infrastructure, arguing that coming improvements in existing air transport and highway systems will carry the state forward for many decades. Still others argue that state funds would be better spent on urban transportation systems, where the majority of trips are made and congestion and pollution problems are concentrated. In addition, there are those who would prefer less government spending on transportation of any sort, and those who would wait to see what emerging technological advances will bring.

It is not clear that public decision-makers, or anyone else for that matter, have the know-how to prioritize intercity transport modes or to evaluate whether new technologies will solve current problems. Technological advances are certainly bringing about new ways of doing things, from 'dematerializing' many products to reducing the need for travel for meetings and other communications. As suggested by Seba (2014), energy and transport systems are likely to be disrupted faster than we can imagine. On the other hand, not every advanced technology will survive its commercial tests. For instance, the cutting-edge but costly supersonic air travel service offered by Concorde planes was finally ended after economic and environmental costs proved too high for the times and the context.

History tells us that transportation technologies can change dramatically over a period of a few years. Early in the twentieth century, automobiles went from being a luxury good for the wealthy to a common household appliance in only two decades. Widespread deployment of the automobile led to changes in urban living that were far-reaching and only partially foreseen. Today, automobiles may be undergoing transformational change. Many elements of automation are already available on personal vehicles – anti-tipping sensors, backup screens and warning signals, dynamic braking. Driverless cars are being tested and their deployment could transform the way we move about, for both passengers and freight. Car connectivity technology seems likely to create new ways of managing safety and congestion impacts. Carsharing programmes could transform vehicle ownership patterns as well.

Air transport changes have been equally dramatic. Human flight went from a short and dangerous moment afloat for the Wright Brothers in 1903 to the first commercial flight in 1914 to millions of miles a year of air passenger transport by the 1960s. Today a single aircraft can carry upwards of 1,000 passengers, and a major airport such as Los Angeles International serves 75 million emplaning passengers a year. The availability of affordable, reliable air transport has changed trade and business patterns, location choices, and recreational options for millions of people.

In thinking about the role of HSR then, the question is not just about competition with existing modes as they currently exist, but with how HSR will compete with or complement modes as they change over time, potentially in revolutionary ways. This is an area of forecasting that is not yet very well developed, however, and so predicting how a mode will compete 30 years in the future is fraught with uncertainty.

Institutional capacity

In many of the countries that have implemented HSR there has been substantial institutional capacity to implement rail projects, including rail projects that require R&D. Capabilities were strong among government agencies, regulators, planning and engineering firms, and academic institutions. In contrast, in the US there has been little public sector attention to rail, which for decades has been deregulated on the freight side and limited mostly to a small and relatively underfunded public corporation providing intercity passenger services. State DOTs do have some rail capacity, but compared to their capacity to work on highway issues, rail capacity is modest indeed. Few university programmes provide more than a course or two on rail, and even fewer focus on design and engineering details.

The redesign of public administration structure, authority, consultation, and controls to deliver HSR in California has been limited. As discussed in Chapter 14, the California High-Speed Rail Authority was originally set up to quickly prepare a plan for the HSR system and then go out of business. It was subsequently given an extended term, and then made permanent, and then moved to Caltrans where it could draw on available planning, engineering, and right-of-way staff for assistance. However, there is really not much relevant domestic experience in the planning and execution of a complex rail project such as the CA HSR. Trains have not been a high priority for the state for many decades, as evidenced by the small budget for rail projects, the continuing gap in passenger services between Bakersfield and Los Angeles, and the 24 mph speed of current rail lines in the Tehachapi Mountains. Likewise there has been relatively little experience with complex financing mechanisms for transportation projects.

Given the limited number of rail experts in the state agencies, major contracts went to consulting firms with expertise in these issues. This, however, proved controversial, raising questions about who could supervise the consultants adequately. Questions also arose about the complex demand forecasting and cost and revenue modelling needed for the project. The solution was to establish 'peer groups' of outside experts with relevant experience to offer independent oversight and advise the staff and the Legislature on these important project aspects.

Interestingly enough, the peer group on finance does not believe its review functions suffice. It has emphasized the need for greater guidance from the Legislature about the HSR project's plans and funding. To move in this direction, the peer group recommended the creation of a select committee of the Legislature to ensure legislative oversight continuity, as well as a dedicated and continuing oversight staff, possibly located in the Legislative Analyst's Office (LAO). As one member of an oversight committee testified to the Legislature, 'The stakes for the state are far too high to rest solely on periodic oversight hearings and audits.'[1]

Summing up

International experience demonstrates that high-speed rail can provide relatively fast, convenient, efficient, safe, cost-effective, and environmentally responsible mobility service and can enhance economic, cultural, and social sustainability. To achieve these outcomes, however, it must be implemented in a supportive context, priced and operated to attract sufficient ridership, and designed to complement urban transport systems while minimizing community disruption and environmental costs.

With its HSR proposal, California has embarked on the most ambitious rail modernization plan in the United States since the transcontinental railways project began in 1863. Despite continuing controversy over the project and many unresolved details, the first steps toward construction are now underway. Still, the future of the project is not yet secure. But a successful profitable initial operating segment such as the new strategy of connecting the Central Valley with Silicon Valley may become the demonstration project or test bed that changes this.

As with any megaproject, the new California HSR system will be vulnerable to risks associated with costs, revenues, and ridership throughout its development (Flyvbjerg, Bruzelius and Rothengatter 2003). However, these may not be the biggest risks. The project will continue to challenge the capacity of political leaders, government officials and agencies in their decision-making, regulatory, and oversight responsibilities. Deciding on the project alignment and implementation priorities and completing the environmental reviews need to be a top priority but will not end the need for proactive political leadership and guidance as well as expert, hands-on management. If the project continues into construction, it will challenge the execution capabilities of those charged with implementing the project.

Perhaps the biggest risk to the California HSR project is political. A credible commitment to the plan is needed if the plan is to maintain public support; it is needed even more if the plan is to attract additional funding from private partners. The risk of the project is just too great as long as so much is in flux. Thus if the project is to proceed, in addition to finishing the engineering, design, and environmental tasks, reaching an understanding about how to move forward over the next two decades must be a major objective for the very near future.

Note

1 Lou Thomson's testimony to the legislature January 2016.

References

Alberti, M, and Susskind, L, 1996, 'Managing urban sustainability: an introduction to the special issue,' *Environmental Impact Assessment Review*, vol. 16, no. 4, pp. 213–221.

Baldassare, M, 2016, 'Californians and their government,' *Public Policy Institute of California – PPIC Statewide Survey*, San Francisco, CA, p. 5.

Brown, BJ, et al., 1987, 'Global sustainability: toward definition,' Environmental management vol. 11, no. 6, pp. 713–719.

Costanza, R, and Patten, BC, 1995, 'Defining and predicting sustainability,' Ecological Economics, vol. 15, no. 3, pp. 193–196.

Flyvbjerg, B, Bruzelius, N, and Rottengatter, W, 2003, Mega-Projects and Risk: An Anatomy of Ambition, Cambridge University Press, Cambridge, UK.

Healey, P, 1998, 'Building institutional capacity through collaborative approaches to urban planning,' Environment and Planning, A, vol. 30, no. 9, pp. 1531–1546.

Holdren, JP, Daily, GC, and Ehrlich, PR, 1995, 'The meaning of sustainability: biogeophysical aspects,' in Munasinghe, M and Walter, S, eds, Defining and Measuring Sustainability, The Biogeophysical Foundations, Washington: The World Bank.

Litman, T, and Burwell, D, 2006, 'Issues in sustainable transportation,' International Journal of Global Environmental Issues, vol. 6, no. 4, pp. 331–347.

Mazzucato, M, 2015, The Entrepreneurial State, Debunking Public Vs. Private Sector Myths, Revised Edition, Public Affairs, Perseus Books Group, New York, NY.

Seba, T, 2014, Clean Disruption of Energy and Transportation: How Silicon Valley Will Make Oil, Nuclear, Natural Gas, Coal, Electric Utilities and Conventional Cars Obsolete by 2030. Self-published.

The Economist, 2011, 'The perils of extreme democracy,' See: http://www.economist.com/node/18586520 Accessed 31 October 2016.

Thomson, L, 2016, Comments by the Chair of the Peer Review Group on the 2016 Business Plan Developed by the California High-Speed Rail Authority. Letter and Attachment. See: http://www.cahsrprg.com/files/25-March-letter-from-PRG.pdf Accessed 1 August 2016.

Townsend, AM, 2014, Smart Cities, Big Data, Civic Hackers, and the Quest for a New Utopia, W.W. Norton & Company, New York, NY: p. 304.

World Commission on Environment and Development (WCED), 1987, Our Common Future, Oxford and New York: Oxford University Press.

Index

Taylor & Francis eBooks

Helping you to choose the right eBooks for your Library

Add Routledge titles to your library's digital collection today. Taylor and Francis ebooks contains over 50,000 titles in the Humanities, Social Sciences, Behavioural Sciences, Built Environment and Law.

Choose from a range of subject packages or create your own!

Benefits for you

- » Free MARC records
- » COUNTER-compliant usage statistics
- » Flexible purchase and pricing options
- » All titles DRM-free.

REQUEST YOUR FREE INSTITUTIONAL TRIAL TODAY

Free Trials Available
We offer free trials to qualifying academic, corporate and government customers.

Benefits for your user

- » Off-site, anytime access via Athens or referring URL
- » Print or copy pages or chapters
- » Full content search
- » Bookmark, highlight and annotate text
- » Access to thousands of pages of quality research at the click of a button.

eCollections – Choose from over 30 subject eCollections, including:

Archaeology	Language Learning
Architecture	Law
Asian Studies	Literature
Business & Management	Media & Communication
Classical Studies	Middle East Studies
Construction	Music
Creative & Media Arts	Philosophy
Criminology & Criminal Justice	Planning
Economics	Politics
Education	Psychology & Mental Health
Energy	Religion
Engineering	Security
English Language & Linguistics	Social Work
Environment & Sustainability	Sociology
Geography	Sport
Health Studies	Theatre & Performance
History	Tourism, Hospitality & Events

For more information, pricing enquiries or to order a free trial, please contact your local sales team:
www.tandfebooks.com/page/sales

Routledge
Taylor & Francis Group

The home of
Routledge books

www.tandfebooks.com